Blueprints
Tort Law

PEARSON

At Pearson, we have a simple mission: to help people make more of their lives through learning.

We combine innovative learning technology with trusted content and educational expertise to provide engaging and effective learning experiences that serve people wherever and whenever they are learning.

From classroom to boardroom, our curriculum materials, digital learning tools and testing programmes help to educate millions of people worldwide – more than any other private enterprise.

Every day our work helps learning flourish, and wherever learning flourishes, so do people.

To learn more, please visit us at www.pearson.com/uk

EX LIBRIS
COURTNEY
GUDGIN-SKELTON

Blueprints

Your plan for learning

Tort Law

Mariette Jones

PEARSON

Harlow, England • London • New York • Boston • San Francisco • Toronto • Sydney • Auckland • Singapore • Hong Kong
Tokyo • Seoul • Taipei • New Delhi • Cape Town • São Paulo • Mexico City • Madrid • Amsterdam • Munich • Paris • Milan

PEARSON EDUCATION LIMITED
Edinburgh Gate
Harlow CM20 2JE
United Kingdom
Tel: +44 (0)1279 623623
Web: www.pearson.com/uk

First published 2014 (print and electronic)

© Pearson Education Limited 2014 (print and electronic)

The right of Mariette Jones to be identified as author of this work has been asserted by her in accordance with the Copyright, Designs and Patents Act 1988.

The print publication is protected by copyright. Prior to any prohibited reproduction, storage in a retrieval system, distribution or transmission in any form or by any means, electronic, mechanical, recording or otherwise, permission should be obtained from the publisher or, where applicable, a licence permitting restricted copying in the United Kingdom should be obtained from the Copyright Licensing Agency Ltd, Saffron House, 6–10 Kirby Street, London EC1N 8TS.

The ePublication is protected by copyright and must not be copied, reproduced, transferred, distributed, leased, licensed or publicly performed or used in any way except as specifically permitted in writing by the publishers, as allowed under the terms and conditions under which it was purchased, or as strictly permitted by applicable copyright law. Any unauthorised distribution or use of this text may be a direct infringement of the author's and the publishers' rights and those responsible may be liable in law accordingly.

ISBN: 978-1-4479-2002-1 (print)
    978-1-4479-2003-8 (PDF)
    978-1-2920-1511-8 (eText)

British Library Cataloguing-in-Publication Data
A catalogue record for the print edition is available from the British Library

Library of Congress Cataloguing-in-Publication Data
Jones, Mariëtte, author
  Tort law / Mariette Jones.
    pages cm
  Includes index.
  ISBN 978-1-4479-2002-1
  1. Torts – England. I. Title.
  KD1949.6.J66 2014
  346.4203–dc23
              2014002929

10 9 8 7 6 5 4 3 2 1
16 15 14 13 12

Print edition typeset in 10/12pt Helvetica Neue LT Pro by 35
Printed in Great Britain by Henry Ling Ltd, at the Dorset Press, Dorchester, Dorset

NOTE THAT ANY PAGE CROSS REFERENCES REFER TO THE PRINT EDITION

Brief contents

Table of cases **x**
Table of statutes **xvi**
Acknowledgments **xix**
How to use this guide **xx**
What is a Blueprint? **xxiv**
Introduction **xxvi**
Study skills – studying tort **xxix**

PART 1
Negligence 2

1 Tort: overview **5**
2 Negligence: introduction – duty of care **25**
3 Negligence: breach of duty **49**
4 Negligence: causation **65**
5 Negligence: defences **83**

PART 2
Trespass 100

6 Trespass to land and goods **103**
7 Trespass to the person **119**

PART 3
Statutory regimes 142

8 Occupiers' liability **145**
9 Product liability **165**
10 Defamation **185**

PART 4
Miscellaneous torts 210

11 Nuisance and the tort in *Rylands* v. *Fletcher* **213**
12 Employers' (operational) liability and vicarious liability **239**
13 Other torts **261**

Glossary **278**
Index **280**

Contents

Table of cases   x
Table of statutes   xvi
Acknowledgments   xix
How to use this guide   xx
What is a Blueprint?   xxiv
Introduction   xxvi
Study skills – studying tort law   xxix

PART 1
Negligence   2

1 Tort: overview   5

Setting the scene   8
What does tort mean?   8
Basic elements of a tort   10
Aims and objectives of tort law   17
Interests protected by tort law   17
The boundaries of tort law   20
Apportionment of blame   21
Key points   23
Core cases and statutes   23
Further reading   24

2 Negligence: introduction – duty of care   25

Setting the scene   28
Donoghue v. *Stevenson* – the birth of the modern tort of negligence   28
Elements of the tort of negligence   30
Duty of care   31
The role of policy   35
Liability for omissions   40
Liability for psychiatric injury and economic loss   42
Key points   46
Core cases and statutes   46
Further reading   48

3 Negligence: breach of duty   49

Setting the scene   52
Negligence: breach of duty   52
Proving breach of duty   60

Key points 63
Core cases and statutes 63
Further reading 64

 Negligence: causation 65

Setting the scene 68
Introduction to causation 68
Causation 69
Factual causation 69
Legal causation (remoteness of damage) 77
Foreseeability: *The Wagon Mound (No. 1)* 78
Key points 80
Core cases and statutes 81
Further reading 82

 Negligence: defences 83

Setting the scene 86
Three main defences to a claim in negligence 86
Volenti non fit injuria 87
Contributory negligence 92
Illegality (*ex turpi causa non oritur actio*) 97
Key points 98
Core cases and statutes 98
Further reading 99

PART 2
Trespass 100

 Trespass to land and goods 103

Setting the scene 106
The meaning of trespass 106
Forms of trespass to land 108
Title of the claimant 112
Defences 113
Remedies 114
Trespass to goods 115
Key points 116
Core cases and statutes 117
Further reading 118

 Trespass to the person 119

Setting the scene 122
Introduction 122
Assault 124
Battery 126

Defences to assault and battery   128
False imprisonment   133
The rule in *Wilkinson* v. *Downton* – liability for causing indirect harm   135
Harassment   137
Key points   138
Core cases and statutes   139
Further reading   140

PART 3
Statutory regimes   142

8 Occupiers' liability   145
Setting the scene   148
Introduction   148
Occupier   149
Occupiers' Liability Act 1957: occupiers' liability to lawful visitors   151
Occupiers' Liability Act 1984: liability to trespassers and non-visitors   158
Key points   161
Core cases and statutes   162
Further reading   163

9 Product liability   165
Setting the scene   168
Liability in contract and consumer law   168
Common law liability in negligence   169
Statutory liability – the Consumer Protection Act 1987   173
Defences under the Consumer Protection Act 1987   179
Key points   181
Core cases and statutes   181
Further reading   183

10 Defamation   185
Setting the scene   188
Introduction   188
Libel and slander   189
Elements of defamation   191
Who can claim?   195
Who may be sued?   196
What makes/made defamation special?   197
Defences   201
Remedies   205
Key points   206
Core cases and statutes   207
Further reading   208

PART 4
Miscellaneous torts 210

11 Nuisance and the tort in Rylands v. Fletcher 213
Setting the scene 216
Introduction 216
Statutory nuisance 216
Private nuisance 217
Public nuisance 226
Defences to nuisance 229
Remedies for nuisance 232
The tort in *Rylands* v. *Fletcher* 233
Key points 236
Core cases and statutes 237
Further reading 238

12 Employers' (operational) liability and vicarious liability 239
Setting the scene 242
Distinction between personal (primary) and vicarious (secondary) liability 242
Employer's liability/principles of operational liability 243
Vicarious liability 250
Employers' vicarious liability: elements 251
Key points 258
Core cases and statutes 258
Further reading 259

13 Other torts 261
Setting the scene 264
Liability for animals 264
Economic torts 270
Key points 276
Core cases and statutes 276
Further reading 277

Glossary 278
Index 280

Table of cases

CASES

A v. Hoare and other appeals [2008] UKHL 6; [2008] 1 AC 844 **121, 132, 133, 139**
A v. National Blood Authority [2001] 3 All ER 289 **167, 177, 179, 180, 182, 183**
Abouzaid v. Mothercare (UK) Ltd [2000] EWCA Civ 348; [2000] All ER (D) 2436 **167, 179, 180, 182**
Adam v. Ward [1917] AC 309 **203**
Alanov v. Chief Constable of Sussex Police [2012] EWCA Civ 234; [2012] All ER (D) 17 (Mar) **134**
Alcock v. Chief Constable of the South Yorkshire Police [1991] 4 All ER 907 **xxxiii, 27, 42, 43, 47, 247, 248**
Allen v. British Rail Engineering Ltd [2001] EWCA Civ 242; [2001] All ER (D) 291 (Feb) **58**
Allen v. Gulf Oil Refining Ltd [1981] AC 1001 **230**
AMF International Ltd v. Magnet Bowling Ltd [1968] 1 WLR 1028 **150**
Andreae v. Selfridge & Co Ltd [1938] Ch 1 **225**
Anns v. Merton London Borough Council [1978] AC 728 **32, 33, 35, 44, 45**
Attorney-General v. PYA Quarries [1957] 2 QB 169 **215, 227, 237**
Austin v. Commissioner of Police for the Metropolis [2008] 1 All ER 564 **135**
B (adult: refusal of medical treatment), Re [2002] EWHC 429 (Fam); [2002] 2 All ER 449 **129**
Bailey v. Armes [1999] EGCS 21 **149, 62**
Bailey v. Ministry of Defence [2008] EWCA Civ 883; [2009] 1 WLR 1052 **70, 71**
Baker v. TE Hopkins & Son Ltd [1959] 1 WLR 966 **94**

Baker v. Quantum Clothing Group [2011] UKSC 17; [2011] 4 All ER 223 **246, 247, 258**
Baker v. Willoughby [1970] AC 467 (HL) **75, 76**
Barber v. Somerset County Council [2004] UKHL 13; [2004] 2 All ER 385 **248**
Barker v. Corus (UK) [2006] 2 WLR 1027 **72, 81**
Barnett v. Chelsea and Kensington Hospital Management Committee [1969] 1 QB 428 **69**
Barrett v. Enfield London Borough Council [2001] 2 AC 550 **37, 47**
Barrett v. Ministry of Defence [1995] 1 WLR 1217 **40**
Barr v. Biffa Waste Services Ltd [2012] EWCA Civ 312; [2013] QB 455 **225, 230, 231, 238**
Bellew v. Cement Co [1948] Ir R 61 **232**
Benjamin v. Storr (1874) LR 9 CP 400 **228**
Bernstein v. Skyviews and General Ltd [1978] QB 479 **109, 117**
Bin Mahfouz v. Ehrenfeld [2005] EWHC 1156 (QB); [2005] All ER (D) 361 (Jul) **199**
Bird v. Jones (1845) 7 QB 742 **121, 134, 139**
Birch v. University College London Hospital NHS Foundation Trust [2008] EWHC 2237 (QB); [2008] All ER (D) 113 (Sep) **129**
Blyth v. Proprietors of the Birmingham Waterworks (1856) 11 Exch 781 **31, 52, 62, 63**
Bocardo SA v. Star Energy UK Onshore Ltd and another [2010] UKSC 35; [2010] 3 All ER 975 **105, 109, 117**
Bolam v. Friern Hospital Management Committee [1957] 1 WLR 582 **31, 51, 54, 55, 63, 75, 128, 129**

Bolitho *v.* City and Hackney Health Authority [1997] 4 All ER 771 **31, 51, 54, 55, 63, 67, 74, 75, 80, 129**
Bolton *v.* Stone [1951] 1 All ER 1078 **56–8, 225**
Bonnington Castings Ltd *v.* Wardlaw [1956] AC 613 **70, 71, 81**
Bradford Corporation *v.* Pickles [1895] AC 587 **7, 15, 16, 23, 226**
Bridlington Relay Ltd. v. Yorkshire Electricity Board [1965] Ch 436 **222**
British Railways Board *v.* Herrington [1972] AC 877 **154, 158**
Brooks *v.* Commissioner of the Metropolis [2005] 2 All ER 489 **39**
Brown *v.* Cotterill (1934) 51 TLR 21 **170**
Brown *v.* Rolls Royce Ltd [1960] 1 WLR 210 **58**
Bunt *v.* Tilley [2006] 3 All ER 336 **197**
Butchart *v.* Home Office [2006] 1 WLR 1155 **32**
Caldwell *v.* Maguire [2001] EWCA Civ 1054: [2001] All ER (D) 363 (Jun) **91**
Calgarth (The) [1927] P 93 **105, 110, 152**
Cambridge Water *v.* Eastern Counties Leather plc [1994] 2 WLR 53 **236**
Campbell *v.* Mirror Group Newspapers Plc [2004] 2 AC 457 **189**
Caparo Industries plc *v.* Dickman [1990] 1 All ER 568 **3, 27, 31, 33–5, 38, 44–7**
Carmarthenshire County Council *v.* Lewis [1955] AC 549 **41**
Carslogie Steamship Co *v.* Royal Norwegian Government [1952] AC 292 **77**
Cassidy *v.* Daily Mirror Newspaper [1929] 2 KB 331 **187, 192, 207**
Cassidy *v.* Ministry of Health [1951] 1 All ER 574 **251, 255**
Century Insurance *v.* Northern Ireland Regional Transport Board [1942] AC 509 **256**
Chatterton *v.* Gerson [1981] QB 432 **129**
Chaudry *v.* Prabhaker [1988] 3 All ER 718 **45**
Chic Fashions (West Wales) Ltd *v.* Jones [1968] 2 QB 299 **111**
Christie *v.* Davey [1893] 1 Ch 316 **226**
Cinnamond *v.* BAA [1980] 1 WLR 582 **111**

City of London Corpn *v.* Samede and others [2012] EWCA Civ 160; [2012] 2 All ER 1039 **109**
Cole *v.* Turner (1704) 6 Mod Rep 149 **127**
Collins *v.* Wilcock [1984] 3 All ER 374 **127**
Condon *v.* Basi [1985] 2 All ER 453 **90**
Conway *v.* George Wimpey & Co Ltd [1951] 2 KB 266 **106, 117**
Corby Group Litigation Claimants *v.* Corby BC [2008] EWCA Civ 463; [2009] QB 335 **228**
Cork *v.* Kirby MacLean Ltd [1952] 2 All ER 402 **7, 11, 12, 23, 31, 67, 69, 80, 81**
Cornish *v.* Midland Bank plc [1985] 3 All ER 513 **45**
Cruddas *v.* Calvert [2013] EWCA Civ 748; [2013] All ER (D) 198 (Jun) **273, 276**
Crown River Cruises Ltd *v.* Kimbolton Fireworks Ltd [1999] 2 Lloyd's Rep 533 **218**
Cummings *v.* Granger [1977] 1 All ER 104 **270**
Cutler v. United Dairies (London) Ltd [1933] 2 KB 297 **90**
Dann *v.* Hamilton [1939] 1 KB 509 **85, 91, 98**
De Beers Abrasive Products Ltd *v.* International General Electric Co of New York [1975] 1 WLR 972 **272**
Derry *v.* Peek (1889) 14 App Cas 337 **263, 271**
Dobson *v.* Thames Water Utilities Ltd [2009] EWCA Civ 28; [2009] 3 All ER 319 **218**
Donoghue *v.* Stevenson [1932] AC 562 **xxii, 3, 4, 7, 13, 19, 23, 27–33, 35, 40, 44–6, 143, 167–9, 171, 181**
Donoghue *v.* Folkestone Properties Ltd [2003] EWCA Civ 231; [2003] QB 1008 **160**
Douglas, Zeta Jones and Northern and Shell plc *v.* Hello! Ltd (No 1) [2001] QB 967 **189**
Drane *v.* Evangelou [1978] 1 WLR 455 **112**
Draper *v.* Hodder [1972] 2 QB 556 **263, 264, 276**
DPP *v.* Jones [1999] 2 All ER 257 **109**
E *v.* English Province of Our Lady of Charity and another [2013] 2 WLR 958 **257**
Eaton Mansions (Westminster) Ltd *v.* Stinger Compania de Inversion SA [2011] EWCA Civ 607; [2011] All ER (D) 168 (May) **110**
Edward Wong Finance Co. Ltd v. Johnson Stokes & Master [1984] AC 296 **55**

Edwards v. Railway Executive [1952] AC 737 **152**
Elias v. Passmore [1934] 2 KB 164 **111**
Enfield LBC v. Outdoor Plus Ltd [2012] EWCA Civ 608; [2012] All ER (D) 87 (May) **114**
Erven Warnink BV v. J Townend & Sons (Hull) Ltd [1979] AC 731 **263, 275, 276**
F v. West Berkshire Health Authority [1989] 2 All ER 545 **127, 130, 139**
Fairchild v. Glenhaven Funeral Services Ltd [2002] UKHL 22; [2002] 3 All ER 305 **67, 75, 67, 72, 73, 81**
Ferguson v. British Gas Trading Ltd [2009] EWCA Civ 46; [2009] 3 All ER 304 **137**
Ferguson v. Welsh [1987] 1 WLR 1553 **152, 153, 162**
Fowler v. Lanning [1959] 1 QB 426 **123**
Froom v. Butcher [1976] QB 286 **xxxviii, 85, 95, 96, 99**
Geary v. JD Wetherspoon plc [2011] EWHC 1506 (QB); [2011] All ER (D) 97 (Jun) **154, 160**
General Cleaning Contractors v. Christmas [1953] AC 180 **246**
Glasgow Corporation v. Taylor [1922] 1 AC 44 **155, 158, 162**
Goldman v. Hargrave [1967] 1 AC 645 **41, 220, 225, 234**
Gough v. Thorne [1966] 1 WLR 1387 **94**
Gouldsmith v. Mid Staffordshire General Hospitals NHS Trust [2007] EWCA Civ 397; [2007] All ER (D) 257 (Apr) **56**
Gray v. Thames Trains Ltd [2009] UKHL 33; [2009] AC 1339 **97**
Grant v. Australian Knitting Mills [1936] AC 85 **170, 172**
Gregg v. Scott [2005] 2 WLR 268 **74**
Hall v. Brooklands Auto-Racing Club [1933] 1 KB 205 **52**
Haley v. London Electricity Board [1965] AC 778 **57**
Halsey v. Esso Petroleum Co. Ltd. [1961] 1 WLR 683 **215, 222, 224–6, 228, 238**
Harris v. Birkenhead Corporation [1976] 1 WLR 279 **149**
Haseldine v. Daw [1941] 2 KB 343 **32, 157, 169, 170, 181**

Hatton v. Sutherland [2002] EWCA Civ 76; [2002] 2 All ER 1 **248, 258, 259**
Hawley v. Luminar Leisure Ltd [2006] EWCA Civ 18; [2006] All ER (D) 158 (Jan) **253, 254**
Haynes v. Harwood [1935] 1 KB 146 **90**
Hedley Byrne & Co v. Heller & Partners [1964] AC 465 **45, 270**
Henderson v. Merrett Syndicates Ltd [1995] 2 AC 145 **19**
Hickman v. Maisey [1900] 1 QB 752 **109, 117**
Hill v. Chief Constable of West Yorkshire [1988] 2 All ER 238 **33, 35, 36, 38, 39, 46**
Hills v. Potter [1984] 1 WLR 641 **129**
Higgs v. WH Foster (trading as Avalon Coaches) [2004] EWCA Civ 843; [2004] All ER (D) 21 (Jul) **160**
Holbeck Hall Hotel Ltd v. Scarborough Borough Council [2000] 2 All ER 705 **220**
Hollywood Silver Fox Farm v. Emmett [1936] 2 KB 468 **226**
Home Office v. Dorset Yacht Club [1970] AC 1004 **41, 77, 250**
Hotson v. East Berkshire Health Authority [1987] 1 All ER 210 **74, 81**
Hunter v. Canary Wharf Ltd [1997] 2 All ER 426 **215, 218, 219, 236–8**
Hurst v. Picture Theatres Ltd [1915] 1 KB 1 **105, 113, 117**
Hussain v. Lancaster City Council [2000] QB 1 **219**
Hutchinson v. York, Newcastle and Berwick Railway Company (1850) 5 Ex 343 **244**
ICI Ltd v. Shatwell [1965] AC 656 **89**
Inverugie Investments Ltd v. Hackett [1995] 1 WLR 713 **114**
Jameel v. Dow Jones & Co Inc [2005] 2 WLR 1614 189, 194, 207, 208
Jameel v. Wall Street Journal Europe SPRL (No. 3) [2006] UKHL 44; [2006] 4 All ER 1279 **200**
J A Pye (Oxford) Ltd v. Graham and another [2002] UKHL 30; [2002] 3 All ER 865 **112**
Jobling v. Associated Dairies Ltd [1982] AC 794 **75, 77**
Joel v. Morrison (1834) 6 C & P 501 **256**
John v. Mirror Group Newspapers [1996] 2 All ER 35 **199**

John Summers and Sons Ltd *v.* Frost [1955] AC 740 **250, 258**
Jolley *v.* London Borough of Sutton [2000] 3 All ER 409 **155, 156, 162**
Jones *v.* Livox Quarries Ltd [1952] 2 QB 608 **xxxviii, 94, 95**
Jones *v.* Wright [1991] 2 WLR 814 **xxxiii**
Joseph *v.* Spiller [2010] UKSC 53; [2011] 1 All ER 947 **202**
Junior Brooks *v.* Veitchi Co Ltd [1983] 1 AC 520 **44**
Kaye *v.* Robertson [1991] FSR 62 **274**
Kent *v.* Griffiths, Roberts and London Ambulance Service [1998] EWCA Civ 1941; (1998) 47 BMLR 125 **39**
Keown *v.* Coventry Healthcare NHS Trust [2006] EWCA Civ 39; [2006] 1 WLR 953 **56, 155, 159, 162**
Khorasandjian *v.* Bush [1993] 3 WLR 476 **xxvii, 21, 217**
Kirk *v.* Gregory (1876) 1 Ex D 55 **116**
Knightley *v.* Johns [1982] 1 All ER 851 **77**
Knowles *v.* Liverpool CC [1993] 1 WLR 1428 **245, 247**
Knupffer *v.* London Express [1944] AC 116 **194**
Kubach *v.* Hollands [1937] 3 All ER 907 **172**
Lamb *v.* Camden Borough Council [1981] QB 625 **77**
Lane *v.* Holloway [1968] 1 QB 379 **130, 139**
Latimer *v.* AEC Ltd [1953] AC 643 **246, 247, 258**
Lawrence *v.* Coventry (t/a RDC Promotions [2012] EWCA Civ 26; [2012] 1 WLR 2127 **231**
Lawrence *v.* Fen Tigers Ltd [2012] EWCA Civ 26; [2012] 3 All ER 168 **231**
League against Cruel Sports *v.* Scott [1986] QB 240 **108**
Leakey *v.* The National Trust [1980] QB 485 **220**
Leeman *v.* Montague [1936] 2 All ER 1677 **266**
Letang *v.* Cooper [1965] 1 QB 232 **108, 121, 123, 139**
Lippiatt *v.* South Gloustershire CC [2000] QB 51 **219, 220**
Lister *v.* Hesley Hall Ltd [2002] 1 AC 215 **241, 255, 256, 257, 259**
Lowery *v.* Walker [1911] AC 10 **147, 152, 162**
Ludsin Overseas Ltd *v.* Eco3 Capital Ltd [2013] EWCA Civ 413; [2013] All ER (D) 172 (Apr) **271**
Majrowski *v.* Guy's and St Thomas's NHS Trust [2006] UKHL 34; [2007] 1 AC 224 **252, 257–9**
Malone *v.* Laskey [1907] 2 KB 141 **217**
Marcic *v.* Thames Water Utilities Ltd [2003] UKHL 66; [2004] 2 AC 42 **216, 237**
Mbasogo *v.* Logo Ltd (No 1) [2006] EWCA Civ 1370; [2007] QB 846 **124**
McDonalds Corp. *v.* Steel [1995] 3 All ER 615 **190, 195, 196**
McFarlane *v.* Tayside Health Board [1999] 3 WLR 1301 **52**
McGhee *v.* National Coal Board [1973] 3 All ER 1008 **70, 72, 81**
McKenna *v.* British Aluminium [2002] Env LR 30 **218**
McKew *v.* Holland & Hannen & Cubbits (Scotland) Ltd [1969] 3 All ER 1621 **77**
McLoughlin *v.* O'Brian [1983] 1 AC 410 **43**
Miles *v.* Forest Rock Granite Co (Leicestershire) Ltd (1918) 34 TLR 500 **235**
Miller *v.* Jackson [1977] QB 966 **57, 232**
Ministry of Defence *v.* Radclyffe [2009] EWCA Civ 635; [2009] All ER (D) 299 (Jun) **96**
Moloney *v.* Lambeth London Borough Council (1966) 64 LGR 440 **155**
Morgan *v.* Odhams Press [1971] 1 WLR 1239 **193**
Morris *v.* Murray [1991] 2 QB 6 **85, 88, 98**
Mullin *v.* Richards [1998] 1 All ER 920 **56**
Murray *v.* Ministry of Defence [1988] 2 All ER 521 **134**
Murphy *v.* Brentwood District Council [1990] 3 WLR 414 **34, 35, 45**
Nettleship *v.* Weston [1971] 2 QB 691 **53, 63**
O'Byrne *v.* Aventis Pasteur SA [2010] UKSC 23, [2010] 4 All ER 1 **167, 175**
Ogwo *v.* Taylor [1988] AC 431 **156**
Osman *v.* UK [1999] 1 FLR 193 **38, 39, 47**
Overseas Tankship (UK) Ltd v. Morts Dock and Engineering Co. Ltd (The Wagon Mound) (No 1) [1961] AC 388 **31, 67, 78–81, 156**
Page *v.* Smith [1996] AC 155 **43**

Parabola Investments Ltd v. Browallia Cal Ltd [2010] EWCA Civ 486; [2011] QB 477 **272**
Paris v. Stepney Borough Council [1951] AC 367 **57**
Performance Cars v. Abraham [1962] 1 QB 33 **71**
Phelps v. Hillingdon London Borough Council [2000] 4 All ER 504 **38, 39, 47**
Phipps v. Rochester Corporation [1955] 1 QB 450 **155**
Polemis and Furness, Withy & Co [1921] 3 KB 560 **78, 79**
Pollard v. Tesco Stores [2006] EWCA Civ 393; [2006] All ER (D) 186 (Apr) **167, 178–80, 182**
Pritchard v. Co-operative Group Ltd [2011] EWCA Civ 329; [2012] QB 320 **132**
R v. Ireland [1997] 4 All ER 225 **125, 139**
R v. Rimmington [2005] UKHL 63; [2006] 1 AC 459 **227**
R (on the application of Moos and McClure) v. Commissioner of Police of the Metropolis [2011] EWHC 957 (Admin); [2011] All ER (D) 146 (Apr) **135**
R (on the application of Lumba) v. Secretary of State for the Home Department [2011] UKSC 12; [2012] 1 AC 245 **133, 134**
Read v. J Lyons & Co Ltd [1947] AC 156 **235**
Ready-Mixed Concrete (South East) Ltd v. Minister of Pensions and National Insurance [1965] 2 QB 497 **241, 253, 254, 258**
Reckitt & Coleman Products v. Borden Inc [1990] 1 All ER 873 **275**
Reeves v. Commissioner of Police [2000] 1 AC 360 **154**
Revill v. Newbery [1996] QB 567 **130, 148**
Reynolds v. Times Newspapers Ltd [1999] 4 All ER 609 **187, 203, 204–7**
Richardson v. LRC Products [2000] Lloyd's Rep Med 280 **177**
Rickards v. Lothian [1913] AC 280 **235**
Rigby v. Chief Constable of Northamptonshire [1985] 2 All ER 985 **113**
Robinson v. Kilvert (1889) 41 Ch D 88 **226**
Robson v. Hallett [1967] 2 All ER 407 **110**
Roe v. Minister of Health [1954] 2 QB 66 **56, 58**

Roles v. Nathan [1963] 1 WLR 1117 **156**
Rose v. Plenty [1976] 1 WLR 141 **256**
Rylands v. Fletcher (1868) LR 3 HL 330; [1861–73] All ER Rep 1 **xxiii, xxxix, 12, 97, 211–38**
S v. W (child abuse: damages) [1995] 1 FLR 862 **131**
St George v. Home Office [2008] EWCA Civ 1068; [2008] 4 All ER 1039 **93**
Scott v. London and St Katherine Docks Co [1861–73] All ER Rep 246 **61**
Sedleigh Denfield v. O'Callaghan [1940] AC 880 **215, 217, 219, 223, 237**
Shine v. London Borough of Tower Hamlets [2006] All ER (D) 79 **57**
Sidaway v. Bethlem Royal Hospital [1985] AC 871 **128**
Sienkiewicz v. Greif (UK) Ltd [2011] 2 AC 229 **73**
Sim v. Stretch [1936] 2 All ER 1237 **188, 192**
Six Carpenters' Case (1610) 8 Co Rep 146a **105, 111**
Smith v. Charles Baker & Sons [1891] AC 325 **85, 89, 98**
Smith v. Chief Constable of Sussex Police [2008] UKHL 50; [2009] AC 225 **39, 40**
Smith v. Finch [2009] EWHC 53 (QB); [2009] All ER (D) 158 (Jan) **96**
Smith v. Leech Brain & Co Ltd [1962] 2 WB 405 **80**
Smith v. Littlewoods Organisation Ltd [1987] 1 All ER 710 **40, 47**
Smith v. Stone (1647) Sty 65 **105, 107, 117**
Southwark London Borough Council v. Williams [1971] Ch 734 **114**
Spartan Steel v. Martin & Co Contractors Ltd [1973] 1 QB 27 **44**
Speed v. Thomas Swift & Co Ltd [1943] KB 557 **245, 247**
Spicer v. Smee [1946] 1 All ER 489 **225**
Stannard (t/a Wyvern Tyres) v. Gore [2012] EWCA Civ 1248; [2013] 1 All ER 694 **235**
Stanton v. Collinson [2010] EWCA Civ 81; [2010] All ER (D) 276 (Feb) **95**
Stapley v. Gypsum Mines [1953] AC 663 **90**
Steel and Morris v. UK [2005] 18 BHRC 545 **xxxv, 191, 198**

Stennett v. Hancock [1939] 2 All ER 578 **170**
Stephens v. Myers (1830) 4 C&P 349 **126**
Stermer v. Lawson [1977] 5 WWR 628 **85, 88, 98**
Stevenson Jordan & Harrison v. Macdonald & Evans [1952] 1 TLR 101 **253**
St Helen's Smelting Co v. Tipping (1865) 11 HLC 642 **222, 224**
Stovin v. Wise, Norfolk County Council (Third Party) [1996] 3 WLR 15 **36, 39**
Stubbings v. Webb [1992] AC 498 **123, 131–3**
Sturges v. Bridgman (1879) 11 Ch D 852 **224, 230**
Tate and Lyle Industries v. Greater London Council [1983] 2 AC 509 **228**
Tetley and others v. Chitty and others [1986] 1 All ER 663 **220**
Thomas v. National Union of Mineworkers [1985] 2 All ER 1 **124**
Thompson v. T Lohan (Plant Hire) Ltd [1987] 1 WLR 649 **254**
Tolstoy Miloslavsky v. United Kingdom [1996] EMLR 152 **199**
Tomlinson v. Congleton Borough Council [2002] EWCA Civ 309; [2003] 3 All ER 1122 **59, 147, 153, 160, 162**
Topp v. London Country Buses Ltd [1993] 3 All ER 448 **41**
Transco plc v. Stockport Metropolitan Borough Council [2003] UKHL 61; [2004] 2 AC 1 **235, 236**
Turberville v. Savage (1669) 1 Mod Rep 3 **124**
Turnbull v. Warrener [2012] EWCA Civ 412; [2012] All ER (D) 51 (Apr) **263, 268, 270, 276**
Van Colle and another v. Chief Constable of the Hertfordshire Police [2008] UKHL 50; [2009] AC 225 **39, 40**
Various Claimants v. Institute of the Brothers of the Christian Schools [2012] 3 WLR 1319 **257**

Wainwright v. Home Office [2003] 4 All ER 969 **128, 136**
Walker v. Northumberland County Council [1995] 1 All ER 737 **57, 80, 247**
Walsh v. Lonsdale (1882) 21 Ch D 9 **64**
Wandsworth LBC v. Railtrack plc [2001] 1 WLR 368 **266**
Ward v. Tesco Stores Ltd [1976] 1 WLR 810 **61**
Watson and Others v. Croft Promo-Sport Ltd [2009] 3 All ER 249 **232**
Watt v. Hertfordshire County Council [1954] 1 WLR 835 **59**
Weddall v. Barchester Healthcare Ltd [2012] EWCA Civ 25; [2012] All ER (D) 01 (Feb) **259**
Welsh v. Stokes [2007] EWCA Civ 796; [2008] 1 All ER 921 **268, 276**
Wheat v. E Lacon & Co Ltd [1966] AC 522 **147, 149, 150, 152, 161, 162**
White v. Chief Constable of South Yorkshire [1999] 1 All ER 1 **248**
Wieland v. Cyril Lord Carpets Ltd [1969] 3 All ER 1006 **77**
Wilkinson v. Downton [1897] 2 QB 57 **120, 121, 135–40**
Wilsher v. Essex Area Health Authority [1988] AC 1074 **71**
Wilson v. Pringle [1986] 2 All ER 440 **121, 127, 139**
Wilsons & Clyde Coal Co v. English [1938] AC 57 **31, 241, 244, 245, 258**
Woodward v. Mayor of Hastings [1954] KB 74 **157**
Wooldridge v. Sumner [1963] 2 QB 53 **58, 91**
Woolley v. Ultimate Products Ltd [2012] EWCA Civ 1038; [2012] All ER (D) 282 (Jul) **275, 277**
X (Minors) v. Bedfordshire County Council [1995] 3 WLR 152 **27, 35–8, 47, 249**
Yachuk v. Oliver Blais [1949] AC 386 **94**
Young v. Kent County Council [2005] EWHC 1342 (QB); [2005] All ER (D) 217 (Mar) **159**
Z v. UK [2001] FLR 193 **38, 47**

Table of statutes

Animals Act 1971 **16, 262, 263, 266, 269, 276, 277**
   s. 2 **268, 277**
      (1) **262, 268**
      (2) **262, 263, 267, 268, 276**
         (a) **267**
         (b) **267, 268**
         (c) **267, 268**
   s. 3 **270**
   s. 4 **269**
   s. 5 **262, 276, 277**
      (1)–(3) **270**
   s. 6(2) **262, 266**
      (a), (b) **266**
   s. 8 **269**
   s. 9 **270**
Bill of Rights 1688
   Art. 9 **202**
Civil Aviation Act 1982 **109**
   s. 77 **214, 230, 237**
      (1), (2) **230, 237**
Civil Evidence Act 1968 **60**
   s. 11 **50, 60–2, 64**
Civil Liability (Contribution) Act 1978 **6, 22, 23**
Compensation Act 2006 **73**
   s. 1 **50, 59, 64**
   s. 3 **66, 73, 80, 81**
      (2) **81**
Congenital Disabilities (Civil Liability) Act 1976 **32**
   s. 1(2) **177**
   s. 2(1) **175**
      (2) **175**
      (5) **177**
         (3), (4) **176**
   s. 3 **177, 180, 182**
      (1) **178, 182**

s. 4 **179, 182**
   (1) **179**
s. 6(8) **177**
s. 7 **178**
Consumer Protection Act 1987 **xxxv, 16, 143, 144, 166, 169, 173–83, 278**
Contracts (Rights of Third Parties) Act 1999 **168**
Countryside and Rights of Way Act 2000 **151**
Criminal Law Act 1977 **104, 115**
   s. 6–10 **108**
Dangerous Dogs Act 1991 **266**
Defamation Act 1996 **186, 202**
   s. 2 **205**
   s. 7 **202**
   s. 14 **208**
   s. 15 **202, 208**
Defamation Act 2013 **xxxiv, 143, 144, 186–208**
   s. 1 **190, 191, 195, 200, 201, 206**
      (1) **195**
      (2) **190, 195, 196, 201**
   s. 2 **201, 205**
      (3) **201**
   s. 3 **202, 205**
      (5) **202**
   s. 4(2) **204**
   s. 5 **204**
   s. 6 **203, 205**
   s. 7 **203, 205**
   s. 8 **196, 197**
   s. 9 **200**
   s. 10 **204**
   s. 11 **199, 206, 208**
   s. 12 **206**
   s. 13 **206**
   s. 14 **190**

Defective Premises Act 1972 **32, 148, 161, 203**
Employers' Liability (Defective Equipment) Act 1969 **245**
　s. 1 **240**
　　(1) **245**
Enterprise and Regulatory Reform Act 2013 **249**
　s. 69 **249**
Factories Act 1937
　s. 4(1) **250**
Factories Act 1961 **246**
Guard Dogs Act 1975 **270**
Health and Safety at Work etc. Act 1974 **248, 249**
Human Rights Act 1998 **6, 9, 19, 20, 26, 36, 37, 195, 199, 215, 218**
　s. 6 **39**
　s. 12 **189**
　s. 25(11) **64**
Land Registration Act 2002 **112**
Law Commissions Act 1965 **xxxvi**
Law Reform (Contributory Negligence) Act 1945 **22, 84, 93, 132, 240**
　s. 1(1) **93, 99**
　s. 4 **96**
Law Reform (Personal Injuries) Act 1948 **244**
Legal Aid, Sentencing and Punishment of Offenders Act 2012 **118**
　s. 144 **112**
Limitation Act 1980 **131–3, 139, 140**
　s. 2 **120, 131–3, 140**
　s. 4A **197**
　s. 11 **120, 131–3, 139, 140**
　s. 15 **112**
　s. 33 **131–3**
Local Government Act 1972
　s. 222 **227**
Malicious Communications Act 1985 **227**
Mental Health Act 1983 **135**
　s. 37 **97**
　s. 53 **130**
Mines (Working Facilities and Support) Act 1966 **109**
National Parks and Access to the Countryside Act 1949 **151, 159**

Occupiers' Liability Act 1957 **32, 143, 146–9, 151, 152, 158, 160, 161, 163, 249, 279**
　s. 1 **147, 151**
　　(3) **153**
　　(4) **151**
　s. 2(1) **146, 151, 154, 157**
　　(2) **152–5**
　　(3) **155**
　　　(a) **155**
　　　(b) **156**
　　(4) **153**
　　　(a) **146, 157**
　　　(b) **153, 157**
　　(5) **158**
Occupiers' Liability Act 1984 **32, 143, 144, 146–9, 151, 155, 157–61, 163, 249, 279**
　s. 1(1) **159**
　　(a) **146, 147, 159**
　　(4) **159**
　　(5) **160**
　　(7) **147, 159**
Police and Criminal Evidence Act 1984 **130, 140**
　ss. 8–22 **116**
　ss. 15–19 **113**
　s. 24 **134**
　s. 25 **134**
Protection from Eviction Act 1977 **115**
Protection from Harassment Act 1997 **xxxvii, 21, 115, 120, 125, 137, 138, 217, 218, 278**
　s. 1(1) **137**
　s. 3 **252**
　s. 7(3) **137**
Race Relations Act 1976 **249**
Rights of Entry (Gas and Electricity) Boards Act 1954 **113**
Road Traffic Act 1988 **61**
　s. 149(3) **84, 91, 99**
Safety of Sports Grounds Act 1975 **249**
Sale and Supply of Goods Act 1994 **168**
Sale of Goods Act 1893 **168**
Sale of Goods Act 1979 **19, 168, 176**
Securing the Protection of Our Enduring and Established Constitutional Heritage (SPEECH) Act 2010 (US) **199**

Senior Courts Act 1981
   s. 49 **64**
Theft Act 1968
   s. 9 **108, 117**
Torts (Interference with Goods) Act 1977 **104, 115**
   s. 3 **116**
   s. 8 **116**
Unfair Contract Terms Act 1977 **21, 157, 168, 178, 255**
   s. 2(1) **92**
Vagrancy Act 1824
   s. 4 **108, 117**

Statutory Instruments

Noise at Work Regulations 1989, SI 1989/635 **246, 247**
Provision and Use of Work Equipment Regulations 1998, SI 1998/2306 **245**
Unfair Terms in Consumer Contract Regulations 1999, SI 1999/2083 **168**

European legislation

Directives

Directive 85/374/EEC Liability for Defective Products **xxxv, 166, 167, 174**

Conventions

European Convention for the Protection of Human Rights and Fundamental Freedoms **9, 19, 20, 38, 39**
   Art. 6 **26, 38, 47**
   Art. 8 **218**
   Art. 10 **189, 195, 199**
   Art. 13 **38**

Acknowledgements

I am grateful to the anonymous referees from academic institutions whose valuable comments and suggestions have been instrumental in the production of this text. Any errors or omissions remain the author's. Many thanks also to my colleagues at Middlesex University, London, with whom I am privileged to teach students from across the globe. The inspiring and creative team at Pearson, and in particular my editor, Christine Statham, deserve special thanks.

Finally, but most of all, heartfelt thanks to my long-suffering and patient James.

Mariette Jones
Middlesex University

How to use this guide

Blueprints was created for students searching for a smarter introductory guide to their legal studies

This guide will serve as a primer for deeper study of the law – enabling you to get the most out of your lectures and studies by giving you a way in to the subject which is more substantial than a revision guide, but more succinct than your course textbook. The series is designed to give you an overview of the law, so you can see the structure of the subject and understand how the topics you will study throughout your course fit together in the big picture. It will help you keep your bearings as you move through your course study.

Blueprints recognises that students want to succeed in their course modules

This requires more than a basic grasp of key legislation; you will need knowledge of the historical and social context of the law, recognition of the key debates, an ability to think critically and to draw connections between topics.

Blueprints addresses the various aspects of legal study, using assorted text features and visual tools

Each Blueprints guide begins with an **Introduction**, outlining the parameters of the subject and the challenges you might face in your studies. This includes a **Map** of the subject highlighting the major areas of study.

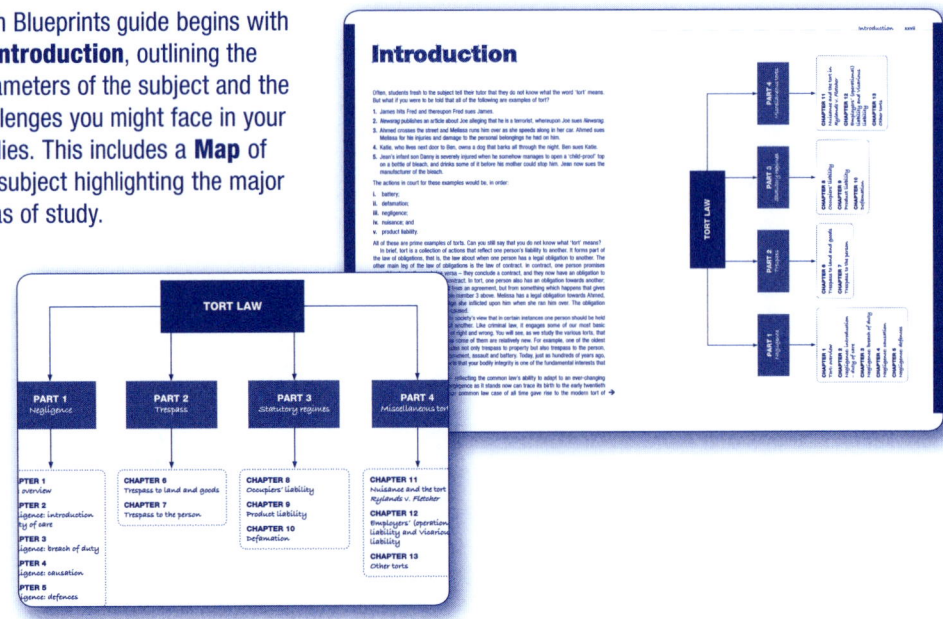

How to use this guide xxi

Each **Part** of the guide also begins with an Introduction and a Map of the main topics you need to grasp and how they fit together.

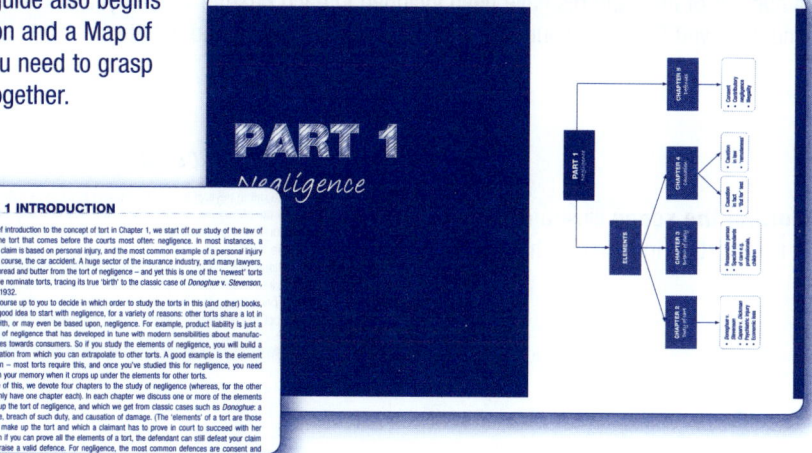

Each guide includes advice on the specific **study skills** you will need to do well in the subject.

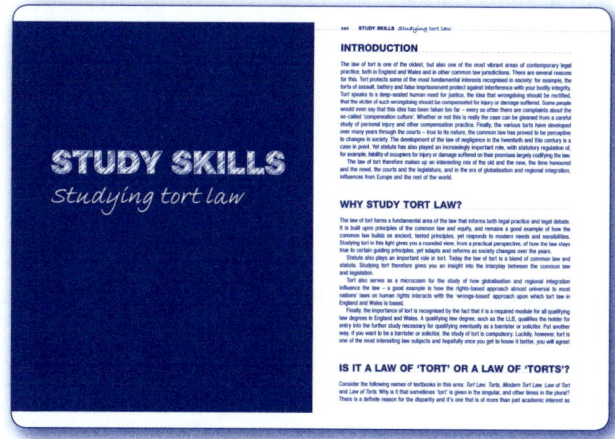

Each chapter starts with a **Blueprint** of the topic area to provide a visual overview of the fundamental buildings blocks of each topic, and the academic questions and the various outside influences that converge in the study of law.

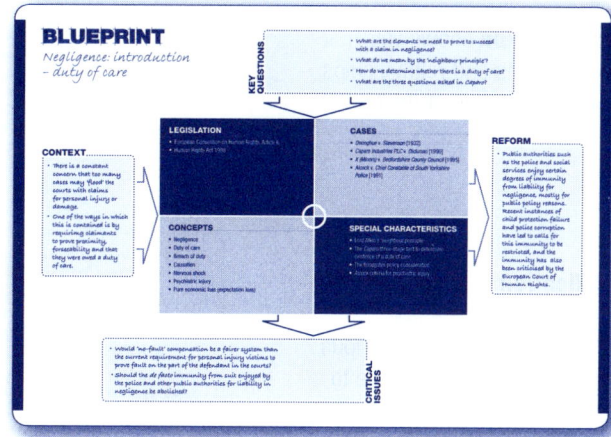

How to use this guide

A number of text features have been included in each chapter to help you better understand the law and push you further in your appreciation of the subtleties and debates:

Setting the scene illustrates why it is important to study each topic.

Setting the scene

Negligence in tort can mean several things. It can refer to careless behaviour or negligent conduct in the ordinary sense of the phrase, or it could refer to the legal concept of **fault**, which is a requirement for liability in most civil and criminal actions. For example, in criminal law if you intentionally kill someone, you may be found guilty of murder; if you negligently cause someone's death, you may be found guilty of manslaughter. 'Fault' here includes intention, or negligence. In this sense negligence as a fault element is important to us, because for many torts 'fault' is a requirement for liability. For now, though, we concentrate on the third possible meaning of negligence, namely as a tort in its own right. In short, the tort of negligence means that if you negligently or carelessly cause damage or injury to someone, you may be held liable for it.

Cornerstone highlights the fundamental building blocks of the law.

CORNERSTONE

Reasonable person test

Whichever analogy is used, the point is that we are dealing with the average person. This is an objective test, which means that we compare the specific defendant against a fictional standard. We do not enquire into the defendant's own, subjective, standards but hold her to the standard set for all.

Application shows how the law applies in the real world.

APPLICATION

G is driving his car over the speed limit, and knocks down a pedestrian at a crossing. The pedestrian, F, happens to suffer from brittle bone diseases and as a result of being knocked down, suffers severe spinal injuries and is now paralysed. G's lawyer points out to court that G had not been exceeding the speed limit very much, and also that even though he could foresee that his negligent action could knock someone over, any normal person would at most have suffered a broken bone or two. The court does not accept this and states that G must take his victim as he found her. It was foreseeable that there could be injury, it did not need to be foreseeable too that the injury would be that severe.

Intersection shows you connections and relationships with other areas of the law.

INTERSECTION

What about words or actions on their own, absent the apprehension of imminent harm? The courts for some time tried to make this actionable, but the enactment of the Protection from Harassment Act 1997 solved the problem of what amounted really to a gap in the law. We briefly look at the Harassment Act at the end of this chapter.

Reflection helps you think critically about the law, introducing you to the various complexities that give rise to debate and controversy.

REFLECTION

Is the House of Lords' approval of the practice of kettling justified?
McBride and Bagshaw (2012: 37) state that:

'[i]t is surprising that of the nine judges who ended up considering the case of *Austin* . . . not one could be found to speak for the idea that it is unlawful to imprison an innocent person, whether or not doing so is necessary in order to prevent a breach of the peace.'

This decision was subsequently watered down slightly when it was decided in *R (on the application of Moos and McClure)* v. *Commissioner of Police of the Metropolis* [2011] EWHC 957 that kettling may only be used as a last resort, but it may nevertheless be concluded that the courts are still favouring public order over individual freedom – something which traditionally does not sit well with the common law.

How to use this guide xxiii

Context fills in some of the historical and cultural background knowledge that will help you understand and appreciate the legal issues of today.

> **CONTEXT**
> Before 1957, the common law prescribed that you owed a duty to lawful visitors, but that duty varied according to whether the visitor entered by contract or as an invitee or licensee. Thus, varying levels of duty were owed to various kinds of visitors. The Occupiers' Liability Act 1957(OLA 1957) simplified matters by abolishing these 'occupancy duties' and replacing them with the single common duty of care, owed to a single category of visitor, the lawful visitor.

Take note offers advice that can save you time and trouble in your studies.

> *Take note*
> *Intermediate examination is only relevant if it would be reasonable to expect somebody (such as the retailer, or the consumer, or anybody else) actually to inspect the product. If a product is supposed to go onto the market 'as is', it would not be reasonable to*

defendant to show that the damage was caused by the *manufacturer's* negligence. This is even more so if there is a clear warning by the manufacturer that the product should be inspected. *Kubach* v. *Hollands* [1937] 3 All ER 907 a schoolgirl was injured when the chemicals she used at school in an experiment caused an explosion. It turned out that the retailer who supplied the chemicals to the school had not tested the product as per the manufacturer's instructions. The court held that the retailer could be held liable but not the manufacturer.

Exclusion of liability

Key points lists the main things to know about each topic.

> ## KEY POINTS
> - Defamation protects an individual's reputation and is the defamatory publication of an untrue statement which lowers the claimant in the eyes of society.
> - The law of defamation has recently been the subject of major reform, resulting in the enactment of the Defamation Act 2013.
> - There are two kinds of defamation: libel and slander, of which the former is more important.

Core cases and statutes summarises the major case law and legislation in the topic.

> ## CORE CASES AND STATUTES
>
> | Case | About | Importance |
> |---|---|---|
> | Marcic v. Thames Water Utilities Ltd [2003] UKHL 66 | Claim in nuisance | Where a statutory regime covers a nuisance situation, the claim has to be instituted in terms of the statute. |
> | Hunter v. Canary Wharf Ltd [1997] 2 All ER 426 | Locus standi in private nuisance | One has to have a legal right in the affected land in order to be able to sue in private nuisance. |
> | Sedleigh Denfield v. | Private nuisance | Even if you did not create a |

Further reading directs you to select primary and secondary sources as a springboard to further studies.

> ## FURTHER READING
> Barrett, B. (2006) Vicarious liability for harassment by an employee. *ILJ* 35(4), p. 431
> This is a case comment on the House of Lords' decision in *Majrowski* v. *Guy's and St Thomas' NHS Trust* [2006] UKHL 34, and explains in clear terms how employers are held vicariously liable for both common law and statutory torts committed by an employee.
>
> general principles relating to employers' liability towards their employees.
>
> Pawlowska, C. (2012) Vicarious liability is now more about value judgment than law. *SJ* 156(11), pp. 12–13
> In this easy-to-read article in the *Solicitors' Journal*, the author examines cases after the decision in *Lister* v. *Hesley Hall*, where the

A **glossary** provides helpful definitions of key terms.

> **actionable *per se*** A claim which is actionable without proof of damage.
> **assault** Tort consisting of the threat of immediate harm to the claimant.
> **battery** Tort consisting of unlawful touching or touching with hostile intent.
> **burden of proof** This indicates who has the burden or duty to prove something in court.
> **causation** The element needed in most torts showing that the action forming the tort caused the damage sued for.
>
> **false imprisonment** Tort consisting of fully restricting a person's ability to move from a place.
> **fault** A requirement for many torts, consisting of either intention or negligence.
> **harassment** A course of conduct causing distress or alarm, in terms of the Protection from Harassment Act 1997.
> **injunction** A court order to prevent something from happening, or if it is happening already, to stop it from recurring or continuing.

What is a Blueprint?

Blueprints provide a unique plan for studying the law, giving you a visual overview of the fundamental buildings blocks of each topic, and the academic questions and the various outside influences that converge in the study of law.

At the centre are the 'black-letter' elements, the fundamental building blocks that make up what the law says and how it works.

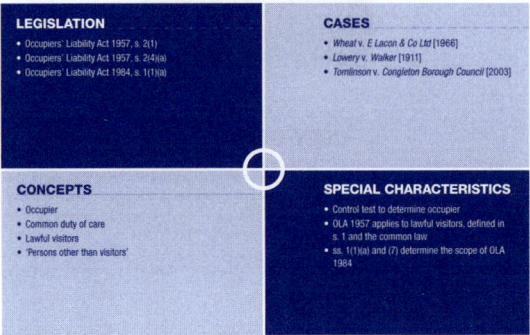

As a law student you will need to learn what questions or problems the law attempts to address, and what sort of issues arise from the way it does this that require critical reflection.

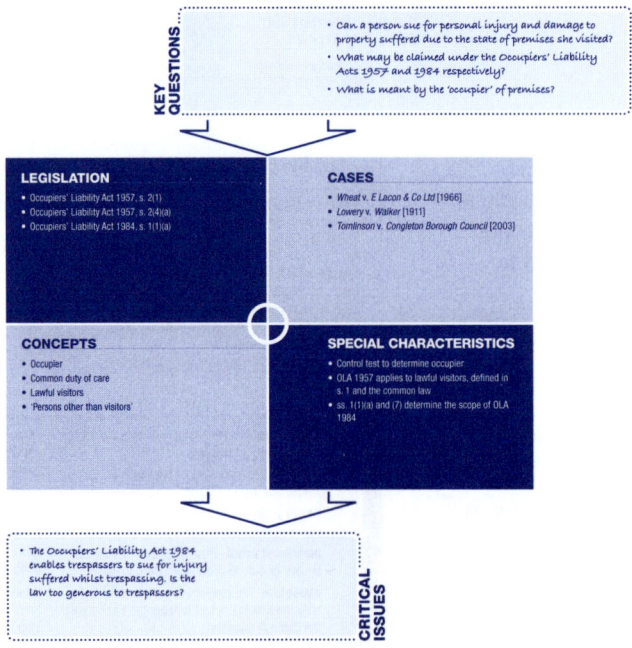

What is a Blueprint? xxv

To gain a more complete understanding of the role of law in society you will need to know what influencing factors have shaped the law in the past, and how the law may develop in the near future.

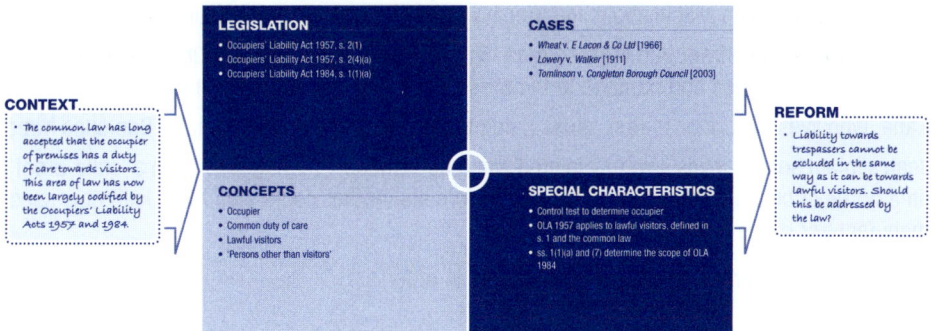

You can use the Blueprint for each topic as a framework for building your knowledge in the subject.

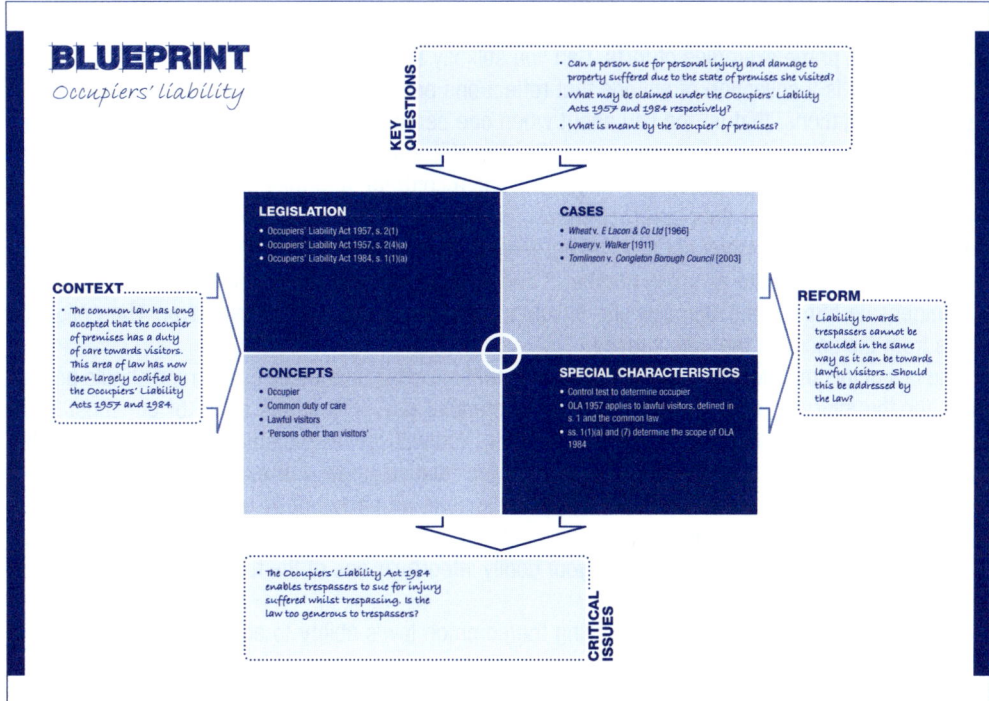

Introduction

Often, students fresh to the subject tell their tutor that they do not know what the word 'tort' means. But what if you were to be told that all of the following are examples of tort?

1. James hits Fred and thereupon Fred sues James.
2. *Newsrag* publishes an article about Joe alleging that he is a terrorist, whereupon Joe sues *Newsrag*.
3. Ahmed crosses the street and Melissa runs him over as she speeds along in her car. Ahmed sues Melissa for his injuries and damage to the personal belongings he had on him.
4. Katie, who lives next door to Ben, owns a dog that barks all through the night. Ben sues Katie.
5. Jean's infant son Danny is severely injured when he somehow manages to open a 'child-proof' top on a bottle of bleach, and drinks some of it before his mother could stop him. Jean now sues the manufacturer of the bleach.

The actions in court for these examples would be, in order:

i. battery;
ii. defamation;
iii. negligence;
iv. nuisance; and
v. product liability.

All of these are prime examples of torts. Can you still say that you do not know what 'tort' means?

In brief, tort is a collection of actions that reflect one person's liability to another. It forms part of the law of obligations, that is, the law about when one person has a legal obligation to another. The other main leg of the law of obligations is the law of contract. In contract, one person promises something to another and vice versa – they conclude a contract, and they now have an obligation to one another arising out of their contract. In tort, one person also has an obligation towards another; however the obligation comes not from an agreement, but from something which happens that gives rise to the obligation. Take example number 3 above. Melissa has a legal obligation towards Ahmed, to compensate him for the damage she inflicted upon him when she ran him over. The obligation arises from the accident that she caused.

The law of tort therefore reflects society's view that in certain instances one person should be held liable for the injury or damage of another. Like criminal law, it engages some of our most basic concepts of justice and our ideas of right and wrong. You will see, as we study the various torts, that some of them are ancient whereas some of them are relatively new. For example, one of the oldest torts is that of trespass: this includes not only trespass to property but also trespass to the person, which in turn includes false imprisonment, assault and battery. Today, just as hundreds of years ago, the law still recognises in these torts that your bodily integrity is one of the fundamental interests that the law should protect.

Other torts are relatively new – reflecting the common law's ability to adapt to an ever-changing society. For example, the tort of negligence as it stands now can trace its birth to the early twentieth century. Arguably the most famous common law case of all time gave rise to the modern tort of →

Introduction xxvii

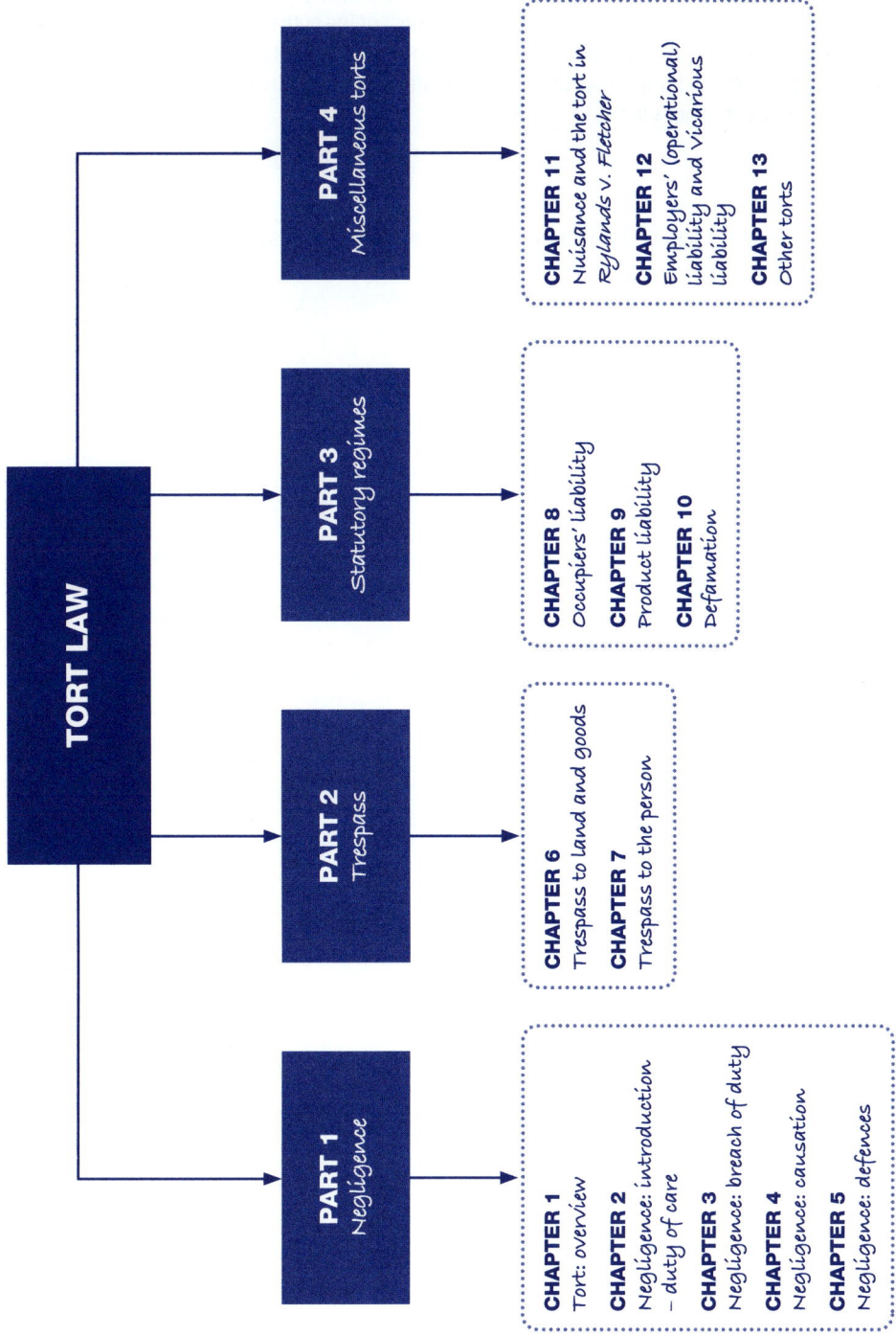

negligence, namely *Donoghue* v. *Stevenson* [1932] AC 562. You will soon be introduced to the famous snail in the ginger beer that led to this judgment, but also to many other very interesting cases.

Because of the focus of tort – our everyday lives – most of the court cases you will encounter make very engaging reading. In this book we try to give you a map to guide you towards a basic understanding of the most important torts. If this taster leaves you thinking; 'I want to know more', we have succeeded in what we set out to do.

Note: References to the feminine gender include reference to the masculine and vice versa.

STUDY SKILLS
studying tort law

INTRODUCTION

The law of tort is one of the oldest, but also one of the most vibrant areas of contemporary legal practice, both in England and Wales and in other common law jurisdictions. There are several reasons for this. Tort protects some of the most fundamental interests recognised in society: for example, the torts of assault, battery and false imprisonment protect against interference with your bodily integrity. Tort speaks to a deep-seated human need for justice, the idea that wrongdoing should be rectified, that the victim of such wrongdoing should be compensated for injury or damage suffered. Some people would even say that this idea has been taken too far – every so often there are complaints about the so-called 'compensation culture'. Whether or not this is really the case can be gleaned from a careful study of personal injury and other compensation practice. Finally, the various torts have developed over many years through the courts – true to its nature, the common law has proved to be perceptive to changes in society. The development of the law of negligence in the twentieth and this century is a case in point. Yet statute has also played an increasingly important role, with statutory regulation of, for example, liability of occupiers for injury or damage suffered on their premises largely codifying the law.

The law of tort therefore makes up an interesting mix of the old and the new, the time honoured and the novel, the courts and the legislature, and in the era of globalisation and regional integration, influences from Europe and the rest of the world.

WHY STUDY TORT LAW?

The law of tort forms a fundamental area of the law that informs both legal practice and legal debate. It is built upon principles of the common law and equity, and remains a good example of how the common law builds on ancient, tested principles, yet responds to modern needs and sensibilities. Studying tort in this light gives you a rounded view, from a practical perspective, of how the law stays true to certain guiding principles, yet adapts and reforms as society changes over the years.

Statute also plays an important role in tort. Today the law of tort is a blend of common law and statute. Studying tort therefore gives you an insight into the interplay between the common law and legislation.

Tort also serves as a microcosm for the study of how globalisation and regional integration influence the law – a good example is how the rights-based approach almost universal to most nations' laws on human rights interacts with the 'wrongs-based' approach upon which tort law in England and Wales is based.

Finally, the importance of tort is recognised by the fact that it is a required module for all qualifying law degrees in England and Wales. A qualifying law degree, such as the LLB, qualifies the holder for entry into the further study necessary for qualifying eventually as a barrister or solicitor. Put another way, if you want to be a barrister or solicitor, the study of tort is compulsory. Luckily, however, tort is one of the most interesting law subjects and hopefully once you get to know it better, you will agree!

IS IT A LAW OF 'TORT' OR A LAW OF 'TORTS'?

Consider the following names of textbooks in this area: *Tort Law*, *Torts*, *Modern Tort Law*, *Law of Tort* and *Law of Torts*. Why is it that sometimes 'tort' is given in the singular, and other times in the plural? There is a definite reason for the disparity and it's one that is of more than just academic interest as it affects the way in which you should approach the study of tort. One camp is of the opinion that there are certain underlying, universal principles to all torts, and that we can therefore talk of 'tort', as a unitary concept. In the other camp are those who believe that this area of the law deals with various very different torts, and that we should recognise this fact by acknowledging that there are not one but many torts – in the plural.

So how is this debate of significance to you as a student embarking on your study of this area of law? First, it should flag up to you that there *are* indeed various different torts, and you should therefore expect to have to get to know these and that each of the torts has its own rules, elements and principles which you need to master. Secondly, this should inform the way in which you approach reading relevant case law.

Tort law in action: unitary or disparate view of tort?

The decision in *Khorasandjian* v. *Bush* [1993] 3 WLR 476, which considered the possibility of a new tort of harassment, provides support for the general, unitary view. However, after that decision, the Protection from Harassment Act 1997 was enacted, which again could indicate a swing towards a more disparate view of torts.

THE COMMON DENOMINATORS AND THE VARIOUS NOMINATE TORTS

First, you need to try to learn at least the names of the most important nominate (named) torts. This is relatively easy to do – have a look at the tables of contents of a variety of textbooks on tort and you will quickly be able to make a list. For now, here are some of the most important torts:

- Negligence
- Nuisance
- Trespass
- Occupiers' liability
- Defamation.

Then, keeping in mind that there are various disparate torts, your strategy for learning tort should recognise that there are indeed elements that are to be found in multiple torts (even if they are not *common* to all torts). For this reason this book (and most other textbooks on tort) starts off by looking at these common denominators or common principles. Thus, an important skill for you to master in order to succeed with studying tort is to recognise that although there are various nominate torts, there are some elements which are common to some of them – further, where an element *is* to be found in different torts, in most cases they are fairly similar. Recognising this will save you a lot of time when you learn the various torts, as you will know that, at least for some elements, you will probably have learnt the relevant rules already. For example, similar rules about factual causation apply to virtually all torts that have this as an element.

So it makes sense to look at the most commonly encountered elements first and then at the nominate torts and which elements each contains. In this book, we do this by examining the commonly encountered elements first in the introductory chapter.

This also explains why, out of all the nominate torts, we start off with negligence – most of the elements common to other torts are to be found in negligence.

WHY IS THERE SO MUCH FOCUS ON THE TORT OF NEGLIGENCE?

You will notice that most textbooks (including this one) devote more space to negligence than to most of the other torts. There are several reasons for this. First, negligence is the most important modern tort, as it is the one which gives rise to the most litigation and is therefore dealt with in the courts more often. There is a wealth of reported judgments on negligence.

Secondly, the principles underlying the tort are applicable to many other torts: for example, the principles surrounding causation. So dealing with these elements here gives you a sound understanding not only of negligence, but of principles also underlying other torts. You will therefore note that, in the later chapters, you will be referred back to principles already dealt with under negligence, as they are applicable in the same manner.

A good strategy, therefore, is for you to study negligence really thoroughly, because you will be learning principles that you will be applying to the other torts (and also, if you intend to practise personal injury law at some stage, in the courts).

THE NOMINATE TORTS

Having first looked at the most common principles underlying tort law, we study a variety of the most important torts. These are named, hence the term 'nominate torts'. In this book, we focus on the elements that you need to prove for each nominate tort as a learning strategy.

Learn the elements of each tort

When we refer to the 'elements' of a tort, we mean those things that both make up the tort and that have to be proved in court for a successful claim in that specific tort. As you learn about more torts, you will note that for some of them the elements overlap. Or, put another way, some elements are common to multiple torts.

> ### Example: the elements of negligence
> As an example, let's look at the elements that you have to prove for the tort of negligence. These include that you have to prove that there was a duty of care, that there was breach of such duty of care, which caused damage, and that such damage was not too remote.

At this stage, it is a good strategy to make a flowchart of the elements for the tort you are studying. Then, following your own flowchart, you can easily work out whether the tort has been committed or not. Let's look at the elements for negligence again, this time using a flowchart to determine whether there was negligence.

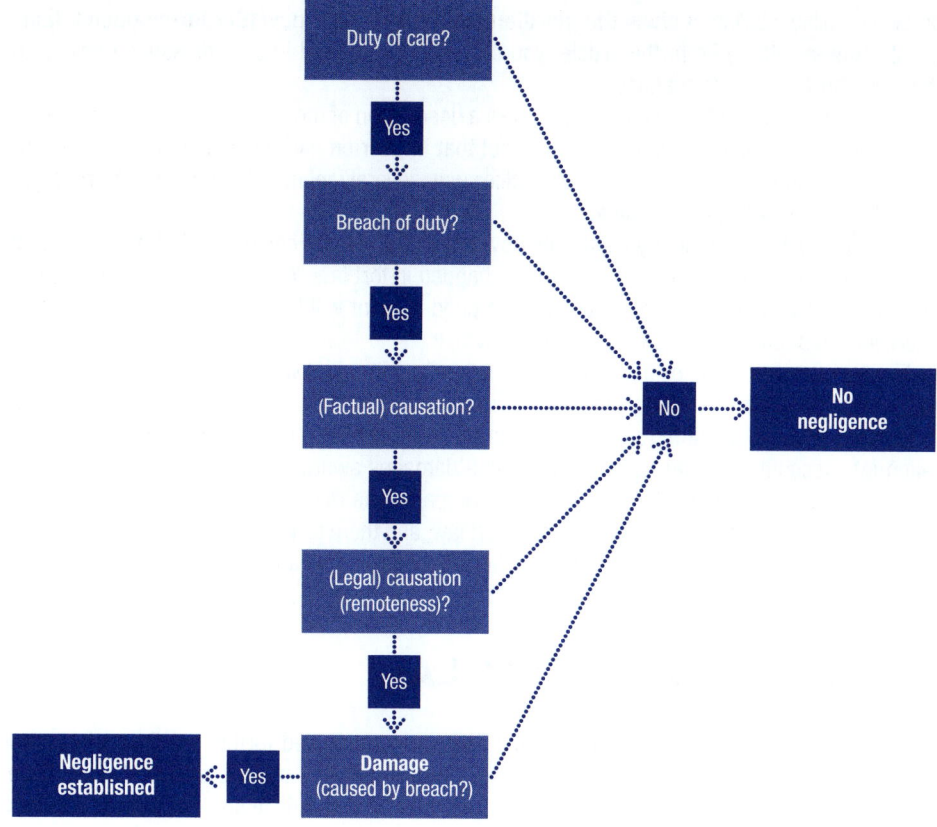

Figure 1 Elements of negligence flowchart

Using a flowchart such as this is useful for several reasons: when faced with a problem-type question for coursework, it provides a logical template for answering the question. For the same reason, it comes in handy in exams. But, most importantly, it is valuable in real life – in practice, when you have to advise a client or prove the matter in court.

Tort law in action

An article in the *Guardian* newspaper of 19 November 2012 entitled: 'Compensation award for car crash girl sets personal injury record at £23m' reported on compensation awarded to a young woman called Agnes Collier, who suffered very severe spinal injuries due to a motor vehicle accident which the defendant had caused by his negligent driving. Ms Collier also lost her mother in the accident.

Damages were awarded against the insurers of Anthony Norton, the motorist who had caused the accident. In a criminal trial, Mr Norton was given a suspended sentence and was banned from driving for 18 months. He was also ordered to do 300 hours' unpaid community work. (The full article is available online at **www.theguardian.com/world/2012/nov/19/23m-compensation-crash-agnes-collier**.) From the article, you can see how several important issues relevant to the law of tort operate in practice.

First, if you read the facts you will recognise a description of most of the elements necessary to succeed with a claim in negligence: the fact that Mr Norton had been driving carelessly, for example, and that as a result of this Ms Collier was severely injured. Here we have breach of duty of care, causation and damage.

Secondly, this article clearly illustrates how one set of events could lead to both a criminal and a civil case – something which can often happen in tort law. You should always remember that the law seldom operates in a vacuum – a good student will keep various possibilities and intersections of different areas of the law in mind.

Finally, the article focuses on the record-breaking amount that was awarded to the claimant, explaining it in terms of the care that she would continue to need for the rest of her life, the loss of enjoyment of life she suffers because of being paralysed, etc. These are all factors that are taken into account when the court decides on a damages award; yet it is also significant that the claim was instituted against an insurance company. The role and influence (and availability or otherwise) of insurance is a major factor in tort law, and there is a debate about how pragmatic we should be in allowing this to influence judicial thinking in this area.

READING ABOUT TORT LAW

At the end of each chapter in this book you will find some suggested further reading, which should help you to delve into the material more fully. Remember that this book is intended as a guide, a blueprint mapping an outline, and that it is up to you to fill in that outline so that it forms a coherent and detailed whole. The suggested reading in each chapter is annotated, meaning that a brief explanation is provided as to why it is thought the suggested piece of reading would be of use to you. Sometimes this would be a chapter or two out of authoritative books, and sometimes you would be advised to read core cases. The inclusion of cases as further reading is rare, however, because it is understood that you will know that the cases referred to in the text are all important and that you need to read them in any case. So if you encounter a case in the suggested further reading section, it is an indication that the case itself is *very* important, or that there is some area of the decision of which you need to take special note.

More often you will be directed to legal journal articles.

What makes legal journal articles so special?

In the age of information at your fingertips via the internet (more often than not via Wikipedia), it is very easy to make the mistake of thinking that all information is equal. Please dispel that notion from your mind.

As a student of the common law, you know by now that the *only* authoritative sources of the law are cases (following, of course, the hierarchy of cases and the precedent system) and legislation. But what about what is written about the law? Why do tutors applaud when you refer to an article from, say, the *Modern Law Review*, but not from Wikipedia?

The difference lies in the process that the different articles underwent prior to publication. To be published in an academic journal, an article is submitted to a panel of experts in the field who, mostly without being known to each other or the author, carefully scrutinise the article for veracity, currency and overall quality. This means that by the time you as a student get to read the article, you are already assured of a product that is highly regarded by academics in the field. This is called 'peer review'. The same does not apply to internet blogs, etc.

Just to make things even more complicated, not all law journals are equal! Some are more highly ranked (or regarded) than others. For example, the *Modern Law Review* is arguably the highest-ranking law journal in the United Kingdom and competition by academics to get published in this journal is fierce. Other high-ranking law journals include publications such as the *Law Quarterly Review* and the *Oxford Journal of Legal Studies*. So how do you as a student know which law journals are ranked highly, and more importantly, does it matter? The ranking of journals is by no means a scientific endeavour and there is no 'ranking authority' where you can find out which journal is 'best'. Instead, academics go largely by measuring who publishes where, how many times articles are cited, etc. For now, do not worry too much about the ranking of journals. Instead, it is enough for you to be aware that some journals are ranked higher than others. It does not mean that the lesser-ranked journals are not valuable – these tend to be journals publishing articles aimed at practitioners such as solicitors or barristers or even law students such as yourself and may, for that reason, be more accessible. The aim is to get you reading, and reading *widely*. So if you read an article on a topic in a journal, and it seems to be impenetrable for whatever reason – perhaps the prose is difficult to follow, or the reasoning too abstract – do not get discouraged. It may be that articles in other journals may be written more clearly and more accessibly.

Journal rankings – does it matter?

We hope that you will read widely enough for you eventually to make up your own mind about this question. For now, you may wish to read an article from a 'highly ranked' journal, and compare it to an article from a 'lesser ranked' journal. Both are on an important topic in tort, namely 'causation' – the legal rules about whether an action caused the claimant's damage:

Compare Lord Hoffmann, 'Causation' (2005) 121 *Law Quarterly Review* 592, with Lord Neuberger of Abbotsbury, 'Loss of a Chance and Causation' (2008) 224(4) *Professional Negligence* 206. (You may also be interested to note that Lord Neuberger is the current President of the Supreme Court of the UK. So it cannot be said that highly respected lawyers do not publish in lower-ranked journals!)

Excerpts from journals may be found in collections such as Jenny Steele's *Tort Law: Text, Cases and Materials* (2nd edition, Oxford University Press, 2010). Collections such as these are helpful if you want to have a snapshot of what has been written about a particular subject. It is always preferable, though, to read the entire journal article itself.

One of the core skills you need as a law student and as a practising lawyer is to find information about a given topic. Familiarise yourself with the electronic databases to which your university may subscribe, such as Westlaw. You need to know how to search for journal articles using terms, authors or titles.

There are numerous journals that publish authoritative articles on tort law, both in the UK and in other common law jurisdictions. These include both specialist journals and journals that have a wider law-focused approach, which may from time to time include tort articles.

Specialist journals include:

- *Tort Law Review* (Tort L Rev)

Journals focusing on personal injury include:

- *Journal of Personal Injury Law* (JPI Law)
- *Personal Injury Law Journal* (PILJ)
- *Professional Negligence* (Prof Neg)

Highly ranked journals of general academic interest with occasional articles on tort law include:

- *Law Quarterly Review* (LQR)
- *Modern Law Review* (MLR)
- *Oxford Journal of Legal Studies* (OJLS)

Other journals of general academic interest include:

- *New Law Journal* (NLJ)

Law journal abbreviations

Sometimes you have a reference for a journal article with only an abbreviation for the journal name. How do you find out which journal it is? You can search for the journal abbreviation online using the *Cardiff Index to Legal Abbreviations* at **www.legalabbrevs.cardiff.ac.uk/site/index** or you can have a look at D. Raistick, *Index to Legal Citations and Abbreviations* (available in the reference section of most law libraries). The latter is *very* thorough – it contains almost 500 pages of abbreviations!

It cannot be stressed how important it is to read widely – but be discerning in what you read! Always aim to read from academic journals to ensure that what you read has been peer reviewed and is authoritative. Let's emphasise again the difference in quality between, say, an anonymous blog posted on the internet, and an article that's been subjected to rigorous academic scrutiny before being published in a reputable journal. By reading widely, you will not only improve your insight and knowledge of the law of tort, but also learn how to write good essays by seeing how it's done by the professionals.

Apart from being discerning in what you read, to really excel in tort, you also need to pay attention to *how* you read. This is imperative because of the sheer volume of material available on the subject – spanning not only a multitude of recent cases, articles and statutes, but also hundreds of years of common law on the subject. You need to be able to distil the ocean of information to a manageable size. How to do that?

First, you *have* to read widely, as this is the only way in which you will start to get a feel for common themes. If something crops up again and again in your reading, pay attention. Secondly, take notes, and be as concise as possible. As a rule you should try mostly to read with a pen and paper (or some other note-taking device) at hand and make notes as you go along. Ask yourself whether you agree with what the writer is saying. How well does the argument bear logical analysis? Is it based on solid law, i.e. does it truly reflect what the courts and statutes have to say on the law? Has it identified anything new that needs attention, or does it draw our attention to a deficiency or some point not raised before? It doesn't hurt, if you are an imaginative person, to see your job in reading about the law as going on an intelligence-gathering mission, or preparing for a major court case.

KEEPING UP TO DATE

Despite being an old and established discipline of the law, tort is a fast-changing area, illustrating the unique responsiveness of the common law to changes in society. Therefore, one of the skills you need to cultivate in studying (or practising) tort law includes the habit of keeping up to date with what is happening in the courts. This in turn means that you have to cultivate the habit of reading court cases (yes, groan) *in the original*.

Case law in tort

Not surprisingly, given that it is such an old and established part of the common law, you will note that there is a lot of case law in tort. Having said that you need to cultivate the habit of reading cases in the original (i.e. as published in the law reports), this should be qualified by a bit of realism. As a law student (and possibly as a lawyer afterwards), you will find that you usually have more reading to do than you have available time to do said reading in. Once again, the solution lies in being discerning in your reading. Not all sources are equal, and neither are all court cases!

Usually, you learn very early on in your legal studies about the hierarchy of courts and the system of precedent. This helps you to pick which report to target – if a matter started off in the High Court, went to the Court of Appeal, and ended up being adjudicated in the Supreme Court, it is logical if you are pressed for time to select the Supreme Court decision. In fact, it is imperative to make sure you read the latest and highest decision in a matter, as you do not want to confidently repeat a decision that was later overturned in a higher court!

Example: the Hillsborough litigation

In 1989, 95 people died and hundreds needed hospitalisation after more people were allowed into a stadium to watch a football match than could be accommodated. The events were witnessed in real time by thousands of people – at the stadium, on television, and on the radio. Many people sued the authority who was responsible for policing the event for the psychiatric harm they suffered after witnessing such a horrific event.

Start off by reading *Jones* v. *Wright* [1991] 2 WLR 814 and then the decision of the House of Lords in *Alcock* v. *Chief Constable of the South Yorkshire Police* [1991] 4 All ER 907.

→

> For our purposes at present, you need to take note that the matter went through two appeal stages, both to the Court of Appeal and to the House of Lords. For now, read all the cases and make sure you understand how the focus shifted from seeing the problem purely in terms of foreseeability to one addressing the issue of a more workable test for duty of care in psychiatric injury cases. Summarise the findings in the court of first instance, the Court of Appeal and the House of Lords, and then compare them. Were the findings upheld or overruled at each appeal stage? Hopefully you will glean from this exercise how important it is to be able to find out what constitute the final words of the highest court in adjudicating a matter.

Together with being able to identify which court was the highest (and therefore had the final say) involved in adjudicating any given matter (using your knowledge of the hierarchy of courts), once you have identified the final judgment, it is important to know how to read it. Here, other important skills you learn in your first year of legal study come in usefully, namely your knowledge about the structure of a reported case. You get taught about *ratio decidendi* (reasons for the decision) and *obiter dicta* (things said by the by) for a reason! One of these is the fact that English judges are not in general known for their brevity. You need to be able to wade through long judgments and glean only the most important parts – the reasons for judgments. Here, knowing what a headnote is certainly comes in handy as usually this will give you an indication of what the most important parts of the judgment relate to. It also helps to read case commentaries published in legal journals, and compare what is said there with your own notes and impressions about the case.

In short, with cases you need to make summaries, be aware of the hierarchy of courts (and the possibility of a higher court having overruled a lower court's judgment), and constantly keep an eye out for recent judgments that may modify earlier ones.

Statutes in tort

Increasingly, legislation is playing an important part in the law of tort. This could happen if the common law crystallises into a set interpretation of the law from which there is no real prospect of deviation due to the clear nature of relevant precedent, yet calls for amendment of the law are imperative.

Example: defamation

The most recent example of parliamentary intervention in the area of tort is the enactment of the Defamation Act 2013. There was increasing criticism of the defamation laws as they stood, as defamation was alleged to be skewed in favour of the rich and powerful. Although the courts showed themselves willing to respond to some of these policy concerns, they were very restricted due to the clear nature of precedent in this area. This meant that the only way to effect change far reaching enough was to legislate.

This Act, which is not in total effect yet, is discussed in Chapter 10.

It could also happen that there are *lacunae*, or gaps, in the law which need to be filled. Or it could be that the legislature is compelled to give effect to obligations undertaken by the state to legislate upon something agreed to internationally – EC directives and their implementation should be kept in mind here.

> ### Example: product liability
>
> During the 1960s a number of babies whose mothers had taken the drug Thalidomide during pregnancy were born with birth defects. Although the common law principles of negligence made it possible to claim for this in theory, it proved to be virtually impossible in practice to hold the manufacturers liable, because it was so difficult to prove fault on the part of the manufacturers. This, together with other concerns prompted the EU to take action to protect consumers injured by defective products and to make it easier for them to claim compensation. The idea was to introduce strict liability for defective products. The European Directive on Liability for Defective Products 1985 (85/374/EEC) was therefore passed, which in turn led to the enactment of the Consumer Protection Act 1987.

So there are various reasons why Parliament may decide to legislate. Sometimes the legislation supplements the common law, at other times it codifies the law, or it could usher in a totally new regime. What does it mean to you in practice? In tort, you need to know which torts are governed mostly by the common law, and which are governed by statute and, if the latter, to what extent the common law still applies. Take the example of liability for injury caused by defective products above. You should know that the Consumer Protection Act 1987 is applicable, and what the elements are that you need to prove for liability. But you should *also* know that, at the same time, there may be common law liability in negligence, based on the same facts. This is important because, with the evidence to hand, you may be able to succeed with one claim where you fail with the other – something very important when working out a litigation strategy for a client – or answering an exam or coursework question!

Finally, also keep an eye on what is being decided in Strasbourg, as this often leads to changes in the law so as to keep in line with human rights law.

> ### Example: *Steel and Morris* v. *UK* [2005] 18 BHRC 545
>
> In Chapter 11 when we look at defamation, we discuss this case in which the European Court of Human Rights held that denying legal aid to defendants in a libel action was an infringement of the right to a fair trial. As a consequence of this decision by the Strasbourg court, the law was amended so that legal aid is now available to the defendant in a libel action, but only if it was brought by a multinational corporation.

Background reading

It has already been stressed how important it is to read academic journals. Added to that, it is a good idea to make a habit of regularly reading news reports about legal matters. The reason is because, in this way, you will be able to keep up to date with areas of immediate concern in the law. As always, be discerning and consult reputable news media. The following list of useful websites should give you an idea of where to start for tort law.

Useful websites	
Description	Website
The *Guardian* newspaper's highly regarded law page, which includes blogs from respected legal commentators on topical legal issues.	www.theguardian.com/law
This is the website of the judiciary of England and Wales, including tribunals. A very handy feature of this website is the very up to date reporting of topical cases – in some instances, on the day of the judgment itself.	www.judiciary.gov.uk/
The Ministry of Justice website provides up-to-date commentary and links on topical legal issues including many relating directly to tort law, such as compensation claims. It also provides statistics that could be helpful in academic and practical research.	www.gov.uk/government/organisations/ministry-of-justice
The Law Commission is the statutory independent body created by the Law Commissions Act 1965 to keep the law under review and to recommend reform where it is needed. It is a good idea always to keep an eye on what the Law Commission is doing, as their findings often form the basis of law reform. Areas related to tort law will mostly be found in the 'commercial and common law' section of their website. The example here concerns damages for personal injury.	http://lawcommission.justice.gov.uk/areas/damages-for-personal-injury-collateral-benefits.htm
The Cardiff Index to Legal Abbreviations maintained by the University of Cardiff is a useful tool when conducting law research where you have the abbreviation of a law journal but not its full name, or *vice versa*.	www.legalabbrevs.cardiff.ac.uk/

HOW TO APPROACH COURSEWORK IN TORT

Coursework in tort mostly takes the form of either a problem or an essay-type question. The rationale behind these two choices is that tutors attempt to mimic real life in your assessment – the aim is to teach you how to apply the law and also how to think critically about the law. Both of these are important skills in tort, as this is an area of law heavily present in legal practice, and also closely influenced by changes in policy and societal thinking.

In general, for either kind of coursework, you should ensure that you support your arguments with authorities. These could consist of ratios from case law, sections of statutes, sections from EU Law and/or decisions from the European Court of Human Rights etc. Remember that the *only* sources of law are judgments from courts and statute!

To supplement the law as it is, which you've identified from judgments or statutes, you should include references to commentary on the law. The best way of doing this is to refer to articles from academic legal journals. Very sparing use, for example to give context, could be made of news articles from reputable newspapers or websites.

Problem-type questions in tort law

Problem-type questions are very common in tort law. But why do tutors so frequently set these kinds of questions? There are two main reasons. First, being able to answer a question like this demonstrates that you not only know the law, but are also able to apply it. Secondly, questions like these are aimed at mimicking real life: you may be asked to advise a hypothetical client – as a lawyer this is your daily task. As such, an abstract understanding of law is not enough. By solving many problem-type questions you gain valuable skills that are directly applicable in the workplace.

Keeping in mind, then, that problem-type questions are aimed at problem solving, imagine you are in a real-life situation: what would your client really want to know? Would she like to know about the historical development of the applicable tort? Or the policy reasons behind applicable legislation? Maybe, if she is the sort of person who has an interest in this sort of thing. But given that she is paying you by the hour, it is more likely that she would like to hear concise, definite (or as definite as possible) answers to practical questions such as: 'Do I have a case?', 'Will I win?', and 'What will I get?' Similarly, in approaching a problem-type question, you will quickly realise that you need to cut out discussions of extraneous matters and focus on solving the problem.

The 'IPAC' technique described by Finch and Fafinski in Chapter 12 of their book *Legal Skills* (Oxford University Press, 2007) is very useful when approaching problem-type questions whether in coursework or in the exam. This is an easy way to both approach a problem question, and to make sure that you do so in as thorough a manner as possible. 'IPAC' is an abbreviation for Issue, Principle, Application and Conclusion. Some writers refer to this technique as the IRAC technique, preferring to refer to a Rule rather than Principle, but the meaning stays the same.

Applying IPAC, in your problem you first identify the issue, i.e. the question that needs to be answered. Then you identify the applicable legal principle (or rule). This means that in practical terms you have to state the law that enables the question to be answered. The next step is application: work out how the law would operate in relation to the question identified. That is, apply the law to the facts. Your final step is to draw a conclusion. This in effect is the answer to the question. Be careful to ensure that your conclusion is supported by the evidence you have led. Also, remember to apply this technique to every aspect of the question, including the main question and any sub-questions that the main question may include.

Let's now look at an example of using this technique to a tort question. Imagine that the following very simple question formed part of your coursework.

Issue	⇐	Identify the question you need to answer
Principle/**R**ule	⇐	State the law you need to answer the question
Application	⇐	Explain how the law applies to the question identified
Conclusion	⇐	State the answer to the question

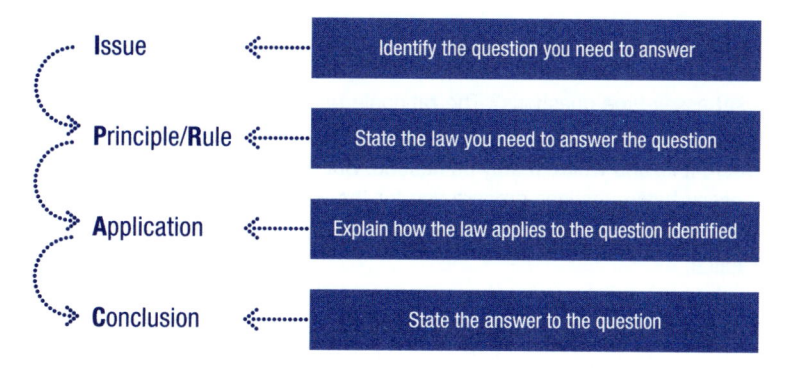

Figure 2 IPAC/IRAC problem-solving technique

> ### Putting what you learnt into practice: the 'IPAC' technique in a tort problem
>
> 'Sharon was speeding along the road at almost twice the speed limit when she lost control of her car, mounted the kerb and drove into a tree. Jane, who was a passenger in the car, was severely injured as she was flung through the front windscreen. It was found that she suffered brain damage which would impede her speech for ever, and also that she would have to undergo very expensive reconstructive surgery. In an action in negligence against Sharon, the court agreed that Jane's damages amount to £100,000. However, the court also held that Jane, by not wearing a safety belt at the time of the accident, was 20 per cent responsible for her own injuries. Advise Sharon as to the amount of damages she is liable to pay.'
>
> **Issue:** First, you will identify the question as being *how much* damage Sharon will have to pay to Jane, given that Jane was contributorily negligent.
>
> **Principle/rule:** Secondly, you will identify the applicable law. Here the question is to do with the tort of negligence, and it could have demanded an explanation of negligence. Depending on the marks indicated, you may have to include a brief explanation of the theory around negligence, explaining which elements need to be proved, and which cases are applicable. However, the main question relates to damages, and the legal rule or principle you have to discuss in detail is that of *contributory negligence*. Describe how it operates and refer to case law as examples (such as *Jones* v. *Livox Quarries Ltd* [1952] 2 QB 608 or, for not wearing a seat belt, *Froom* v. *Butcher* [1976] QB 286). You will also need to refer to the Law Reform (Contributory Negligence) Act 1945.
>
> **Application:** Once you've finished discussing the theory, apply the law to the facts. In this instance, the court has already held that there was 20 per cent contributory negligence on the part of Jane. Now you need to show how this is translated into a reduction in the amount of damages Jane has to pay. The award of £100,000 will be reduced by 20 per cent.
>
> **Conclusion:** Having tested the law against the facts, you now need to give a conclusion. To do this, go back and see what the question was that you have identified. Here the question was how much Sharon will have to pay Jane, and the answer based on your discussion should be £80,000. (Remember that your conclusion may validly be 'inconclusive' too, depending on the facts of the question.)

Essay questions in tort law

Why do tutors set essay-type questions? The rationale behind this type of question is different from problem-type questions. Attempting an essay forces you to think about not only what the law is, but how it got to where it is, and where it may be headed. But do not think that this is a purely theoretical exercise. Even essay-type questions prepare you for the world of work, because large parts of what lawyers do consist of advising clients about the law. You may think of this as similar to writing letters of advice in practice.

Because the aim here is not purely solving a problem, it allows the opportunity for speculation, for you to look at various sides of an issue, to ask 'what if?' A good strategy for essay questions would be to start off with a brief introduction, followed by the evidence you have gathered (cases, statutes, academic commentary, etc.), and to finish with a brief conclusion.

HOW TO PREPARE FOR EXAMS IN TORT

Questions you are likely to encounter in tort exams tend to follow the same pattern as those for coursework, in that they usually consist of either problem statements or more theoretical essay-type questions. You can therefore use the same approach to these questions, keeping in mind that you will inevitably have to memorise large chunks of work (even if your institution allows open book examinations).

Many students find it a bit overwhelming trying to study for an exam in tort, because of the sheer volume of material to be mastered – just the amount of case law is already daunting. The only way to deal with this is to whittle the volume of information down to a manageable size. For this to work as a strategy it is imperative to commence your exam preparation *at the start* of the year and to *keep at it* continuously, by making summaries as you go through the work. If you find that even at this stage you tend to get lost in the volume of information, it may be a good idea to *start off* (rather than see it as an end of year 'crammer') with a revision guide such as one of the *Law Express* books published by Pearson, or this book. Your university handbook should also form a manageable introductory text. Once you've cemented the basic principles from such a concise source, you will find it easier to then read deeper about the subject in the more substantial textbooks, journals and law reports. Think of the process as building up a solid skeleton (summaries) and then putting some meat on the bones (reading further, fleshing out your understanding).

Another common problem is getting confused by the various nominate torts, especially where there are torts that are related to each other or that share certain elements. This is something that often, unfortunately, becomes clear when tutors mark exams. The trick is to recognise beforehand that such confusion is a definite possibility, and to ensure that you know the nominate torts well enough to keep them separate in your mind, bearing in mind that this will be more difficult under the stressful atmosphere of an exam. Some students may adopt the strategy of thinking comparatively when it comes to the various torts.

You may consider drawing up a large comparison table with the nominate torts (or certain nominate torts). In this way you can visually represent similarities and differences across the torts. A good example of such a type of table is found in one of the 'Law Express' revision guides published by Pearson: E. Finch and S. Fafinski, *Tort Law* (2nd edition, 2009) on p. 127. The table compares the tort in *Rylands* v. *Fletcher* (1868) LR 3 HL 330, negligence, private nuisance and trespass to land on criteria such as the possible claimant, the possible defendant, the type of interference making up the tort, and whether damage is required. This is what the first row of Finch and Fafinski's table looks like:

	Rylands v. *Fletcher*	Negligence	Private nuisance	Trespass to land
Who can sue?	A person whose land or property is harmed by the escape of a dangerous thing	A person who has suffered personal harm to property as a result of a breach of duty of care	A person with a proprietary interest in land who has suffered interference with the quiet enjoyment of land	A person in possession of land who suffers unjustified and direct interference with that land

You can make comparison tables for all or some of the torts, and may wish to include the commonly encountered elements such as causation, fault, damage, etc. Such a table can be a most useful revision tool as it gives you an overview of a large body of work – very effective to combat getting lost in the volume of work. It could also help in fostering the habit of thinking of more than one tort perhaps being applicable to a set of facts.

Advice based on common mistakes made in exams is the same as for several other examined law modules. Make sure to use your time effectively and answer all the questions you are set, and *only* the question set. Tutors often find that students answer the question they *wished* had been set – unfortunately, this will not be awarded any marks if it does not relate to the question *actually* asked. Also remember that your answer should present a logical argument (consider using a flowchart, discussed above) and should be substantiated. This means that for each statement of law you have to give proof, either in the form of a relevant judgment or legislation. Always keep in mind that one set of facts in a problem question could encompass more than one tort – and often includes vicarious liability. Make sure all your bases are covered, but at the same time remember that you will likely lose marks if you discuss irrelevancies. It is therefore very important that you know your work well enough to know what is applicable and what is not! The last thing you should remember is to include a valid (i.e. logically arising from the evidence you led) conclusion. Without a conclusion, you have not answered the question. But remember that a valid conclusion does not need to be definite – on the evidence you could validly come to the conclusion that it is impossible to predict what the position is, that more facts are needed, etc.

Finally, remember to *enjoy* the learning process. Tort is a very interesting and constantly evolving part of the living law, and what you learn now will not only come in very handy in legal practice you may undertake later in life, but in broadening your understanding of how society attempts to restore balance in the area of civil liability.

SUMMARY

- Tort is one of the key areas of modern law, based on ancient principles of the common law.
- Tort overlaps with several other areas of the law, such as criminal law, consumer law and employment law, amongst others. Therefore, the study and practice of tort law should always occur in a wider context.
- There are various nominate torts that each has its own rules, processes and outcomes, yet there are principles that may be shared amongst various configurations of these torts. Recognising this should inform the way in which you approach studying tort.
- The tort of negligence encompasses most of the elements found in many other torts, and is an important tort in terms of volume of litigation and compensation awards generated.
- Both the common law and statute play important parts in the law of tort. Therefore, both case law and legislation need to be studied.
- Tort continues to evolve and therefore it is imperative to keep up to date with recent court judgments and legislative enactments.

PART 1
Negligence

PART 1: Negligence

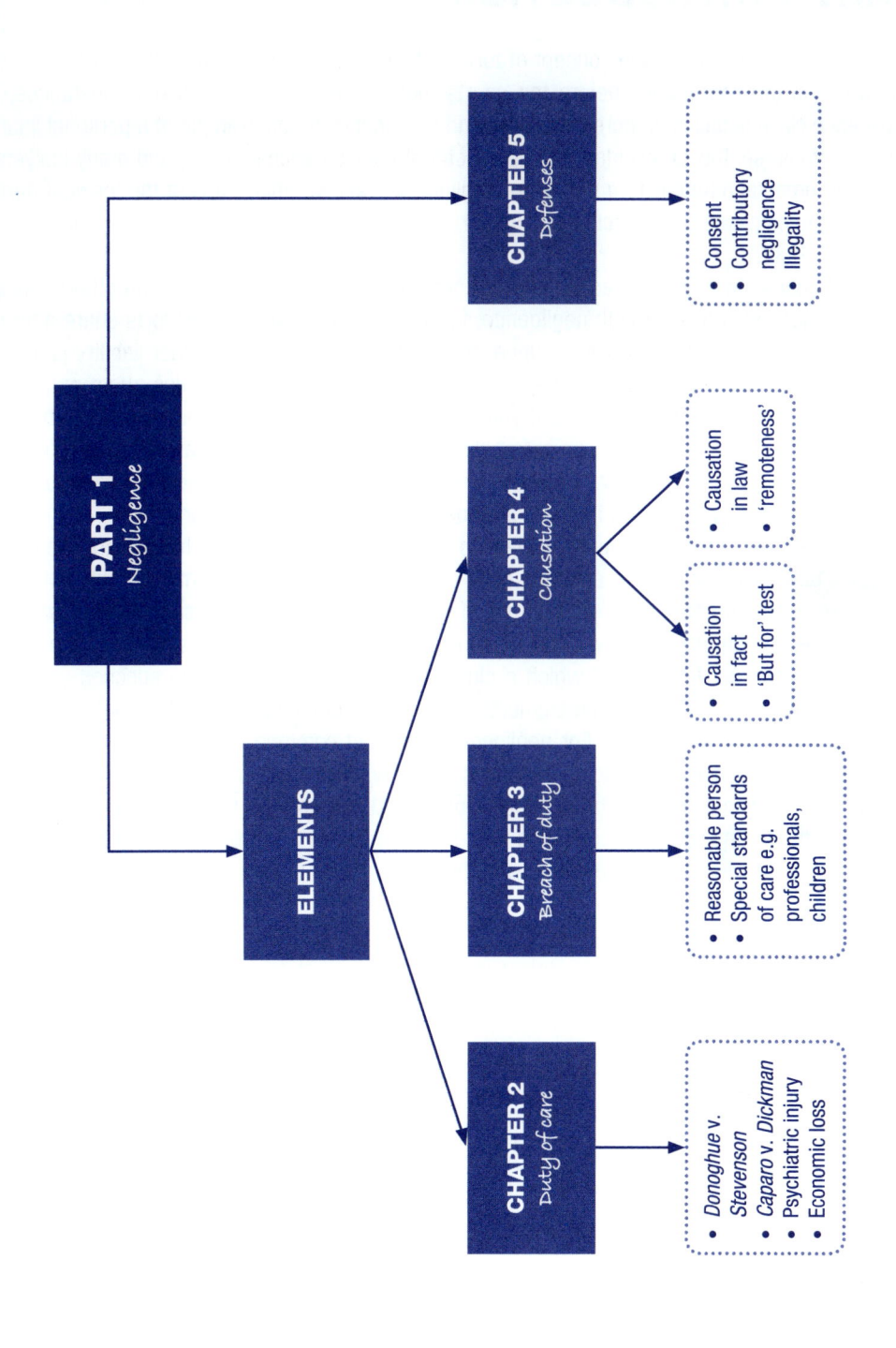

ELEMENTS

CHAPTER 2: Duty of care
- *Donoghue v. Stevenson*
- *Caparo v. Dickman*
- Psychiatric injury
- Economic loss

CHAPTER 3: Breach of duty
- Reasonable person
- Special standards of care e.g. professionals, children

CHAPTER 4: Causation
- Causation in fact 'But for' test
- Causation in law 'remoteness'

CHAPTER 5: Defenses
- Consent
- Contributory negligence
- Illegality

PART 1 INTRODUCTION

After a brief introduction to the concept of tort in Chapter 1, we start off our study of the law of tort with the tort that comes before the courts most often: negligence. In most instances, a negligence claim is based on personal injury, and the most common example of a personal injury claim is, of course, the car accident. A huge sector of the insurance industry, and many lawyers, earn their bread and butter from the tort of negligence – and yet this is one of the 'newest' torts amongst the nominate torts, tracing its true 'birth' to the classic case of *Donoghue* v. *Stevenson*, decided in 1932.

It is of course up to you to decide in which order to study the torts in this (and other) books, but it is a good idea to start with negligence, for a variety of reasons: other torts share a lot in common with, or may even be based upon, negligence. For example, product liability is just a subspecies of negligence that has developed in tune with modern sensibilities about manufacturers' duties towards consumers. So if you study the elements of negligence, you will build a solid foundation from which you can extrapolate to other torts. A good example is the element of causation – most torts require this, and once you've studied this for negligence, you need only refresh your memory when it crops up under the elements for other torts.

Because of this, we devote four chapters to the study of negligence (whereas, for the other torts, we only have one chapter each). In each chapter we discuss one or more of the elements that make up the tort of negligence, and which we get from classic cases such as *Donoghue*: a duty of care, breach of such duty, and causation of damage. (The 'elements' of a tort are those things that make up the tort and which a claimant has to prove in court to succeed with her claim.) Even if you can prove all the elements of a tort, the defendant can still defeat your claim if she can raise a valid defence. For negligence, the most common defences are consent and contributory negligence and, in some instances, illegality. Because these defences are important not only for negligence but also for a variety of other torts, we spend a whole chapter (Chapter 5) examining them. Once again, study these well, because it will make your work easier when you study other torts where the same defences apply.

CHAPTER 1

Tort: overview

BLUEPRINT
Tort: overview

KEY QUESTIONS

LEGISLATION
- Human Rights Act 1998
- Civil Liability (Contribution) Act 1978

CONTEXT
- The law of torts forms part of the law of obligations, as does the law of contract. These areas of law recognise that one person owes (has an obligation towards) another.

CONCEPTS
- Civil liability
- 'Damage' v. 'damages'
- Actionable *per se*
- Fault
- Strict liability

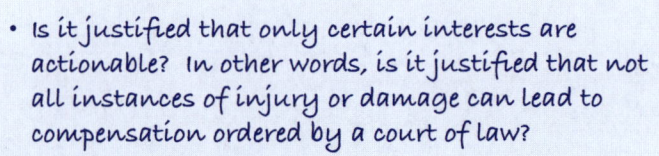

- Is it justified that only certain interests are actionable? In other words, is it justified that not all instances of injury or damage can lead to compensation ordered by a court of law?
- Does the availability of insurance play too large a role in courts' decisions in tort actions?

- Is it a law of tort or a law of torts? i.e. can we identify enough common features to talk of 'tort' in general, or do the individual torts differ so much from each other that we have to think of them in distinct terms?
- What is a civil wrong and in which instances could it lead to liability?
- How does civil liability differ from criminal liability?
- What are the main nominate torts?

CASES
- Cork v. Kirby MacLean Ltd [1952]
- Donoghue v. Stevenson [1932]
- Bradford Corporation v. Pickles [1895]

REFORM
- Will the courts move towards a more unitary approach to tort law, or will the distinctions between the various nominate torts continue to be entrenched?
- With the increasing emphasis on the rights-based approach of human rights litigation, will the 'wrongs-based' nature of the law of tort change?

SPECIAL CHARACTERISTICS
- Tort law recognises that a wrong should be compensated
- Causation is mostly determined using the 'but for' test
- Fault for the purposes of tort relates mostly to negligence or intention

CRITICAL ISSUES

Setting the scene

What do we mean by 'tort'? Can we talk of tort in general, or is it only a collective term for a variety of actions? The first thing you need to know is that tort relates to civil liability. It refers to a variety of ways in which one person may be held liable in law to another. These make up the law of torts and are various nominate (named) torts. Examples of torts include trespass, negligence, nuisance and defamation. Employers could also be held liable towards their employees, producers towards consumers of their products, and occupiers towards people on their land.

From this you can see that the law of torts aims at protecting a variety of interests, such as bodily integrity or property rights. The main way in which this is done is by trying to compensate the 'victim' for the wrongdoing by the person who had committed the tort (the 'tortfeasor').

To start off, we will look at some of the more common themes of tort, and then focus on some of the more prevalent nominate torts. To do this we will focus on interests, rights and duties in tort, assessment of damages, limitation of actions, the role of other branches of law, legal capacity, vicarious and personal liability and joint and several tortfeasors. In this introductory chapter our objective is to get to grips with the basics, in order to enable you better to understand the more complex concepts and detailed rules that follow in the rest of the book.

WHAT DOES TORT MEAN?

Many law subjects' meanings are clear from the start. For example, when you start a course in criminal law, you probably already have an idea of what the course will cover – crimes and how the law deals with them. The same goes for other law subjects, such as the law of contract. Not so with tort law. If you happen to walk into your first class without knowing what the word 'tort' means, do not feel discouraged! You may not recognise the word, but usually, once your lecturer starts giving examples of tort, you realise that you already do know some torts. The classic example of a tort these days is the motor vehicle accident.

APPLICATION

> If D drives into the back of C's car while C is stationary at traffic lights, D would be held liable for damage to C's car, as well as any resultant injuries C may suffer. Another example: D publishes an unflattering story about C. C may possibly hold D liable for harming C's reputation. Or, let's say D operates a mechanical workshop in his garage and this damages his neighbour, C's, garden. C would likewise probably have a claim.

All of these are examples of possible claims in tort. In short, if you know that you can sue another under circumstances where you suffered damage due to that other person's actions, then you already have an idea of what tort is all about.

The word 'tort' itself is a rather archaic word, which used commonly to mean a 'wrong'. Today we only use it when we talk about the legal concept of a wrong that could lead to **civil liability**.

CORNERSTONE

Civil liability

With civil liability, the alleged wrongdoer potentially faces being held responsible for payment of damages or another form of legal sanction, because she is being sued by another person or institution. Contrast this to criminal liability, which refers to liability for the alleged commission of a crime and which follows prosecution by the Crown.

In fact, the concept of 'civil liability' lies at the heart of tort law. Many students find it useful, at the beginning, to think of tort as the civil equivalent of criminal law – instead of the state or the crown prosecuting the alleged wrongdoer, the 'victim' herself sues the wrongdoer for damages. (As you will see later, there are many similarities between criminal law and tort, but also some significant differences.)

It is difficult to give a simple, generic definition of tort. One of the reasons for this is that the law of tort is made up of various *nominate torts*, each with its own and often differing elements.

> Nominate torts means all the named torts we have, such as assault, defamation, negligence etc.

CONTEXT

There is a lot to be said for studying the nominate torts individually and then returning to the problem of a definition at the end! The following are the principal nominate torts: *trespass to land* occurs when one person unlawfully or unjustifiably interferes directly with another person's land, whilst *trespass to the person* happens when a person unlawfully and intentionally assaults or batters or falsely imprisons another person. Currently, the most far-reaching tort is the tort of **negligence**, when a person breaches a duty of care owed to and causing damage to another. Other nominate torts include **nuisance**, which is when one person unlawfully interferes indirectly with another person's use and enjoyment of land (private nuisance) or where a person does something which materially interferes with the reasonable comfort and convenience of a class of people (public nuisance). **Defamation** protects a person's reputation. It is still possible for new nominate torts to emerge and case law following the recognition of the European Convention on Human Rights by the Human Rights Act 1998 raises a question as to whether there is already a separate tort protecting privacy.

You should understand by now that there is no 'generic' tort, no umbrella term that encompasses all torts. Bearing this in mind, we can, however, point out certain common features. For example, most (but not all!) torts require that you should prove that you have suffered damages. Now we can fruitfully look at the most commonly encountered elements of torts. Before we do so, have a look at Figure 1.1 which mentions some of the concepts that you will have to learn in order to appreciate fully what is meant by 'tort'.

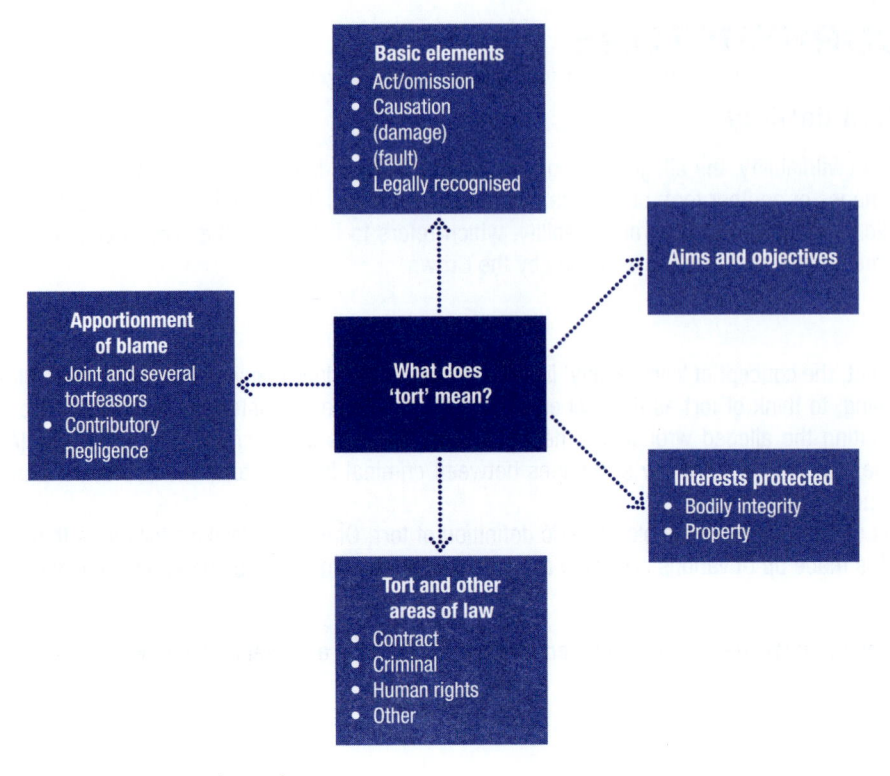

Figure 1.1 What does 'tort' mean?

Basic elements
- Act/omission
- Causation
- (damage)
- (fault)
- Legally recognised

Aims and objectives

Apportionment of blame
- Joint and several tortfeasors
- Contributory negligence

What does 'tort' mean?

Interests protected
- Bodily integrity
- Property

Tort and other areas of law
- Contract
- Criminal
- Human rights
- Other

BASIC ELEMENTS OF A TORT

We look first at the most common elements of torts, and then at the main deviations. Most torts consist of the following elements:

- An **act/omission** by the defendant;
- **causation**;
- **damage/injury** to the claimant;
- due to the defendant's **fault**;
- resulting in harm that is **legally recognised**.

The elements that all torts have in common are that they must consist of some act – or, in certain instances, an omission – legally recognised as a tort. But from here things may deviate! The other elements may, or may not be required, depending on the kind of tort you are dealing with – have a look at Figure 1.2 below, where these elements are indicated in brackets.

A good strategy is to learn the essential elements required for each tort. This means that you know exactly what the claimant must prove to succeed in her action for the specific tort. As a rule of thumb, you should consider:

- what conduct makes up the tort;
- whether the claimant must also prove fault (and, if so, what type of fault); and
- whether the claimant must prove damage.

Basic elements of a tort

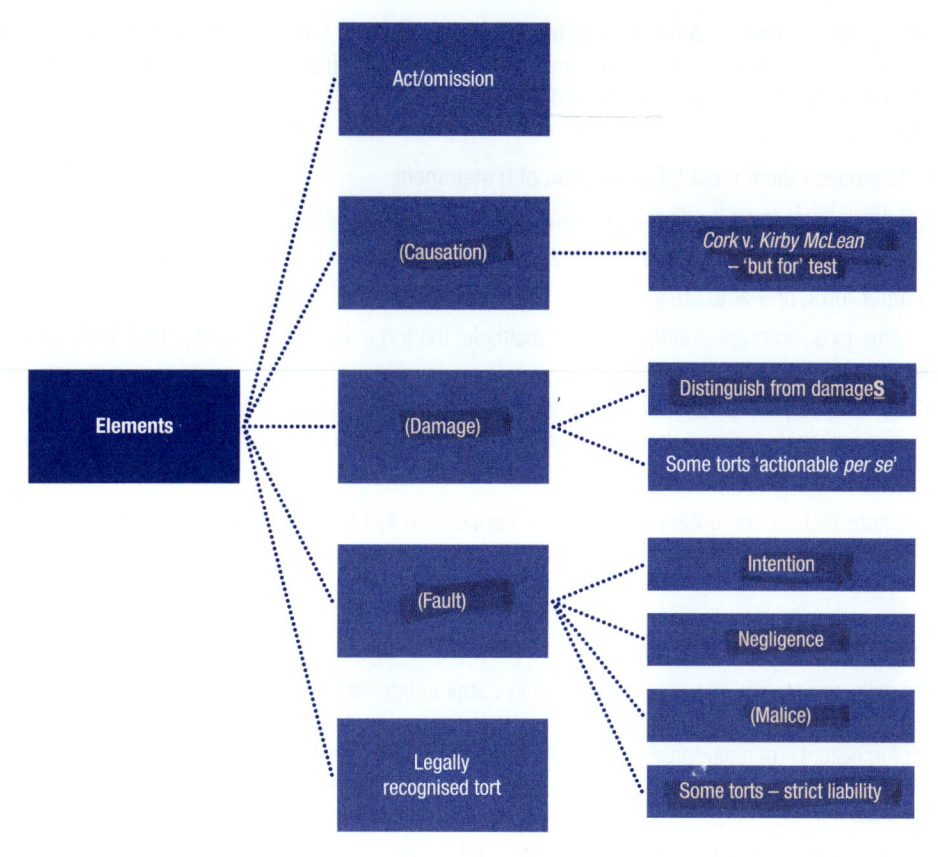

[Figure 1.2 diagram: Elements branching to Act/omission, (Causation) — Cork v. Kirby McLean – 'but for' test, (Damage) — Distinguish from damage**s**, Some torts 'actionable *per se*', (Fault) — Intention, Negligence, (Malice), Some torts – strict liability, Legally recognised tort]

Figure 1.2 Elements of tort

In what follows we will look at each of the elements only briefly, as we will examine them in more detail in the rest of the book.

As in most civil actions, the burden of proving the elements of a tort usually falls on the claimant (an exception which shifts the burden are so-called **res ipsa loquitur** situations), and likewise the standard of proof is the usual civil standard of a balance of probabilities.

> *Res ipsa loquitur* is a Latin term that means 'the thing speaks for itself'. It is usually a rebuttable presumption or inference in favour of the claimant that negligence has taken place.

CONTEXT

Let's now look at each of the elements in more detail.

Act or omission

In most instances a tort consists of an action, because in general there is no liability for *not* doing something. However, as almost always in law, there are exceptions where one could be held liable for *not* acting. We say that in such instances there is a duty to act. If there is a duty to act, and you fail to do so, such failure may be a tort. Mostly there is a duty to act positively if there is a special relationship between the parties, such as a parent and child.

The conduct (act/omission) that a claimant must prove varies from tort to tort. For example:

- In defamation there must be publication of a statement.
- In battery there must be direct, physical contact with the claimant.
- In some torts, the conduct may be an act or it may be an omission – for example, negligence.
- In other torts, only acts are sufficient – for example, battery.
- In some torts, an event is sufficient – for example, the tort in *Rylands* v. *Fletcher* (1868) LR 3 HL 330 requires an escape of something.
- Many torts require proof that the conduct took place in certain circumstances – for example, private nuisance requires that the interference was unreasonable, and trespass to land requires proof that the land was in the possession of another.

Finally, note that an involuntary action is not 'conduct' in tort law. For example, if I am thrown on to your land, I have not committed trespass, since my entry was not voluntary.

APPLICATION

We discuss acts/omissions in negligence in detail in later chapters. For now, just think of it as liability for damage caused negligently by the act – or, in limited circumstances, the failure to act (omission) – of a person. For example, if D was driving along too fast and as a result crashed into C's car, D would be held liable for her act of negligent driving. Or, imagine D is a parent and, because she did not supervise her child properly, the child caused damage to C. C could then hold D liable for her (D's) failure (omission) to take care.

Causation

For most torts, the claimant must show that the defendant's act/omission *caused* the damage. We say that there must be **causation**, or a *causal link*, between the act/omission and the damage suffered. Lawyers often refer to this as the 'chain of causation'. We will return to causation when we look at negligence, but for now keep in mind that the test we use to determine causation is the 'but for' test.

CORNERSTONE

Cork v. *Kirby Maclean Ltd* [1952] 2 All ER 402 (CA)

The 'but for' test was formulated by Lord Denning in this case, and works as follows:

'. . . if the damage would not have happened *but for* a particular fault, then that fault is the cause of the damage; if it would have happened just the same, fault or no fault, the fault is not the cause of the damage.' (emphasis added)

Damage

In general, one has to prove a loss of some sort in order to be successful with a tort claim.

CORNERSTONE

Damage v. damages

Ensure that you understand that these two words have different meanings in law! 'Damage' refers to injury or harm to a person or property, whereas 'damages' (in the plural) relates to the monetary compensation that a court may award for suffering damage.

There are rules about which losses are and which are not recoverable, which we will look at later on. However, once again there are exceptions. In some instances conduct can be actionable even though no damage has been caused. The Latin term for this is *injuria sine damno*, and an example could be where you are held liable when you trespass on someone's property even if you have not caused any damage. Where you can sue someone in tort without having to prove damage it is said to be '**actionable per se**'.

> **Take note**
> Students often confuse the term 'actionable per se' with 'strict liability', which we look at under fault. Remember that the term 'actionable per se' relates to the element of damages, while the term 'strict liability' falls under the element of fault.

Fault

Usually it is not enough to prove that the defendant's action or omission caused you damage in order to succeed with a claim – you would also have to prove that she was at **fault**.

CORNERSTONE

Donoghue v. Stevenson [1932] AC 562

In this, one of the most famous cases in the common law (and one we look at in detail in Chapter 2), Lord Atkin said that the law of tort is 'based upon a general public sentiment of moral wrongdoing for which the offender must pay'. Generally speaking this means that there must be fault to establish liability.

(You will see later that there are some instances, however, where one could be held liable even in the absence of fault – the so-called '**strict liability**' torts.)

CORNERSTONE

Meaning of 'fault'

In tort, the word 'fault' refers to malice, intention or negligence, with malice playing a minor role.

Let's now look at the various kinds of fault that may be required in a tortious action.

Intention

For some torts you have to prove intention on the part of the defendant. An example is trespass to the person. However, note that we encounter two kinds of intention here – either the intention to actually commit the tort, or another, lesser kind of intention such as intending to do something but not intending your action to be a tort, or not intending the consequences that may result from such action. Frequently, it is only the latter, i.e. the conduct, that must be shown to have been intentional, and not necessarily the circumstances or consequences of it. Thus D may be liable if she deliberately touched C even though she did not intend to cause C any damage. In fact, she may be held liable even if her touch did not cause any damage at all. In tort law, I intend something not only if it is my purpose, but also if it is a natural consequence of my conduct.

Negligence

Negligence may be the fault element of a tort. In this context, negligence means 'failing to take reasonable care'. Sometimes proving this could be as simple as showing that the defendant did not behave like the reasonable person. Once again, remember that it is important to distinguish negligence as a fault element from the tort of negligence! Remember, though, that for the tort of negligence you have to prove that the fault element consisted of (the state of mind of) negligence. If the act or omission was intentional, then you do not have the tort of negligence, but it may be some other tort. For example, if I daydream while driving my car and crash into the back of another's car, this may be (the tort of) negligence. If I deliberately drive into the back of another's car, this cannot be negligence. It could be, for example, trespass to goods, or trespass to the person, both of which are torts whose fault requirement consists of intention.

A final word on the distinction between the tort of negligence and negligence as a kind of fault: as a tort, negligence requires proof of more than a failure to take care. It requires proof of a duty to take reasonable care, a failure to take reasonable care, and damage suffered as a consequence. Negligence is a very important tort nowadays, so we will devote a number of chapters to exploring it more fully. For now, remember that you need to prove fault in the form of negligence to succeed with a claim in negligence.

Some torts are satisfied by proof either of intention or of negligence. An example is trespass to land. Thus, if I enter your land, either intentionally or negligently, I may trespass on it.

Malice

Malice has two meanings in tort law. It may be used in the sense of intention. Thus, to say that I harmed you maliciously may mean that I deliberately harmed you. Alternatively, malice could mean ill will or spite. Generally, malice in this second sense is irrelevant to liability.

Put another way, a malicious motive in itself is not enough to found liability. The basic principle is that if a person has a right to do something, then her motive in doing it is irrelevant. In principle, a lawful act does not become unlawful simply because it is done with malice.

CORNERSTONE

Bradford Corporation v. Pickles [1895] AC 587 (HL)

The defendant, Mr Pickles, owned land through which water percolated in undefined, underground channels to land owned by Bradford Corporation. Pickles sank shafts in his own land, which diverted and discoloured the water that reached the Corporation's reservoirs. It was suggested that the defendant's motive was to try and get the plaintiff to buy his land. The House of Lords decided that Mr Pickles had not committed a tort.

Malice is, however, relevant where it is an essential element of a specific nominate tort, such as 'malicious prosecution', or where it serves to indicate unreasonableness, such as in the tort of nuisance.

APPLICATION

If I have not committed the elements of a tort, the fact that I acted out of improper motive will not make me liable. In the same way, if I have committed the elements of a tort, a good motive will not (usually) exonerate me.

Strict (no-fault) liability

There is an old legal adage that says, 'There can be no liability without fault'. Mostly, tort law still adheres to this notion, which reflects a sense of justice (in that the wrongdoer, and only the wrongdoer, gets punished, and that this serves as a deterrent which regulates behaviour in society). However, fault-based liability does leave us with some problems. For example, it can be very difficult in certain circumstances to prove fault. It may also be that society feels that, in some instances, if there was damage, there should be compensation – regardless of who is to blame for the damage. For these and other reasons, some torts are actionable without proof of fault.

CORNERSTONE

Strict liability

Where a defendant is held liable even though she did not act or cause damage intentionally or negligently, we call it no-fault, or strict, liability.

Remember that 'fault' is just one of the elements that usually form part of a tort – you would still have to prove the other elements to succeed with a claim based on a strict liability tort. Also take care to note that 'strict liability' does not mean 'absolute liability' – usually there are defences available to the defendant even if she can in theory be held liable in the absence of intent or negligence.

Examples of strict liability torts include liability under the Consumer Protection Act 1987 and the Animals Act 1971.

Legally recognised liability

Tort law does not protect all interests. So, some persons could be injured by what the defendant does and yet, because their interests or the specific type of injury they suffered are not protected, they will have no right to sue. These are called situations of *damnum sine injuria*. Think of these as situations where damage or injury occur, yet there exists no legal cause of action.

In tort, you may find the word 'injury' used in one of two ways:

- If I say, 'Fred injured me', I may be using the word in the sense of 'damage, harm or loss'. I mean 'Fred harmed me' or 'Fred caused me loss/damage' – this is what is meant by the Latin expression *damnum*.

- Alternatively, I might be using the word in the sense of 'a wrong which gives rise to a right to sue'. I mean 'Fred committed a legal wrong against me' – this is what is meant by the Latin expression *injuria*.

CORNERSTONE

Bradford Corporation v. *Pickles* [1895] AC 587 (HL)

Let's return to the case of *Bradford Corporation* v. *Pickles* [1894] AC 587 (HL), in which we saw that an otherwise legal action cannot lead to a claim in tort purely because of an immoral motive. More specifically, the House of Lords decided that Mr Pickles had not committed a tort because, although the Corporation had suffered damage (*damnum*), it had no *right* to the water (as it was not in a watercourse, such as a stream) and so Pickles was entitled to do what he liked on his own land. Thus Bradford Corporation had suffered no legal wrong (*injuria*).

To recap: if your claim is not recognised as a tort (i.e. it is not actionable), you cannot sue on it, even if you did suffer damage or injury.

However, the converse can also be true in tort: there are instances where the law recognises a claim even in the absence of injury or damage. Lawyers refer to this as *injuria sine damno*, or a claim that is 'actionable *per se*'. You should realise by now that most torts require the claimant to prove that she has suffered some damage or harm or loss. But, there are some torts (such as trespass and libel), which do not require proof of damage – a claimant may sue even though no damage has been done. These torts actionable *per se* are instances where the law has been broken (*injuria*) but no loss has been suffered (*sine damno*). Such cases usually arise in situations where the right to be protected is extremely important in itself. For example, the law puts a high premium on bodily integrity. Therefore, if someone touches you without your consent she may be found liable for battery, even if the touch did not hurt you physically in any way.

CORNERSTONE

Actionable *per se*

Do not confuse *damnum sine injuria* with *injuria sine damno*! The latter refers to a situation where the defendant may be held liable even if the claimant cannot prove loss or damage, and it's best to remember this as 'actionable *per se*'. The former refers to the situation where, although there is damage, there is no cause of action, or the case is not actionable. Also, do not confuse the term 'actionable *per se*', with the term 'strict liability' – remember that they relate to different elements of tort. Strict liability means you do not have to prove fault, while with a tort 'actionable *per se*' you do not have to prove damages.

Figure 1.2 summarises the most important concepts you need to learn concerning the basic elements of most torts, which we have just looked at. Note that those that may be omitted from some torts are indicated in brackets.

AIMS AND OBJECTIVES OF TORT LAW

Up to now, we have looked at tort in general, and at the various elements that many of them have in common. Once you are sure you understand the elements, you can move on to deepen your understanding of the law of torts by concentrating on its functions and aims, and by distinguishing it from other branches of law.

The law of torts aims to achieve several things: compensation, retribution, deterrence, and loss distribution, to name but a few. In practice, tort mainly aims to compensate financially a person who has suffered an injury. The intention is to try and put the claimant in the position she would have been in but for the occurrence of the tort. (Contrast this 'backward in time' view with the aim of damages in contract, which is to put the claimant in the position she would have been in had the contract been duly discharged – a view that looks 'forward in time'.)

INTERESTS PROTECTED BY TORT LAW

Tort protects a number of interests in a number of ways. For example, the interest we all have in bodily security is protected by, amongst others, the torts of negligence, public nuisance and trespass to the person. The interest we may have in real property is protected by the torts of negligence, private and public nuisance and trespass to land. Other interests protected include reputation (defamation), economic and business interests.

When tort law declares that an interest is protected, some academics suggest that it is creating a right on the part of the claimant to claim against invasions of that interest (i.e. a right of action may underlie any of the nominate torts: negligence, trespass, nuisance and defamation). At the same time it imposes a duty or obligation on a defendant not to invade that interest.

INTERSECTION

> Apart from breaking tort down into its constituent elements, and looking at its functions in protecting certain interests, you can also deepen your understanding of this area of law by looking at it in relation to, or in context with, other areas of the law. We already know that tort falls under civil law, in that it entails a private person or corporation suing another private person or corporation.

Tort and criminal law

Tort and crime are similar in many ways. Both set a standard of behaviour and both attach legal consequences to behaviour that falls below that standard. In fact one action may lead to both criminal prosecution and a civil action in tort. We will get back to this later, but for now let's look at the apparent differences between crime and tort.

The main difference is, of course, that tort forms part of civil law while crime falls under public law. This means various things: in tort, one person (either a human or a legal person such as a company) sues another person, the alleged **tortfeasor**, while in crime the Crown *prosecutes* an alleged offender. In a tort action, as in all civil actions, the court finds *in favour* of either the claimant or the defendant – contrast this to a criminal case, where if the Crown wins its case, we say that the accused is found *guilty* of a crime, and where the Crown fails to win, the court *acquits* the accused.

The outcomes also differ. If a claimant wins her case, the court may award her a monetary award of damages, or another remedy such as an **injunction**. The focus is very much on the victim of the wrongdoing and in placing her in the position she would have been in had the tort not occurred – in other words, the focus is on *compensation*. In criminal matters, the focus is much wider. Whilst it is possible for the victim of crime to obtain compensation (e.g. through the Criminal Injuries Compensation Authority or through a criminal compensation order), a crime is considered to be damaging to society as a whole, and seen as reprehensible enough that it requires *punishment*, usually in the form of a fine or a custodial order.

There are also procedural and evidentiary differences between the two. As a civil matter, the **standard of proof** is a balance of probabilities, which is much easier to attain than the standard in criminal matters, namely 'beyond a reasonable doubt'.

> **Standard of proof** relates to how high the bar is set in terms of convincing the judge or jury of your case: in criminal matters, the bar is higher (beyond reasonable doubt) than in civil matters (on a balance of probabilities).
>
> CONTEXT

Because the standard of proof is lower in civil matters, it could (and does) happen that a person is acquitted of a crime but, on the same set of facts, held liable in a civil court. (Think of the OJ Simpson case.)

While in the criminal law the penalty imposed will reflect the severity of the criminal conduct, in tort a defendant who has done little wrong may nevertheless have to pay a large sum in compensation, because a minor lapse may cause a lot of damage.

Tort and contract law

Tort and contract are similar because both aim to ensure that a person fulfils a lawful duty. The difference is that usually, in contract law, the defendant has undertaken the duty voluntarily when she concluded the contract, whilst, with tort, the duty is imposed by law, without the defendant's consent being necessary. The limitation periods also differ.

However, it can justly be said that the distinctions between tort and contract are more apparent than real. For example, it is no longer true to say that all contractual duties arise from agreement – the duties imposed in contract by the Sale of Goods Act 1979, to take just one example, are created by statute law. It is also difficult to draw a clear line between tort and contract. For a long time, if you entered a contract due to the deliberate misrepresentation by another, your only remedy would have been to rely on the tort of deceit. Contractual and tortious duties may co-exist on the same facts. For example, in the classic case of *Donoghue* v. *Stevenson* [1932] AC 502, when a contractual remedy proved to be impossible for the claimant, the court developed tort in order to give her a remedy.

In *Henderson* v. *Merrett Syndicates* Ltd [1995] 2 AC 145 the House of Lords affirmed the principle of concurrent liability, and suggested that a claimant was entitled to take advantage of the remedy which was more advantageous to him/her. This has led many to think that we may be moving to a general law of obligations or of restitution.

Contract law protects the expectation interest (pure economic loss) and tort generally does not. Through a series of cases dealing with economic loss in the tort of negligence, it seemed for some time that tort was coming close to allowing actions for loss of expectation. For some time, claimants have been able to sue either in tort or in contract where the facts allow for both. Nevertheless, the courts have made it clear that they will not allow tort law to be used as a vehicle for avoiding difficulties that might arise with a contractual duty on the same facts.

The courts will also not allow reliance on a tortious duty that was greater than that imposed under a contract.

Important examples of situations where the claimant may elect to sue in either contract or tort are where the claimant has suffered personal injury as a result of negligent breach of a contract of employment, or a contract of carriage. Normally, however, in both these situations the claim will be brought in tort.

Other differences between tort and contract relate to issues such as remoteness of damage, service of writs outside the jurisdiction, costs and minors' liability.

Tort and human rights

The Human Rights Act 1998 incorporated the European Convention for the Protection of Human Rights and Fundamental Freedoms (ECHR) into national law.

CORNERSTONE

Human Rights Act 1998

This Act enables individuals to challenge the legitimacy of acts or omissions by the state/public bodies and/or the failures of the law to protect those fundamental rights protected by the Convention. These can now be challenged in the national courts, rather than litigants having to go →

> the European Court of Human Rights (ECtHR) in Strasbourg to pursue their case. The Act can indirectly be of benefit in a dispute between individuals, because a court is itself a public body and must therefore ensure compatibility with the Convention by, amongst others, exercising judicial discretion in a way which gives effect to such rights, interpreting legislation in accordance with the Convention, developing the common law so that it is compatible with Convention rights and also by creating a remedy in private disputes where it is necessary in order to protect an individual's right.
>
> In any action before a court or tribunal, the court or tribunal must take account of the relevant articles of the ECHR and any relevant case law of the ECtHR.

The Human Rights Act 1998 poses a problem for English tort law because the jurisprudence of the ECHR is different from English law. The ECHR gives a right and the state is then allowed to derogate from this right in certain circumstances for particular purposes. The state has a 'margin of appreciation' in this, but any derogation must be proportionate and necessary for the protection of the stated aims. The court will balance the violation of the right with the harm caused by upholding it. The case law of the ECtHR is thus based on rights, while English tort law is based on the commission of a wrong. It may be helpful to think of this situation as a 'rights-based regime' meeting a 'wrong-based regime'.

The Human Rights Act 1998 continues to impact on the development of tort law. For example, it has broadened the circumstances in which claimants are entitled to sue in the tort of negligence, as we shall see later. Because its impact, or potential impact, is so wide-ranging, we will look at Human Rights, where applicable, throughout this book.

Tort and other areas of law

Remember that tort law does not operate in a vacuum. You should always be aware of the context in which actions occur, as well as the fact that more than one area of law may be applicable to a set of facts. We have already seen that one set of facts may give rise to tortious as well as criminal consequences. Similarly, the boundaries between tort and contract may blur. For some torts it may be necessary for you to understand other areas of the law – for example, for the torts of trespass to land and *Rylands* v. *Fletcher* you need to understand certain land law principles, especially relating to title to land.

THE BOUNDARIES OF TORT LAW

We have already looked at some of the boundaries of tort law. You should understand now that there is no 'general' right to claim, that damages suffered do not necessarily entitle you to a claim. You also know that the boundaries are sometimes very blurry between tort and other areas of law, where the proper cause of action would not lie in tort but maybe in some other area of law, e.g. contract. Now take note that, apart from these, there are other issues within which the law of tort operates. We will now briefly just look at a couple of these.

Limitations of actions

A right to sue may be extinguished by the expiry of the limitation period. A tortious remedy may be extinguished in other ways – for example, by satisfaction, judgment or release or, where the law permits this, exclusion of liability (see e.g. the Unfair Contract Terms Act 1977).

Is it a 'law of tort' or a 'law of torts'?

You may have noticed that the titles of textbooks differ in how they refer to this area of law: some refer to a 'law of tort' or 'tort', in the singular, whilst others refer to 'torts', in the plural. This represents a difference in view as to the foundation of tortious liability: some are of the view that there is a *general principle* underlying the various disparate torts; others believe that there is simply a *body of rules* creating specific torts, which cannot be referred to any general principle of liability.

The difference between the two is not purely academic: it also affects how the courts view the development of new areas of liability. Were they to adopt a 'general principles' (or unitary) view, then, whenever unjustifiable harm was done, the presumption would be in favour of tortious liability. Were they to adopt a 'body of rules' (or disparate torts) view, the presumption might be less favourable.

> The decision in *Khorasandjian* v. *Bush* [1993] 3 WLR 476, which considered the possibility of a new tort of harassment, provides support for the general, unitary view. However, after that decision the Protection from Harassment Act 1997 was enacted, which again could indicate a swing towards a more disparate view of torts.

REFLECTION

Tort and insurance

If victims have a choice as to whom to sue, they will often choose wealthy defendants, e.g. corporations, or they will choose to sue people the law requires to have insurance, e.g. drivers and employers. Social security and personal insurance can also play a part in supporting accident victims.

APPORTIONMENT OF BLAME

Think back to our discussion of fault as one of the elements that you need to prove for a tortious action. Keeping in mind that sometimes we have no-fault liability, nevertheless it seems just that the wrongdoer should compensate the 'victim'. Things are seldom clear-cut, however. What if there are several persons who have caused the harm? Or what if the victim herself were somehow to blame as well? In instances like this we have to look at ways in which we can relate the proportion of fault to the proportion of compensation to be paid.

Joint and several tortfeasors

It could be that more than one person causes damage to another. For example, C could have been beaten up by two men, A and D, in which case C would have a claim in battery against both A and D as *joint* tortfeasors. In other words, one tortious act caused by more than one person. With joint liability, each of the tortfeasors is liable for the full damage, but the claimant can only claim her full damage once.

CORNERSTONE

Civil Liability (Contribution) Act 1978

For example, if A and D beat up C to such an extent that she is rendered disabled and faces medical bills of £50,000, C could claim the £50,000 from both A and D in one action. Alternatively, she could decide to sue only one of them for the full amount. What she cannot do is to sue A for £50,000 and also sue D for £50,000. If she sued A and he paid up, he will then have the right to sue D for his (D's) contribution (Civil Liability (Contribution) Act 1978).

If there is more than one tortfeasor, each acting independently, but causing cumulative harm, we talk about *several* or *concurrent* tortfeasors. Again, provided the claimant suffered one indivisible injury as a result, she could claim from one or more or all the tortfeasors for her full damages. (Remember the requirement of *causation* here!) If a single defendant is held liable, she would then in her turn have to try and recoup contributions from the other tortfeasors, as described above. This may be difficult if the other tortfeasors are insolvent, or do not exist any more. We will look at this interesting area again in our discussion of negligence later in the book.

Contributory negligence

It may also happen that the 'victim' herself may be partly to blame for her damages. A good example here would be a motor vehicle accident.

APPLICATION

Let's say D negligently drove into C while C was stationary at traffic lights, and caused damage to her car as well as a neck injury to C. It's pretty clear that D is to blame and will have to pay for C's injury. However, let's say that C was not wearing her safety belt and it is established that, if she had worn one at the time of the accident, her injury would have been less. In such an instance it's partly her fault that she suffered the injury to the extent that she did. What the court will now do is to apportion the blame between the two parties (in terms of the Law Reform (Contributory Negligence) Act 1945). For example, the court may decide that the injury was 80 per cent D's fault, and that C's negligence contributed 20 per cent to her injury. If the damage is calculated at, say, £10,000, that would mean that D would have to pay £8,000 and C will have to bear the shortfall of £2,000.

Contributory negligence is a partial defence and we will look at it in detail under the discussion of the tort of negligence.

KEY POINTS

- 'Tort' is the umbrella term we use for a number of instances that the common law recognises as giving rise to civil liability. Examples include negligence, trespass, assault and battery, and defamation.
- Tort always consists of an act (or sometimes an omission) giving cause for a legal action. Usually fault and damage are required, but not always.
- The main aim of tort is to provide compensation for civil injury, and it does so by protecting a variety of interests, such as bodily integrity (the tort of assault and battery).
- The law usually requires fault (usually in the form of either negligence or intent) for tortious liability, but there are a few exceptions which we call *strict* or no-fault liability
- Tort law intersects with a number of areas of law, such as criminal law, human rights, or contract law.

CORE CASES AND STATUTES

Case	About	Importance
Cork v. *Kirby MacLean Ltd* [1952] 2 All ER 402	Element of (factual) causation	(If) the damage would not have happened *but for* a particular fault, then that fault is the cause of the damage; if it would have happened just the same, fault or no fault, the fault is not the cause of the damage (per Lord Denning).
Donoghue v. *Stevenson* [1932] AC 562	Element of fault, negligence	(This case is dealt with in detail in Part 1: Negligence.) For now, know that the case established the rule that one owes a duty of care to certain classes of people.
Bradford Corporation v. *Pickles* [1895] AC 587	Element of intention, malice	An otherwise legal action cannot lead to a claim in tort purely because of an immoral motive.

Statute	About	Importance
Civil Liability (Contribution) Act 1978, ss. 1 and 2	Joint and several liability	The common law rule was that joint or several tortfeasors could not recover a contribution or indemnity from other tortfeasors in the absence of an agreement between them. Now the 1978 Act states that if the claimant recovered damages from one of several tortfeasors, such tortfeasor will have the right to recover contributions from the others (we will look at how this is calculated later).

FURTHER READING

Atiyah, P.S. (1997) *The Damages Lottery.* **Oxford: Hart Publishing**
For anyone interested in the law of tort and personal injury law in particular, this book was written by an academic authority.

Murphy, J. (2008) Rights, reductionism and tort law. *OJLS* **28, p. 393**
This article gives an explanation of the classification and elements of tort law.

Parker, A. (2006) Changing the claims culture. *New Law Journal* **p. 702**
For students who are interested in the compensatory nature of most torts, this is a good article to read.

Lewis, R. (2005) Insurance and the tort system. *Legal Studies* **25(1), p. 85**
Stapleton, J. (1995) Tort, insurance and ideology. *MLR* **58, p. 820**
Both these articles examine the relationship between tort law and the insurance industry.

CHAPTER 2

Negligence: Introduction – duty of care

BLUEPRINT

Negligence: introduction – duty of care

KEY QUESTIONS

CONTEXT

- There is a constant concern that too many cases may 'flood' the courts with claims for personal injury or damage.
- One of the ways in which this is contained is by requiring claimants to prove proximity, forseeability and that they were owed a duty of care.

LEGISLATION

- European Convention on Human Rights, Article 6
- Human Rights Act 1998

CONCEPTS

- Negligence
- Duty of care
- Breach of duty
- Causation
- Nervous shock
- Psychiatric injury
- Pure economic loss (expectation loss)

- Would 'no-fault' compensation be a fairer system than the current requirement for personal injury victims to prove fault on the part of the defendant in the courts?
- Should the *de facto* immunity from suit enjoyed by the police and other public authorities for liability in negligence be abolished?

- What are the elements we need to prove to succeed with a claim in negligence?
- What do we mean by the 'neighbour principle'?
- How do we determine whether there is a duty of care?
- What are the three questions asked in *Caparo*?

CASES
- *Donoghue* v. *Stevenson* [1932]
- *Caparo Industries PLC* v. *Dickman* [1990]
- *X (Minors)* v. *Bedfordshire County Council* [1995]
- *Alcock* v. *Chief Constable of South Yorkshire Police* [1991]

SPECIAL CHARACTERISTICS
- Lord Atkin's 'neighbour principle'
- The *Caparo* three-stage test to determine existence of a duty of care
- The floodgates policy consideration
- *Alcock* criteria for psychiatric injury

REFORM
- Public authorities such as the police and social services enjoy certain degrees of immunity from liability for negligence, mostly for public policy reasons. Recent instances of child protection failure and police corruption have led to calls for this immunity to be restricted, and the immunity has also been criticised by the European Court of Human Rights.

CRITICAL ISSUES

Setting the scene

Negligence in tort can mean several things. It can refer to careless behaviour or negligent conduct in the ordinary sense of the phrase, or it could refer to the legal concept of **fault**, which is a requirement for liability in most civil and criminal actions. For example, in criminal law if you intentionally kill someone, you may be found guilty of murder; if you negligently cause someone's death, you may be found guilty of manslaughter. 'Fault' here includes intention, or negligence. In this sense negligence as a fault element is important to us, because for many torts 'fault' is a requirement for liability. For now, though, we concentrate on the third possible meaning of negligence, namely as a tort in its own right. In short, the tort of negligence means that if you negligently or carelessly cause damage or injury to someone, you may be held liable for it.

Negligence is arguably the most important of the modern torts, because it is the most frequently used of all torts. It traces its acceptance as a tort in its own right to a landmark case in the early twentieth century – *Donoghue* v. *Stevenson*. Negligence protects against three types of harm: personal injury, damage to property and (rarely) economic loss. The tort of negligence is thus concerned with compensating people who have suffered damage as a result of the carelessness of other people.

Think about this for a moment. Life is full of mishaps, and accidents – as they say – do happen. If everyone who suffers an accident is able to claim damages, the courts would be flooded with claimants, and we then run the risk that people would be so afraid of being sued that they cease to pursue otherwise enjoyable or beneficial activities.

For this reason (the so-called floodgates argument), the law does not provide a remedy for everyone who suffers due to negligence. The main way in which liability is kept in check is by means of the doctrine of the duty of care. A person will only be liable to another for negligence if she has a duty of care towards the other and she has breached that duty and caused damage to the other. This is the concept of the 'reasonable person' – we ask whether the conduct of the defendant was less than what we would expect from a reasonable person in her position.

Let's now examine the tort of negligence in more detail, as well as one of its vital components, the duty of care.

DONOGHUE v. STEVENSON – THE BIRTH OF THE MODERN TORT OF NEGLIGENCE

Traditionally to succeed with a claim in tort, you had to prove that there was intentional and direct interference with your person or your property. However, careless acts seemed to cause more loss or injury than intentional acts. It therefore followed that claimants could sometimes make out a case for liability for careless, and not just intentional, deeds that caused foreseeable loss or injury. The courts sometimes allowed such claims, but not very consistently and usually with some extra element required, such as fraud. Therefore, there was no general duty of care.

This changed after the landmark case of *Donoghue* v. *Stevenson* [1932] AC 562, in which negligence was established as a separate tort in its own right. The case formulated a way to determine whether negligence had occurred, mainly by establishing a test to determine whether a duty of care existed in each specific case.

Donoghue v. Stevenson – the birth of the modern tort of negligence

CORNERSTONE

Donoghue v. Stevenson [1932] AC 562

Mrs Donoghue's friend bought her a bottle of ginger beer, which she enjoyed until a half-decomposed snail was poured out of the opaque bottle into her glass. As a result of having drunk some of the tainted ginger beer before seeing the snail in the remainder, Mrs Donoghue contracted gastro-enteritis. If Mrs Donoghue had bought the drink for herself, her personal injury claim would have been straightforward – she would have had a contractual claim because of being party to a contract of sale. However, she could not, because in contract law the doctrine of privity restricts contractual claims to parties to the contract only. The House of Lords, by a majority of three to two, instead allowed her a remedy in tort. Lord Atkin, addressing the principle that the unavailability of an action in contract left the claimant without any remedy, stated:

> 'If this were the result of the authorities, I should consider the result a grave defect in the law . . . I do not think so ill of our jurisprudence as to suppose that its principles are so remote from the ordinary needs of civilised society and the ordinary claims it makes upon its members as to deny a legal remedy where there is so obviously a social wrong.'

There are two important tort principles arising from this case. The first relates to product liability, and is expressed in the narrow *ratio decidendi* ('reason for decision') of the case. In short, the narrow *ratio* of *Donoghue* v. *Stevenson* is the principle that a manufacturer owes a duty of care in negligence to the ultimate consumer of her products, which she sells in such form as to show that she intends them to reach the consumer in that form without reasonable possibility of intermediate examination, and with the knowledge that the absence of reasonable care in the preparation of the products will result in injury to the consumer's life or property. (We will examine product liability in detail in Chapter 9.)

The second principle, which is more important to us at present as it can be said to form the foundation of the tort of negligence, arises out of the famous wider *ratio* or *obiter dictum* by Lord Atkin:

> 'The rule that you are to love your neighbour becomes in law, you must not injure your neighbour; and the lawyer's question, Who is my neighbour? receives a restricted reply. You must take reasonable care to avoid acts or omissions which you can reasonably foresee would be likely to injure your neighbour. Who, then, in law is my neighbour? The answer seems to be – persons who are so closely and directly affected by my act that I ought reasonably to have them in contemplation as being so affected when I am directing my mind to the acts or omissions which are called in question.'

As mentioned above, the floodgates argument was one of the main reasons why, before *Donoghue*, the courts were reluctant even to entertain the idea of a general duty of care. Put another way, they feared potentially limitless liability, with the courts overwhelmed with claimants. So it should be no surprise that in *Donoghue*, the court was at pains to restrict the operation of claims in negligence.

Let's look at Lord Atkin's judgment again, from which we extract two further important concepts in a claim in negligence: First, there is the *reasonable foreseeability principle*:

'You must take reasonable care to avoid acts or omissions which you *can reasonably foresee* would be likely to injure your neighbour.' (emphasis added)

Secondly, we have the *principle of proximity*, which Lord Atkin formulated Three he answered his own question, 'Who, then, in law is my neighbour?' as:

'. . . persons who are *so closely and directly affected* by my act that I ought reasonably to have them in contemplation as being so affected when I am directing my mind to the acts or omissions which are called in question.' (emphasis added)

ELEMENTS OF THE TORT OF NEGLIGENCE

To succeed with a claim in negligence, the **burden of proof** is on the claimant to prove three elements.

CORNERSTONE

Elements of negligence

The claimant will have to prove that:

1. the defendant owed the claimant a *duty of care*;
2. the defendant has acted in *breach* of that duty;
3. the defendant's breach *caused* the claimant's *damage* or injury. (Causation is in turn made up of two elements, factual causation and 'causation in law' which means that the damage must not be too remote a consequence of the defendant's breach.) (More about this in Chapter 4.)

These are the three elements of the tort of negligence and it is up to the claimant to prove each one. You will see that there is a large degree of overlap and that the three elements can sometimes merge. We will look at each of these elements, and the cases that explain them in detail as we discuss negligence. For now, the whole process can be visualised as shown in Figure 2.1.

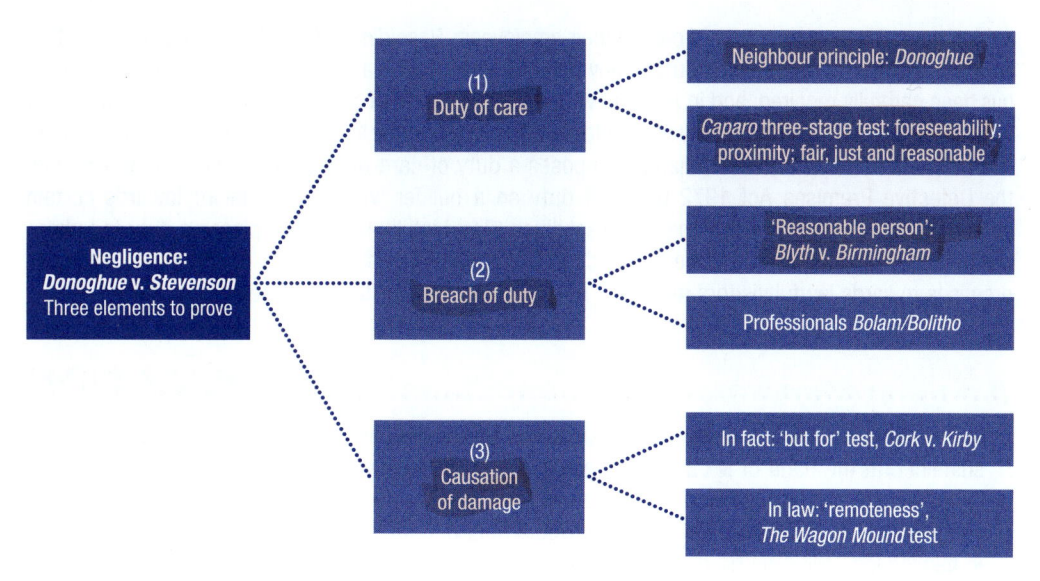

Figure 2.1 Negligence grid

Negligence: *Donoghue* v. *Stevenson* — Three elements to prove

- (1) Duty of care
  - Neighbour principle: *Donoghue*
  - *Caparo* three-stage test: foreseeability; proximity; fair, just and reasonable
- (2) Breach of duty
  - 'Reasonable person': *Blyth* v. *Birmingham*
  - Professionals *Bolam/Bolitho*
- (3) Causation of damage
  - In fact: 'but for' test, *Cork* v. *Kirby*
  - In law: 'remoteness', *The Wagon Mound* test

> **REFLECTION**
>
> From time to time, it is suggested that the law should do away with the requirement of fault for personal injury claims, particularly in relation to accident compensation and medical negligence cases. Reformers argue that having to prove that the defendant was at fault (i.e. either acted intentionally or negligently) is time consuming and expensive, and that the process of proving a claim overburdens the courts. People also ask why the victim of another's careless act should be compensated whilst the victim of a disease, for example, is not. In New Zealand a 'no fault' compensation scheme was launched, but that proved to be very costly too. What do you think?

DUTY OF CARE

Let's start with the first element, the duty of care. Note that part of this entails that a duty is owed *to* someone, and this 'someone' is the 'neighbour' contemplated in *Donoghue* – those people who are so closely affected by our deeds that we have a duty to take care to avoid harming them. This is purposely vague – what was meant was that, in each case, the court would have to decide whether there was a duty of care or not, and also whether such duty was owed to the specific claimant before the court. This was what happened, in fact, both before and after *Donoghue*, with cases clarifying instances where there is a recognised duty of care. There are, of course, instances where it is accepted that there is a duty of care due to the relationship between the parties. These established duty situations include the duties of, for example, a doctor to a patient, a solicitor to a client, or a road user to other road users. In less clear instances, case law shows the way.

The *Donoghue* case itself, for example, established a duty of care for manufacturers (towards the consumer). Apart from this, the duty of care is identified, on a case-by-case basis, to a number of different relationships. To name but a few: In *Wilsons & Clyde Coal Co* v. *English* [1938] AC 57 it was held that employers owe a duty of care to their employees; *Haseldine* v. *Daw* [1941] 2 KB 343 held that the repairer of an article owes a duty to any person by whom the article is lawfully used to see that it has been carefully repaired; and in *Butchart* v. *Home Office* [2006] 1 WLR 1155 the Court of Appeal held that a prison authority owed a duty of care towards a prisoner they knew to be depressed and suicidal.

In a number of instances, Parliament imposes a duty of care by enacting statutes. For example, the Defective Premises Act 1972 places a duty on a builder, vendor or landlord towards certain categories of purchaser; the Congenital Disabilities (Civil Liability) Act 1976 places a duty to unborn children on certain people; and the two Occupiers' Liability Acts place a duty of care on occupiers of premises towards lawful visitors (the 1957 Act) and trespassers (the 1984 Act) respectively.

APPLICATION

> Imagine that you are a solicitor. Mrs A asks you whether she can claim for a personal injury she sustained at the hand of Mr B. Mrs A tells you that she believes that Mr B did not cause the injury wilfully, but accidentally. You therefore think about a possible claim in negligence. First, you will have to establish whether Mr B owed a duty of care to Mrs A. If not, there is no claim in negligence. (We may be dealing with another tort, but let's just think about negligence for now.) How would you find out whether there was a duty of care? Start by looking at statute law – is there a relevant statute that imposes a duty of care in this instance? Also look for an applicable precedent – are there any cases with similar facts where the court acknowledged a duty of care? If you can find a precedent you save yourself a lot of work, because now you will not have to start at the beginning and try to convince the court that there *should* be a recognised duty of care. Your next step will then be to prove that there was breach of the duty, that the breach caused your client's injury, and that the damage was not too remote (in other words, the other elements of negligence, which we look at later).

Development of the duty of care

Let us just repeat again what we learnt from *Donoghue*: the law recognises that a person has a duty to take reasonable care to avoid doing something which she can reasonably foresee would be likely to injure her neighbour. This is not an absolute duty, owed everywhere to everybody. It is left to the courts to decide when there is such a duty, and to whom.

The neighbour principle

Donoghue established the neighbour principle, by which we basically ask whether a person should be regarded, in each specific situation before the court, as a 'neighbour' to whom a duty of care is owed. If the answer is yes, the court then has to decide (either based on precedent or in principle) whether there was a duty of care. For a while, though, this process was reversed. The prime example of the disparity in thinking was the case of *Anns* v. *Merton London Borough Council* [1978] AC 728.

The *Anns* test

Lord Wilberforce in *Anns* formulated a new two-part test to determine whether the defendant owed a duty of care to the claimant. First, he held, provided there is a sufficient relationship of proximity or neighbourhood between the parties, a **prima facie** duty of care arises. Secondly, if the first question is answered affirmatively, then the court has to consider whether there are reasons to reduce or limit the scope of the duty, or the class of person to whom it is owed or the damages to which a breach of it may give rise.

This approach effectively turned the test in *Donoghue* on its head. The difference worked like this: provided there was proximity between the parties, in *Donoghue* the claimant would then have to convince the court that there was good reason to acknowledge a duty of care, whilst in *Anns* it was assumed that there is a duty of care, and it would then be up to the court to decide whether there was good reason *not* to impose a duty of care.

Anns, therefore, made it very easy for a claimant, by doing away with the requirement to convince the court of a duty of care. You can see how this had the potential of encouraging more litigants.

The three-stage *Caparo* test

Not surprisingly, given the constant fear of opening the floodgates of litigation, many cases criticised the decision in *Anns.* Finally, it was overturned in the following key case.

CORNERSTONE

Caparo Industries plc v. Dickman [1990] 1 All ER 568

In this case a company's auditors negligently compiled and certified an audit of Company F's accounts. Another company then made a take-over bid for F, in reliance on the negligently made audit. In the end it lost money on the transaction, and therefore sued for its financial losses. The court had to determine whether the auditors owed a duty of care to the claimants.

The court rejected the assumption of a duty of care, and went back to a three-stage test for imposing liability. Three questions will need to be asked by the courts:

1. Was the damage *reasonably foreseeable*?
2. Was there a *relationship of proximity* between defendant and claimant?
3. Is it *fair, just and reasonable* in all the circumstances to impose a duty of care?

(The court then decided, based on policy, that there was no reason why auditors should be deemed to have a special relationship with non-shareholders, and therefore the auditors had not owed any duty of care to the claimants in respect of their purchase of F.)

If this three-stage test sounds familiar, it should! The first question echoes the foreseeability requirement formulated in *Donoghue*, while the second test similarly reflects its famous neighbour principle. The main addition is the fact that it is spelt out in so many words in the third *Caparo* requirement that the courts take policy issues into account when deciding on a duty of care. This is not that new a requirement, though, because questions of policy have been taken into account already by the courts, for example, on answering the question whether or not the required degree of proximity exists in a given situation.

A good example of how this worked is the case of *Hill* v. *Chief Constable of West Yorkshire* [1988] 2 All ER 238. In this case the mother of one of the Yorkshire Ripper's victims sued the police in negligence, averring that if they had taken proper care in their investigation, they could have caught the killer before he murdered her daughter. The court held that there was not sufficient proximity between the police and the general public to establish a duty of care to individual members of the public. The reason for the immunity from suit that the police enjoy is pure policy: it is in the public interest that the police do their work unfettered by having to worry about everything they do for fear of being sued. The third condition (policy) therefore means that the courts will limit liability and that no duty will be imposed unless it is just in all the circumstances. We examine policy in more detail later in this chapter.

The House of Lords endorsed the *Caparo* three-stage test in *Murphy* v. *Brentwood District Council* [1990] 3 WLR 414, which overruled *Anns*. Note that the courts do not always clearly and methodically use the test in a three-step process – this is because the three conditions of the *Caparo* test overlap and are interrelated.

The current approach

A number of subsequent cases have confirmed the *Caparo* three-stage test as good law. Remember that the three issues overlap and may also have a bearing on each other. For example, the closer the

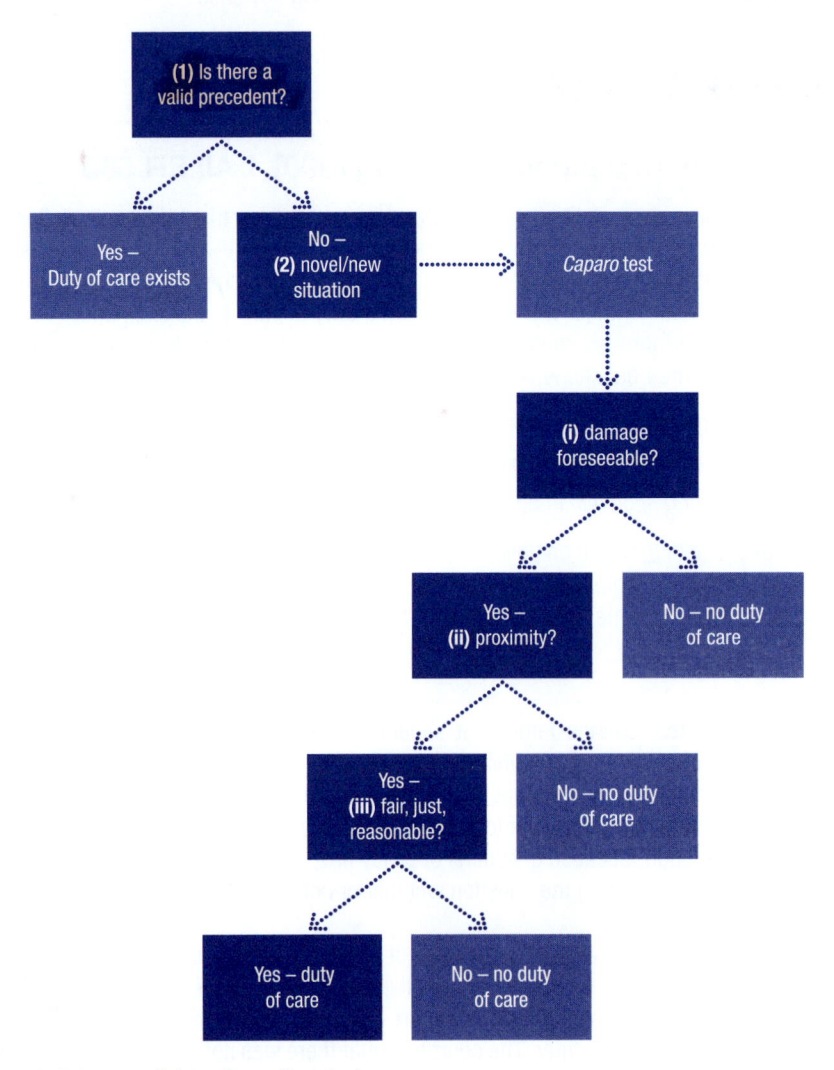

Figure 2.2 Existence of duty of care flowchart

proximity between defendant and claimant the more likely it would be that it would be fair, just and reasonable to impose a duty of care.

Also remember that you should always think of precedent first – is there a relevant case or an established analogous area that resemble the particular set of facts you are dealing with? It is only in the absence of precedent, i.e. in novel instances, that we use the three-stage test to determine whether there should be liability. The flowchart in Figure 2.2 explains the procedure.

THE ROLE OF POLICY

We have already noted that policy has always played a major role in determining liability for negligence. If we look at case law we see that in many instances the courts limit possible liability on policy grounds. For example, it has been stated in many cases that the police, in general, enjoy immunity as they are not held to have a duty of care towards the public at large, or to any particular individual in general. Many policy considerations entail a balancing exercise. In the *Hill* case, above, it is clear that the individual claimant's interest in a remedy for her loss is balanced against society's interest in maintaining a fearless police force. The same reasoning is to be found in a case that dealt with actions taken or not taken by relevant local authorities in child abuse situations: the court held in *X (Minors)* v. *Bedfordshire CC* [1995] 3 WLR 152 that the imposition of a duty of care by local authorities to individuals might make local authorities adopt an overly cautious approach, to the detriment of children.

This does not mean that policy dictates that police, local authorities, etc. are always immune from being sued – it just means that the courts will balance the individual's right to a remedy in cases of negligence with society's interest in public authorities that are able to carry out their functions effectively. Against this background, let us look more closely at the liability (or lack thereof!) of public authorities.

Liability of public authorities

There is nothing in our law that prevents a public authority being liable just like any other person for *foreseeable physical injury* brought about by a *positive act*. The trouble with public authorities, however, is that it's rarely that simple – their potential liability is problematic for several reasons. Let's examine some.

In many instances, the behaviour complained of comprises an omission (failure to act) – e.g. the police failing to act on

> **Take note**
> Before we move on, let's just recap where we are in our discussion of negligence. The claimant has to prove three elements: that she was owed a duty of care; that there was breach of this duty; and that this caused her damage. We are looking, in this chapter, at the first element only: whether there is a duty of care. The classic case, Donoghue v. Stevenson, gave us the neighbour principle to determine whether the defendant owed the claimant a duty of care. In each case the court had to decide whether there was such a 'neighbour' relationship and thus a duty. In the case of Anns, the court ruled that a duty of care was assumed – the claimant did not have to prove it, but the defendant could disprove it. This made things very easy for claimants and raised concerns about the courts being flooded with claims. Therefore, in Murphy v. Brentwood, the Anns case was overruled, and the position now is that a claimant has to prove a duty of care (i.e. we returned to the position under Donoghue). A further key case, Caparo Industries v. Dickman, sets out a handy three-stage test to determine whether there is a duty of care.

> **Take note**
>
> Most public bodies derive their power from statute, and usually the enabling statute tells us what the powers and duties of such a body are. Do not, however, assume that there is a breach of duty if the relevant body does not perform the duty or exercise the power given to it by statute, and that therefore, without further ado, you have a claim in tort. The courts have held that statutory bodies will not incur liability in tort merely for failing to perform a statutory duty or for failing to exercise a statutory power. You therefore need to establish independently whether there was a common law duty of care on the part of the body. (We examine breach of statutory duty as a tort in more detail in Chapter 13.)

information that might have prevented a crime (*Hill*), or a local authority failing to take a child into care with the result that the child is abused (*X*). Liability for omissions (as opposed to actions) is controversial and not readily granted, as you will see from our discussion later. Similarly controversial in tort is liability for the acts of third parties, which also happens frequently in the context of public authorities. This, too, we will discuss in detail later (see Chapter 12).

Very often the loss complained of by the claimant comprises not physical injury or damage to property, but less easily proven damage due to the loss of a chance, or pure economic loss, which in general cannot be claimed in tort. Sometimes public law, rather than tort, would be more appropriate given the public nature of the defendant. For the same reason, i.e. because we are dealing with public bodies, the Human Rights Act 1998 and human rights law in general also play a role. Finally, as we have seen, the issue of public policy plays a significant role when the courts are faced with a public authority defendant, because of the balancing question mentioned earlier (individual interests of claimant versus society's interest).

The leading case about public authorities' liability, before the Human Rights Act 1998 took effect, was *Stovin* v. *Wise, Norfolk County Council (Third Party)* [1996] 3 WLR 15. This case considered the situation where the complaint was that the public authority failed to do something that they had a statutory power, but no statutory duty, to do. In this case, the local highway authority failed to remove a bank of earth at a junction, which made it difficult for drivers turning right to see approaching traffic. W, as a result, collided with S's motorcycle. W's insurers paid S, and then claimed for a contribution from the highway authority, alleging that they were negligent in failing to implement an earlier decision to remove the bank of earth. The highway agency had the power to do this in terms of statute. The House of Lords held that the highway authority was not liable. Three principles became clear from this judgment:

1. There is no liability on the part of the authority for a pure omission.

2. The court made a distinction between a statutory power and a statutory duty – with a statutory power it is within the discretion of the authority whether to act or not.

3. Even if there was a statutory duty, it does not necessarily follow that failure to fulfil the duty will lead to a private right to sue – it depends on the will of Parliament in drafting the statute.

Therefore, the court held that in these situations liability under the common law of negligence can only arise if it had been irrational not to exercise the power and if the policy of the statute was compatible with awarding compensation. The effect of this decision was somewhat modified when the Human Rights Act 1998 started to play a significant role in this area (more about this below).

As far as public services are concerned, certain types of defendant may escape negligence liability because the courts have held that they owe no duty, whilst others are judged by the standard of

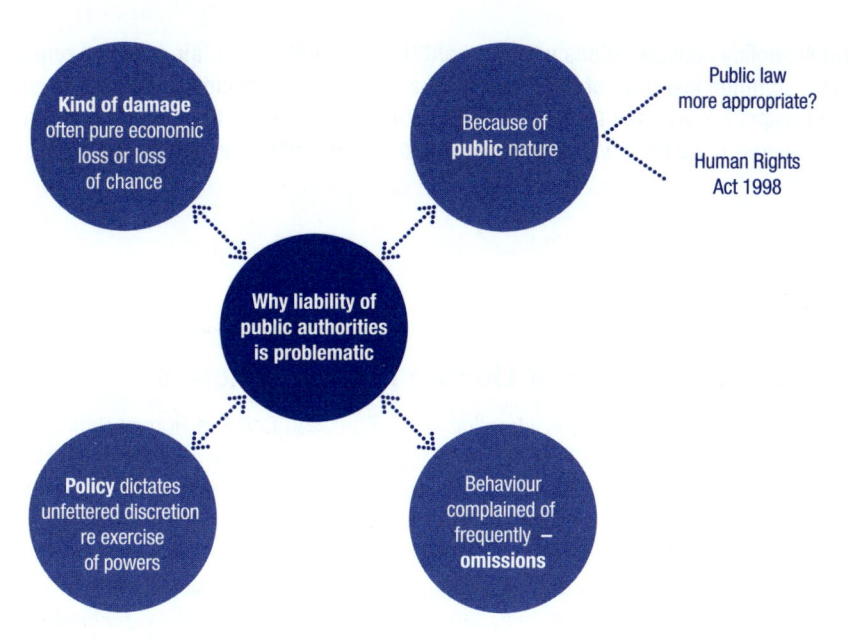

Figure 2.3 Why liability of public authorities is problematic

[Diagram centre: Why liability of public authorities is problematic — surrounded by: Kind of damage often pure economic loss or loss of chance; Because of public nature (Public law more appropriate? Human Rights Act 1998); Policy dictates unfettered discretion re exercise of powers; Behaviour complained of frequently – omissions]

their profession. We will now look at local authorities and other public servants (such as the police, fire brigade, ambulance service, NHS etc.).

Local authorities

The courts are relatively loath to impose a liability in negligence on local authorities, mainly as it is feared that fear of liability would hobble them in their ability to perform their functions, which in turn would be contrary to the public interest. Or, as Deakin (2008: 210) puts it: 'the courts will not hold public bodies liable in tort if to do so involves entering into areas of policy which are not properly *justiciable*'.

CORNERSTONE

X (Minors) v. Bedfordshire County Council [1995] 2 AC 633

In this case the House of Lords held that in most instances an action in negligence against a public authority carrying out its delegated powers would fail. In this case, a local authority failed to exercise its power to take a child who was the victim of abuse into care.

From this and similar cases it seemed that the English courts lean in favour of society's overriding interest in unfettered functioning of public or statutory bodies. However, public authorities do not enjoy absolute immunity. This is borne out by the House of Lords' judgment in *Barrett* v. *Enfield London Borough Council* [2001] 2 AC 550, where it was decided that:

'the public policy considerations which meant that it would not be fair, just and reasonable to impose a common law duty of care on a local authority when deciding whether or not to take action in respect of a case of suspected child abuse did not have the same force in respect of decisions taken *once the child was already in local authority care.*' (emphasis added)

CORNERSTONE

European Convention of Human Rights, Article 6

The matter has also had some consideration at the European Court of Human Rights (ECtHR). In *Osman* v. *UK* [1999] 1 FLR 193 the ECtHR held that police immunity violated Article 6 of the European Convention of Human Rights (ECHR), which guarantees an individual access to court, or put another way, a right to a fair hearing. Later on, however, when some of the claimants in *X* v. *Bedfordshire CC* took their case to the same court, it held that the partial immunity from suit enjoyed by the local authorities did *not* violate Article 6. In this decision by the ECtHR (*Z* v. *UK* [2001] FLR 193) the reasoning was that, although the House of Lords in *X* v. *Bedfordshire CC* had held that the authorities did not owe a duty of care towards the individual claimants, it came to that decision after a judicial process of weighing up the competing interests. Therefore, the ECtHR held, there was indeed access to court and a fair hearing for the claimants and Article 6 was not violated.

(The court did, however, rule in favour of the claimants on other European Convention of Human Rights grounds, such as the right to a remedy contained in Article 13.)

From the above it is therefore clear that policy issues as determinants in deciding whether or not there is a duty of care should not be seen in isolation, nor as cast in stone.

You will note that the application and consideration of human rights law started to affect courts' consideration of public authorities' actions. Also take care to note that public authorities' actions are justiciable, provided it does not involve weighing social policy considerations which themselves are not justiciable. This approach was confirmed by the House of Lords in *Phelps* v. *Hillingdon London Borough Council* [2000] 4 All ER 504, which dealt with the so-called 'education cases', where professionals in education failed to do their job properly (for example, failing to diagnose a claimant's dyslexia in one instance, and in another failing to provide a student with muscular dystrophy with the proper equipment needed, such as a computer). The House of Lords held, in effect, that everything a public authority does is in principle justiciable, but in such cases it is subject to the tripartite *Caparo* test by the court to see whether or not a duty of care exists. The one exception is those decisions made under a discretion which clearly involve the weighing of considerations of a social policy kind about which Parliament cannot have intended the court to substitute its views for those of ministers and officials.

Other public servants

The courts have found that the *police* do not owe a general duty of care towards any particular individual. As we saw in *Hill* v. *Chief Constable of West Yorkshire* [1989] AC 53 (HL), the duty of the police is to the public at large. *Hill* was confirmed in the more recent House of Lords decision of *Brooks* v. *Commissioner of the Metropolis* [2005] 2 All ER 489. The same reasoning applies to other emergency services such as the coast guard and the fire service, in that they are not held liable for failing to act. Similarly, the ambulance service does not have a general duty to respond to a call. However, in *Kent* v. *Griffiths, Roberts and London Ambulance Service* [1998] EWCA Civ 1941 it was decided that once a call has been accepted, the service owes a duty to the named individual at the specified address – provided that it is just, fair and reasonable to impose such a duty.

The influence of human rights

We should remind ourselves at this stage that the police, local authorities, and also the courts, are all public authorities.

CORNERSTONE

Human Rights Act 1998, section 6

Section 6 of the Human Rights Act 1998 imposes a duty on all public authorities to act in a manner consistent with human rights.

Logically, then, as they are public authorities, the courts, police and local authorities owe a direct duty to the populace to act in a manner consistent with their rights. In addition to this, as a signatory to the European Convention of Human Rights, the UK has a duty to ensure that its domestic common law is consistent with Convention rights. It is possible that cases involving serious failures by the state (which includes the police) to protect public safety and private life will in some instances have to be decided in favour of the claimant otherwise the law will be inconsistent with, amongst others, Article 2 (right to life) and Article 6 (right to trial) of the ECHR.

For example, the European Court of Human Rights held in *Osman* v. *United Kingdom* [1999] EHRR 245 that the existence of 'blanket immunity' in such cases is contrary to Article 6 of the ECHR. Thus, cases that would previously have been automatically struck out on the grounds that it is not fair, just and reasonable to impose a duty on police in relation to suppression and detection of crime will now have to go to trial and be decided on their facts.

As to other public authorities, we already saw that there has been a shift from near immunity of public authorities (*Stovin*) to the recognition of justiciability (*Phelps*).

So, the current situation is that cases that previously would not have made it to court, do. But what happens once they get there is another question, and once again one heavily influenced by policy considerations. It could be argued that, even if such cases get to court, the likelihood of a claim succeeding is very low, because the courts tend to place very stringent criteria in place. For example, the court in *Van Colle and Another* v. *Chief Constable of the Hertfordshire Police* [2008] All ER (D) 408 (HL) and *Smith* v. *Chief Constable of Sussex Police* [2008] UKHL 50 held that the police would only be under a duty to take action when they 'knew or ought to have known of a real and immediate risk to life'. The court set the foreseeability bar very high indeed – this becomes clear when you consider that in both cases the victims had reported to the police that specific persons were making threats of violence; but in neither case did the police take steps to protect the victim. In both instances the court held that the police were not liable.

> **REFLECTION**
>
> In *Van Colle*, a prosecution witness was shot dead by the accused shortly before he was due to give evidence at the latter's trial for theft. In the weeks preceding the trial there were instances where the accused had approached the witness, and tried to dissuade him from giving evidence. Over the same period the witness's property had been damaged. Just before the witness was murdered, he received two telephone calls from the accused, the final one being very aggressive and threatening. These phone calls and some of the incidents had been reported to the police.
>
> In *Smith*, the facts were even more damning of the police's failure to act: after the claimant broke up with his former partner, the latter sent him persistent and threatening phone, text and internet messages, including threats to kill him. The claimant reported all this to the police, and also provided the officers with details of his former partner's previous history of violence. The officers declined to look at or record the messages, took no statement from him and completed no crime form. However, they took steps to trace the calls and informed him of the progress of that investigation. Shortly thereafter he was attacked at his home by his former partner and sustained severe and continuing injuries.
>
> Given the facts of cases such as *Van Colle* and *Smith*, can you think of instances where the police will be held to have breached a duty to an individual?

LIABILITY FOR OMISSIONS

From our discussion of the difficulties in holding public bodies liable for negligence, we have learnt that one of the problems is that in many cases the behaviour complained about was a failure to act – an omission. Even though *Donoghue* v. *Stevenson* states that acts 'or omissions' may form the basis of the negligence action, nevertheless there is no general liability for failure to act in the English law. In other words, there is no general duty to help others. This is not absolute, however. There are instances where the law places a duty on a person to act, and if that person then omits to act, she may be held liable.

The key case informing us when there will be a duty to act is *Smith* v. *Littlewoods Organisation Ltd* [1987] 1 All ER 710. In this case the defendant bought a cinema with the intention of demolishing it. Unknown vandals got into the empty building and started a fire which then damaged the claimants' property. The court held that there was no general duty to act, but that there were certain exceptions to this principle: where there was a relationship between the parties creating an assumption of responsibility; where there was a relationship of control between the defendant and the person who caused the damage; and where the defendant created or failed to remove a source of danger.

Assumption of responsibility

Where the defendant took on the responsibility for something, and then failed to do what was expected of her, she may be held liable. Sometimes it is clear that there is an assumption of responsibility – for example, a contractual relationship between parties usually creates a duty on the defendant to take positive steps to protect the claimant from loss. Even where it is less explicit, it could be clear from the facts of any given situation that the defendant assumed responsibility towards the claimant.

In *Barrett* v. *Ministry of Defence* [1995] 1 WLR 1217 a soldier got very drunk at a celebration. A duty officer took him to his room and left him there, where the soldier subsequently died as a result of his inebriation. The court held that the duty officer, by starting to take care of the soldier, had assumed a duty of care towards him and should have taken further steps to ensure his well-being.

Relationship of control between the defendant and a third party

Where the defendant is in control of somebody else, and fails to exercise such control, she may be held liable. In *Carmarthenshire County Council* v. *Lewis* [1955] AC 549 a teacher was left in charge of a playground where there were a number of very small children. She had to go into the school building and while she was there one of the children walked out of the playground on to the road. A lorry driver swerved to avoid the child, hit a tree and was killed. The teachers at the school and the County Council were held to have been jointly in control of the child: they therefore had a duty to take reasonable steps to prevent them becoming a danger to others. (On the facts the teacher was held to not have breached this duty, but remember that the question of a duty of care is the start, and that is followed by the question of breach of such duty, which we look at in the next chapter.)

Another case that illustrates liability for omitting to control a third party is *Home Office* v. *Dorset Yacht Club* [1970] AC 1004. Prison authorities allowed Borstal inmates to escape and cause damage to the claimants. The court held that the prison authorities had a custodial duty, and therefore a relationship of control over the detainees.

Creation of or failure to remove a danger or source of danger

In *Goldman* v. *Hargrave* [1967] 1 AC 645 a tall tree on the defendant's land was struck by lightning and ignited. The defendant cleared the land around the tree and chopped up the tree into sections, leaving it to burn out. A wind rose and spread sparks from the tree to a neighbour's land, causing a fire which in turn caused extensive damage. The court held the defendant liable as he failed to do something which he could have done with little cost or effort, i.e. to put the fire out.

In cases like this, whether or not there is a duty of care depends very much on the facts of each individual case. You may find it very surprising that in the following case no liability was imposed: In *Topp* v. *London Country Buses Ltd* [1993] 3 All ER 448, a bus was left empty with the keys in the ignition, awaiting a relief driver who did not turn up. Punters from a nearby pub got into the bus, took it for a ride and caused damage. The court held that the bus company could not have known the 'character' of the usual clientele of that particular pub, and that the subsequent events were therefore not foreseeable.

INTERSECTION

The general rule in our law is that a person who commits a tort will be personally liable. There are exceptions to this, however, where another will be held vicariously liable. The question here is: when will A be liable to B for the negligent act of C? This question is closely related to liability for omissions (discussed above) because A's liability will normally concern his omission to exercise control over C. We will examine vicarious liability in detail later (Chapter 12), but for now, take note that exceptionally, one may be held liable for a tort committed by another. Review the cases above and see how they illustrate a situation where A is held liable to C based on a tort committed by B – we see that examples include the following relationships: prison officers and prisoners (*Home Office* v. *Dorset Yacht Co. Ltd* [1970] AC 1004); employer and employee (*Topp* v. *London Country Buses (South West) Ltd* [1993] 3 All ER 448); and parent (or person '*in loco parentis*') and child (*Carmarthenshire County Council* v. *Lewis* [1955] AC 549).

LIABILITY FOR PSYCHIATRIC INJURY AND ECONOMIC LOSS

Originally, tort law was based only upon losses in the form of *physical injury* or *property damage*. Psychological injury and purely economic loss went largely uncompensated, unless it occurred as a consequence of physical injury or property damage. The reason for this was mainly because it was feared that potentially limitless claims could follow from a single event – the 'floodgates' argument. However, the twentieth century saw a significant development of duties of care in these areas.

Psychiatric injury

> **CONTEXT**
>
> Older cases refer to '**nervous shock**'. Nowadays we talk of **psychiatric injury**, which is a more accurate term. Nevertheless nervous shock is still useful as it reminds us that the kind of psychiatric injury one can claim for is usually caused by a single, one-off incident – a 'shock', in other words.

To claim compensation for **psychiatric injury** in negligence, one has to prove several things (in addition to the usual elements for negligence, namely a duty of care, breach and causation). The claimant must have an actual recognised psychiatric condition capable of resulting from the shock of the incident and recognised as having long-term effects. Mere grief, distress or anger is not enough. In addition, the injury must have been caused by a sudden event.

Next, we need to determine whether the claimant is a primary or a secondary victim, as that determines what else needs to be proved. If the claimant was physically injured or in danger of physical injury then she is a *primary victim* and can claim under the normal rules of negligence.

If the claimant was not physically injured or in physical danger, she can still claim as a *secondary victim*. To succeed with her claim she will have to satisfy the so-called *Alcock* criteria for claims for psychiatric injury, formulated in the following case.

CORNERSTONE

Alcock v. *Chief Constable of South Yorkshire Police* [1991] 4 All ER 907

This case arose out of the Hillsborough football disaster, where the police allowed a large crowd of football supporters into an already overcrowded stadium, leading to severe injuries and even loss of life. Friends and family witnessed the event on radio and television, and several of them claimed for their resultant nervous shock. The court held that in such instances, i.e. where the claimant was not physically in danger of injury, she needs to prove the following:

1. a sufficiently close tie of love and affection with the primary victim; and
2. proximity to the accident or the immediate aftermath, which was sufficiently close in time and space; and
3. she was suffering nervous shock through what was seen or heard of the accident or its immediate aftermath.

```
                        ┌─────────────────────────┐         ┌─────────────────────────┐
                        │ • Only recognised       │ ······▶ │ Primary victim          │
                        │   psychiatric condition │         │ Normal rules of         │
                        │ • Sudden event          │         │ negligence              │
                        └───────────┬─────────────┘         └─────────────────────────┘
                                    │
                                    ▼
                        ┌─────────────────────────┐
                        │    Secondary victim     │
                        │    Alcock criteria:     │
                        │  Alcock v. Chief Constable │
                        │  of South Yorkshire Police │
                        └───────────┬─────────────┘
                ┌───────────────────┼───────────────────┐
                ▼                   ▼                   ▼
   ┌─────────────────────┐ ┌─────────────────────┐ ┌─────────────────────┐
   │ (1) Sufficiently    │ │ (2) Proximity (in   │ │ (3) Nervous shock   │
   │ close tie of love   │ │ space and time) to  │ │ result of what was  │
   │ and affection with  │ │ accident / immediate│ │ seen/heard of       │
   │ primary victim      │ │ aftermath           │ │ accident/immediate  │
   │                     │ │                     │ │ aftermath           │
   └─────────────────────┘ └─────────────────────┘ └─────────────────────┘
```

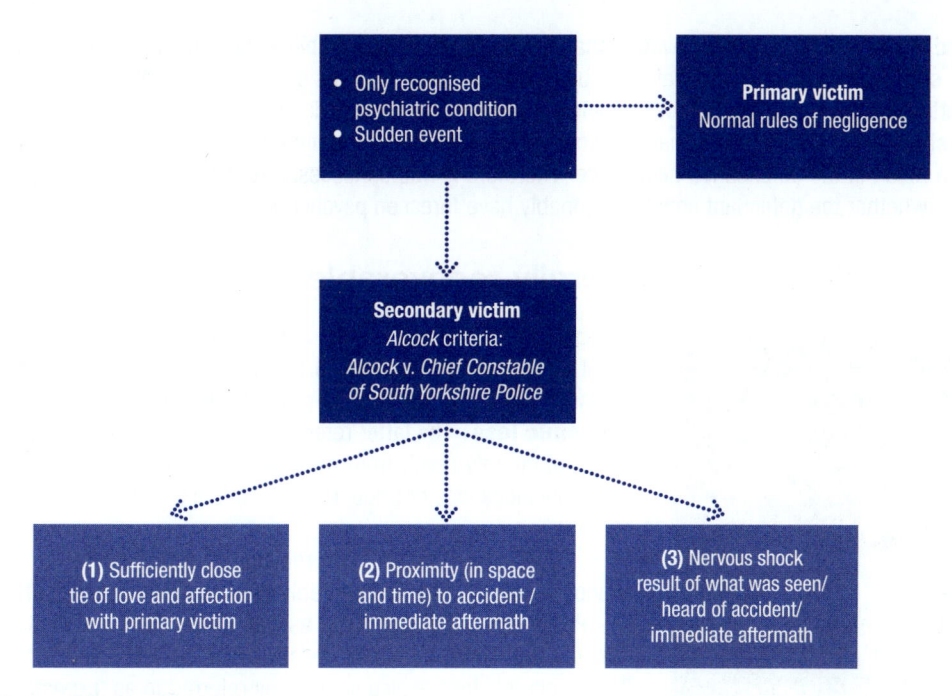

Figure 2.4 Psychiatric injury

Look at the three *Alcock* criteria again. For a secondary victim, there is a requirement of proximity. But how close does she need to be?

In *McLoughlin* v. *O'Brian* [1983] 1 AC 410 the House of Lords *extended* liability for nervous shock by widening the concept of 'proximity'. In this case Mrs McLoughlin was at home when she was told that her husband and children had been in a road accident. She went to the hospital where she saw how badly her family was injured – one of her children had been killed and her other children and her husband severely injured. As a result of what she had heard and subsequently saw at the hospital, she suffered severe nervous shock, for which she claimed damages. The House of Lords found in her favour. The significance of this is that in doing so, the House extended liability for psychiatric injury to all cases where it was *reasonably foreseeable* that the plaintiff would suffer such injury, irrespective of any limitations of time and space. In other words, the ordinary test of reasonable foreseeability is applied for psychiatric injury, same as for other kinds of injury. The 'proximity' requirement of *Alcock* was therefore watered down.

INTERSECTION

> We look at the requirement that the injury or damage need to have been foreseeable in more detail in our discussion of the element of causation (Chapter 4). For now, be aware of the fact that if the damage was not foreseeable, there will be no liability (because the causation element would not be proved).

When we say, then, that the damage need to be foreseeable, do we mean in general, or do we mean that the *specific kind* of damage had to be foreseeable? In *Page* v. *Smith* [1996] AC 155 the House of Lords answered this question in the light of a claim for psychiatric injury by a victim of a road accident. The defendant averred that he should not be held liable as he could not have foreseen the specific kind of injury the claimant suffered. The House of Lords disagreed and held that it did not matter whether the injury in fact sustained was physical, psychiatric or both. It was sufficient to ask whether the defendant should have reasonably foreseen that the claimant might suffer personal injury as a result of the defendant's negligence. Therefore it was unnecessary to ask, as a separate question, whether the defendant should reasonably have foreseen psychiatric injury, specifically.

Economic loss not generally recoverable

> **Take note**
>
> Do not get confused here – in certain instances economic loss as such can be claimed. But 'pure' economic loss cannot be claimed. What then, is the difference between these two concepts? The facts of the next case we look at will make it clear.

In legal claims for negligence, a financial compensation is the usual remedy. It is important to understand, from the start, that personal injury and damage to property are distinct from '**pure economic loss**'. The latter refers to damage suffered and which does *not* directly result from personal injury or damage to property. It includes loss of trade, loss of profit and loss of investment revenue.

The courts have always been reluctant to allow liability for pure economic loss, as this was primarily seen as falling under contract law. Policy reasons played a role as well. The general rule was and remains that 'pure economic loss' cannot be recovered in tort. Pure economic loss is also sometimes referred to as 'expectation loss', as what it usually boils down to is a claim for what was *expected* instead of what was *actually* lost.

If the economic loss was the *direct consequence* of *physical damage*, it may be recovered. If not, it is 'pure' economic loss and cannot be recovered. In *Spartan Steel* v. *Martin & Co Contractors Ltd* [1973] 1 QB 27 the defendants caused a power failure lasting some time. The claimants had to scrap the batch of steel it was then smelting and this reduced its value by £368. They would also have been able to smelt several other batches of steel, but could not and therefore suffered a loss of profit. The court held that the loss of profit in the melt in progress was directly caused by the physical damage and could therefore be recovered. But the loss of profit not related to any physical damage (i.e. the batches they were planning to, but could not smelt) could not be recovered.

For a while, it appeared to be possible to recover for pure economic loss caused by negligent acts. In *Anns* v. *Merton London Borough Council* [1978] AC 728 the defendant council were held liable to tenants for loss suffered due to shoddy building. The House of Lords held that the council owed a duty of care and was liable even though the loss suffered was pure economic loss. In *Junior Books Ltd* v. *Veitchi Co Ltd* [1983] 1 AC 520 the court allowed a claim against a subcontractor that had laid faulty flooring. (Note that here the court pointed out that the relationship between the parties were 'just short of a direct contractual relationship'. This is very rare and *Junior Books* has not been followed.)

INTERSECTION

Remember that we encountered *Anns* when we looked at the two-stage test for determination of a duty of care. *Anns* provided that, given the necessary proximity, a duty of care is presumed and it would then be up to the defendant to prove why such duty should *not* be accepted. *Caparo Industries* v. *Dickman* subsequently reverted to the reasoning in *Donoghue*, namely that the presumption should be that there is no duty and that it should be proven that there is a duty of care.

Liability for psychiatric injury and economic loss   45

This expansion of liability was much criticised and finally *Anns* was overruled by *Murphy* v. *Brentwood District Council* [1991] 1 AC 398 (HL). The facts in this case were very similar to those of *Anns*. The House of Lords found that the council was not liable in the absence of physical injury. Therefore, there is no liability for pure economic loss arising from negligent acts and it is not recoverable in negligence.

Exceptions to the rule that economic loss cannot be claimed in tort

An exception to this rule is when we are dealing with *negligent misstatements*. This exception is based on the decision in *Hedley Byrne & Co* v. *Heller & Partners* [1964] AC 465. The claimants relied on a reference given by the defendants, and on the strength of that contracted with X. X went into liquidation and it was discovered that the reference given by the defendant was prepared without any prior checks. The claimant succeeded in recovering its losses from the defendant on the basis of its negligent misstatement. Note that we are dealing here with *purely* economic loss – the loss the claimants suffered was not connected to any physical injury or to any damage to property. The House of Lords laid down a number of requirements which claimants would have to satisfy in order to establish a duty of care for negligent misstatements. There must be:

1. A *special relationship* between the parties – for example a friend buying a car on his friend's behalf (*Chaudry* v. *Prabhaker* [1988] 3 All ER 718), or a bank clerk advising on a mortgage (*Cornish* v. *Midland Bank plc* [1985] 3 All ER 513).
2. A voluntary *assumption of responsibility* by the party giving the advice
3. *Reliance* on that advice by the party receiving it, and
4. It must be *reasonable* for the party to have relied on that advice.

As we wrap up our examination of the duty of care, let's take a moment to remember that establishing a duty of care is only the start – once a duty of care is recognised, there are still other factors that have to be proven to succeed with a claim in negligence. Visually, this is where we are:

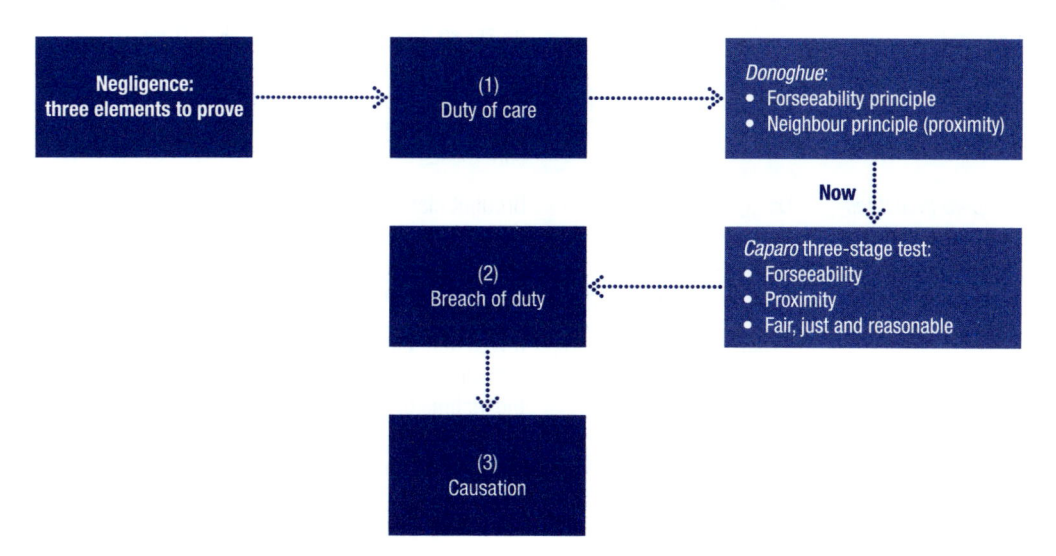

Figure 2.5 Duty of care: where does it fit in?

KEY POINTS

- Negligence refers to two concepts: negligence as an element of fault means carelessness, but negligence also means a tort in its own right.
- The three elements which together establish liability in the tort of negligence are a duty of care, breach of such duty, and causation of damage.
- *Donoghue* v. *Stevenson* is arguably the most famous case in the common law, and to a large extent it 'created' the modern tort of negligence.
- The *Caparo* test describes three questions to be asked to determine whether the defendant owed the claimant a duty of care. These are whether the damage was foreseeable, whether there was proximity between the claimant and defendant, and whether it is fair, just and reasonable to impose a duty of care.
- Liability for omission occurs only in exceptional circumstances.
- Psychiatric injury can be claimed but are subject to strict rules such as that it must be a recognised psychiatric condition.
- Pure economic loss can only be claimed in exceptional circumstances.
- The courts are very loath to impose a duty of care on public authorities, based on policy considerations.

CORE CASES AND STATUTES

Case	About	Importance
Donoghue v. *Stevenson* [1932] AC 562	Claim in negligence as a tort in its own right	House of Lords established principle that under certain circumstances if a duty of care is breached there may lie a claim in tort for damages negligently caused. Established the modern tort of negligence and formulated the neighbour principle to determine when a duty of care exists.
Caparo Industries plc v. *Dickman* [1990] 1 All ER 568	Using proximity, foreseeability and policy considerations to establish a duty of care	Brought clarity regarding the duty of care element in negligence claims by establishing a three-part test and indicating that policy considerations form part of the process.
Hill v. *Chief Constable of Yorkshire* [1988] 2 All ER 238	Police do not owe a duty of care to the public at large	It was held that in general there is not sufficient proximity of relationship between the police and the victims of crime to establish a general duty of care on the part of the police, to the public at large, and also that it is in the public interest that police were immune from actions for negligence in respect of their activities in the investigation and suppression of crime.

Core cases and statutes 47

Case	About	Importance
X (Minors) v. Bedfordshire CC [1995] 2 AC 633	Local authorities negligently did not take abused children into care, but were held not liable	It was held on the grounds of public policy that the imposition of a duty of care by local authorities to individuals might make local authorities adopt an overly cautious approach, which would work to the detriment of children.
Barrett v. Enfield London Borough Council [2001] 2 AC 550	Local authorities who had children taken into care were held to have a duty of care	The House of Lords held that if a decision has been taken to take a child into care, the same public policy considerations, which had to be taken into account when an authority had to decide whether or not to take a child into care, did not apply.
Z v. UK [2001] FLR 193	Some of the claimants in X v. Bedfordshire CC argued that local authorities' immunity from suit infringed Art. 6 of the ECHR	The ECtHR decided that because the UK courts weighed up the claimants's Art. 6 rights against the interests of society, they did have a fair hearing and therefore their right to a fair trial was not infringed.
Phelps v. Hillingdon London Borough Council [2000] 4 All ER 504	Failure of education professionals to perform jobs properly	Court held that actions, including failure to act, by local authorities are justiciable according to usual Caparo criteria, save where policy decisions were made under a discretion, about which Parliament cannot have intended the court to substitute its views for those of ministers and officials.
Smith v. Littlewoods Organisation [1987] 1 All ER 710	Defendant failed to secure its derelict cinema, vandals set it alight, causing damage to neighbours	The court set out under which circumstances one may be held liable for a failure to act: 1. Assumption of responsibility 2. Relationship of control 3. Creation of – or failure to remove – danger.
Alcock v. Chief Constable of South Yorkshire Police [1991] 4 All ER 907	Nervous shock	Criteria for claims for psychiatric injury of secondary victims: 1. Sufficiently close tie of love and affection with primary victim 2. Proximity 3. Nervous shock as result of accident or immediate aftermath.

Statute	About	Importance
European Convention of Human Rights, Art. 6	Right to a fair trial	Successfully used by the claimant in Osman v. UK but held not to have been an issue in Z v. UK by the ECtHR.

FURTHER READING

Deakin, S., Johnston, A. and Markesinis, B (2008) *Markesinis and Deakin's Tort Law.* **Oxford: Oxford University Press, pp. 208–17**
This is a highly regarded (and you will note, very weighty) textbook on tort. In this extract, the authors discuss why certain defendants have (or seem to have) immunity from suit. Reading these pages will help you understand why the courts are reluctant to impose liability on certain classes of defendants, such as the police, local authorities, social workers, etc.

Howarth, D. (2006) Many duties of care – or a duty of care? Notes from the underground. *OJLS* **26, p. 449**
The author argues that, instead of many duties of care, we all owe one overarching duty of care. Reading this article will help you think critically about the reasons why duty of care is recognised in court or not.

Morgan, J. (2006) The rise and fall of the general duty of care. *PN* **22(4), p. 206**
This article provides an in-depth analysis of the duty of care as a requirement for negligence, and also examines the extent to which policy considerations play a role in courts' decisions in this area.

Smith, J. C. and Burns, P. (1983) *Donoghue* **v.** *Stevenson* **– the not so golden anniversary.** *MLR* **46, p. 147**
The authors discuss how useful the various tests to determine whether one owes a duty of care are.

Witting, C. (2005) Duty of care – an analytical approach. *OJLS* **25, p. 417**
This article will help you to get to grips with the theoretical basis upon which the duty of care is based.

CHAPTER 3

Negligence: breach of duty

BLUEPRINT
Negligence: breach of duty

KEY QUESTIONS

LEGISLATION
- Compensation Act 2006, s. 1
- Civil Evidence Act 1968, s. 11

CONTEXT
- After proving that you were owed a duty of care, the next element to prove is that such duty was breached.
- This is done by means of an objective test, asking whether the defendant's conduct fell below what is to be expected of a reasonable person.

CONCEPTS
- Duty of care
- Breach
- Standard of care
- Professional standard of care
- State of the art
- *Res ipsa loquitur*

- The *Bolam* test provides that as long as a medical practitioner can prove that her conduct accords with an accepted course of action, even if this is a minority, she will escape liability in negligence. Is this justified?

- Who carries the burden of proof in negligence cases?
- What is the standard of care in negligence cases?
- What is meant by the reasonable person test and is this text universally applied?

CASES

- *Bolam* v. *Friern Hospital Management Committee* [1957]
- *Bolitho* v. *City and Hackney Health Authority* [1997]

SPECIAL CHARACTERISTICS

- Reasonable person test
- *Bolam* test for professional standard of care
- State of the art defence

REFORM

- The *Bolam* test for professional liability of doctors has been modified somewhat by the case of *Bolitho*, in which the court confirmed that expert evidence about medical practice still needs to be able to withstand logical analysis by the court.

CRITICAL ISSUES

Setting the scene

To recap: liability for the tort of negligence occurs when the defendant had a duty of care to the claimant, breached that duty and this breach was the cause of the claimant's damage. To prove a breach of duty, the claimant must show that the defendant's conduct has fallen below the appropriate standard of care. It is decided on a case-by-case basis *what* precisely the appropriate standard of care *is*. In general, however, the standard of care required is the standard which would have been adopted by the 'reasonable person' (in older cases called the 'reasonable man') who finds herself in the same circumstances as the defendant. It is an *objective test*.

Take note

Do not confuse the terms 'burden of proof' with 'standard of proof'. The former relates to who has to prove her case in court. Usually this is the claimant, following the adage of 'he who avers has to prove'. When we say that the burden of proof is reversed, we mean that it shifts from the claimant to the defendant – something which is fairly unusual and which happens by exception only.

The standard of proof tells us to what extent proof is required. For civil cases, the standard of proof is 'on a balance of probabilities' – merely tipping the scale in your favour would suffice, in other words. For criminal cases, the standard of proof is 'beyond reasonable doubt' – your proof has to be almost 100 per cent.

NEGLIGENCE: BREACH OF DUTY

Once the claimant has proven that the defendant owed her a duty of care, the next step is to establish whether this duty has been breached. The burden of proving this falls on the claimant.

Specifically for negligence cases, however, how do the courts judge whether a particular defendant breached her duty of care towards the claimant?

Standard of care: the reasonable person test

The standard of the 'reasonable man' was first established in *Blyth* v. *Proprietors of the Birmingham Waterworks* (1856) 11 Exch 781. According to Lord Alderson:

'Negligence is the omission to do something which a reasonable man, guided upon those considerations which ordinarily regulate human affairs, would do, or doing something which a prudent and reasonable man would not do.'

In *Hall* v. *Brooklands Auto-Racing Club* [1933] 1 KB 205 the 'average man' was described as 'the man on the Clapham Omnibus'. More recently the fictional 'reasonable man' was described in *McFarlane* v. *Tayside Health Board* [1999] 3 WLR 1301 as a traveller on the London Underground. Of course it also has to be taken into account that defendants are nowadays likely to be corporations – but again, even though corporations are seen as legal persons, they cannot function without humans.

CORNERSTONE

Reasonable person test

Whichever analogy is used, the point is that we are dealing with the average person. This is an objective test, which means that we compare the specific defendant against a fictional standard. We do not enquire into the defendant's own, subjective, standards but hold her to the standard set for all.

Because the reasonable person test is objective and not subjective, it means that no allowance is made for the inexperience or lack of skill of the particular defendant before the court. For example, in *Nettleship* v. *Weston* [1971] 2 QB 691 it was found that the same standard of care is expected of all motorists, regardless of their age or experience, and this includes learner drivers.

In certain instances, however, the reasonable person test is not used, and other factors are taken into account. If the defendant is a professional, or particularly skilled, then she will be judged on a higher standard, against her natural peers. For example, a doctor will be judged against the 'reasonable doctor'. Further, if the defendant is a child, obviously they cannot be judged against the standard of the average person. Rather the child will be judged against children of the same age and ability. It may also happen that people engage in activities where, as a result of the nature of the activities, a lesser or higher standard of care may be required (such as taking part in sport, or being a spectator at a sporting event). In such instances the courts apply a different standard of care from that of the reasonable person. Finally, if a person acts in an emergency, the circumstances surrounding the emergency will be taken into account when looking at the expected standard of care.

Special standards of care

Skilled or professional defendants

What is the standard of care expected of people who present themselves as having specialist skills by having a particular trade or profession, like doctors? The standard would be higher than that of the average person, but the test will still be objective in that the defendant will be judged against her peers. In other words, a professional is compared with her peer group: a surgeon should act as a reasonable surgeon would, a lawyer as a reasonable lawyer and so on.

> **Take note**
> In examining the duty of care and breach of duty, we deal with matters of law as well as matters of fact. A matter of law is set by statute or case law or any other source of law. For example, it is a matter of law that the standard of care expected in negligence cases is that of the reasonable person. A matter of fact means that the focus now moves to the facts of the particular case before the court, and the court (either the judge, or in criminal cases the jury) must test the facts against the standards set by the law. For example, in negligence cases, the judge will examine whether the actions of the defendant fell below the standard set by law, i.e. whether the defendant's actions were less than what we would expect from a reasonable person.

For doctors, then, the standard would be the 'reasonable doctor'. But having established this, we come to an important question, namely determining what such reasonable doctor would have done. How does the court decide what a 'reasonable doctor' would have done? In such instances the courts will used the so-called '*Bolam* test', as laid down in the case of *Bolam* v. *Friern Hospital Management Committee* [1957] 1 WLR 582:

'... the standard of care expected of professionals is not that of the reasonable lay person, but that of a reasonable person having the same skills as the defendant has.'

CORNERSTONE

Bolam v. *Friern Hospital Management Committee* [1957] 1 WLR 382

The claimant suffered fractures while undergoing electro-convulsive therapy under the direction of the defendant. Whilst being treated, the doctor did not restrain the claimant, nor was he given any muscle relaxants, and it was alleged that if this had been done, he would not have suffered the fractures whilst convulsing.

At the trial, expert evidence was led that reflected medical views in favour of giving muscle relaxants and constraining a patient whilst administering shock treatment, but for the defence contrary medical opinion was given.

The court held the defendant not liable, holding that as long as the doctor acts in accordance with 'a practice accepted as proper by a responsible body of medical men skilled in that particular art', she will be taken as having acted as a reasonable doctor and accordingly there would be no breach of duty and no liability.

This is controversial, as the case established that a professional defendant will not be held liable if her conduct accorded with one view of responsible common practice, even though some other members of her profession hold another opinion. Thus, the standard expected of professionals is that of *a* competent body of professional opinion, not of professional opinion *generally*. It could therefore conceivably be a practice that is only accepted by a minority of professionals.

It has been argued that the court thereby allowed doctors to set their own standards, and even that the court abdicated its adjudicatory function in doing so.

The *Bolam* test has caused controversy and was subject to much criticism, but the House of Lords has approved the test in relation to various aspects of medical treatment. However, the test appears to have been modified somewhat by the House of Lords in the following case.

CORNERSTONE

Bolitho v. *City and Hackney Health Authority* [1997] 4 All ER 771

The claimant's two-year-old son was admitted to hospital with respiratory difficulties. Over the course of his stay, he appeared to get better at stages, and at stages his condition appeared to deteriorate. Finally, he deteriorated to such extent that he did not get enough oxygen, suffered brain damage and subsequently died. One of the issues before the court related to whether a reasonable doctor would have intubated the child or not. The claimant in this case was able to produce an expert witness who said that the boy in question should have been intubated, while the doctor in this case was able to produce an expert witness to say that intubation would not have been the correct treatment.

In this situation, the *Bolam* principle had always been taken as suggesting that the doctor was therefore not negligent – other medical opinion might disagree with what she did, but she could produce evidence that it was a practice accepted by a responsible body of medical opinion.

However, Lord Browne-Wilkinson, with whom the other Law Lords agreed, thought differently. While agreeing that the *Bolam* test was still the correct one to apply, he said that the court was not obliged to hold that a doctor was not liable for negligence simply because some medical experts had testified that the doctor's actions were in line with accepted practice. The court had to satisfy itself that the medical expert's opinion was reasonable, in that they had weighed up the risks and benefits, and had a logical basis for their conclusion.

In other words, following the *ratio* in *Bolitho*, the court cannot abdicate its role of adjudicating evidence.

There are some signs that the *Bolam* test is no longer applied quite as strictly as before, and that the *Bolitho* case is being used to hold medical opinion to a proper standard of reasonableness. For example, in *Gouldsmith* v. *Mid Staffordshire General Hospitals NHS Trust* [2007] EWCA Civ 397, the claimant's fingers were amputated and she submitted expert medical opinion that, had she been referred for specialist care, this could have been avoided by surgery. The Court of Appeal, applying *Bolitho*, held that the trial judge should have considered whether the specialist would have been negligent in not conducting the operation.

Lord Browne-Wilkinson himself in *Bolitho* pointed out (at 242), that in other professional areas, the courts do not abdicate their function of weighing up expert evidence. For example, in *Edward Wong Finance Co. Ltd.* v. *Johnson Stokes & Master* [1984] AC 296, the defendant's solicitors had completed a mortgage transaction in local 'Hong Kong style' rather than English style. This enabled a dishonest solicitor for the borrower to abscond with the loan money. Expert evidence was led that completion in Hong Kong style was almost universally adopted in Hong Kong and was therefore in accordance with a body of professional opinion there. Nevertheless, the defendant's solicitors were held liable for negligence by the Privy Council because it accepted that there was an obvious risk which could have been guarded against. Thus, in the view of the court, the body of professional opinion, though almost universally held, was not reasonable or responsible and was therefore not compelling.

> **Take note**
>
> Even though *Bolitho* seems to restore to the court its role of weighing evidence, *Bolam* is still applied. Lord Browne-Wilkinson held that a judge would only be entitled to reject expert medical evidence in the very rare case where it had been demonstrated that the professional opinion was incapable of withstanding logical analysis. He further held that in most cases the fact that distinguished experts in the field were of a particular opinion would demonstrate the reasonableness of that opinion.
>
> The defendant's course of action would therefore only be judged as falling below the standard of care if it was backed up by very poor medical evidence indeed!

State of the art defence

In areas such as medicine and technology, the state of knowledge about a particular subject may change rapidly, so that procedures and techniques which are approved as safe and effective might very quickly become outdated, and even be discovered to be dangerous.

CORNERSTONE

State of the art defence

The case of *Roe* v. *Minister of Health* [1954] 2 QB 66 established that, where this happens, a defendant is entitled to be judged according to the standards that were accepted at the time when they acted.

In *Roe*, the claimant was paralysed after receiving an injection containing a contaminated anaesthetic. Unknown to the defendants at the time (1947), it is possible for contaminants to enter glass ampoules through minuscule cracks. In this instance, the phenol in which the ampoule containing the anaesthesia was stored, entered into the syringe with which the claimant was injected. The Court of Appeal (hearing the matter much later) applied the test of what was the standard of medical knowledge in 1947 in respect to the detection of the presence of the phenol in the ampoules and held the defendants not liable. This is called the 'state of the art' argument which a defendant can use as a defence to a claim.

Children

The standard of care owed by a child is that which can be expected of a reasonable child of the defendant's own age. In *Mullin* v. *Richards* [1998] 1 All ER 920 the claimant's eye was seriously injured after she and the defendant played at fencing with plastic rulers. Both were 15 years old at the time. The court held that, while an ordinary, reasonable adult would not normally play around in such a manner, it was entirely in accord with what could be expected of an ordinary, reasonable 15-year-old.

Similarly, in *Keown* v. *Coventry Healthcare NHS Trust* [2006] EWCA Civ 39 it was held that there was no liability when an 11-year-old boy fell while climbing on a fire escape, as at that age the child knew the risk of what he was doing.

Other considerations to determine standard of care

Apart from setting the standard higher for professionals, and lower for children, the courts take several other factors into account when determining the standard of care.

Likelihood of harm

Where one person owes a duty to another, she must guard against the risk of causing harm. The court will consider the likelihood that harm will occur. In *Bolton* v. *Stone* [1951] AC 850 (HL) there was held to be no liability when a cricket ball was hit out of cricket grounds and hit the claimant while she was walking in the road. The court examined the frequency of this kind of risk occurring and on the facts (evidence showed that balls had been hit into the road only approximately six times in the preceding 30 years) held that it was rare enough not to make the reasonable man think twice about playing on those grounds. In contrast, in *Miller* v. *Jackson* [1977] QB 966 (CA), on similar facts, there was held to be liability because cricket balls were hit out of the ground frequently.

The defendant must also take into account any factors that might increase the risk of harm occurring. In *Haley* v. *London Electricity Board* [1965] AC 778 the defendants had excavated a trench along a pavement to effect electrical repairs. They put up a railing, but unfortunately this was two feet off the ground, which meant that when the claimant, who was blind, tapped along with his stick he missed the railing and fell into the trench. As a result he suffered severe damage to his hearing and was rendered almost totally deaf. The House of Lords held that the defendants owed a duty of care towards people who walked along the pavement, and that such duty included blind people. On the facts it was held that by not putting the barrier where a blind person, who in his turn took the kind of precautions to be expected from his disability (such as using a stick), could perceive it, they had breached their duty and were held liable.

The extent of the possible harm

The court will also ask, if harm does occur, how serious is it likely to be? If it is likely to be relatively minor, it is unlikely that the court would decide that a reasonable person (who is not overcautious) would have had second thoughts about proceeding with the action complained of. However, if the consequences of things going wrong are likely to be significant, it is less likely that a reasonable person would have continued with the action.

In *Paris* v. *Stepney Borough Council* [1951] AC 367 an employer did not supply an employee who was blind in one eye with safety goggles. In the industry concerned (motor vehicle repairs) it was standard practice to provide safety goggles. The court held that the defendants had owed a higher duty of care towards the claimant, because it was known that an injury to his 'good' eye could have dire consequences – which in this case did come to pass – namely blindness.

Similarly, in *Walker* v. *Northumberland County Council* [1995] 1 All ER 737 the defendant was held to have owed a higher duty of care to the claimant because they were aware of his fragile state of mind (which was caused by overloading him with work).

Cost and practicability of precautions

If there is a risk, it is only necessary to do what is reasonable to try and avoid causing harm. There is no obligation to go to extraordinary lengths, especially where the risk is small. The court engages in a balancing exercise – the risk, on the one hand, is considered against the cost and practicability of taking precautions. We have already seen in *Bolton* v. *Stone* that the defendants escaped liability due the small risk of cricket balls being hit out of the relevant grounds.

However, if precautions are relatively easy and cheap to take, this is also taken into account and it is more likely that the defendant will be held liable. The Court of Appeal confirmed this in *Shine* v. *London Borough of Tower Hamlets* [2006] All ER (D) 79, where a small boy was injured when he tried to 'leapfrog' a bollard which the local council had not kept in proper repair. Lord Buxton

> **Take note**
> Be careful not to confuse this somewhat special duty of care with the so-called 'thin skull rule', which only applies once we get to the stage where the court considers causation. We examine the thin skull rule in more detail later (Chapter 4). For now just note that it means that, should the claimant have some condition or peculiarity which means that her damages would be more than for the average person, it's too bad for the defendant. If it was proved that the defendant breached a duty to the claimant and this caused the claimant's damage, liability will be for the full extent of the damage. In short, the thin skull rule says that a defendant should 'take his victim as he finds him'.

contrasted the relatively easy and cheap precaution of repairing a bollard which the council admitted it had a duty to, and was planning to repair in any case, with the facts in *Bolton* v. *Stone*:

> 'On the one hand the accident, although it was held to be foreseeable, was the result of a prodigious and unprecedented hit of the cricket ball out of the ground, on some computations a shot that travelled more than 100 yards; against on the other hand the only way of preventing that possible occurrence being either to shut down the cricket ground altogether or place fences around it of an excessive and no doubt unsightly nature. Although the case is authority for the general principle that there should be a balance, it goes no further than that. Applying the balance in this case, it seems clear to me that the balance comes down firmly on the side of saying that it would not be an unreasonable burden on the local authority to have taken the precaution in this case of getting their bollard into its proper state.'

Further, the higher the risk of damage, or the more serious the possible consequences, the more likely that a reasonable person would take proper precautions. What is proper and appropriate will be a matter to be decided on the facts of each case.

Reasonable foreseeability

The reasonable person cannot be expected to take precautions against risks that are not foreseeable: see *Roe* v. *Minister of Health*, above, where at the time the medical practitioners could not have foreseen that phenol can seep through minuscule cracks in the glass ampoules storing anaesthetics.

Common practice

Failure to conform to a common practice of taking safety precautions can be evidence of negligence because it shows that the defendant has not done what others in the community regarded as reasonable. However, it cannot be regarded as conclusive evidence, because the claimant will still have to prove that the failure was the cause of her loss. So it will not be enough to say 'the defendant did not follow common (or industry) practice'.

Brown v. *Rolls Royce Ltd* [1960] 1 WLR 210 illustrates this. A factory worker contracted dermatitis and sued his employer in negligence, alleging that it was common practice for employees doing his type of work to be supplied with barrier cream, something which his employers failed to do. The House of Lords held that proof of a common practice may be compelling evidence assisting a claimant in proving negligence, but that in itself it is not enough to found negligence. In *Allen* v. *British Rail Engineering Ltd* [2001] EWCA Civ 242, the claimants sued the defendants for injury to their hands caused by the use of vibrating tools in the course of their employment. The defendants showed that it was only some years after the tools were used that it became known that they could cause damage. The court agreed that the defendants should only be held liable for that time and accordingly reduced (apportioned) the damages that the claimants were awarded.

On the other hand, this works the other way around too. Where a defendant can show that she has complied with common practice as regards safety precautions, this can provide good evidence that she was not negligent, although it is not conclusive because a particular conduct may be negligent despite it being common practice.

In other words, it will not be a defence to say 'everybody else was doing it'.

Sporting events

At a sporting event the competitors and spectators may be owed a *lower* standard of care than the general standard. It is assumed that, by participating in sport, or even by attending as a spectator, one consents to some risk. In *Wooldridge* v. *Sumner* [1963] 2 QB 43 (CA) a photographer at a horse show was injured when the defendant, a rider, took a corner fast and crashed into him. The defendant was not held liable, and the court stated that the duty of care at a sporting event would only be breached if the competitor displayed a 'reckless disregard' for the safety of the spectator.

Social value of the activity

The defendant will not be held liable in negligence if there is a justification for taking the risk in question. Put another way, if what is being done is of social value, a lower standard of care may be required. For example, if the purpose is to save somebody's life, it may be justified to take an abnormal risk. Another example would be speed limits on roads – without doubt a speed limit of 10 mph would significantly lower the risk of motor vehicle accidents, but the social utility of speedy transportation outweighs such a measure.

Some values are obviously worth taking risks for. For example, in *Watt* v. *Hertfordshire County Council* [1954] 1 WLR 835 a fireman was injured by an improperly secured jack whilst on his way to save the life of a woman trapped under a car. His claim failed.

Other values are less easy to assess and the balancing exercise may be more difficult.

> **REFLECTION**
>
> One often hears urban myths about apparently harmless activities being prevented on 'health and safety' grounds – i.e. for fear of being sued in case of injury. Still, the law itself takes a more common sense approach in weighing up the social utility of an activity against the risk of injury or damage – and here social utility includes leisure activities. Think, for example, of the weight given to the social utility of playing cricket in *Bolton* v. *Stone*. Another case is illustrative. We look at the case of *Tomlinson* v. *Congleton Borough Council* [2003] 3 All ER 1122 in detail later (in Chapter 8) but it is useful briefly to consider its impact on this area of law. In this case the claimant dived into the shallow end of a lake owned by the defendant council, struck his head and suffered a severe spinal injury. The House of Lords, in considering whether a beach, used by many people and if used properly for permitted purposes posed little risk, should be closed by the council for fear of liability in case of injury. The House struck a blow for common sense, making it clear that the social utility of the amenity in this case outweighed the risk, especially given the fact that the risk was exacerbated by the irresponsible behaviour of the claimant himself.

There is also statutory recognition of the common sense approach.

CORNERSTONE

Compensation Act 2006, section 1

Section 1 of the Compensation Act 2006 states:

> 'A court considering a claim in negligence or breach of statutory duty may, in determining whether the defendant should have taken particular steps to meet a standard of care (whether by taking precautions against a risk or otherwise), have regard to whether a requirement to take those steps might –
>
> (a) prevent a desirable activity from being undertaken at all, to a particular extent or in a particular way, or
>
> (b) discourage persons from undertaking functions in connection with a desirable activity.'

Before we move on to a couple of instances that may help the claimant to prove breach of duty, let's just recap what we have learnt about how we use the standard of care to determine breach of duty.

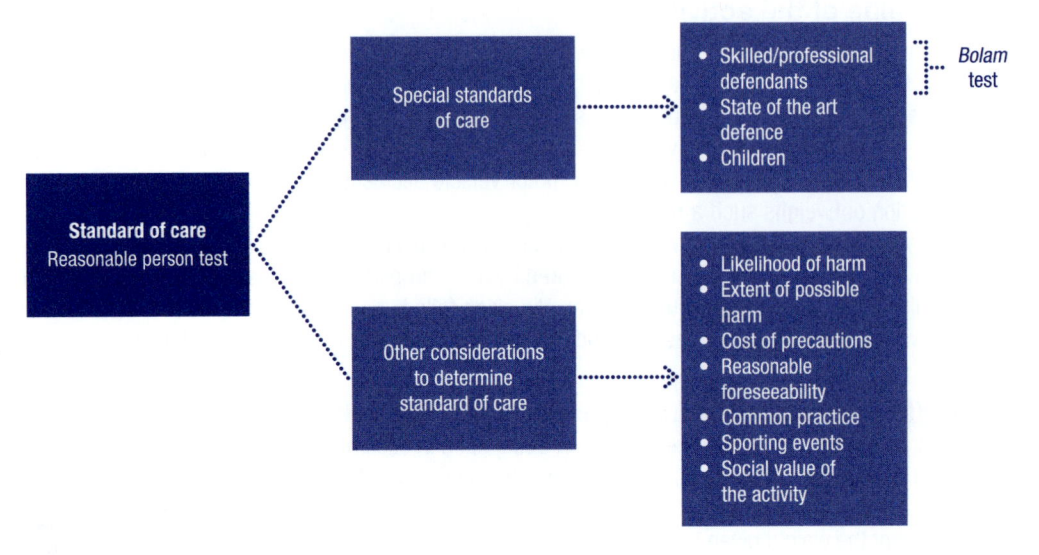

Figure 3.1 Standard of care: reasonable person test

PROVING BREACH OF DUTY

As with most civil actions, the burden of proof falls on the claimant, and the standard of proof required is the 'balance of probabilities'. In two instances, however, the claimant is assisted, namely where the maxim *res ipsa loquitur* or section 11 of the Civil Evidence Act 1968 apply.

Civil Evidence Act 1968

This statutory provision provides considerable assistance to the claimant, in cases where the event complained of also constituted a crime.

CORNERSTONE

Civil Evidence Act 1968, section 11

Section 11 of this Act states that, if a person is proved to have been convicted of an offence, '... he shall be taken to have committed that offence unless the contrary is proved ...'

What this means is best illustrated by an example.

C was walking his dog one night when D, driving at 60 mph in a residential area and simultaneously talking on his mobile phone, mounted the pavement and crashed into C and his dog Lassie. Both

C and Lassie were seriously injured – C's leg had to be amputated and Lassie had to undergo several operations at the veterinary surgery, at a great cost to C, who loved his dog and would not let her be put down while her life could be saved.

D, in the meantime, was found guilty of several offences under the Road Traffic Act 1988, amongst which was dangerous driving.

C decides to sue D for his personal injuries and also for damage to his property (Lassie). In a 'normal' negligence case, C would have to prove all the usual elements – duty of care, breach, etc. In this scenario, however, section 11 of the Civil Evidence Act saves C a lot of work. He will not have to prove that D was negligent – that is already proved by D's conviction in a criminal court of a crime that includes an element of negligence. All that C will have to prove is that D's action caused his damage.

Res ipsa loquitur

CORNERSTONE

Res ipsa loquitur

This is a Latin phrase which translates loosely as 'the facts speak for themselves'. It is used as an aid in court proceedings to prevent claimants having to waste time 'proving the obvious'.

The classic judgment in this area is that of Erle CJ in *Scott* v. *London and St Katherine Docks Co* [1861–73] All ER Rep 246 at 248:

'. . . where the thing is shown to be under the management of the defendant or his servants, and the accident is such as in the ordinary course of things does not happen if those who have the management use proper care, it affords reasonable evidence, in the absence of explanation by the defendants that the accident arose from want of care.'

In this case a bag of sugar fell on the head of a dockworker. The court's decision was therefore that it was self-evident that there was negligence. The judgment contains three elements that need to be there for 'the thing to speak for itself' in negligence cases:

1. the thing causing the damage must have been under the exclusive control of the defendant;
2. the accident must be of the kind which does not normally happen in the absence of negligence; and
3. there must be no explanation of the cause of the accident.

An example of how *res ipsa loquitur* works can be found in the case of *Ward* v. *Tesco Stores Ltd* [1976] 1 WLR 810 (CA). The claimant slid on yoghurt spilt on the floor of the defendant supermarket, and claimed in negligence. The court held that there was an inference of liability – nothing else could have caused the claimant's injury, the floor and its state was under exclusive control of the defendant, and the defendant could not prove sufficiently that their procedures for keeping the floor clean were sufficient to trump the inference of negligence.

Take note

Res ipsa loquitur makes it easier for a claimant to prove her case – but make sure you understand that the claimant still actually has to prove her case. The burden of proof remains with the claimant. It is a mistake to think that the burden of proof shifts from the claimant (to prove negligence) to the defendant (to disprove negligence). The burden of proof stays with the claimant throughout. If the defendant, however, can 'knock out' one of the three legs of res ipsa loquitur, the claimant would have a much more difficult task in proving negligence. For example, if the defendant in Ward v. Tesco could have produced better evidence that there was an efficient system of keeping the floor clean, it is not impossible that the claimant would not have been successful with her claim.

The main legal points surrounding breach of duty can be summarised visually as follows:

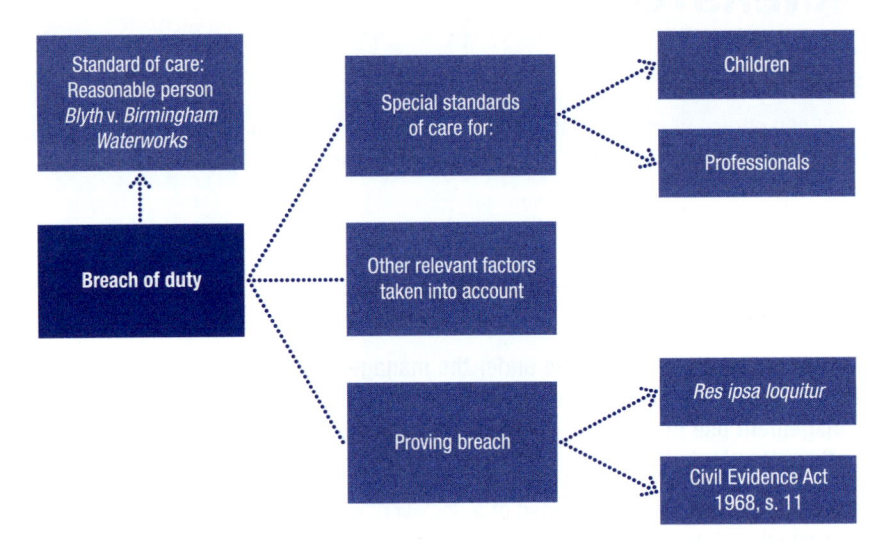

Figure 3.2 Breach of duty

KEY POINTS

- After the claimant proved that she was owed a duty of care, the next element to prove is that such duty was breached.
- To prove breach of duty we first have to determine what the relevant standard of care was. The courts use an objective standard called the reasonable person test.
- In some instances there will be deviation from this standard of care, notably when we deal with children or with specialists such as professionally qualified persons.
- The *Bolam* case, modified somewhat by the *Bolitho* case, sets the standard of care for professionals essentially as being common professional practice.
- Other considerations such as the utility of the activity, etc. are taken into account when determining whether or not breach had occurred.

CORE CASES AND STATUTES

Case	About	Importance
Blyth v. *Birmingham Waterworks* (1856) 11 Exch 781	Standard of care in negligence	Set the standard as being that of a 'prudent and reasonable man'.
Bolam v. *Friern Hospital Management Committee* [1957] 1 WLR 582	Medical negligence, whether the standard of care was breached	As long as a doctor acts in accordance with a competent body of medical opinion, even if it reflects a minority view, the standard of care cannot be held to have fallen below that expected from a reasonably competent medical practitioner.
Bolitho v. *City and Hackney Health Authority* [1997] 4 All ER 771	Clarified application of *Bolam*, medical negligence	Courts are not to accept expert medical evidence that is not able to withstand logical analysis.
Nettleship v. *Weston* [1971] 2 QB 691	Standard of care expected of unskilled defendants	The standard of care is objective. Subjective factors, such as the lack of skill of a learner driver, are irrelevant: such a driver is still tested against a reasonably competent driver.

Statute	About	Importance
Judicature Act 1873, s. 25(11) (the rule is now in s. 49 of the Senior Courts Act 1981)	Where the rules of equity and common law conflict then equity shall prevail	Applied in cases (e.g. *Walsh* v. *Lonsdale* (1882)) where the rules of equity and common law give different answers to a legal problem.
Civil Evidence Act 1968, s. 11	Convictions as evidence in civil proceedings	Criminal convictions eliciting an element of negligence can be taken as proof of such negligent action in civil claims.
Compensation Act 2006, s. 1	Factors of social utility to be considered in negligence claims	Courts are to take into account, when examining the standard of care in negligence cases, whether steps taken to address risk may prevent desirable activity from taking place, or discourage persons from undertaking such desirable activities.

FURTHER READING

Atiyah, P. (1972) *Res ipsa loquitur* in England and Australia. *MLR* 35, p. 337
Professor Atiyah discusses whether *res ipsa loquitur* serves as merely an aide to an inference of negligence, or whether it shifts the burden of proof to the defendant. Also read, in answer to this question, the Privy Council decision in *Ng Chun Pui* v. *Lee Cheun Tat* [1988] RTR 298 (PC).

***Bolitho* v. *City and Hackney Health Authority* [1997] 4 All ER 771**
This judgment clarifies the standard of care in negligence cases, particularly that relating to professionals and discusses the application of the decision in *Bolam* v. *Friern Hospital Management Committee* [1957] 1 WLR 582. Take note also of the application of principles of causation, which are discussed in the next chapter.

Hoyano, L. (2002) Misconceptions about wrongful conception. *MLR* 65, p. 883
Reading this article will help you to further understand the issues surrounding the *Caparo* decision, and how policy influences the courts' thinking on the duty of care issue.

Williams, K. (2005) Legislating in the echo chamber? *NLJ* 155, p. 1938
This article examines clause 1 of the Compensation Bill 2005, which was enacted in 2006 as section 1 of the Compensation Act 2006. This section tries to prevent people from *not* pursuing activities for fear of litigation, and this article asks how effective this effort is.

CHAPTER 4
Negligence: causation

BLUEPRINT
Negligence: causation

KEY QUESTIONS

LEGISLATION
- Compensation Act 2006, s. 3

CONTEXT
- Causation limits negligence claims to instances where claimants can prove that their damage was caused by the defendant, and that such damage was foreseeable.
- Legal causation seeks to limit liability to only those instances where damage is foreseeable or not too remote.

CONCEPTS
- Factual and legal causation
- Joint and several liability
- Proportional liability
- *Novus actus interveniens*
- Legal causation or remoteness of damage

- The Compensation Act, s. 3, makes it easier for the victim of mesothelioma (asbestos poisoning) to prove causation than other victims of tort. Is this justified on policy and legal grounds, given the unique nature of the disease?
- Does foreseeability as a legal requirement import too much uncertainty into the law on negligence?

- What do we mean by causation?
- How does factual causation differ from legal causation?
- What are the tests we use to determine factual and legal causation?

CASES
- *Cork* v. *Kirby MacLean Ltd* [1952]
- *Fairchild* v. *Glenhaven Funeral Services Ltd* [2002]
- *Bolitho* v. *Hackney Health Authority* [1997]
- *The Wagon Mound (No. 1)* [1961]

SPECIAL CHARACTERISTICS
- The 'but for' test for factual causation
- *The Wagon Mound* test for legal causation
- Thin skull rule re damage

REFORM
- As medical knowledge advances, will mesothelioma victims retain the evidentiary advantage they currently enjoy?

CRITICAL ISSUES

Setting the scene

Let's recap what we have learnt so far regarding the tort of negligence.

A claimant suing someone in negligence must prove, on the balance of probabilities, that a duty of care exists and then that the defendant acted in breach of this duty of care. She would do that by proving that the defendant's actions were less than what we would expect of a reasonable person. If she proved that, we have negligence, but that does not end the matter. She then has to prove that the breach caused her to suffer damage as a result. Put another way, she has to prove that the breach *caused* her damage or injury. Lawyers refer to this as *causation* – the requirement that the claimant has to prove that there is a direct link between the act/omission of the defendant and the damage suffered.

INTRODUCTION TO CAUSATION

On the face of it causation seems straightforward: A did B and B caused C's damage therefore A is liable to C. But there are factors that complicate the issue of causality. For example, more than one possible cause could be identified. Or an *omission* could be at issue – how does one establish that failing to act caused damage?

Closely related to the term 'causation' is the concept of 'the causal chain', which becomes important when we have multiple causes of damage. Think, for example, of a motorway pile-up: A negligently runs across a motorway, causing B, who was travelling too fast, to swerve and collide with C, who in turn was talking on her mobile phone and not paying proper attention to her driving, and in her turn collided with D. The chain of causation clearly stretches from D all the way back to A. But will D be able to hold A liable? Did anything happen to 'break' the chain between A and D? In such a case, A would not be liable to D (someone else may be, e.g. the intervening action that broke the chain of causation may establish such person's action as causing D's damage).

Causation is important because it is not only required as an element to prove the tort of negligence but also for the other torts. Even if the claimant does not need to prove fault (the strict liability torts), she must still show a direct link between the defendant's acts or omissions and the damage suffered.

CORNERSTONE

Factual and legal causation

Causation is sometimes referred to as factual causation, which is largely self-explanatory, and legal causation. Legal causation is an additional requirement to fulfil after it was proved on the facts that A did cause B's damage – the question is then how closely connected the damage is to the causative event. Put another way, it asks how remote the damages are. If it is held that the damage is very remote, the claim will not succeed.

Let us now examine these issues in more detail.

CAUSATION

Where a breach of a duty of care is proved or admitted, the burden still lies on the claimant to prove, on the balance of probabilities, that such breach *caused* the injury suffered. In all cases the primary question is one of fact: did the wrongful act cause the injury?

Causation is measured in two ways.

Causation in fact or the 'but for' test

Here we look at the cause of damage. The 'but for' test is the starting point for determining causation, and the central question is whether what the defendant did (or omitted to do) was the factual cause of the claimant's loss or whether it was caused by something else.

Causation in law/remoteness of damage

In addition to factual causation, it must be proved that the damage is still sufficiently approximate in law to hold the defendant liable to compensate the victim. In other words, in certain cases, even where it is proved that the act/omission in fact caused the claimant's damage, the courts may find that nevertheless the defendant is not liable because the loss is too 'remote'. The damage may be too unusual or too far removed as a consequence of the act or omission of the defendant.

FACTUAL CAUSATION

The breach of duty must be the fact that caused the damage – it must be the factual cause of the damage. Traditionally the test that the courts use to determine factual causation is the 'but-for' test.

CORNERSTONE

The 'but for' test: *Cork* v. *Kirby MacLean* [1952] 2 All ER 402

To establish causation in fact the 'but for' test asks whether the claimant would not have suffered the damage but for the defendant's negligent act or omission. As Lord Denning put it in the case of *Cork* v. *Kirby MacLean Ltd* [1952] 2 All ER 402:

'. . . if the damage would not have happened *but for* a particular fault, then that fault is the cause of the damage, if it would have happened just the same, fault or no fault, the fault is not the cause of the damage.' (emphasis added)

Let us apply this to a case to see how it works:

In *Barnett* v. *Chelsea and Kensington Hospital Management Committee* [1969] 1 QB 428 a man drank contaminated tea and was taken ill. Upon attending hospital he was turned away from its casualty department and later died from arsenic poisoning. The court held that, without doubt the casualty officer should have seen and examined the deceased, and that his failure to do either was negligence. So the court took the first two elements of negligence to be proved (duty of care and breach of such duty). But the claimant's widow's claim fell apart on the basis of causation. It was proved that he would have died even if the doctor at casualty had treated him. Therefore, he would not have died, 'but for' the hospital's failure to treat him – he would have died anyway. The hospital was held not liable.

Although the 'but for' test is generally straightforward, there are some instances where it causes confusion. This can happen where there were multiple causes of damage, where there was a 'lost chance' of recovery, where there are multiple *consecutive* causes and also where there may have been a new, intervening act which broke the chain of causation.

Multiple causes of damage

Problems with the 'but for' test occur where the claimant's damage is the result of more than one cause. In such cases it is difficult to identify the precise cause of the damage and the case law is often quite inconsistent when trying to deal with this. It may be of some use to you to think of this in two ways – the multiple causes may be simultaneous (happening at the same time) or consecutive (happening one after the other). Let's start by looking at the former.

Materially contributed to the damage

In general, the claimant does not have to prove that the defendant's breach was the only or even the main cause of the damage: in *Bonnington Castings Ltd* v. *Wardlaw* [1956] AC 613 the House of Lords found that the claimant needed to show that a defendant's breach of duty *'materially contributed to the damage'*. In that case, a workman was exposed to two sorts of dust at his workplace, over a number of years. He contracted a lung disease, but it could not be proved which of the two kinds of dust caused it. By law, the employer was under a duty to extract one of the kinds of dust – so if it could be proved that this dust caused his illness, liability would have been inferred much more readily. However, even though it could not be established, the court held that the employer was liable as the dust at least partially caused the illness. The key phrase here is 'materially contributed to the damage'.

Materially increased the risk of damage

Courts may also decide a multiple causes case by asking whether the negligence of the defendant has *'materially increased the risk'* of damage. If it has, the defendant should be held liable for damages: two cases that were decided on this basis are illustrative. In *McGhee* v. *National Coal Board* [1973] 3 All ER 1008 the claimant contracted dermatitis after working in hot, dusty conditions for years. He alleged that having no choice but to cycle home covered in dust caused him to suffer his illness. The court held in his favour as it was of the opinion that the employer materially increased the claimant's risk of contracting dermatitis by not providing adequate washing up facilities. In *Bailey* v. *Ministry of Defence* [2008] EWCA Civ 883, the claimant was ill and in a weakened state, and was treated in a hospital managed by the defendant. In part due to her weakened state but also in part because of the hospital's inadequate care, she suffered brain damage. The court held that the inadequate care materially contributed to her injury and her claim succeeded.

More than two or three possible causes: operative cause of damage

In *Bonnington* and in *Bailey* only two things could have caused the damage. Where there are a variety of possible causes it is more complicated – then it has to be proved which of them actually did cause the damage. Why? Remember that the claimant has to prove her case on a balance of probabilities. This is easy to do if there are only two possible causes, maybe even if there are three. Much more than that and statistically it would be very difficult indeed to convince the court on a 51 per cent basis which one/more of the possible factors caused your damage. For example, in *Wilsher* v. *Essex Area Health Authority* [1988] AC 1074 (HL) a claimant was born prematurely and was given oxygen. He became blind and it was found that the oxygen might have been one of five possible reasons for it. The House of Lords found that in the absence of conclusive evidence that the hospital's negligence had been the *operative cause* of the damage, it could not be held liable.

Multiple consecutive causes

Where there are multiple *consecutive* causes the liability remains generally with the first defendant unless the later cause increased the damage. The 'but for' test will be applied to the original defendant. In *Performance Cars* v. *Abraham* [1962] 1 QB 33 (CA) A negligently drove into B, and later C also negligently struck B. The court held that A remained liable – C was not held liable for respraying B's car as the car already needed a respray due to A's collision by the time C hit it.

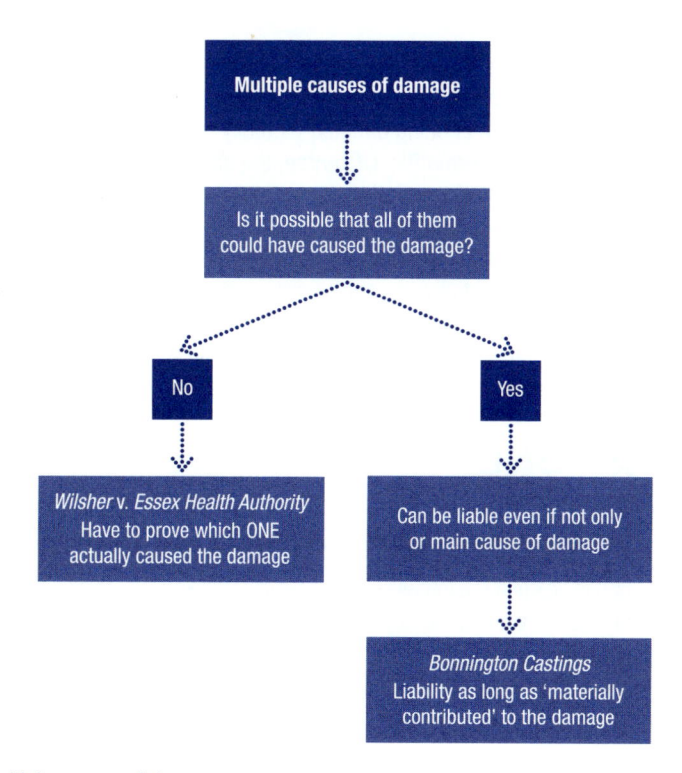

Figure 4.1 Multiple causes of damage

The mesothelioma cases

CORNERSTONE

Joint and several versus proportional liability

What would be the case if, over his lifetime, an employee worked for several different employers and in the end contracted a work-related illness that could have been caused at any of his former workplaces? Who would be held liable? If one cannot be pinpointed, would none be held liable? Or would all of them be held liable, and if so on what basis?

Joint and several liability could mean that one employer could end up paying everything, even though it may not have caused the illness. Joint and several liability means that the claimant can decide to hold all the defendants liable or she could hold one liable, who in his turn could then ask his co-defendants to repay him their contributions. From the standpoint of the claimant, this is ideal, as she would demand payment from the most economically viable defendant and not have to worry whether other impecunious defendants can pay or not.

Proportional liability could mean that those who were not liable have to pay, and could also mean that the claimant ends up under-compensated (for example, if four out of his five previous employers had become bankrupt).

Think back to the *McGhee* case, above. That case is, to an extent, a departure from the normal approach in as much as, though the defendant is being deemed factually to have *contributed* to the dermatitis, he is being held liable for the *whole* dermatitis. Of course, the problem the court had was that it could not evaluate the extent of the material contribution by the defendant to the claimant's injury.

It would have been hard on the claimant to respond to this obstacle by providing no compensation but is it really common sense, justice or legitimate policy to make the defendant wholly liable for something that is very likely only partially its fault? Perhaps a better approach would have been to provide compensation for 50 per cent of the injury?

This problem was paramount in the House of Lords case dealing with a form of lung cancer caused by asbestos called mesothelioma.

CORNERSTONE

Fairchild v. *Glenhaven Funeral Services Ltd* [2002] 3 All ER 305

The claimant, who had developed mesothelioma, had been employed, over time, by several employers. It was clear that the disease was caused by exposure to asbestos dust at work, but it could not be established which employer was liable. The House of Lords held that all the employers were jointly and severally liable, leaving employers to seek contribution amongst themselves.

This case is relatively unusual, mainly because of the unique nature of mesothelioma – it could be caused by a single, minuscule strand of asbestos. It would therefore be very difficult indeed ever to find out which of the employers was responsible. The House of Lords' decision also had a strong policy element. It pointed out that two injustices needed to be weighed up: on the one hand, it is unjust to hold somebody jointly liable with someone else if there is a chance that she did not contribute to the damage; but on the other hand, it would be unjust to deny the claimants in this unique situation a remedy.

You can imagine that the insurance industry was not happy with the judgment in *Fairchild*, and indeed they challenged it in a subsequent, similar case: In *Barker* v. *Corus (UK)* [2006] 2 WLR 1027 (HL) the claimant's husband, who died of mesothelioma, had been exposed to asbestos during three periods in his working life; first, while working for a company which had since become insolvent; secondly, while working for the defendant and thirdly while self-employed. The House of Lords partially overruled its decision in *Fairchild*. It confirmed that there is an exception in mesothelioma cases to the normal rules on liability in negligence, whereby any relevant employer could be liable in relation to mesothelioma caused by wrongful exposure of an employee to asbestos. But, it held, it is fair that where more than one person was in breach of duty and might have been responsible, liability should be attributed according to the defendant's relative degree of contribution to the risk, probably measured by the duration and intensity of the exposure involved. Therefore, it held, the defendants' liability was several only. This meant that a deduction was made in proportion to the claimant's own contribution to his illness. Further significance of several liability (i.e. proportional liability) became clear from the co-joined claims to this case, where claimants with mesothelioma were employed by employers who subsequently became bankrupt – several liability now meant they could only claim from the remaining, solvent employers for their proportional contribution. If they could claim on the *Fairchild* basis, they would have been able to claim their full damage from one of the solvent employers.

Barker, therefore, was bad news for the unfortunate victims of asbestos exposure, and as a result of resistance to this ruling, the Compensation Act 2006 was enacted.

CORNERSTONE

Compensation Act 2006, section 3

This section provides that, where a person negligently or in breach of a statutory duty exposed another to asbestos, and the victim contracted mesothelioma, then the responsible person or persons will be held liable for the *whole* of the damage.

This applies regardless of whether there was more than one responsible person, non-tortious exposure by a responsible person or exposure by the victim herself.

In other words, as far as mesothelioma victims are concerned, this overrules *Barker*.

The Supreme Court confirmed this position in *Sienkiewicz* v. *Greif (UK) Ltd* [2011] 2 AC 229. In this case, the claimants were exposed to asbestos at work but it was also proved that there was general atmospheric asbestos exposure. It was calculated in the instance of one of the claimants for example, that the defendants' exposure could have been as little as 18 per cent. Nevertheless, the Court of Appeal and then the Supreme Court held the defendants liable in terms of the common law (*Glenhaven*) and section 3 of the Compensation Act 2006, dealing in mesothelioma cases involving multiple defendants: a claimant could establish liability by demonstrating that the defendant had been in breach of duty by exposing her to asbestos fibres and had thereby materially increased the risk that she would develop mesothelioma. In such instances, the word 'material' simply means a degree which is more than minimal. This is of course much easier to prove than on a balance of probabilities, which is the usual standard! Why? The Supreme Court pointed out that so long as medical science is unable to pinpoint, precisely, causation in mesothelioma cases there can be no place for the conventional test of causation (i.e. on the balance of probabilities). The defendants were therefore held liable to the full extent of the claimants' damage.

Loss of a chance

When the claimant's damage consists of a 'loss of a chance', for example, where the defendant's negligence robbed the claimant's chance of avoiding a poor outcome, or increased the likelihood of a poor outcome, the courts are very reluctant to impose liability. The courts are especially reluctant to find liability for the loss of a chance in medical negligence cases. For example, in *Gregg* v. *Scott* [2005] 2 WLR 268 a doctor misdiagnosed a lump under the claimant's arm. Later it was found to be cancerous. Mr Gregg could not prove that he had a likelihood of survival higher than 50 per cent, even at the time of his first visit to Dr Scott. Although his chance of survival was diminished by the original misdiagnosis, it was not enough to found liability.

Also in *Hotson* v. *East Berkshire Health Authority* [1987] 1 All ER 210, a boy's fracture was misdiagnosed and he later developed a hip deformity. Experts confirmed that, even if the diagnosis was correct, there was a 75 per cent chance that he would have developed the deformity anyway. The House of Lords held that, as there was only a 25 per cent chance that the negligence had caused the deformity, this did not satisfy the balance of probabilities.

Omissions

Related to the loss of a chance is the vexing question of 'what if' posed by failures to act. We have already looked at this in some detail (in Chapter 1) and you will remember that in general there is no duty to act. But suppose there was found to be a duty under the exceptional circumstances relating to omissions, and there was breach of a duty to act, the next question then becomes: what then, should have been done? It is only when you can make out a clear case that something specific should have been done that you will be able to satisfy the requirement of causation. To illustrate the difficulties in causation related to this, let's re-visit the case of *Bolitho*, which we already examined (in Chapter 3).

CORNERSTONE

Bolitho v. *Hackney Health Authority* [1997] 4 All ER 771

A young boy, P, was admitted to hospital with respiratory difficulties. At hospital, his condition deteriorated, but despite calls from the attending nurse, the responsible doctor did not come to see P or treat him. He eventually went into respiratory failure and cardiac arrest and suffered severe brain damage. Not long after that, he died. P's mother, as administrator of his deceased estate, sued the hospital (as vicariously liable for the actions of its employee doctor) in negligence.

The defendants accepted that the responsible doctor was in breach of her duty of care not to have attended P or arranged for a suitable deputy to do so.

Lord Browne-Wilkinson went on to point out that, having a duty of care, and clear breach of such duty having been proved, negligence had been established. But that was not the end of the case, because the question of *causation* also had to be decided.

The matter was complicated here because the behaviour complained of was in the form of an omission, a failure to act. The question was therefore: would the cardiac arrest have been avoided if the doctor had attended as she should have done? The next question is then, what *should* she have done? It is only if the court could pinpoint what she should have done – let's call it 'Action X', and it was clear that she would not have performed 'Action X', that we would be able to answer the question of causation. Put another way, the question then becomes: Did her failure to perform X cause P's death? But first the court had to find out what 'Action X' was supposed to be. This turned out to be a dispute about whether a competent doctor would have decided to intubate P.

Intubation involves surgically inserting an oxygen tube into the chest. All the parties accepted that, in hindsight, intubation would have saved P. But hindsight is, as they say, 20–20, and the issue before the court was twofold – first, what would the relevant doctor, in fact, have done, and secondly, would this course of action have been in accordance with accepted medical practice? The doctor admitted that even had she been there, she would *not* have intubated. The question then is, would that decision have been contrary to accepted medical practice? (In our terminology, would 'Action X' have been intubation?) If the claimant could prove that the doctor acted against accepted medical practice, she would have proved causation and her claim would succeed.

The claimant submitted expert medical evidence that intubation should have been indicated for this situation. The defence, on the other hand, submitted expert medical evidence to the effect that in such a situation, intubation should *not* have been the chosen course of action.

We therefore had, in *Bolitho*, the kind of situation addressed by the *Bolam* test – two conflicting sets of expert medical opinion. A strict application of *Bolam* would have meant that the matter ended there – the doctor could back her actions up as being in line with an accepted medical practice. As we have seen (in Chapter 3), however, the court in *Bolitho* pointed out that it is possible to discount expert evidence if the court is convinced that it does not withstand logical analysis. In the event, the court found that both sets of medical expert evidence were credible and as they were, the court had to accept the defendant's version. (Revise Chapter 3 to make sure you understand the reasoning.)

New act intervening (*novus actus interveniens*)

'*Novus actus interveniens*' is a Latin phrase that means 'a new act intervenes' in the chain of causation, breaking it. If this happens, the new intervening act would be the cause of the damage, not the original act.

A new act intervening is therefore an effective defence for the defendant against a claim for negligence. If the court accepts the intervening act as the true cause of the claimant's damage, then the defendant is not held liable, even if she has been negligent. In *Jobling* v. *Associated Dairies Ltd* [1982] AC 794 (HL) the claimant suffered a back injury at work due to the negligence of his employer, resulting in loss of 50 per cent of his earning capacity. Later, and unrelated to the accident, he developed a spinal disease which totally incapacitated him. The court held that the disease of the spine was a *novus actus interveniens* which broke the chain of causation.

If the court does *not* accept the intervening act as the true cause of the damage, then the chain is unbroken and the defendant is held liable. For example, in *Baker* v. *Willoughby* [1970] AC 467 (HL) the claimant was knocked down by a car and suffered a stiff leg as a result, which in turn compelled him to downgrade his job. Later he was shot in the same leg and as a result the leg had to be amputated. The defendant claimed that his liability for the leg injury should cease at the time of the second injury, but the House of Lords held that the claimant's loss of earnings was a result of the original injury.

Bermingham and Brennan (2011: ch. 6) explain the apparent inconsistency between *Jobling* and *Baker* in the following way: *Baker* involved two torts whereas in *Jobling* a tort was followed by a

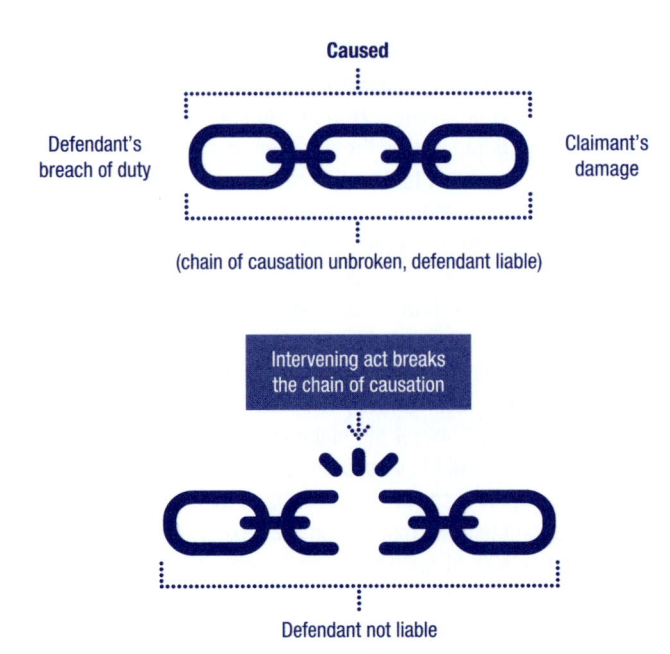

Figure 4.2 The chain of causation

naturally occurring disease. In *Baker*, it was highly unlikely that compensation would be available from those who shot the plaintiff and therefore if the first defendant's liability ceased at the time of amputation, there was a real risk of under-compensation for the plaintiff. This only partially explains the differences as of course, compensation cannot be claimed from a naturally occurring disease either.

There are three categories of intervening acts – by the claimant herself, by an act of nature and by a third party. Let's examine each in turn.

An intervening act of the claimant

The defendant can plead that the claimant herself is responsible for her own damage.

CORNERSTONE

Novus actus or contributory negligence?

Whether the claimant's own behaviour counts as a *novus actus* or merely as contributory negligence is a matter of degree and has to be judged on the facts of each case. The effects are very different, though. If the court decides that the claimant was contributorily negligent, the defendant will still be held liable but the damages owed will be lowered proportionally. For example, X wins a negligence case against Y but the court held that X contributed 10 per cent to her own damages. (Imagine, for example, that Y was driving negligently and crashed a car he and X was in, but that X was also negligent because she was not wearing her seatbelt.) If damages are set at £1000, we need to subtract 10 per cent to see how much X will get: £900. X is entitled to her damages, albeit less because of her own negligent action, because she did not break the chain of causation.

If, on the other hand, X did something which broke the chain of causation, she will not be entitled to *any* damages from Y.

The test applied by the courts in these cases is whether the claimant was acting reasonably in the circumstances. In *McKew* v. *Holland & Hannen & Cubbits (Scotland) Ltd* [1969] 3 All ER 1621 an employer was liable for a work-related injury sustained by the claimant. The claimant, after the accident, and knowing that his injury had weakened his leg, went down a steep staircase with no handrail, fell and broke his ankle. The court held that his action amounted to a *novus actus* because he unreasonably put himself in a dangerous situation. Compare this to the very similar facts in *Wieland* v. *Cyril Lord Carpets Ltd* [1969] 3 All ER 1006. Again, the claimant suffered an injury at work for which her employer was liable. Due to this injury she had to wear a neck brace, and because of this brace she could not see out of her glasses properly. She slipped and fell down some steps. The court held that in this instance the claimant's action was not unreasonable, and the defendant had to pay for the further injuries she suffered because of the fall.

An intervening act of nature

The defendant might not be held liable if she can show that the act of nature is unforeseeable and independent of her own negligence. Take note that it is *only* if the event was unforeseen and independent that the chain of causation would be broken – in the majority of instances this will not be the case. For example, in *Carslogie Steamship Co* v. *Royal Norwegian Government* [1952] AC 292 the defendant negligently caused a collision with the claimant's ship. Some temporary repairs were made and the ship set sail for the United States, where it would be repaired in full. En route a storm broke out and the ship sustained further heavy damage. The court held that the storm was unforeseeable and separate from the initial collision. As a result the defendants could not be held liable for the further damage.

An intervening act of a third party

The defendant must show that the act of the third party also caused the claimant damage and that the act was of such magnitude that it did in fact break the chain of causation. A third party may intervene in a variety of ways. This is best illustrated by looking at some cases. One example is to be found in the case of *Jobling* v. *Associated Dairies*, which we discussed above.

In *Knightley* v. *Johns* [1982] 1 All ER 851 Mr Johns caused an accident in a one-way tunnel ('accident 1'). The police, attending the scene, closed the end of the tunnel but also told two motorcyclists to drive through the tunnel (going the wrong way). A car then hit one of the motorcyclists ('accident 2'). The question was whether Mr Johns could be held liable to the injured motorcyclist, or whether the police's negligent action was a *novus actus interveniens*. The court held that the police negligence did indeed disturb the sequence of events and counted as a new intervening act.

If the intervening act should have been foreseen, the original wrongdoer will be held liable. In *Lamb* v. *Camden Borough Council* [1981] QB 625 the defendant's workmen flooded the claimant's house and, while the house was vacated for repairs, it was occupied by squatters who caused further damage. The court held that, although this was foreseeable, it wasn't foreseeable to such an extent that the defendant could be held liable for the actions of the squatters – for that, the outcome was seen as too remote. Contrast this to the case of *Home Office* v. *Dorset Yacht Co* (which we discussed in Chapter 2), where it was held that it was foreseeable that the escaped Borstal boys would cause damage, and that their actions were therefore not in and of themselves a new intervening act that broke the chain of causation – the defendants were still held liable.

LEGAL CAUSATION (REMOTENESS OF DAMAGE)

Once factual causation has been proved, damages might still be denied to the claimant if the damages suffered are too remote a consequence of the defendant's breach.

CORNERSTONE

Remoteness of damage

The test is a question of law rather than fact and here policy plays a part in the court's considerations. The main reason is that the law should draw a line somewhere, otherwise defendants face potentially limitless liability arising from one tort.

Direct consequence: *Re Polemis*

Until 1961, the test of remoteness used by the courts was whether the damage was a *direct consequence* of the breach of duty. This was regardless of how foreseeable this loss was: *Re Polemis and Furness, Withy & Co* [1921] 3 KB 560. In this case, charterers of a ship filled the hold with containers of benzene. This leaked and filled the hold with vapour. When the ship was unloaded, a stevedore negligently dropped a plank into the hold. A spark ignited the vapours and the ship was destroyed. The Court of Appeal held the charterers, as employers of the stevedores, liable. This was because the damage was a *direct consequence* of the stevedore's negligent act.

INTERSECTION

The employers were held vicariously liable for the negligent action of their employee. (We examine vicarious liability in detail in Chapter 12.)

FORESEEABILITY: *THE WAGON MOUND (NO. 1)*

However, the usual test was changed by the following case.

CORNERSTONE

Overseas Tankship (UK) Ltd v. *Morts Dock & Engineering Co (The Wagon Mound (No. 1))* [1961] AC 388

This decision by the Privy Council, commonly known as *'The Wagon Mound'*, established that the defendant will only be liable if the damage was a *reasonably foreseeable consequence* of the breach of duty. In this case, oil had leaked from a tanker into Sydney harbour due to the defendant's negligence. The oil floated to the claimant's wharf, where another ship was being repaired by welders. The oil caused some damage to the slipway, but then, a few days later, a spark from the welding operations ignited the oil, which had soaked into some cotton wadding that was floating in the water, and caused more serious damage. The trial judge found that the damage to the slipway was reasonably foreseeable but, given that the evidence showed that the oil needed to be raised to a very high temperature before it would catch fire, the fire damage was not reasonably foreseeable. However, under the test in the *Re Polemis* case, he found defendants liable for both damages.

The Privy Council took a different view. It stated that *Re Polemis* was no longer good law. The new test for remoteness was the foresight of the reasonable person: was the kind of damage the claimant suffered reasonably foreseeable at the time of the breach of duty? Under this test, the claimants in the present case were only liable for the damage to the slipway and not for the fire damage.

Thus the reasonable foreseeability test set down in this case is now the test for remoteness of damage (or, if you prefer, for legal causation).

Foreseeability is a more flexible concept than that of directness, and helps the courts to arrive more easily at policy decisions. On the other hand, it should also be noted that foreseeability entails a large measure of unpredictability. What is foreseeable to one person may not be so to another – therefore a subjective element is introduced.

In many instances, application of the test of reasonable foreseeability will not bring a different result from that of directness. Much depends on how widely or narrowly the question of foreseeability is phrased.

The 'thin skull' rule

If the type of injury is foreseeable, but not how severe the injury would be, perhaps because of some pre-existing condition on the part of the claimant, the defendant would still be held liable for all of the losses.

> **Take note**
> Although *Re Polemis* has not yet been overruled, the reasonable foreseeability test from *The Wagon Mound (No. 1)* is accepted by the courts as the relevant test to follow in questions of remoteness. However, for cases of intentional torts (actionable per se), such as trespass to the person, *Re Polemis* remains good law and therefore one would use the direct consequence test to evaluate remoteness.

CORNERSTONE

The thin skull rule

This rule means that the defendant will 'have to take the claimant how she finds her' and that she will be liable for the full extent of the injuries suffered by the claimant.

The thin skull rule is also known as the 'egg-shell skull' rule. Note that this rule only comes into operation once all the other elements for negligence have been proved.

APPLICATION

G is driving his car over the speed limit, and knocks down a pedestrian at a crossing. The pedestrian, F, happens to suffer from brittle bone diseases and as a result of being knocked down, suffers severe spinal injuries and is now paralysed. G's lawyer points out to court that G had not been exceeding the speed limit very much, and also that even though he could foresee that his negligent action could knock someone over, any normal person would at most have suffered a broken bone or two. The court does not accept this and states that G must take his victim as he found her. It was foreseeable that there could be injury, it did not need to be foreseeable too that the injury would be that severe.

Let's also look at a real-life example: in *Smith* v. *Leech Brain & Co Ltd* [1962] 2 WB 405 (CA) the claimant suffered a burn to his lip due to his employer's negligence. It turned out that the claimant's lip was pre-malignant before the burn and that it resulted in cancer, from which the claimant died. Despite the fact that cancer was not foreseeable, the employer was held liable.

The thin skull rule can also apply where the harm is psychiatric damage: *Walker* v. *Northumberland CC* [1995] 1 All ER 737; or where the expected damage is physical injury but the claimant suffers shock instead and has a particular sensitivity. It can also apply to economic weakness. So, if damage is caused in a foreseeable way the defendant is liable for the full extent of the damage even if this is exceptional, e.g. the claimant is suffering from cardiac failure or the property damaged is very valuable.

To recap, causation can be visualised in the following way:

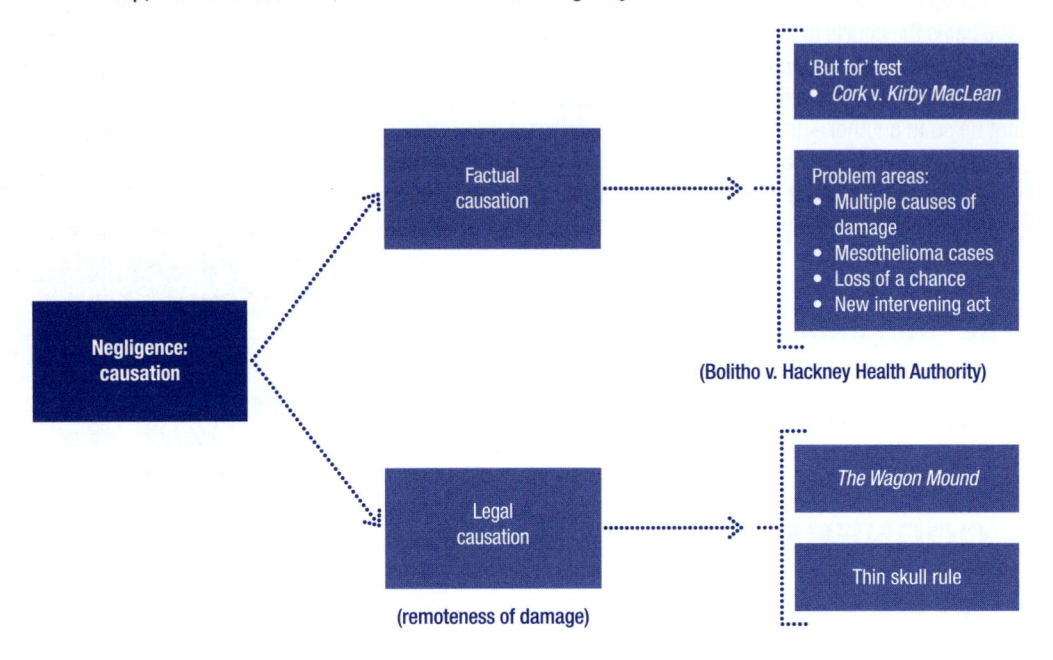

Figure 4.3 Negligence: causation

KEY POINTS

- Together with proving a duty of care and breach of such duty, the claimant in a negligence case has to prove that such breach caused her damage. This is referred to as 'causation'.
- Causation in fact means the factual evidence and is determined by the 'but for' test formulated by Lord Denning in *Cork* v. *Kirby MacLean*.
- The so-called asbestos cases and section 3 of the Compensation Act 2006 make it easier for mesothelioma (asbestos poisoning) victims to hold defendants liable in that the causation element is watered down somewhat for such cases.
- Causation in law means that even if the breach did in fact cause the damage, the claimant still has to prove that the damage was not too remote, i.e. that it was foreseeable. This is a policy requirement aimed at preventing limitless liability, i.e. the floodgates argument.

CORE CASES AND STATUTES

Case	About	Importance
Cork v. Kirby MacLean [1952] 2 All ER 402	'But for' test established for factual causation	To determine factual causation, we ask: 'but for' the defendant's action, would the damage have happened?
Bonnington Castings Ltd v. Wardlaw [1956] AC 613	Multiple causes of damage	Claimant can claim provided he can show that the defendant's breach of duty 'materially contributed' to the damage.
McGhee v. National Coal Board [1973] 3 All ER 1008	Multiple causes of damage	Employer found liable as its action materially increased the risk of damage.
Fairchild v. Glenhaven Funeral Service Ltd [2002] 3 All ER 305	Joint and several liability of multiple defendants to mesothelioma victims	Various employers who may have contributed to the defendant's having contracted mesothelioma from asbestos exposure were held liable on a 'joint and several' basis.
Barker v. Corus (UK) [2006] 2 WLR 1027	Mesothelioma victims: several liability only	Partially overruled Fairchild, holding that liability among multiple defendants in mesothelioma cases were to be several only. Later overruled by the Compensation Act, s. 3.
Hotson v. East Berkshire Area Health Authority [1987] 1 All ER 210	It is difficult to prove causation if the action complained of resulted in a 'loss of a chance'	In this case there was only a 25 per cent chance that the negligence had caused the claimant's injuries, therefore the balance of probabilities was not satisfied.
The Wagon Mound (No. 1) [1961] AC 388	Sets out the 'legal causation' leg of the causation requirement	Once factual causation is proved, the claimant still has to prove that the damage was not too remote in law. For this the test if whether the kind or type of damage in fact suffered by the claimant was reasonably foreseeable.

Statute	About	Importance
Compensation Act 2006, s. 3(2)	Liability towards mesothelioma victims	Reverses decision in Barker v. Corus, re-establishes joint and several liability as per Fairchild v. Glenhaven Funeral Services Ltd for mesothelioma victims.

FURTHER READING

Bermingham, V. and Brennan, C. (2011) Tort Law: Directions. 3rd edition, Oxford: Oxford University Press, Chapter 6
It is important that you fully understand both factual and legal causation. Issues such as multiple consecutive and multiple simultaneous causes often cause misunderstanding. This chapter in Bermingham and Brennan provides a clear and easy to follow explanation of key concepts in causation, and can be read as a starting point from which to further deepen your understanding of causation.

Hoffmann, L. (2005) Causation. LQR 121, p. 592
Places the issue of causation in context through an excellent discussion of why it is relevant to everyday life, as well as focusing on the intersections with other elements of the tort of negligence.

Khoury, L. (2008) Causation and risk in the highest courts of Canada, England and France. LQR 124, p. 103
This article highlights the problems that courts face in establishing causation and assigning liability for injuries where there are multiple defendants all with differing levels of contribution to the damage. Reading this article will show you some comparisons with other jurisdictions, and will also help you further understand the risk-based system followed in UK case law, specifically the House of Lords ruling in *Barker* v. *Corus UK Ltd*.

Morgan, A. (2002) Inference, principle and the proof of causation. NLJ p. 1060
This article discusses causation well and also looks at the landmark case of *Fairchild* v. *Glenhaven Funeral Services*.

Zahn, B. (2011) Harmful conduct as the touchstone of causation: an analytical comparison of Barker v. Corus and Julian. Edin LR 15(2), p. 197
If you find the mesothelioma cases interesting, this article gives a useful overview of *Fairchild* and *Barker*.

CHAPTER 5
Negligence: defences

BLUEPRINT
Negligence: defences

KEY QUESTIONS

LEGISLATION

- Road Traffic Act 1988, s. 149(3)
- Law Reform (Contributory Negligence) Act 1945

CONTEXT

- Contributory negligence is the most important defence due to its partial nature, and limits liability to reflect a claimant's relative blameworthiness for her own damage.

CONCEPTS

- *Volenti non fit injuria*/consent
- Complete and partial defences
- Contributory negligence
- *Ex turpi causa*/illegality

- If we allow illegality as only a partial defence, does this mean that claimants are able to profit from their own illegal actions?

- What are the main defences to a claim in negligence?
- What is meant by a full or a partial defence?
- How does contributory negligence influence the award of damages?

CASES

- *Stermer* v. *Lawson* [1977]
- *Morris* v. *Murray* [1991]
- *Smith* v. *Charles Baker & Sons* [1891]
- *Dann* v. *Hamilton* [1939]
- *Froom* v. *Butcher* [1976]

REFORM

- The Law Commission in 2010 reported that the courts, in stating the policy reasons behind their decisions based on the defence of illegality, are developing the law in this area satisfactorily (and therefore no legislation is needed).

SPECIAL CHARACTERISTICS

- Consent, full defence – subjective test
- Contributory negligence, partial defence – objective test
- Illegality as a defence reflects policy considerations by courts

CRITICAL ISSUES

Setting the scene

Once a claimant has convinced the court of the merits of her claim in tort, it does not mean that the matter is over and that she has won her case. The next step would be for the court to consider whether the defendant has a legitimate defence. If accepted by the court, such a defence could defeat the claimant's claim (a 'full' defence), or it could serve to partially defeat the claim, in which case the claimant would get only part of what she is claiming for (a partial defence). One should therefore, with each tort, also think about whether there is a possible defence to it. A good example is where a passenger in a motor vehicle accident successfully proves to the court that she could claim against the driver in negligence. If the driver can then prove that the claimant was not wearing a seatbelt and that this contributed to her injuries, the court will accept this as the defence of 'contributory negligence'. This is an important defence in negligence and other torts and entails that the claim will be reduced because of the claimant's own fault in contributing to her damage. Let's first focus on the defences to the most important modern tort, negligence.

We start off by looking at the defence commonly referred to as 'consent'. This is where the defendant voluntarily accepted or consented to the tort or the risk posed by the tortious action. Lawyers refer to this as *volenti non fit injuria*. As it plays an important part in negligence actions, we need to examine it in detail.

We then look at the other defence most relevant to negligence, contributory negligence. This defence recognises that the claimant herself contributed to her own damage, and reduces the damages accordingly. Finally, we also briefly examine the defence of illegality, also referred to as the *ex turpi causa* defence.

THREE MAIN DEFENCES TO A CLAIM IN NEGLIGENCE

It may be useful to start off by looking at an example of the three main types of defence in negligence, before we start looking at the law. Cooke (2013; 214) sets out a hypothetical scenario incorporating all three of the major defences, along the following lines:

APPLICATION

> Steve is walking along the road when his friend Harry screeches to a halt in a BMW next to him, shouting: 'Get in, I've just nicked this car a block away!' Steve hesitates a moment at this news, mainly because he knows his friend Harry has had his licence revoked due to past accidents in cars. But then he jumps in the passenger side and Harry drives off at speed. Because of his driving at 70mph in a 20mph zone, Harry crashes the car into a lamp-post. Steve, who did not bother fastening his seat belt, is thrown through the windscreen and severely injured.
>
> If Steve sued Harry in negligence, he could be met with the defences of contributory negligence or consent (*volenti non fit injuria*) and perhaps *ex turpi causa* as well.
>
> It could be argued that when he got into the car, he fully appreciated the risk as he knew what a bad driver Harry was. In this case, the defence of consent may prevail and if so, Steve's entire claim will be defeated.
>
> If the court does not accept consent, which is a full defence, it is likely that Harry would successfully raise the partial defence of contributory negligence – Steve's damages would be reduced because by not wearing a seatbelt he had contributed to his own injuries.
>
> Finally, the defence of illegality may be raised as they were engaged in a crime by driving in a stolen car.

Let's now look at these defences in more detail.

VOLENTI NON FIT INJURIA

We often refer to **volenti non fit injuria** as the defence of 'consent'. Lawyers also commonly refer to it simply as '*volenti*'. The idea is that if you consent to something happening, you should not be able to later turn around and make someone liable for what has happened. The consent could be to one of two things: consent to damage or injury or consent to the risk that damage or injury may occur.

CORNERSTONE

Volenti non fit injuria

Volenti non fit injuria can be loosely translated as meaning 'there can be no injury to one who consents'. It is a full defence, meaning it completely defeats the claimant's suit, and it is subjective because the court has to consider what the particular claimant thought at the time she allegedly consented to the risk of damage.

In deciding whether the defence of *volenti* should succeed, the court will ask what, exactly, the claimant consented to, as well as whether such consent was given freely. Although consent can be express or implied, it should be given voluntarily and freely in order to count as a defence. As you will see from the cases we will examine, this entails that the defendant will have to show that not only was the claimant aware of the risk, but she nevertheless accepted that risk freely, without coercion. If there is doubt about this the courts tend to disallow the defence.

CORNERSTONE

Complete and partial defences

It is relatively difficult to succeed with a defence of *volenti*. This is because *volenti* is a complete defence, which means that if it is successful it defeats the claim completely and no damages can be recovered. Other examples of full defences include the defence of illegality (**ex turpi causa non oritur actio**) and Acts of God.

If disallowing the defence sounds harsh to you, remember that in many cases the defence of contributory negligence would then be available as an alternative. As you will see below, this is a partial defence, which means that it does not defeat the claim – the claimant's action is successful. But the fact that the claimant is found to have been negligent too then serves to reduce the amount of damages that she can claim.

Volenti is available in two situations: first, where the defendant knows that harm will definitely be inflicted (intentional infliction of harm), and consents to it. A good example of this is where you sign a medical consent form before surgery. Secondly, where there is the possibility of harm, and the claimant voluntarily accepts the risk of injury. This relates to the negligent infliction of harm. An example would be where a person takes part in a rugby game, and understands that this might entail the risk of injury. In both cases, the courts require that consent be given freely and voluntarily.

Broadly speaking, the defendant will have to prove two things: first, that the claimant knew of the precise risk involved and, secondly, that the claimant exercised free choice and voluntarily accepted the risk. Let's examine these requirements in more detail.

Knowledge of the risk

The test here is subjective and we look at the knowledge of the relevant claimant, not of the reasonable person. Put another way, we do not ask what the claimant *ought* to have known, but what she *actually* knew. If the claimant was not aware of the risk or even if she was aware of the risk, but vaguely, the defence will fail. Again, it must be noted that the courts do not easily allow this defence, because it is a total defence and if successfully raised, completely defeats the claim.

Two cases illustrate that the courts look at what the relevant claimant knew about the risk undertaken.

CORNERSTONE

Stermer v. Lawson [1977] 5 WWR 628

In this Canadian case the defendant lent his friend, an inexperienced rider, his 650cc motorbike. He gave him brief instructions as to how to use it, but due to the claimant's inexperience the friend crashed and was injured. The Supreme Court of British Columbia held that because the claimant did not know of the dangers involved in riding this bike he could not be said to have been '*volens*'.

In other words, because he had not appreciated the risk fully, he could not be said to have consented to it. (The court held, however, that the claimant did know that he was inexperienced and that therefore he should have taken steps to see he knew how to ride the bike before he did so. The court held him 50 per cent to blame for his own injuries, meaning that although the defendant failed with the defence of *volenti*, he successfully raised the defence of *contributory negligence*. We look at this defence in more detail below.)

By contrast, in the following case the court considered that the claimant *did* know what he was consenting to.

CORNERSTONE

Morris v. Murray [1991] 2 QB 6

A passenger (who had himself been drinking) knowingly and willingly embarked on a flight with a drunken pilot. The plane crashed, killing the pilot and injuring the claimant, who then sued the pilot's estate in negligence. The Court of Appeal held that his claim was defeated by the defence of *volenti*. The court was convinced that he had realised how drunk the pilot was and therefore that he had implicitly waived his right to sue for damages.

Interestingly, the courts are very reluctant to accept *volenti* as a defence where the claimant got into a car with a drunk driver – see the discussion below.

Voluntary acceptance of the risk

For *volenti* to succeed, the defendant also, in addition to knowledge on the part of the claimant, has to prove that the claimant exercised free choice and voluntarily accepted the risk. This means that just knowing that there is a risk is not enough, the claimant also had thereupon to exercise a free choice to *accept* the risk. Put another way, if you know about a risk, it does not necessarily follow that you have also agreed to the risk. If there is anything that puts doubt in the mind about how freely and voluntarily the risk was accepted, the defence will fail. Let's look at some examples of instances where the courts are very reluctant to find that there was free and voluntary consent.

Special areas

Employees

If an employee suffers damage at work due to the employer's (personal or vicarious) fault, the courts are reluctant to uphold a defence of *volenti* on the part of the employee. Merely continuing to work whilst aware of the risk of doing so, is not enough to imply consent. The following case, much cited (not always favourably, but still good law), illustrates the principle.

CORNERSTONE

Smith v. Charles Baker & Sons [1891] AC 325

Mr Smith was employed by railway contractors to drill holes in a rock cutting. Nearby, other employees of the defendant operated a crane which lifted stones and at times swung them over the plaintiff's head. Mr Smith was fully aware, for months, of the danger to which he was thus exposed by working near the crane. When a rock fell from the crane, injuring him, he sued his employers. They, in turn, pleaded *volenti* as a defence, saying that, in continuing to work whilst being fully aware of the risk, the claimant had consented to the risk.

The House of Lords rejected the defence of *volenti* as on the evidence it was clear that the claimant had not voluntarily undertaken the risk of injury – he had, for example, made sure to get out of the crane's way whenever a warning was shouted or whenever he became aware of the crane swinging over him. However, due to the nature of his work he could not always keep a proper lookout and it was during such an occasion that he was injured.

More recently it has been acknowledged more clearly that many employees, even if they were fully aware of the risk under which they work, would be hesitant to stop working – they might be afraid of losing their jobs. So continuing to work knowing the risk does not imply consent to the risk, because the consent was not given freely.

This does not mean that the defence of *volenti* will always fail against an employer in an employer–employee relationship: in *ICI Ltd.* v. *Shatwell* [1965] AC 656 the claimant disregarded both the employer's instructions as well as statutory safety regulations. The House of Lords held that where two fellow servants combined to disobey an order deliberately though they knew the risk involved, *volenti non fit injuria* was a complete defence if the employer was not himself at fault.

Rescuers

Should a person who, at risk to herself, rescues somebody else, be found to have voluntarily accepted the risk and therefore be precluded from claiming damages? The attitude of the courts seems to be that the voluntary nature of such acts does not imply that they were undertaken freely. It may be more correct to look at this from the point of view of policy: the courts do not want to deter people from acting as rescuers. If rescuers get injured whilst rescuing, in principle they should be able to recover damages and such a claim should not be too easy to defeat with a defence.

In *Haynes* v. *Harwood* [1935] 1 KB 146 a police officer stopped a bolting horse in circumstances where the horse might have injured people. He successfully sued for his personal injury. The court rejected the defence of *volenti*, stating that the claimant, being a police officer and seeing that people were at risk of being injured, felt under both a professional and moral duty to act. As such he had not acted freely out of choice. (The court contrasted this to the case of *Cutler* v. *United Dairies (London) Ltd* [1933] 2 KB 297, where *volenti* was successfully raised against a claimant who was injured when he assisted in trying to recapture a runaway horse. In *Cutler* the horse was not on a public highway, had come to rest in a field and did not seem to be a danger to anyone. In such circumstances, the court held, the claimant had indeed freely and voluntarily accepted risk to himself.)

> **Take note**
>
> Even if the (complete) defence of *volenti* fails, an employer may still succeed in raising the (partial) defence of contributory negligence, which we look at below. *Stapley v. Gypsum Mines* [1953] AC 663 is a good example of contributory negligence in an employer–employee setting. In this case miners disregarded an instruction from their employer and were injured and killed respectively as a result. The widow of the deceased miner sued successfully for damages, but due to the contributory negligence of the deceased, the amount of damages was substantially (and proportionally) reduced.

Sport

Do you consent to injury if you take part in sport, or if you go and watch a sporting event? The courts accept that participants may be held to have accepted the risks which are inherent in the particular sport. It is a question of fact as to which risks are inherent for which sports. For example, horseracing is inherently more dangerous than, say, snooker. But even if you participate in a risky sport, it does not mean that you consent to all kinds of injury – usually you only consent to those that are possible during the course of normal play. In *Condon* v. *Basi* [1985] 2 All ER 453 the claimant suffered serious leg injuries during a football match as a result of a foul tackle by the defendant. The court held the defendant liable in negligence because he had acted in a way to which the other player could not be expected to consent.

APPLICATION

> Ben and James play rugby for their local club. During a friendly match with a rival club, Ben was tackled around his thighs by Jason, and dislocated his knee as a result. Because tackles like these are allowed within the rules of the game, Ben will not succeed with a claim for damages as he will be seen as having consented to the risk of injury incidental to a contact sport such as rugby.
>
> In the same match, James was also tackled by Jason, but this time the tackle was around James's neck – an illegal manoeuvre in rugby. James suffered spinal injuries as a result. In this instance James may be able to recover damages, as he will not be taken to have consented to risks outside of the rules of the game.

Take note, however, that even if the action complained of falls outside the rules of the game, the courts will still make a value judgement about whether the action reaches the threshold for liability. Put plainly, even if you break the rules in a sport, the mere fact that you broke the rules is not enough to make you liable – it also has to be proved that the action itself was negligent. For example, in *Caldwell* v. *Maguire* [2001] EWCA Civ 1054, a jockey who was injured in a horse race due to another jockey cutting in in front of his mount claimed in negligence. The Court of Appeal dismissed his claim. It recognised that a horse race was a fast-moving sport involving split second decision making and inherent risk. Within that context, the court held that the defendant jockey's failure to follow to the letter the rules of the sport and indeed his carelessness did not amount to negligence.

So the threshold is indeed higher in sport than in everyday life. Similar rules apply to spectators. In *Wooldridge* v. *Sumner* [1963] 2 QB 53, where a spectator was injured at a horse show, Lord Diplock (at 68) put it like this:

> 'A person attending a game or competition takes the risk of any damage caused to him by any act of a participant done in the course of and for the purposes of the game or competition notwithstanding that such act may involve an error of judgment or a lapse of skill, unless the participant's conduct is such as to evince a *reckless disregard* of the spectator's safety.' (emphasis added)

Drunk drivers' passengers

If you get into a car, knowing that the driver is drunk, are you taken to have consented to injury should there be an accident? Again, the courts are reluctant to imply such an agreement.

CORNERSTONE

Dann v. Hamilton [1939] 1 KB 509

The claimant was injured after accepting a lift from a drunk driver. Asquith J held that there may be cases in which the drunkenness of the driver at the material time was so extreme and glaring that to accept a lift from him would have been very dangerous indeed. In such instances, he implied, *volenti* may possibly succeed. However, on the facts of this case he found that the driver's degree of intoxication fell short of this, and he therefore concluded that *volenti* was not applicable.

This reflects the courts' attitude that, because *volenti* is a complete defence, the defendant has to prove that the claimant had *fully* consented to the entire risk.

In *Dann* v. *Hamilton* Asquith J added (at 518) that he thought that it would be unjust that the drunk driver should be protected from suit by the mere fact that he got drunk before committing the act of negligence, whereas, if he had committed the same act when sober, he would have been liable. In this regard also consider section 149(3) of the Road Traffic Act 1988, below.

CORNERSTONE

Road Traffic Act 1988, section 149(3)

This states that *volenti* is not available where a driver's passenger sues her in circumstances where insurance is compulsory. In other words, if the passenger willingly accepted the risk of the driver being negligent, that does not absolve the driver of liability.

Statutory restrictions on the defence

To sum up: *volenti* will succeed as a defence if the defendant can prove that the claimant freely and voluntarily, and appreciating the risk, agreed to accept the risk of damage.

```
Claimant proves claim
worth £10,000
        ↓
Defendant proves claimant
was volens (consented)
        ↓
Full defence defeats claim
        ↓
Claimant loses case
and recovers £0 damages
```

Figure 5.1 Consent/*volenti*

However, even if the defence is made out (and we have seen above that this is not necessarily an easy defence to use), in some instances there are statutory restrictions that restrict the parties' freedom to agree or consent. For example, the Unfair Contract Terms Act 1977, section 2(1) defeats any attempt to restrict or exclude liability for negligence causing death or personal injury. This reflects the courts' reluctance to imply an agreement that the claimant will accept the risk of injury – think of the 'drunk driver' cases we have looked at. The courts are more ready to enforce an agreement concerning the risk of property damage.

INTERSECTION

Consent is very important as a defence to trespass to the person in medical cases. For a discussion of the medical cases under trespass to the person (see Chapter 7).

CONTRIBUTORY NEGLIGENCE

This defence applies where the claimant was partly to blame for her own damage. In other words, her damage was partly caused by her own fault and partly by the fault of the defendant.

CONTEXT

Since 1945, contributory negligence is only a partial defence, in that, if it is successful, the damages awarded will be adjusted. Before that time it was a complete defence and just like *volenti*, operated to negate the claimant's entire claim. For example, if C successfully proved negligence against D, but D could prove that C in her turn was even just 1 per cent contributorily negligent, that would mean that D lost her case and would not be able to recover any damages at all. The operation of contributory negligence as a full defence was recognised to be too harsh and eventually, in 1945, it was changed to a partial defence by the legislature.

Once you understand that a successful defence of contributory negligence is a partial defence, the next concept is to understand how the courts go about deciding *how* partial the defence is. The court will have to decide the degree of contributory negligence, and reduce the damage awarded by that degree.

CORNERSTONE

Law Reform (Contributory Negligence) Act 1945

The Law Reform (Contributory Negligence) Act 1945 provides in section 1(1):

> 'Where any person suffers damage as the result partly of his own fault and partly of the fault of any other person or persons . . . the damages recoverable in respect thereof shall be reduced to such an extent as the court thinks just and equitable having regard to the claimant's share in the responsibility for the damage.'

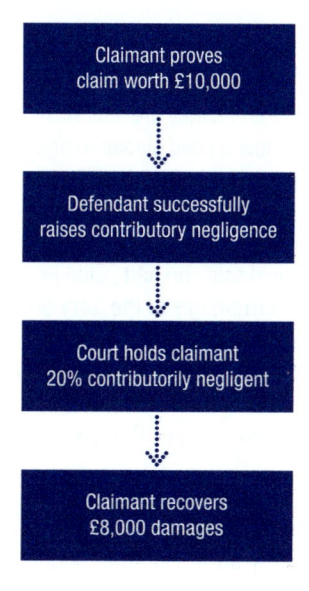

```
Claimant proves
claim worth £10,000
        ↓
Defendant successfully
raises contributory negligence
        ↓
Court holds claimant
20% contributorily negligent
        ↓
Claimant recovers
£8,000 damages
```

Figure 5.2 Contributory negligence

Let us again examine how it works from the beginning. After the claimant has proved her claim against the defendant, it is then up to the defendant to prove that the claimant herself was also negligent and that this caused (part of) her damages. Necessarily this entails that the defendant will have to prove all the elements for negligence against the claimant, including that the claimant failed to take reasonable care for her own safety and that this failure was the cause of her own damage.

Fault

The question here is whether it was partly the claimant's fault that caused the damage. Damage includes damage to property and personal injury. In *St George* v. *Home Office* [2008] EWCA Civ 1068 a long-time drug addict was assigned a top bunk in a prison and, whilst undergoing withdrawal, fell from the bunk and suffered injuries including brain damage. The prison was held liable for his injuries because they had knowingly assigned him the top bunk and this was a direct cause of his injuries. The court had also to decide whether the claimant's drug addiction was partially to blame for his injuries. The court accepted that *but for* his drug addiction, he would not have suffered the damage. However, in terms of section 1(1) of the 1945 Act the court also had to evaluate his *blameworthiness*. Thus, asking themselves whether he was to blame, the court held that his addiction was not the potent cause of his injuries – he became addicted years ago, in his teens. Therefore, it was too remote in place and time to be properly regarded as the cause of the injury and he was not held contributorily negligent.

Standard of care

Objective standard

Just as in establishing negligence, the test for blameworthiness is measured against the standard of the reasonable person. In other words, the test is objective. In *Jones* v. *Livox Quarries Ltd* [1952] 2 QB 608 the claimant was injured when he rode the tow bar of a vehicle at work. In reducing his damages due to his contributory negligence, the court held that he had not acted as a reasonable and prudent man would have.

Exceptional instances

Of course, allowances are made for children as they are less likely than adults to appreciate possible risks to their conduct. The courts will look at how a child similar in age and development would reasonably be expected to behave. For example, a nine-year-old boy was held not to know or to be expected to know the qualities of petrol in *Yachuk* v. *Oliver Blais* [1949] AC 386. In *Gough* v. *Thorne* [1966] 1 WLR 1387 a 13-year-old girl crossed a road obscured by a lorry on the indication that it was safe to do so by the truck driver, and was hit by a car. The court held that she had acted as could be expected of a person her age, that is to say, less cautiously (and more trustingly of the lorry driver) than an older person would have.

The courts also treat rescuers somewhat differently. As pointed out in the discussion of *volenti* above, there are policy reasons not to hold rescuers liable too easily – that may discourage people from coming to the aid of others. Likewise, rescuers will only be held contributorily negligent if they had shown wholly unreasonable disregard for their own safety, as per *Baker* v. *TE Hopkins & Son Ltd* [1959] 1 WLR 966.

Causation

Let's look at an example that is often used to illustrate how the element of causation needs to be proved:

APPLICATION

Imagine that C was injured in a car crash and wants to sue the driver D in negligence. C proves her case against D. In his defence D tells the court that C was not wearing a seatbelt at the time of the accident. The courts readily agree that this is an example of C failing to take care for her own safety. But D's defence will only succeed if he can prove *all* the elements of negligence, including causation. The court will ask the question: *But for* the fact she was not wearing a seatbelt, would she have sustained the relevant injuries? If she would have suffered the injuries *just the same*, the fact that she was not wearing a seatbelt would be irrelevant. Therefore, if the car crashed, and C was thrown forward through the windscreen, the fact that she was not wearing a seatbelt would be very relevant because if she had worn one, her injuries might have been less or absent.

However, let's imagine a stationary car was hit in such a way as to force C back into her seat. In this scenario, wearing a seatbelt would have made no difference to her; her injuries were not caused by her failure to wear a safety belt. The court will not hold her contributorily negligent.

There are several court cases dealing with claimants contributing to their own injuries by not wearing a seatbelt. Let us look at an example.

CORNERSTONE

Froom v. *Butcher* [1976] QB 286

In *Froom* v. *Butcher* the claimant was injured in a motor vehicle accident negligently caused by the defendant. His injuries were found to be worse than they would have been had he been wearing a seatbelt. His damages were therefore reduced by 20 per cent. The court pointed out that the damage was caused in part by the bad driving of the defendant and in part by the claimant's failure to wear a seatbelt. (Note that the court looks at what caused the *damage*, not what caused the *accident*.)

Remember, though, the requirement of causation. In *Stanton* v. *Collinson* [2010] EWCA Civ 81, for example, the Court of Appeal held that not wearing a seat belt would not automatically lead to a finding of contributory negligence – it was held that there should be no reduction where the injury would not have been reduced to 'a considerable extent' by the seatbelt.

Of course, foreseeability forms part of causation. In *Jones* v. *Livox Quarries Ltd* [1952] 2 QB 608 (above) Lord Denning explained (at 615):

'Although contributory negligence does not depend on a duty of care, it does depend on foreseeability. Just as actionable negligence requires the foreseeability of harm to others, so contributory negligence requires the foreseeability of harm to oneself. A person is guilty of contributory negligence if he ought reasonably to have foreseen that, if he did not act as a reasonable, prudent man, he might be hurt himself; and in his reckonings he must take into account the possibility of others being careless.'

Apportionment of damages

Once the defence is allowed, the court then needs to decide *how much* the claimant contributed to her damages. It uses this percentage or fraction to reduce proportionately the damages she can claim from the defendant. The defence therefore does not defeat the claim, but only mitigates the impact of the claim on the defendant by reducing the damage the claimant can recover from the defendant. We say that damages are *apportioned* between the claimant and the defendant, because each is held liable for a *portion* of the damage.

Let's look at a few examples.

In *Froom* v. *Butcher* discussed above, the claimant's damages were reduced by 20 per cent because he contributed to his injuries in that proportion by not wearing a seatbelt.

In *Ministry of Defence* v. *Radclyffe* [2009] EWCA Civ 635 an army officer was injured whilst jumping off a high bridge during an adventure training exercise with his unit. He did so partly because of pressure put on him by his commanding officer. The Court of Appeal held the Ministry of Defence liable for his injuries, but also held that, in bowing to pressure, he had still exercised some discretion and was partially to blame for his own injuries. His damages were therefore reduced by 40 per cent.

Remember that with seatbelts (and helmets) the defendant still has to prove that not wearing it *caused* part of the claimant's damage. For example, in *Smith* v. *Finch* [2009] EWHC 53 a cyclist suffered head injuries when a speeding motorcyclist crashed into him. It was shown that he would have suffered the same severe head injuries even if he had been wearing a cycling helmet, and therefore his failure to wear a helmet did not contribute to his injuries.

CORNERSTONE

Contributory negligence as a partial defence

Contributory negligence serves to reduce the amount of damages the claimant will receive by subtracting the proportion for which the defendant herself was found to be liable. It is therefore a partial defence, because it does not defeat the claim entirely. Because the defence concerns negligence on the part of the defendant, the test is, as in the tort of negligence, objective. The court judges the defendant against what a reasonable person would have done in her situation. Contrast this to the objective nature of the defence of *volenti*, above.

It is important to remember that, although very relevant to it and therefore meriting this chapter's discussion in relation specifically to negligence, neither *volenti* nor contributory negligence are defences solely to negligence. *Volenti*, for example, could also be raised as a defence to battery (trespass to the person) when you sign a medical consent form before surgery.

As to contributory negligence, a better description may have been 'contributory fault' because the courts examine to what extent the claimant's fault contributed to her injury – and fault is an element of other torts apart from negligence. According to section 4 of the Law Reform (Contributory Negligence) Act 1945, fault means:

'. . . negligence, breach of statutory duty or other act or omission which gives rise to liability in tort or would, apart from this Act, give rise to the defence of contributory negligence.'

Therefore, contributory negligence can be raised in, for example, negligence, actions under the rule in *Rylands* v. *Fletcher* (1868) LR 3 HL 330, trespass to the person and nuisance.

ILLEGALITY (*EX TURPI CAUSA NON ORITUR ACTIO*)

Loosely translated, the defence of *ex turpi causa non oritur actio* says that 'from a bad cause, no action can arise', or that no court action can be sustained on the basis of an illegal action. Therefore, if the defendant can prove that the claimant's damage was caused during the commission of something illegal, this could serve as a defence against a claim of negligence.

CORNERSTONE

Illegality as a policy-based defence

The idea behind this defence is that it would be contrary to public policy to allow a claim for damage to someone who was injured whilst knowingly committing a crime. Whether this defence is a full or a partial defence depends on the nature of the illegal act. Because this entails a judgement of moral blameworthiness, a decision on this necessarily reflects policy at the relevant time. The courts are not very consistent in the application of illegality, but as a rule of thumb they seem to be more willing to allow the defence the more serious the illegality, and *vice versa*.

An example of a successful defence of illegality to a claim in negligence can be found in *Grey* v. *Thames Trains Ltd* [2009] 1 AC 1339. The claimant suffered a personality change as a result of a train crash and, a couple of years later, stabbed a man to death. He was found guilty of manslaughter and was ordered to be detained in a hospital under section 37 of the Mental Health Act 1983. He sued the defendants in negligence, amongst others for loss of earnings suffered both before and after his incarceration for the manslaughter. The defendants admitted liability in negligence but raised a defence of illegality against the losses suffered *after* the claimant was found guilty of the crime and incarcerated for it as punishment. The House of Lords agreed and barred his claim for loss of earnings suffered after the killing. The loss of earnings after his arrest is part of the lawful sentence imposed on him for manslaughter. Lord Hoffmann said (at 51):

'. . . it is offensive to public notions of the fair distribution of resources that a claimant should be compensated (usually out of public funds) for the consequences of his own criminal conduct.'

Put another way: if the claimant was allowed to claim for loss of earnings while incarcerated, this would at the least nullify the punishment (part of the aim of incarceration is precisely to take away the prisoner's earning power), and at the worst allow him to profit from his own illegal action.

INTERSECTION

Illegality can also be raised against other torts, such as trespass.

CHAPTER 5 Negligence: defences

KEY POINTS

- The main defences against a claim in negligence are consent (*volenti non fit injuria*), contributory negligence, and to a lesser extent, illegality.
- With the defence of *volenti non fit injuria* the defendant alleges that the claimant consented to the risk of damage and cannot therefore subsequently claim when the damage actually happened. If successful, it is a full defence and defeats the claimant's claim.
- With contributory negligence the defendant alleges that the claimant was also at fault and therefore partially caused her own damage, thus necessitating that her damages be reduced to reflect the degree of her own blameworthiness. As damages are reduced but nevertheless granted, contributory negligence serves as a *partial* defence.
- Illegality can be raised as a defence if the claimant's action is based on facts that constitute the commission of a crime.

CORE CASES AND STATUTES

Case	About	Importance
Stermer v. *Lawson* [1977] 5 WWR 628	Inexperienced rider borrowing a motorbike held not to be *volens*	A person who does not fully understand the risk he is consenting to cannot be taken as having consented to it.
Morris v. *Murray* [1991] 2 QB 6	Claimant voluntarily accompanied drunken pilot	A person who knowingly and willingly undertakes a risk will be barred by the defence of *volenti* to claim in negligence.
Smith v. *Charles Baker & Sons* [1891] AC 325	Employee injured at work after having been aware of the risk for some time	Courts are unlikely to find that continuing to work despite being aware of the risk of injury would constitute implied or tacit consent to the resultant injury.
Dann v. *Hamilton* [1939] 1 KB 509	Passenger injured due to negligence of drunk driver held not to have been *volens*	If *volenti* succeeded as a defence by drunk drivers against liability for injuries they caused to passengers who got in the car knowing the driver was drunk, it would mean that the drunk driver would be protected from suit by the mere fact that he got drunk before committing the act of negligence, whereas, if he had committed the same act when sober, he would have been liable. Therefore, courts are reluctant to hold passengers *volens*.

Case	About	Importance
Froom v. *Butcher* [1976] QB 286	Damages awarded to claimant injured in motor vehicle accident reduced by 20 per cent due to him nor wearing a seatbelt	Illustrates the operation of contributory negligence as a defence. A causal connection between the claimant not wearing his seatbelt and the injuries he sustained was shown. Note that the causation refers to the damage and if causation is not shown, the mere fact of not wearing a seatbelt will not be sufficient to reduce damages.

Statute	About	Importance
Road Traffic Act 1988, s. 149(3)	*Volenti* is not available where a driver's passenger sues her in circumstances where insurance is compulsory	If the passenger willingly accepted the risk of the driver being negligent, that does not absolve the driver of liability.
Law Reform (Contributory Negligence) Act 1945, s. 1(1)	Damages reduced in proportion to claimant's own fault	The claimant's blameworthiness is taken into account when determining how much damage she could recover.

FURTHER READING

Law Commission Report 160 (2001) *The Illegality Defence in Tort*. London: The Stationery Office
The Law Commission finished its examination of the defence of illegality in general in 2010. This report deals with their findings on tort. Reading this in conjunction with cases that have been decided since 2001 will help you understand the defence in more detail.

Cooke, J. (2013) *Law of Tort*. Harlow: Pearson
Chapter 9 in this text by Professor Cooke provides a particularly lucid and interesting discussion of the defences to a claim in negligence.

Davies, P. (2010) The illegality defence: turning back the clock? *Conv* 4, p. 282
This article discusses recent attempts (initiated by the Law Commission) to reform the defence of illegality and reading it will help you understand the context of this evolving defence.

Jaffey, A.J.E. (1985) *Volenti non fit injuria*. CLJ 44, p. 87
This is an older article but gives a good overview of the concept of consent.

Porter, M. (2009) Blame the victim. *NLJ* 159, p. 337
This article deals with the defence of contributory negligence and looks at it specifically in the light of cyclists and the wearing of helmets.

Tan, K. (1995) *Volenti non fit injuria*: an alternative framework. *Tort L Rev* 3, p. 208
Carol Tan here suggested refashioning the defence of *volenti* as an assessment of the claimant's conduct. She suggests that issues such as whether the claimant was a rescuer, or committing a crime or trespassing, for example, should be taken into account in this defence. Reading this article will deepen your understanding of the policy issues surrounding this defence.

PART 2
Trespass

PART 2
Trespass

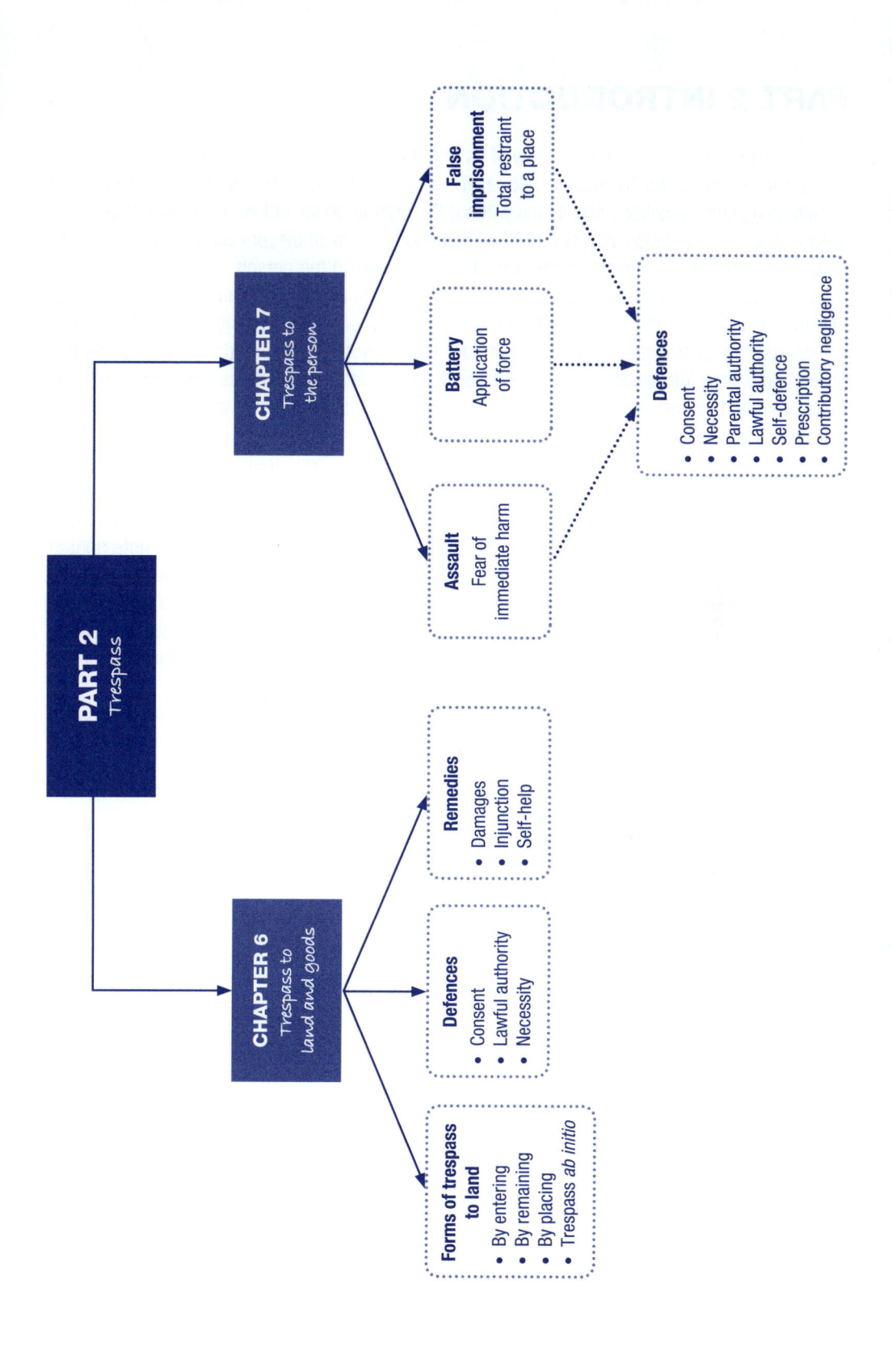

CHAPTER 6
Trespass to land and goods

Forms of trespass to land
- By entering
- By remaining
- By placing
- Trespass *ab initio*

Defences
- Consent
- Lawful authority
- Necessity

Remedies
- Damages
- Injunction
- Self-help

CHAPTER 7
Trespass to the person

Assault
Fear of immediate harm

Battery
Application of force

False imprisonment
Total restraint to a place

Defences
- Consent
- Necessity
- Parental authority
- Lawful authority
- Self-defence
- Prescription
- Contributory negligence

PART 2 INTRODUCTION

When we hear the word 'trespass', many of us first think about somebody entering property with no right to be there. But trespass in the legal sense means more than that. Yes, it includes a person going onto somebody else's land without the right to do so, but some would be surprised to hear that it also includes liability for hitting somebody, for example, or even threatening somebody with words alone. The latter are examples of trespass to the person.

In this part, we look at the two main groups of trespass, namely trespass to land and goods, and then trespass to the person. At first glance it may be a bit puzzling why both of these are termed 'trespass' until you think about your bodily integrity as something worth protecting against unwanted intrusions – it could even be argued that this is perhaps the primary interest to be protected in law! When somebody touches you without your leave, or threatens you with violence, they are trespassing onto your bodily integrity. The same goes for property: if somebody comes into your house uninvited, or overstays her welcome, she is trespassing; or if somebody takes your book without your leave, she is trespassing with regard to your property.

There are certain elements that are common to all the kinds of trespass – all of them consist of a voluntary action, which makes up the *intention* (i.e. fault) part of the tort. Take note right at the start that the intention is about the *action*, not necessarily the tort. So you could innocently walk onto a piece of land believing you had a right to be there, whereas in fact you do not – and that would still constitute trespass, as long as you walked onto the land of your own accord. If, however, you were thrown onto the land, you did not enter it voluntarily and you therefore did not commit trespass.

In Chapter 6 we look at trespass to land and goods, and in Chapter 7 we examine trespass to the person, which in turn consists of assault, battery and false imprisonment.

CHAPTER 6
Trespass to land and goods

BLUEPRINT
Trespass to land and goods

KEY QUESTIONS

LEGISLATION
- Criminal Law Act 1977
- Torts (Interference with Goods) Act 1977

CONTEXT
- Protects <u>possession</u> therefore actionable *per se* (without having to prove damage)

CONCEPTS
- Trespass to land
- Trespass to goods
- Actionable *per se*

- Is trespass *ab initio* an outdated doctrine?

- What is meant by trespass?
- What interests are protected by the tort of trespass to land and goods?

CASES

- *Smith* v. *Stone* [1647]
- *Bocardo SA* v. *Star Energy* [2010]
- *The Calgarth* [1927]
- *Six Carpenters' Case* [1610]
- *Hurst* v. *Picture Theatres Ltd* [1915]

REFORM

- Unclear whether <u>negligent</u> trespass recognised.

SPECIAL CHARACTERISTICS

- Intention needed but only for *action* constituting the tort
- Trespass is actionable *per se*
- Protects *possession* of land/goods

CRITICAL ISSUES

Setting the scene

When we think of **trespass**, the image that comes to mind is that of a person illegally entering private property. This certainly is a form of trespass but it is not the whole picture.

In fact, trespass takes three forms:

1. trespass to the person;
2. trespass to land; and
3. trespass to goods.

Thus, trespass aims to protect people against interference with their bodily integrity and their property, fixed or movable. Think of trespass as helping yourself to what you do not lawfully have a right to: access to somebody else's land, or property, or person. It is also useful to think in examples: if I enter your house without your permission, or if I 'borrow' your book without your permission, I am committing trespass. Similarly, trespass could be directed at a person's bodily integrity: if I threaten you, or touch you without your permission, or keep you captive, I am committing trespass. These instances of trespass to the person are known as **assault**, **battery** and **false imprisonment**.

Of course, there are differences between the types of trespass, most notably the kinds of interests protected, but there are also significant similarities. All three have the same basic characteristics: for all forms of trespass, the *action* making up the trespass must be committed intentionally or deliberately. Note that we refer to the *action* and not the tort itself – it is possible to commit trespass unintentionally. For example, if you walk onto somebody's land erroneously believing that you have the right to do so, you will be committing trespass just the same, irrespective of your belief, because you *walked* onto the land *intentionally*. The defendant will be liable for all the consequences of her actions, whether or not they are foreseeable.

Trespass is actionable *per se*, which of course means that the claimant does not have to prove damages.

THE MEANING OF TRESPASS

We saw above that trespass is the result of an intentional action – and not an intention to commit trespass, necessarily.

CORNERSTONE

Element of intention

To constitute trespass it would be enough that you are on somebody's land intentionally, and it would not be a defence that you (mistakenly) thought that you had a right to be there.

In *Conway* v. *George Wimpey & Co Ltd* [1951] 2 KB 266 a lorry driver was told by his employer to convey only other employees of the company. Nevertheless he gave a lift to the claimant, who was not employed by the defendant. The court held that the claimant, on getting on the lorry, was *prima facie* a trespasser and it was immaterial whether the claimant actually knew he was one or not.

We can think of this as 'innocent trespass'.

Voluntary action

Trespass is the direct result of someone's own voluntary action.

CORNERSTONE

Smith v. Stone (1647) Sty 65

The defendant was carried onto the claimant's land by force and was held not to have committed trespass.

Further, if crossing over the boundary of someone's property is the result of your own action, but an *indirect* result, you will not be liable in trespass. For example, if you lose control of your car and it leaves the road and enters another's land, this will likely be seen as an indirect consequence of your action and therefore not trespass. (You may, however, be held liable in negligence.)

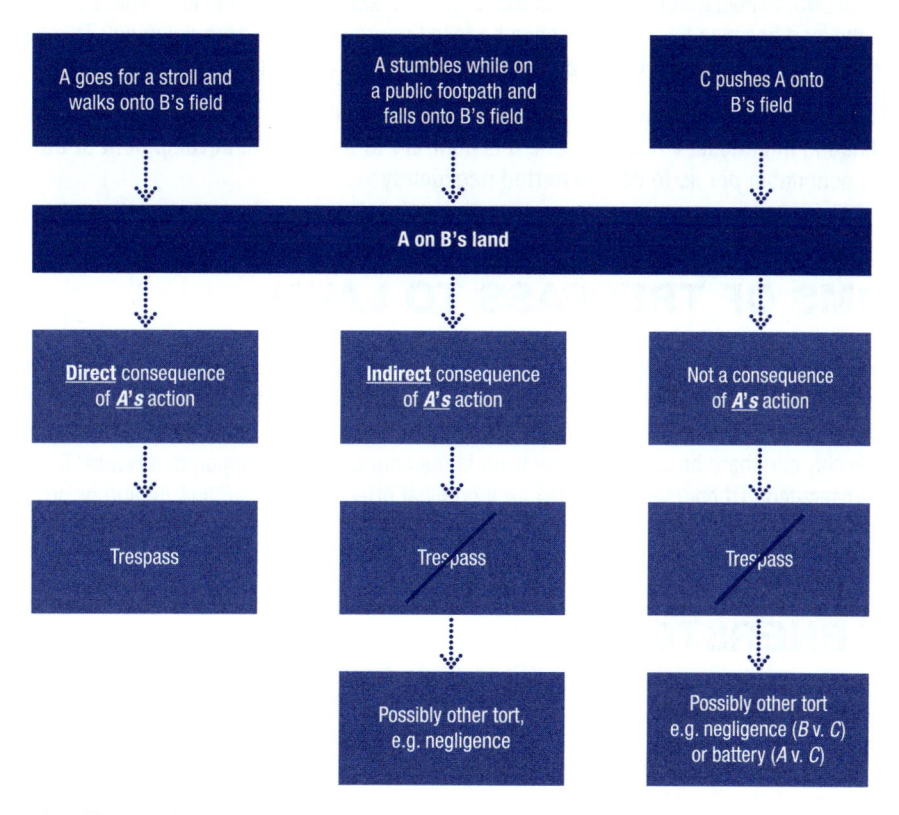

Figure 6.1 Trespass by entering land

CORNERSTONE

Actionable *per se*

The tort of trespass protects your interest in not having your land (or goods, or your body) interfered with by others. As such its aim is not compensatory, and that is why you can succeed with an action in trespass without having to prove that you have suffered actual damage.

Contrast this to negligence, where the aim *is* compensatory, and where you will have to prove damages. Of course, if you have in fact suffered damage because of trespass, you can recover it in your claim.

The question arose whether trespass could be committed negligently. From cases dealing with trespass to the person the answer seems to be no (see *Letang* v. *Cooper* [1965] 1 QB 232 (Chapter 7)). However, the decision in *League against Cruel Sports* v. *Scott* [1986] QB 240 suggests it can. In this case hounds from a hunt entered land belonging to the claimant who, of course, does not approve of such hunting and sued in trespass. The court held that in the case where animals stray onto land their owner will be held liable if he or she intended them to enter the claimant's land. (This is uncontroversial and we will get back to this below when we look at liability for straying animals.) But then the judge went on (at 253) to hold that the master of the hunt could *also* be held liable in trespass if the hounds entered the land because '. . . by negligence he failed to prevent them from doing so'. This has been criticised widely. For example, Giliker and Beckwith (2008: 373–4) write:

> 'it is submitted that a consistent approach should be adopted to trespass, which should be confined to intentional voluntary acts. It is contrary to the general development of the law for a tort actionable *per se* to be committed negligently.'

FORMS OF TRESPASS TO LAND

In most instances trespass is only a tort. There are very few exceptions where it can also be a crime, for example under section 4 of the Vagrancy Act 1824, section 9 of the Theft Act 1968 and sections 6–10 of the Criminal Law Act 1977, offences relating to entering and remaining on property. In these instances only can there be said to be any truth in the commonly seen notice that reads 'Trespassers will be prosecuted'! Of course, it can also be a criminal offence to do damage to land or property on the land *whilst* trespassing.

CORNERSTONE

Trespass to land

Interference with possession of land can take place by entry to land, by unlawfully remaining on land or by putting objects on land.

Trespass by entering land

Physical entry

This is the most common form of trespass: the defendant enters the land of the claimant. First, let's look at what we understand by 'land'. More specifically, does land include airspace above, and substrata below, the surface of the land? Both questions are answered in the affirmative, although in *Bernstein* v. *Skyviews and General Ltd* [1978] QB 479, where a complaint was made about aerial photos taken of land, the court held that the right to ownership of airspace was limited to a height necessary for the ordinary use and enjoyment of the land. The Civil Aviation Act 1982 further provides that civil aircraft commit no trespass where they fly at a reasonable height.

CORNERSTONE

Bocardo SA v. Star Energy UK Onshore Ltd and another [2010] UKSC 35

The defendant drilled for oil below ground on neighbouring land to the claimant's, but then drilled diagonally under the substrata of the claimant's land and extracted oil worth millions of pounds. The claimant won his case in trespass and the Supreme Court held that the title of a freehold owner extended down through the strata beneath the surface of his land.

Even though the claimant in *Bocardo* won its case in trespass, and although the defendant made millions of pounds in profits due to its trespass, the court indicated that the claimant was only entitled to an almost laughably small amount of damages (a figure of £82.50 was given at Para. 92).

> The reason for the small amount of damages awarded in *Bocardo* is because when it came to this kind of operation (drilling for and extracting oil) the Mines (Working Facilities and Support) Act 1966 applies, which operates on the principle of compulsory purchase. The compulsory acquisition of ancillary rights over or under land operated here to deny the claimant from being able to claim for the true worth of a valuable oilfield partially sited beneath its land. Also see the assessment of damages in cases of trespass, which we look at below.

The tort of trespass to land includes abusing the right of entry.

In *Hickman* v. *Maisey* [1900] 1 QB 752 a racing tout used a highway crossing the claimant's land to spy on the form of a racehorse. The court held that this was trespass.

However, the House of Lords more recently held that lawful use of the highway also included reasonable and usual activities consistent with the purpose of passage: in *DPP* v. *Jones* [1999] 2 All ER 257 it was held that a protest that took place on the grass verge of the highway next to Stonehenge was a reasonable use of the highway provided the highway was not blocked or a nuisance committed, and therefore it did not amount to trespass. Contrast this to the Court of Appeal's decision in *City of London Corpn* v. *Samede and others* [2012] EWCA Civ 160 that the 'Occupy London' camp set up in front of St Paul's Cathedral in London was not a reasonable use of the highway.

Trespass by remaining on land after permission is revoked

Trespass is also committed by remaining on land after having been asked to leave. The defendant must have been allowed a reasonable time for leaving. In *Robson* v. *Hallett* [1967] 2 All ER 407 a police officer was invited into the defendant's house, but then asked to leave. He was on his way out when the defendants assaulted him. The court held that when a licence to enter was revoked, as a result of which the licensee had to leave, a reasonable time must be given to him in which to do it.

Trespass by exceeding the extent to which permission is granted

Trespass is also committed by remaining on land after the right of entry has ceased.

It is also trespass when, after being given permission to enter onto land for a certain purpose, the defendant goes beyond that purpose.

For example, a guest on private property who is permitted to walk and do bird-watching on her neighbour's land, would be committing trespass if she then proceeds to gather berries and mushrooms – she would be abusing her licence to be there.

CORNERSTONE

The Calgarth [1927] P 93

Scrutton LJ illustrated the concept of trespass by exceeding permission granted very memorably in this case (at 110):

> 'When you invite a person into your house to use the staircase, you do not invite him to slide down the bannisters, you invite him to use the staircase in the ordinary way in which it is used.'

(This dealt with damage to a canal vessel. It was held that the right to navigate the relevant channel was confined to vessels paying dues to enter or leave the canal, and that the right of navigation did not include a right to ground on the bank.)

Trespass by placing or projecting objects onto land

It is trespass if you place something on somebody else's land, and it continues to be trespass for as long as it remains on the land. It is also sufficient if you *caused* such thing to move onto someone else's land, always provided that it amounted to 'direct' interference.

In *Eaton Mansions (Westminster) Ltd* v. *Stinger Compania de Inversion SA* [2011] EWCA Civ 607 a tenant installed air conditioning units onto the roof of his landlord's building without the latter's consent and was held to have committed trespass.

Trespass *ab initio*

Trespass *ab initio* means that where a defendant has a legal right to enter land and then acts outside the authority granted she becomes a trespasser from the moment she entered the land (i.e. 'from the start'/*ab initio*).

Trespass *ab initio* covers only those defendants who commit positive acts of abuse. It does not cover omissions. Thus, in the following case the doctrine was not applied.

Forms of trespass to land

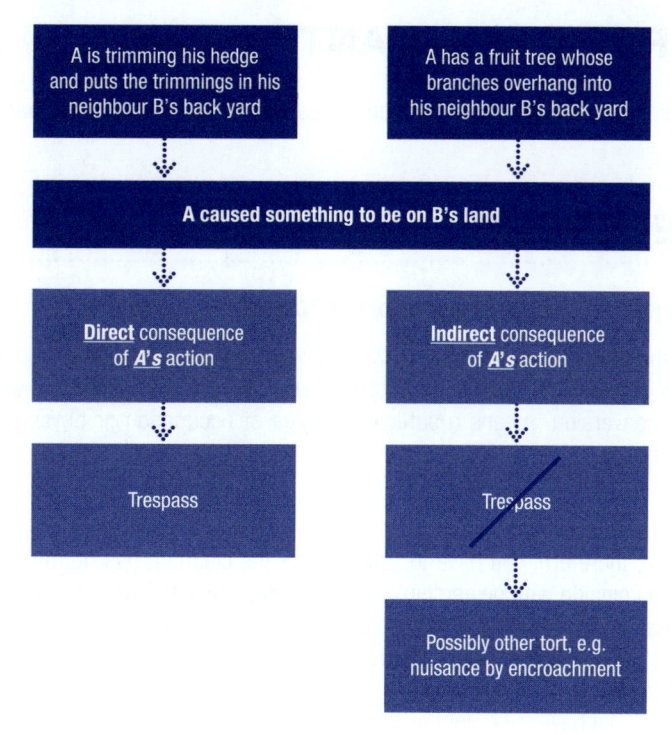

Figure 6.2 Trespass by causing objects to be on land

CORNERSTONE

Six Carpenters' Case (1610) 8 Co Rep 146a

The carpenters in this case ate and drank in an inn and then left without paying, but they were not liable as trespassers *ab initio* since their abuse was simply an omission – the failure to pay.

The doctrine also does not seem to apply to cases of partial abuse: *Elias* v. *Passmore* [1934] 2 KB 164. In *Chic Fashions (West Wales) Ltd* v. *Jones* [1968] 2 QB 299 (CA), Lord Denning expressed the view that the doctrine of trespass *ab initio* was outdated, but he subsequently applied the doctrine in *Cinnamond* v. *BAA* [1980] 1 WLR 582.

> **REFLECTION**
>
> Is trespass *ab initio* an outdated doctrine? It is a generally accepted legal principle that the lawfulness of an act should be judged by the circumstances prevailing *at the time of that act* and *not by later events*. Thus, in effect, later events cannot make unlawful an act that was lawful at the time of commission. Trespass *ab initio* can be criticised because it seems to offend against this principle.
>
> On the other hand, consider the following: one of the defences against trespass includes justification by law, of which the most obvious example is the police entering premises with a search warrant. If such a warrant is abused, the doctrine of trespass *ab initio* can be very useful for protection of one's person, goods and land against abuse of official power.

TITLE OF THE CLAIMANT

Trespass to land aims to protect against direct and unjustifiable interference with a person's possession of land.

CORNERSTONE

Trespass protects *possession of land*

Note that it is the person *in possession of the land* who has the right to sue. In *JA Pye (Oxford) Ltd v. Graham and another* [2002] UKHL 30 Lord Browne-Wilkinson said that the word 'possession' in trespass or conversion, means a sufficient degree of occupation or physical control with an intention to possess.

In each instance, therefore, you have to ask whether the claimant has rightful possession of the land. Often this will coincide with ownership, but not always. The key is to have exclusive possession. Thus, if I let a house to you but invade your privacy there, you (in possession) may well be entitled to sue me (the owner) in trespass: *Drane* v. *Evangelou* [1978] 1 WLR 455 (CA).

For that reason a tenant would also have rightful possession of land (and be able to sue in trespass) whereas a lodger will not have such right to sue. Mere use of the land is insufficient. In the usual case of landlord and tenant, it is the tenant who will have the right to sue in trespass.

Generally, possession of a master's property by a servant is not sufficient title as against the master. Neither does a guest in a hotel room, a lodger in a house or a spectator in a theatre have sufficient possession to sustain an action.

REFLECTION

Should squatters be able to sue in trespass? It used to be settled law that 'possession' did not have to be *legal* possession. The law protected even wrongful possession. Thus squatters could sue for trespass against all but the true owner and those acting on the true owner's behalf. Squatters could also acquire title by adverse possession: Limitation Act 1980, section 15.

However, from September 2012, section 144 of the Legal Aid, Sentencing and Punishment of Offenders Act 2012 provides that it is now a criminal offence to squat in a residential building. For such liability the Act requires that the person enters a residential building intending to live there as a trespasser, having entered it as a trespasser. The Act also requires that she knew or ought to have known that she is a trespasser. The newly created crime of squatting in a residential building is punishable by up to six months' jail and fines up to £5,000.

Walsh (2013: 28) points out that this offence has, in addition to the provisions of the Land Registration Act 2002, made it harder for squatters to obtain title by adverse possession of a residential property. Indeed, it is questionable whether the doctrine of adverse possession survives this legislation (at least, as far as residential property is concerned). The reason is because it seems clear that any person who now makes an application to the Land Registry to be registered as proprietor of a residential building (on the basis of adverse possession) may be admitting, in writing, that she has committed a criminal offence. Even if a person is willing to risk going to jail in order to obtain title to property, we need to keep the *ex turpi causa* doctrine in mind – will the courts allow such a person to benefit from their own illegal act?

DEFENCES

The main defences to the tort of trespass to land are:

- consent (which includes contractual licence);
- lawful authority; and
- necessity.

Consent

A person who has permission to enter is not a trespasser. Consent can be express or implied, and can also be obtained in the form of a licence. Examples include payment of an entry fee to sporting events or purchase of a cinema ticket. However, a licensee can become a trespasser if she exceeds the licence or if it is revoked. On the other hand, the court may find that the licence was revoked unreasonably and that may militate against a finding of trespass. There are several factors which a court could take into account to decide whether a licence was revoked reasonably: whether the licence was a bare licence (i.e. in the absence of consideration) or a contractual licence (such as buying a ticket), whether there are public law limits on the revocation of a licence (where public bodies granted the licence), whether there is a contract with terms to be observed, etc.

CORNERSTONE

Hurst v. Picture Theatres Ltd [1915] 1 KB 1

The claimant had purchased a ticket for a seat at a cinema show. It was mistakenly believed that he had not paid and he was forcibly turned out of his seat. It was held that he had a right to stay and see the film, provided that he behaved properly and complied with the rules of the management, and that the licence granted by the sale of the ticket included a contract not to revoke the licence arbitrarily during the performance.

Lawful authority

Otherwise tortious trespass could be justified by law: for example, the police may enter and search premises under specific conditions such as, for example, under sections 15–19 of the Police and Criminal Evidence Act 1984. Remember, though, that abuse of such legal authority will make the act a trespass *ab initio*. (See the discussion of this doctrine above.)

Other examples of justification by law, or lawful authority include using a public right of way or a private right of way or an easement over somebody else's property; or a person may be entitled to a profit from the land (the owner of a profit is entitled to take away some produce or substance from the land). Rights of entry are also conferred by operation of law, either under the common law (e.g. abatement of a nuisance) or under statute (e.g. the Rights of Entry (Gas and Electricity) Boards Act 1954).

Necessity

Necessity covers action taken in an emergency to deal with a genuinely perceived danger. In *Rigby* v. *Chief Constable of Northamptonshire* [1985] 2 All ER 985 the claimant's shop was burnt out when police fired a canister of CS gas into the building to force out a dangerous psychopath who had broken into it. The claimant sued the police in trespass (amongst others). The court held that the defence of necessity is available in an action for trespass provided there is no negligence on the part of the defendant in creating or contributing to the necessity. On the facts the court held that the only cause of action open to the police had been to fire the canister and their defence of necessity therefore succeeded. (However, the court did find the police liable in negligence, as they had fired the CS gas knowing that they had no fire-fighting equipment with them.)

The courts are reluctant to extend the defence of necessity too far: when squatters raised this defence against an action of trespass the Court of Appeal rejected it in *Southwark London Borough Council* v. *Williams* [1971] Ch 734. (See also the Reflection box discussion of adverse possession and the criminalisation of residential squatting, above.)

REMEDIES

Damages

Damages are awarded for physical damage to land or for sums lost because of being out of possession (the latter is called *mesne profits*). In *Inverugie Investments Ltd* v. *Hackett* [1995] 1 WLR 713 the Privy Council held that that a person who let out goods on hire, or the landlord of residential property, was entitled to recover damages from a trespasser who had wrongfully used his property, whether or not she could show that she would have let the property to anybody else or used it herself.

In *Enfield LBC* v. *Outdoor Plus Ltd* [2012] EWCA Civ 608 the defendants trespassed by placing steel supports to an advertising hoarding on the claimant's land. The court had to ascertain the value of the benefit of that trespass in order to assess the correct level of damages. The court of first instance awarded only *nominal* damages to the claimant. The Court of Appeal overturned this decision and held that the court had to ascertain the value of the benefit of that trespass to a reasonable person in the position of the claimant. The court had the benefit of the expert evidence as to what the hypothetical licence fees would have been, and awarded damages to the claimant on that calculation.

Distress damages feasant

Where something belonging to/under the control of the defendant is unlawfully on the claimant's land and has caused actual damage, the claimant may retain the thing until the damage has been paid for. For example, a football kicked through a window can be retained until the window is paid for.

Injunctions

You may obtain an injunction to stop the trespass being continued or being repeated. Note that the trespass must either be of a continuing nature, or be actually threatened.

Self-help: re-entry

A person who is entitled to possession can enter or re-enter the premises.

CORNERSTONE

Criminal Law Act 1977

Section 6 of this Act makes it a crime to use or threaten violence for the purpose of securing entry to land occupied by another, except for the displaced resident.

Peaceable re-entry is lawful and reasonable force may be used to evict a trespasser.

Ejectment

The action for recovery of land or 'ejectment' is an action to recover possession of land. The action can be brought against a person without a better legal title. But the claimant needs to be aware of the Protection from Eviction Act 1977 and the Protection from Harassment Act 1997.

TRESPASS TO GOODS

CORNERSTONE

Trespass to Goods and the Torts (Interference with Goods) Act 1977

This form of trespass deals with the intentional and direct interference with the possession of goods. The Torts (Interference with Goods) Act 1977 now largely covers this tort.

As in trespass to land, it is possession rather than ownership that is protected. In common with all other forms of trespass, trespass to goods must be direct and intentional and is actionable *per se.*

Conversion

Conversion is another form of trespass to goods and can be described as wilfully dealing with another's property in a way which amounts to a denial of her right over it, or an assertion of a right inconsistent with her right, by wrongfully taking, detaining or disposing of the property. Because the tort does not have an overarching common definition, it is best understood by looking at examples.

APPLICATION

Conversion would take place where:
- D takes possession of goods that are in another's possession, with the intention of keeping them;
- D refuses to hand over goods in her possession that someone else has an immediate right to possess after they had been demanded from her;
- D causes goods to which C has an immediate right to possession, to be delivered into the hands of A;
- D uses, or destroys, goods to which A has an immediate right of possession.

Defences to trespass to goods and to conversion

The defences are similar to those mentioned for other torts of trespass: consent, necessity and lawful authority. As to necessity, if the trespass in question was necessary for the preservation and protection of the goods and reasonable steps were taken to do this, the defendant has a good defence. In *Kirk* v. *Gregory* (1876) 1 Ex D 55 a near relative of a deceased person immediately after the death, removed some jewellery of the deceased from one room to another. The defence of necessity failed because, although the defendant had acted in good faith, it was not proved that the interference was reasonably necessary.

As to lawful authority, note the powers of the police to search for and seize property without liability: see sections 8–22 of the Police and Criminal Evidence Act 1984.

There is also the defence of *jus tertii* (right of a third person): see section 8 of the Torts (Interference with Goods) Act 1977, which provides that the defendant in an action for wrongful interference shall be entitled to show that a third party has a better right to the goods than the claimant. In this way a defendant can protect herself against double liability by identifying who had the interest protected by the tort at the relevant time.

Remedies

The claimant may, upon succeeding with a claim in trespass to goods or conversion retake the goods or claim damages for the value of the goods and any consequential loss which is not too remote. Where the defendant is still in possession of the goods, delivery of the goods with additional damages is also possible (Torts (Interference with Goods) Act 1977, s. 3).

KEY POINTS

- Trespass can be defined as the direct, intentional and unjustified interference with somebody else's possession of land, goods or bodily integrity.
- Trespass takes three forms: to land, to goods and to the person.
- Trespass differs from negligence as it is an intentional tort, although intention relates only to the action constituting the trespass, and not the mental element of consciously committing a tort.
- Trespass differs from nuisance in that it is a direct as opposed to an indirect action.
- Because trespass protects lawful possession of land, owners and other lawful occupiers such as tenants may sue, whereas lodgers, for example, may not.
- Trespass to goods protects against unlawful interference with the possession of goods. Conversion is a type of trespass to goods.
- Defences to trespass to land include consent, licence, lawful authority and necessity.
- Remedies include damages, ejectment, re-entry and injunctions.

CORE CASES AND STATUTES

Case	About	Importance
Smith v. Stone (1647) Sty 65	Not trespass if defendant carried onto claimant's land by force	Trespass is the consequence of one's own action.
Conway v. George Wimpey & Co Ltd [1951] 2 KB 266	Innocent trespass	The intent element in trespass relates to intention to do the action constituting trespass, not necessarily intent to commit trespass.
Bernstein v. Skyviews and General Ltd [1978] QB 479	Whether 'land' for the purpose of trespass includes airspace above the surface	Interest in undisturbed possession of land for purpose of trespass limited to a height necessary for the ordinary use and enjoyment of the land.
Bocardo SA v. Star Energy UK Onshore Ltd and another [2010] UKSC 35	Whether 'land' for the purpose of trespass includes substrata below the surface	Title of a freehold owner extended down through the strata beneath the surface of his land and protected by tort of trespass.
Hickman v. Maisey [1900] 1 QB 752	Racing tout using public highway to spy on racehorse	If right of entry abused it could amount to trespass.
Hurst v. Picture Theatres Ltd [1915] 1 KB	Ejectment of ticket holder	Licence granted by the sale of the ticket included a contract not to revoke the licence arbitrarily.

Statute	About	Importance
Theft Act 1968, s. 9 and Vagrancy Act 1824, s. 4	Offences relating to entering and remaining on property	In very limited circumstances a tort may also constitute a crime.
Torts (Interference with Goods) Act 1977	Trespass to goods	Intentional and direct interference with the possession of goods.

FURTHER READING

Davies, K. (2010) Subterranean trespassers. *NLJ* 160(7442), p. 1597
This article reviews the Supreme Court ruling in *Bocardo SA v. Star Energy UK Onshore Ltd.*

Enfield LBC v. Outdoor Plus Ltd [2012] EWCA Civ 608
Reading this case will deepen your understanding of remedies to trespass. Here the Court of Appeal explains in detail how damages are calculated in cases involving trespass to land.

Giliker, P., and Beckwith, S. (2008) *Tort*. London: Sweet & Maxwell
Reading Chapter 11 in this text will deepen your understanding of trespass.

Walsh, M. (2013) Practitioner page: squatting and commercial leasehold property. *L&T Rev* 17(1), p. 28
This article examines the impact of the Legal Aid, Sentencing and Punishment of Offenders Act 2012 on adverse possession. Reading this article will help you to understand which interests are protected by the tort of trespass, but also to understand that several areas of law influence and interact with each other.

CHAPTER 7
Trespass to the person

BLUEPRINT
Trespass to the person

KEY QUESTIONS

LEGISLATION
- Limitation Act 1980, ss. 2 and 11
- Protection from Harassment Act 1997

CONTEXT
- Trespass to the person is one of longest established torts.
- It protects some of the most fundamental principles in the common law, such as bodily integrity.

CONCEPTS
- Trespass to the person consist of assault, battery and false imprisonment
- The rule in *Wilkinson* v. *Downton*
- Harassment

- Is the House of Lords' approval of 'kettling' justified?

- What is meant by trespass to the person?
- Which form of trespass protects freedom from interference with your person?
- Which form of trespass protects freedom of movement?

CASES

- *Letang* v. *Cooper* [1965]
- *Wilson* v. *Pringle* [1986]
- *A* v. *Hoare and others* [2008]
- *Bird* v. *Jones* [1845]
- *Wilkinson* v. *Downton* [1897]

REFORM

- The House of Lords recently overruled itself to place intentionally caused injury on same footing as negligence in *A* v. *Hoare*.

SPECIAL CHARACTERISTICS

- Assault requires fear of immediate harm (but no contact)
- Battery requires unconsensual contact
- False imprisonment is a total restraint of freedom to move from a certain place
- *Wilkinson* v. *Downton* is an intentional tort requiring harm
- Harassment is not a form of trespass to the person but developed out of it

CRITICAL ISSUES

Setting the scene

Your life, your bodily integrity, and your freedom are surely some of the most fundamental interests any person would expect to be protected in law. The torts collectively known as trespass to the person protect these interests, and the importance of these interests is reflected in the fact that trespass to the person is actionable *per se* (without having to prove damage). In other words, the slightest infringement of bodily integrity, even where no physical harm results, is actionable. It is also for this reason that, even though most personal injury claims nowadays reach the court via negligence actions, the torts of assault, battery, and false imprisonment are still very important. Negligence requires the claimant to prove damages, and although psychiatric injury is also now recognised as a possible actionable damage, we still need trespass to the person to protect interests that go beyond injury or damage to property.

Trespass itself takes three forms: trespass to land, to goods and to the person. These forms of trespass protect claimants against threatened or actual interference with their land, their property and their bodies. Unlike trespass to land and goods, trespass to the person overlaps with the criminal law to a large extent – but you should ensure that you do not confuse the civil law principles of the torts of assault, battery and false imprisonment, with their criminal law counterparts. The most fundamental difference lies in the focus of the two law systems: whereas the criminal law focuses on the perpetrator and her actions, and seek to punish her wrongful action, the civil law (and tort) focuses on the individual subject of the wrongdoing – and seeks to compensate her for damage suffered, or interests infringed.

All three forms of trespass (i.e. to goods, to land and to the person) have the same basic characteristics: there is an element of *intention*. For trespass to land, the *action* constituting the trespass must be committed intentionally or deliberately. (For assault, battery and false imprisonment the intention requirement goes further, as we will see below). Trespass also requires an element of *immediacy*. An action in assault will only succeed, for example, if there is an immediate threat – not if the threat consists of something that might happen in a couple of months' time.

Recently, harassment as a cause of action developed out of the courts' deliberations on trespass to the person. However, note from the start that harassment as such is *not* a form of trespass to the person.

INTRODUCTION

As stated above, personal injury cases (including **nervous shock**) are nowadays mostly based on the tort of negligence. But what about injury *intentionally* inflicted on another? In this instance the tort of trespass to the person comes into its own. Put another way, to succeed in a personal injury case, if the claimant can prove that the defendant intended the action complained of, she may succeed with trespass. If not, she may, alternatively, succeed with a claim in negligence. It is important to distinguish: actions for *intentional, direct* interference with the person lie in trespass, whilst actions for *indirect* interference with the person lie in negligence.

(Unintentional, non-negligent (direct or indirect) interference with a person is not actionable as this would be a plea of inevitable accident.) Let's look at a few cases that illustrate the difference.

Intention essential

In *Fowler* v. *Lanning* [1959] 1 QB 426 the claimant, in his action for trespass to the person, alleged simply that the defendant shot him and caused him to suffer personal injuries. The defendant raised a defence that, because the claimant's statement of claim did not indicate whether the shooting was intentional or negligent, it did not disclose a cause of action. The court agreed with the defendant. It explained that if the claimant could not prove intention on the part of the defendant (or at least something akin to reckless disregard, which we will come to later), the claimant could not succeed in trespass, but could alternatively attempt to hold the defendant liable in negligence. But in such an instance the onus of proving negligence still lay upon the claimant. The claimant failed to plead and give particulars of either intention or negligence and therefore his statement of claim disclosed no cause of action. (The court also held that there would be no trespass to the person if the injury to the claimant was caused unintentionally and without negligence on the defendant's part.)

CORNERSTONE

Letang v. *Cooper* [1965] 1 QB 232

In *Letang* v. *Cooper*, which you will remember we looked at in our discussion of negligence, the court had to decide whether a person who negligently drove over the claimant while she was sunbathing in a car park, could be held liable in trespass to the person or in negligence. (Or, indeed, whether there could be liability for both!) The claimant would have been time-barred (in terms of the limitation legislation then in operation) in a negligence action, and therefore attempted to hold the defendant liable in trespass (which has a longer limitation period). Lord Denning categorically stated that trespass requires intent, and that if the action was negligent, the correct cause of action would be negligence. The claimant's action therefore failed, because it was instituted too late.

The more recent case *Stubbings* v. *Webb* [1992] AC 498 confirmed that trespass to the person is a tort requiring intention and that if the action was unintentional, the correct cause of action therefore would be negligence. We look at this case in more detail below in our discussion of limitation periods.

From the above it should be clear that you can*not* be held liable *both* in negligence *and* in trespass to the person. The one precludes the other.

CORNERSTONE

Trespass to the person consists of assault, battery and false imprisonment

Trespass to the person protects against direct and intentional harm to personal dignity and bodily integrity and could be assault, battery or false imprisonment.

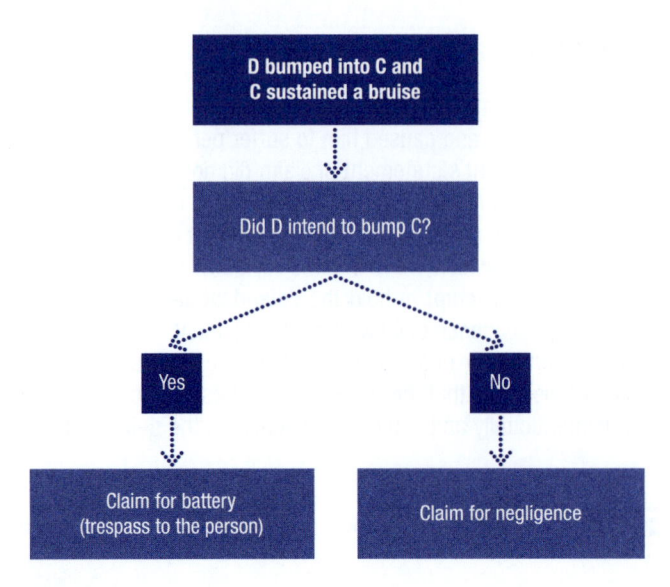

Figure 7.1 Intention

Take note

The Collins English Dictionary defines 'assault' as a violent attack, either physical or verbal. Do not make the mistake of thinking that this is also the legal meaning of assault. The legal meaning of assault precludes physical contact. In legal terms, if contact does follow a verbal threat, that contact would be battery. Do not get confused with assault and battery!

Let's now examine these in turn as each comprises a cause of action in itself, but remember that they may occur in the same set of facts, or together.

ASSAULT

In the case of assault the defendant *does not* make contact with the body of the claimant, but her words and/or actions cause the claimant to apprehend immediate contact.

Can words by themselves amount to assault? Remember for assault, the flip coin of words uttered must be the fear or apprehension induced. If threatening words are uttered but it is objectively clear that the words are empty threats, there is no assault. For example, in *Thomas* v. *National Union of Mineworkers* [1985] 2 All ER 1 striking workers shouted abuse at colleagues who continued to work. They were sued for assault. The court, applying an objective test, held that in this instance we could not talk of assault – the colleagues were at all times safe from attack as they were driven to work and the striking picketers were contained behind a police cordon. The same principle held in *Turberville* v. *Savage* (1669) 1 Mod Rep 3, where it was clear that a threat, backed up with the defendant placing his hand on his sword, amounted to an empty threat – the defendant himself said he would not do anything because the fact that the local assizes (court) were in session prevented him from further action.

More recently, in *Mbasogo* v. *Logo Ltd (No 1)* [2006] EWCA Civ 1370 it was held that mercenaries intercepted in Zimbabwe, on their way to stage an alleged coup against the claimant in Equatorial Guinea, could not be held liable in assault. The claimant would have had to prove that the defendants

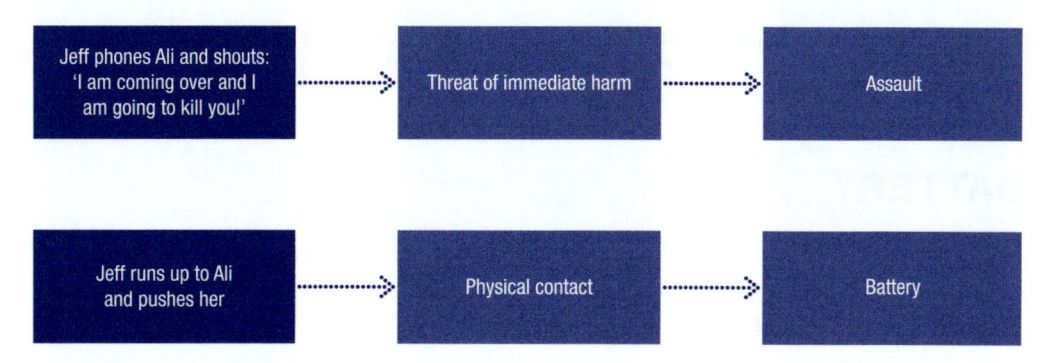

```
┌─────────────────────┐      ┌──────────────────────────┐      ┌──────────────┐
│ Jeff phones Ali     │      │                          │      │              │
│ and shouts:         │·····>│ Threat of immediate harm │·····>│   Assault    │
│ 'I am coming over   │      │                          │      │              │
│ and I am going to   │      │                          │      │              │
│ kill you!'          │      │                          │      │              │
└─────────────────────┘      └──────────────────────────┘      └──────────────┘

┌─────────────────────┐      ┌──────────────────────────┐      ┌──────────────┐
│ Jeff runs up to Ali │·····>│     Physical contact     │·····>│   Battery    │
│ and pushes her      │      │                          │      │              │
└─────────────────────┘      └──────────────────────────┘      └──────────────┘
```

Figure 7.2 Assault and battery

had the capacity to put into effect their intention to commit a battery and there was no suggestion that the advance group in Equatorial Guinea had the capacity to carry out an immediate attack. Neither was there an overt act causing the apprehension of immediate violence.

Is it correct, then, to say that 'fear of immediate harm' is an inherent requirement for assault? First, it is better to talk about 'apprehension' or even 'belief' rather than fear. Even if you do not feel fear but still think that some contact or violence will follow, it will be enough for assault. Nevertheless, fear induced in the claimant is a good indication of assault, provided that it was reasonable fear.

In *R* v. *Ireland* [1997] 4 All ER 225, where the defendant made silent telephone calls to the claimant, sometimes accompanied with heavy breathing, the court held that an assault might be committed by words or gestures alone, depending on the circumstances. As to immediacy, the court stressed that where the making of a silent telephone call caused fear of immediate and unlawful violence, the caller would be guilty of an assault.

So it seems that 'immediate harm' is open to some interpretation: there could be some lapse of time, and 'harm' is interpreted broadly by the courts. Also note that assault does not always need to be made in words.

CORNERSTONE

Assault requires fear of immediate harm (but no bodily contact)

Assault happens when one person by words or actions, occasions fear of immediate harm to another person.

So it seems to be enough if you are put in some uncertainty about when the attack may happen – it is enough if the reasonable fear is that you might be about to be attacked.

INTERSECTION

What about words or actions on their own, absent the apprehension of imminent harm? The courts for some time tried to make this actionable, but the enactment of the Protection from Harassment Act 1997 solved the problem of what amounted really to a gap in the law. We briefly look at the Harassment Act at the end of this chapter.

Where a defendant tried to hit someone but was prevented from doing so by a third party, the tort of assault was held to be committed: *Stephens* v. *Myers* (1830) 4 C&P 349.

BATTERY

Battery often follows assault, as this means that the threat in the assault is carried out.

Direct and intentional application of force

Sometimes, therefore, we can have both an assault as well as a battery in the same set of facts. The two do not always go hand in hand, of course. It is possible for someone to fall victim of a battery without any prior warning.

CORNERSTONE

Battery as non-consensual contact

Battery can be defined as the direct and intentional application of force to another person. It is the actual infliction of unlawful force on another person. 'Force' is open to interpretation as it applies to every form of bodily contact.

By 'unlawful' we mean without lawful justification. Lawful justification could include consent or necessity – we will look at these below when we look at defences.

The tort of battery applies to every form of bodily contact. Let's look at a few examples.

APPLICATION

The following are all examples of battery:

- D punches C in the stomach.
- D slaps C in the face.
- D kisses her assistant, C, against C's will.
- D pushes C out of his way.

The following are *not* battery:

- D operates on C at hospital.
- D and C are boys who play at swords with their rulers, and C gets hurt when D's ruler breaks and a shard hits him in his face.
- D falls onto C when the train they are both travelling in comes to a sudden stop.

It is clear that potentially almost any kind of touching can be seen as 'battery'. So how does the court decide where to draw the line? To succeed in a claim for battery you need to prove three elements:

1. force;
2. direct application; and
3. intent.

Once again, remember that this is a tort that is actionable *per se*, so you can claim even if you suffered no injury or damage.

Hostile intent

In *Collins* v. *Wilcock* [1984] 3 All ER 374 Lord Goff explained that there is a general exception for 'all physical contact which is generally acceptable in the ordinary conduct of daily life'. But what is, and what is not, acceptable in the ordinary conduct of life? Where do you draw the line? Is it, for example, acceptable to pinch a stranger's bottom? Is it assault if a schoolboy injures another whilst playing around? In *Cole* v. *Turner* (1704) 6 Mod Rep 149 Lord Holt attempted to draw the line between actionable batteries and those social contacts which are part of ordinary life by holding that 'the least touching of another *in anger* is a battery'.

While anger is a good marker for the necessary intent in battery, it clearly is not sufficient. What about unwelcome touching *not* conducted in anger? The Court of Appeal in *Wilson* v. *Pringle* [1986] 2 All ER 440 seemed to hold, on the basis of *Cole* v. *Turner*, that battery must be committed with 'hostile intent'.

CORNERSTONE

Wilson v. *Pringle* [1986] 2 All ER 440

The claimant and the defendant were 13-year-old schoolboys. The claimant alleged that the defendant had intentionally jumped on him, as a result of which he suffered serious injuries. He therefore sued the defendant in battery. The defendant denied liability, saying that he was merely playing around and that the injuries were the inadvertent result of ordinary horseplay.

The Court of Appeal held that battery is an intentional and hostile touch or contact. Intent relates to the act of touching, and if that act is done with hostility, it would amount to battery. Take note that the intention does *not* mean that the assailant had to intend *injury*.

Whether or not a touching or contact was hostile was a question of fact to be decided in each case on its own facts. In the instant case, the court held that the defendant's action was not done with hostility.

One of the areas where the 'hostility' test would be useful is medical cases. Let's say a doctor has to operate on a person in an emergency and cannot wait for consent to be given. A court, following *Wilson* v. *Pringle*, would say that there is no battery because there is no hostility on the part of the doctor.

Medical cases

Nevertheless, the hostility requirement appears to have been rejected for medical cases by the House of Lords in *F* v. *West Berkshire Health Authority* [1989] 2 All ER 545, and interpreted rather as actions that were 'unlawful' in the sense of being non-consensual action. We will look at this case in detail when we examine 'consent' as a defence later in this chapter. If the criteria is indeed 'unlawfulness'

> **Take note**
>
> In order to avoid an action for battery, a doctor must show either that consent was given for the touching, or that touching was necessary and in the best interests of the patient.
>
> Note that medical treatment to which the claimant consents does not become battery merely because consent was not 'informed': for example, in *Sidaway* v. *Bethlem Royal Hospital* [1985] AC 871 a doctor did not fully inform the claimant patient of risks involved in a procedure. She averred that her consent had not been informed but the court followed the *Bolam* precedent (see below and also Chapter 3) and acquitted the doctor, because he had followed accepted medical practice at the time by not telling the patient about every possible complication.

in this sense (non-consensus) then it would encompass the situation, for example, where D pinches C's bottom against her will. The finding in *F* was confirmed in *Wainwright* v. *Home Office* [2003] 4 All ER 969. We look at both these cases below.

From the above we can see that there is no absolute test used by the courts to gauge every kind of touch. Instead, the courts tend to take a common sense approach, discounting touch in the ordinary course of human interaction, and for the rest using the 'hostility' test as well as gauging whether a touch was unlawful in the sense of not being consented to. It is worth remembering that battery, as a form of trespass, remains actionable *per se* and that the slightest touch could therefore amount to battery. Of course, if physical harm results, the claimant would be entitled to full compensatory damages.

DEFENCES TO ASSAULT AND BATTERY

If you still feel that it is difficult to define what *precisely* would constitute an assault or battery, do not be alarmed – this is a question that continues to exercise the best legal minds in our courts so you are in good company! The picture may become clearer when we look at the most common defences that can be raised against assault and battery.

Consent

Consent is available as a defence to trespass to the person. Consent here is similar to the defence of voluntary assumption of risk in negligence – *volenti non fit injuria* (no injury is done to one who consents). The consent can be express or implied. There is no difficulty if express consent is given by an adult person who is of sound mind. In such an instance the burden of proof is on the defendant. The defendant will have to prove that the claimant consented to the action that was performed and that it was real consent, not induced by misrepresentation, stress or duress.

INTERSECTION

If this terminology sounds familiar to you, it should. Revise the decisions we examined (in Chapter 3) when we briefly looked at medical negligence: for example, revise *Bolam* v. *Friern Hospital Management Committee* [1957] 1 WLR 582, where it was held that as long as the doctor acts in accordance with 'a practice accepted as proper by a responsible body of medical men skilled in that particular art', she will be taken as having acted reasonably (and thus, non-negligently).

The victim must understand what it is she is consenting to and must give her consent freely. In medical cases, a person with capacity has an absolute right to give or withhold consent to treatment, and capacity will be assumed unless shown otherwise. In Re B (adult: refusal of Medical treatment) [2002] EWHC 429 (Fam) the patient withdrew consent to being kept on artificial respiration machines. The medical personnel who were caring for her knew that, if this were done, she would die. Nevertheless, the court held that, as the patient was in sound mind and refused consent to treatment, continuing treatment would constitute trespass to her person.

Where a person lacks capacity to make their own decision, treatment will be lawful if it is in that person's best interests.

The concept of 'informed consent'

In the USA, in medical cases, consent is not valid unless the patient has enough information to make an *informed* choice. A doctor is under a duty to disclose to the patient the choices available and to warn of any associated risks/dangers in the proposed treatment.

In the UK, however, it is enough that a patient is told of the general nature of proposed treatment. Any complaint about the adequacy of the information or advice must be pursued in negligence. Failure to give full and proper advice does not affect the validity of consent to battery. Thus in *Hills* v. *Potter* [1984] 1 WLR 641 there was no battery when the patient was informed that the operation was serious but was not informed of the risk of paralysis following it. C's consent prevented a battery. The court also stated that where the surgeon or doctor gives advice prior to an operation they do not have to inform the patient of all the details of the proposed treatment or the likely outcome and the risks involved. All that is required is to give the patient *sufficient* information to enable her to decide whether or not to undergo the operation, and the doctor would be giving sufficient information if she does so in accordance with a practice accepted as proper by a responsible body of skilled medical practitioners (again, as per the decision in *Bolam* as adapted in *Bolitho* (see above and Chapter 3)).

Of course, it is a matter of fact whether or not sufficient information is given to a patient in any given situation. To give an example where a doctor was held liable in negligence: in *Birch* v. *University College London Hospital NHS Foundation Trust* [2008] EWHC 2237 a surgeon informed a patient about the risks associated with the procedure he was proposing to have her undergo, but he did not tell her about a less invasive option for which she was initially scheduled. The patient suffered a stroke as a result of the procedure she underwent and claimed in negligence. The court agreed that, had she known of the less invasive option, she would have chosen it and the doctor was held liable.

Take note

An interesting question here is whether, in giving consent, the principles of battery or negligence apply. The court gave an answer in *Chatterton* v. *Gerson* [1981] QB 432, where a patient for whom an operation went wrong sued the operating doctor in both trespass and negligence, averring that the doctor had not explained the possible consequences of the procedure.

So, for our purposes, the question is whether the doctor could be held liable in trespass or in negligence.

The court held that you have to ask two questions. First, did the doctor fail to explain the general nature of the operation? If so, then we cannot speak of consent, and the doctor would be liable in trespass. However, if the doctor had explained the general nature of the operation, the patient is precluded from suing in trespass, but we can then ask a second question which may indicate negligence. So, secondly, we ask is whether the doctor failed to go into the risks and implications of the procedure. If so, the plaintiff could possibly prove that consent would not have been forthcoming had the risks been known (and then the doctor may be held liable in negligence).

Necessity

This defence allows the defendant to intervene to prevent greater harm to the public, a third party, the defendant or the claimant. The courts will only allow this defence if the defendant has acted reasonably in all the circumstances. The defence could be used in medical cases to justify treatment of someone who lacks capacity, for example emergency treatment of an unconscious accident victim.

In *F* v. *West Berkshire Health Authority* [1989] 2 All ER 545 the court held that doctors may intervene in the best interest of the patient where it is necessary to act in circumstances where it is not practicable to communicate with the defendant; and the action taken is such as a reasonable person would in all the circumstances take, acting in the best interests of the person. In *F*, a female mental patient was involved in sexual relationship with another patient, and her doctors asked the court for permission to sterilise her. The court allowed this as falling under necessity, as the patient could not consent for herself. Sterilisation may seem harsh but in the case the authorities had to take into account that contraception was not practicable, and the only other option would have been to break up *F*'s love affair. So in this case, *F* had a happy outcome, all things considered.

Parental authority

Parents are allowed to exercise reasonable restraint or chastisement on their children, without being guilty of trespass to the person. The child must understand the purpose of the punishment, which must be reasonable and proportionate to the wrong committed.

Lawful authority

In some instances statute authorises interference with the person. There are two main groups: the Police and Criminal Evidence Act 1984 enables the police to use reasonable force in furtherance of arrest, and section 63 of the Mental Health Act 1983 deals with health professionals who have to restrain or detain people with mental illness.

Self-defence

Anyone is entitled to use reasonable force in self-defence or to protect others or to prevent a crime or tort being committed. However, the force used must be both necessary and proportionate to the danger. This will be a question of fact.

In *Lane* v. *Holloway* [1968] 1 QB 379 the claimant, an aged, drunken man, verbally abused the defendant's wife in the street by calling her a 'monkey-faced tart'. The defendant came down from his bedroom to the street and struck the claimant with such savagery that the blow required 19 stitches. It was held that this was not force proportionate to a verbal threat and an ineffectual punch from a drunken old man. Indeed, threats and insults may not justify the use of greater force than it was necessary in the circumstances.

INTERSECTION

> Revise the case of *Revill* v. *Newbery* [1996] QB 567 (discussed in Chapter 8), where a householder who shot a burglar was held not to have acted proportionately and thus failed to make out a defence of self-defence.

Prescription

As we have seen under the tort of negligence as well as the defences to negligence, civil actions are time-barred, with different limitation periods in operation for different kinds of action.

CORNERSTONE

Limitation Act 1980

The general rule, contained in section 2 of the Limitation Act 1980, is that the period of limitation for an action in tort is six years from the date on which the cause of action accrued. For trespass to the person, the limitation period is fixed at six years.

The limitation period for negligence actions, however, is generally *three* years. This is because section 11 of the 1980 Act covers actions for damages based on negligence, nuisance or breach of duty where the damages were in respect of personal injuries. The limitation period for such actions is three years, either from the date on which the cause of action accrued or the date of knowledge of the person injured. Furthermore, section 33 of the Limitation Act gives the court the discretion to extend the three-year period if the court is of the opinion that it would be equitable to do so.

The interplay between these three sections of the Limitations Act 1980 was starkly illustrated in the House of Lords' decision in *Stubbings* v. *Webb* [1992] AC 498. S sued her stepfather and stepbrother, many years after reaching majority, for abusing and raping her while she was a child. S had not realised, until much later, that the psychological problems she was suffering, were the result of that abuse. She therefore argued that her cause of action was governed by section 11, which specified three years from the time when the victim of personal injuries *first had knowledge that significant injury had resulted from wrongful behaviour*. The House of Lords held that section 11, by which limitation ran from the date of knowledge, applied only to cases of accidentally caused personal injury. The claim by S was therefore time-barred – she lost her case. From this decision it was clear that section 11 was extendable, while section 2 was *not*.

The decision in *Stubbings* v. *Webb* was criticised. Courts tried to distinguish the case on facts – for example, in *S* v. *W (child abuse: damages)* [1995] 1 FLR 862, where the claimant was time-barred to sue her father, who had abused her as a child (an intentional act, therefore subject to s. 2), it was held that there was also *negligence* involved (subject to s. 11), as the mother should have

Take note

The interpretation of sections 2 and 11 of the 1980 Act in *Stubbings* v. *Webb* meant that for negligently inflicted injury, the claimant could be assisted by the court if she was 'out of time' – either because of the wording of section 11 itself, which refers to the time that the claimant first becomes aware of the injury, or by the application of section 33, which allows the court to extend the actionable period on equity grounds. In contrast, for the victim of an intentionally inflicted injury, no extension of the six-year limit in section 2 was possible. The implications of this were especially harsh for victims of sexual assault or abuse, which →

> by definition are intentional actions: for example, the victim of rape or sexual abuse would be limited to the six-year period, whilst the victim of, say, a motor vehicle accident, would have the possibility of claiming outside of the limitation period.

known about the abuse and had a duty of care to prevent it, and so she succeeded in her claim against the mother. The Law Commission also criticised the situation and recommended to Parliament in 2001 that section 2 of the Limitation Act 1980 should operate in the same manner as section 11 (Limitation of Actions (2001) (Law Com No 270)). Parliament did not legislate upon this recommendation, but in 2008 the House of Lords itself had an opportunity to revisit this area, and took the rare step of overruling its own previous decision.

CORNERSTONE

A v. Hoare and other appeals [2008] UKHL 6

The interplay between the different limitation periods was at issue in the conjoined appeal of several cases in *A* v. *Hoare and other appeals* [2008] UKHL 6. All of the cases related to sexual assault, which for various reasons were not pursued in court until several years *after* the alleged abuses took place. We will look at the facts of only one of these appeals namely that involving the defendant Mr Hoare, who was convicted of raping the claimant, A, and sent to prison for life. A did not, at the time, sue him in tort as it would have made no sense – he was impecunious (he had no money and, being in prison, would not have the opportunity to earn money – so suing him would have been a waste of the courts' time).

A few years down the line Mr Hoare, whilst on day release, won £7million in the lottery. A thereupon sued him in trespass to the person. Hoare's defence was that her claim, relating to an intentional action, was time-barred by section 2 of the Limitation Act 1980.

The House unanimously found in favour of the claimant. Lord Hoffmann noted the recommendations by the Law Commission, as well as (at Para. 25) the 'increasing degree of artificiality' to which courts resort to try and circumvent the harsh results of *Stubbings*. It was therefore held that *Stubbings* had been wrongly decided and that the correct interpretation of the Limitation Act 1980 was that personal injury resulting from intentional trespass to the person did indeed fall within section 11 and therefore the court would have the discretion to use section 33 to extend the limitation period in favour of the claimant.

Contributory negligence

Assault and battery are both torts that require intentional action. Therefore, it would seem that contributory negligence should not be an allowable defence. This was confirmed by the Court of Appeal in *Pritchard* v. *Co-operative Group Ltd* [2011] EWCA Civ 329, where the claimant successfully sued her employer for assault and battery following an attack by her manager in which she was injured. The court had to consider whether the defence of contributory negligence could be raised, as there was evidence that the claimant had provoked her manager. The court held that there is no defence of contributory negligence to an intentional tort such as assault and battery, neither in terms of the common law, nor in terms of the Law Reform (Contributory Negligence) Act 1945 (we looked at this Act in Chapter 4).

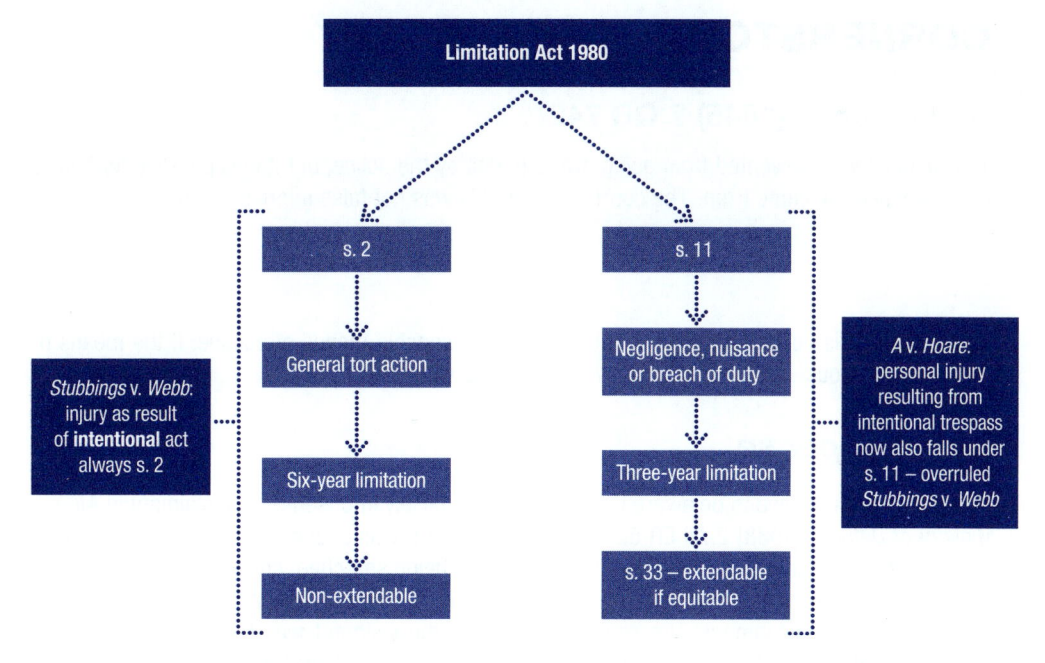

Figure 7.3 Limitation Act 1980

FALSE IMPRISONMENT

This tort is concerned with a person's freedom of movement.

CORNERSTONE

False imprisonment entails total restraint of freedom to move from a certain place

Cooke (2013: 427) writes: 'false imprisonment is the unlawful imposition of constraint on another's freedom of movement from a particular place'. Any restraint of a person's freedom of movement counts as false imprisonment, and examples include arrest, detention, and confinement.

Being held in prison would be a good example: In *R (on the application of Lumba)* v. *Secretary of State for the Home Department* [2011] UKSC 12 the Supreme Court held the Secretary of State for the Home Department liable for the false imprisonment of two foreign national prisoners who were held after serving their prison terms but pending their deportation, without lawful justification.

Total restraint

To count as false imprisonment the restraint must be total, meaning that the claimant cannot go anywhere else.

CORNERSTONE

Bird v. Jones (1845) 7 QB 742

The claimant was prevented from going over a bridge by the police, but it was possible for him to go back where he came from. The court held that this was not false imprisonment.

Similarly, there is no false imprisonment if there is reasonable means of escape. If the means of escape are dangerous, however, we *do* have false imprisonment.

Actionable *per se*

The claimant does not have to be aware that she has been falsely imprisoned. The claimant in *Murray v. Ministry of Defence* [1988] 2 All ER 521 was arrested but it was unclear whether she was aware that, in the period before her arrest, while her house was being searched, she was not free to leave and was, in fact, being detained. The House of Lords held that this was nevertheless a detention for purposes of false imprisonment. The court added that if the claimant was falsely imprisoned but suffered no harm, he could normally expect to recover only nominal damages.

This is, of course, correct because you will remember that as a form of trespass, false imprisonment is actionable *per se*. In *Lumba* (above), the claimants succeeded with their false imprisonment claim but were awarded only nominal damages.

Strict liability

False imprisonment is also a strict liability tort, so fault does not have to be proved. The claimant will have to prove that the defendant intended to impede her freedom of movement, but she does not have to prove that the defendant intended to commit the tort of false imprisonment.

Defences to false imprisonment

Just as for assault and battery, lawful authority, consent, necessity and self-defence are all defences against false imprisonment. We will look at only two of these in brief.

Lawful authority: arrest

A lawful arrest made in accordance with statute cannot amount to false imprisonment, whether made by a police officer or by a private person, although a police officer has stronger protection than a private person. The Police and Criminal Evidence Act 1984, sections 24 and 25 deal with arrest. In *Alanov* v. *Chief Constable of Sussex* [2012] EWCA Civ 234 the Court of Appeal held that even though the threshold for lawful arrest was low, the court still has to decide, using an objective standard, whether an arrest was reasonable. Here, there was no evidence on which to suspect, reasonably and objectively, that the claimant was the alleged rapist the police was looking for, save for his unwillingness to cooperate and his aggression. When they arrested him, therefore, it was on unreasonable grounds and amounted to a trespass to the person.

Necessity

It could be argued that restraining a person's freedom of movement is necessary to protect somebody else, or the public. Recent policing methods, especially the use of '**kettling**' (shepherding demonstrators into a constrained space) came under consideration in *Austin* v. *Commissioner of Police for the Metropolis* [2008] 1 All ER 564. This case was brought by two claimants: A was a mother who came to London on May Day 2001 to take part in a demonstration; S was in London on business and was innocently caught up in the events of the day. Both were detained by the police when the latter 'kettled' the demonstration in Oxford Circus. A pleaded with the police to be allowed to go and collect her child from crèche, to no avail, whilst S's protestations that he had no part in the demonstration similarly fell on deaf ears. Take note that neither of them, at any stage, acted unlawfully or committed any offence. Both sued the police for false imprisonment. The House of Lords held that this was a case of false imprisonment but that the detention was justified as it had been done to prevent an imminent breach of the peace.

> Is the House of Lords' approval of the practice of kettling justified?
> McBride and Bagshaw (2012: 37) state that:
>
> > '[i]t is surprising that of the nine judges who ended up considering the case of *Austin* . . . not one could be found to speak for the idea that it is unlawful to imprison an innocent person, whether or not doing so is necessary in order to prevent a breach of the peace.'
>
> This decision was subsequently watered down slightly when it was decided in *R (on the application of Moos and McClure)* v. *Commissioner of Police of the Metropolis* [2011] EWHC 957 that kettling may only be used as a last resort, but it may nevertheless be concluded that the courts are still favouring public order over individual freedom – something which traditionally does not sit well with the common law.
>
> Do you consider this to be the case and, if so, do modern circumstances justify the public good to triumph over individual rights and freedoms?

Detention for medical purposes can also be a defence, but only if the provisions of the Mental Health Act 1983 for the lawful detention of persons suffering from mental disorder are strictly followed.

THE RULE IN *WILKINSON* v. *DOWNTON* – LIABILITY FOR CAUSING INDIRECT HARM

The three forms of trespass to the person deal with intentional, direct acts, which are actionable without proof of harm (actionable *per se*). And, as we have seen earlier, negligence also deals with direct harm, but which is unintentionally caused. However, what if *indirect harm* is caused *intentionally*?

APPLICATION

Say, for example, that B suffered injuries due to shock occasioned by A's practical joke? B would not be able to sue A in trespass to the person as there was no assault or battery. B would also not be able to sue A in negligence because what A did was intentional.

The following case recognised this and created a new tort which afterwards bore the name of the case.

CORNERSTONE

Wilkinson v. *Downton* [1897] 2 QB 57

The defendant played a practical joke on the claimant, by telling her that her husband had been seriously injured in an accident. The claimant believed him and as a result suffered physical injuries due to shock. The court could not hold the defendant liable for the claimant's nervous shock as there was no threat of violence (assault), nor was there any contact, which is of course required for battery. Nevertheless, the court held that a person who wilfully caused injury in the manner described should be held liable. Since then, this kind of action (for intentional but indirectly caused injury) has been known as the rule in *Wilkinson* v. *Downton*.

It is clear that, unlike for assault and battery, the rule in *Wilkinson* v. *Downton* concerns an intentional (i.e. fault-based) tort occasioning actual injury (physical or psychiatric).

CORNERSTONE

The tort in *Wilkinson* v. *Downton*

The tort in *Wilkinson* v. *Downton* is an intentional tort which indirectly causes harm. The three elements to prove are therefore:

1. intention;
2. harm; and
3. that the harm was caused indirectly.

As harm needs to be proved, this tort is not actionable *per se*. This was confirmed by the House of Lords in *Wainwright* v. *Home Office* [2004] AC 406, where it was decided that no liability exists for distress which falls short of a recognised psychiatric injury. In this case, the question whether the rule in *Wilkinson* (intentional wrongdoing) could apply to claimants who had been strip-searched in breach of Prison Service rules, whilst visiting a relative in prison, and the test to be applied were considered. It was held that there must be extreme and outrageous conduct intentionally or recklessly causing bodily harm or psychiatric injury, and not merely emotional distress.

To sum up then, *Wilkinson* is only available for claims for indirectly inflicted physical and recognised psychiatric injury.

HARASSMENT

Does the harm requirement in *Wilkinson* mean that emotional distress is not actionable? Let's look at what we have learnt so far. For assault, there has to be a fear of immediate harm. For battery, there has to be physical contact. In *Wilkinson* we have just seen that a key requirement is recognised psychiatric injury, for which emotional distress falls short.

CORNERSTONE

Harassment not a form of trespass

If emotional distress is caused by an *on-going* series of events, it may be actionable as **harassment**.

This is certainly not a form of trespass to the person, but it can be argued that it developed partially out of trespass (and other tortious) cases recognising that there should be an action for this kind of wrong.

The legislature recognised that the common law did not address this kind of distress, and therefore enacted the Protection from Harassment Act 1997.

CORNERSTONE

Protection from Harassment Act 1997

The Protection from Harassment Act 1997 provides a remedy for persons who have suffered harassment, which is defined in section 1(1) as a 'course of conduct' amounting to harassment. In section 7(3) it clarifies that by 'course of conduct' is meant conduct on at least two occasions. No actual physical or psychiatric harm or distress need to have resulted from the harassment, alarm or distress is sufficient. The defendant's intention is irrelevant. The Act makes harassment a criminal offence but also provides the victim with a civil remedy.

A good example of a successful suit under this act is to be found in *Ferguson* v. *British Gas Trading Ltd* [2009] EWCA Civ 46. Here the defendant continued to send threatening letters and bills to the claimant. The claimant on several occasions wrote to the defendant telling them that she had paid all bills to them and indeed did not have an account with them any more, yet the letters from them continued. The court held that this constituted harassment and that it was no defence for the defendant to allege that the letters were computer generated – ultimately, a human being was in charge of the computers.

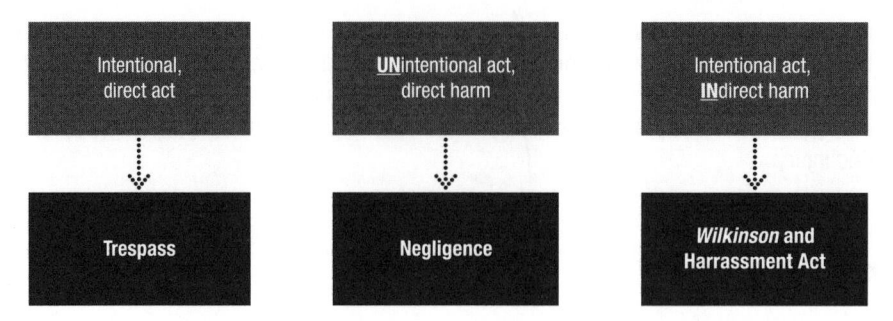

Figure 7.4 The rule in *Wilkinson* v. *Downton*

KEY POINTS

- Trespass to the person entails the protection of the most fundamental interests in society: bodily integrity and freedom of movement. As such it also forms part of some of the longest established torts in our legal system. The interests protected are regarded as so fundamental that the tort of trespass to the person is actionable *per se* (without having to prove damage).
- Trespass to the person consists of three torts: assault, battery and false imprisonment.
- Assault is where one person fears immediate harm due to the words or conduct of another.
- Battery consists of the unjustified and non-consensual application of 'force' to another. 'Force' can be the slightest touch.
- False imprisonment is the total restraint of somebody's ability to move from a certain place.
- The tort in *Wilkinson* v. *Downton* is the intentional but indirect occasioning of harm. It differs from trespass to the person because trespass is a *direct* action, and trespass is actionable *per se*, whereas for *Wilkinson*, damage needs to be proved.
- The most common defences to trespass to the person includes self-defence, necessity, lawful authority and prescription.
- The statutory tort of harassment developed out of a gap in the law of trespass and seeks to compensate people who have suffered emotional distress caused by an *on-going* series of events amounting to harassment.

CORE CASES AND STATUTES

Case	About	Importance
Letang v. *Cooper* [1965] 1 QB 232	Defendant drove over claimant sunbathing in car park by accident, whether this was trespass	Trespass requires intent. If the action was unintentional it cannot be trespass but can be negligence.
R v. *Ireland* [1997] 4 All ER 225	Whether silent phone calls could be assault	Assault might be committed by words or gestures, as long as there is fear of an immediate and unlawful attack.
Wilson v. *Pringle* [1986] 2 All ER 440	Schoolboy injured when a playmate jumped on his back, whether this was battery	For battery, the contact had to be made with 'hostile intent'. Subsequently interpreted as meaning unlawful or non-consensual touching.
F v. *West Berkshire Health Authority* [1989] 2 All ER 545	Doctors asked leave to sterilise a mental patient under their care on ground of necessity	Doctors may intervene in the best interest of the patient where it is necessary to act in circumstances where it is not practicable to communicate with the defendant.
Lane v. *Holloway* [1968] 1 QB 379	Self-defence as defence to trespass to the person	Self-defence has to be proportional: a blow requiring 19 stitches following an ineffectual shove from a drunk person was not proportionate.
A v. *Hoare and other appeals* [2008] UKHL 6	Whether intentional torts such as sexual assault could be treated as favourably as negligence in terms of the Limitation Act 1980	Personal injury resulting from intentional trespass to the person did indeed fall within s. 11 of the Limitation Act 1980 and therefore the court would have the discretion to use s. 33 to extend the limitation period in favour of the claimant.
Bird v. *Jones* (1845) 7 QB 742	Whether preventing claimant from crossing bridge false imprisonment	False imprisonment only happens when there is a total restraint of freedom of movement.
Wilkinson v. *Downton* [1897] 2 QB 57	Whether indirectly but intentionally caused harm actionable	A practical joke resulting in the claimant suffering nervous shock did not occasion a claim in assault or batter, or in negligence, but was held to be actionable.

Statute	About	Importance
Police and Criminal Evidence Act 1984	Lawful arrest a defence against a claim of false imprisonment	Although the bar is set low for police arrests, there still has to be reasonable grounds for the arrest in order for it to be a defence against false imprisonment.
Limitation Act 1980	Extendability of time limits for torts under ss. 2 and 11	Following the interpretation in *A* v. *Hoare* both now extendable under s. 33 (i.e. at the discretion of the court).

FURTHER READING

Cane, P. (2000) *Mens rea* in tort law. *OJLS* p. 533
The element of intention in trespass differs very subtly from that in other torts. It is crucial that you understand this, and reading this article will aid in that process.

Cooke, J. (2013) *Law of Tort*. Harlow: Pearson, Chapter 19
Professor Cooke's textbook on tort is known for being authoritative yet accessible. In Chapter 19 of the 11th edition he discusses trespass to the person, and here we direct you to pp. 427 onward for his discussion of false imprisonment and related issues such as lawful arrest. Students sometimes focus on assault and battery, paying less attention to false imprisonment. Reading this discussion will help you understand the importance of this tort in modern life.

Levinson, J. (2005) Vicarious liability for intentional torts. *JPIL* p. 304
This article specifically focuses on torts against the person such as assault and battery, and should aid your understanding of the torts and their elements.

Lunney, M. (2002) Practical joking and its penalty: *Wilkinson* v. *Downton* in context. *Tort Law Review* 10, p. 168
This article provides a good explanation of the often misunderstood tort in *Wilkinson* v. *Downton*.

McBride, N.J. and Bagshaw, R. (2012) *Tort Law.* Harlow: Pearson
In Chapter 2 of this book, the authors discuss trespass to the person in a thought-provoking and innovative way which will help you to look at this area from a fresh angle.

Trindade, F.A. (1982) Intentional torts: some thoughts on assault and battery. *OJLS* 2, p. 211
This article provides an in-depth discussion of the torts of assault and battery and will help you to broaden your understanding of the elements required for trespass to the person.

PART 3
Statutory regimes

PART 3
Statutory regimes

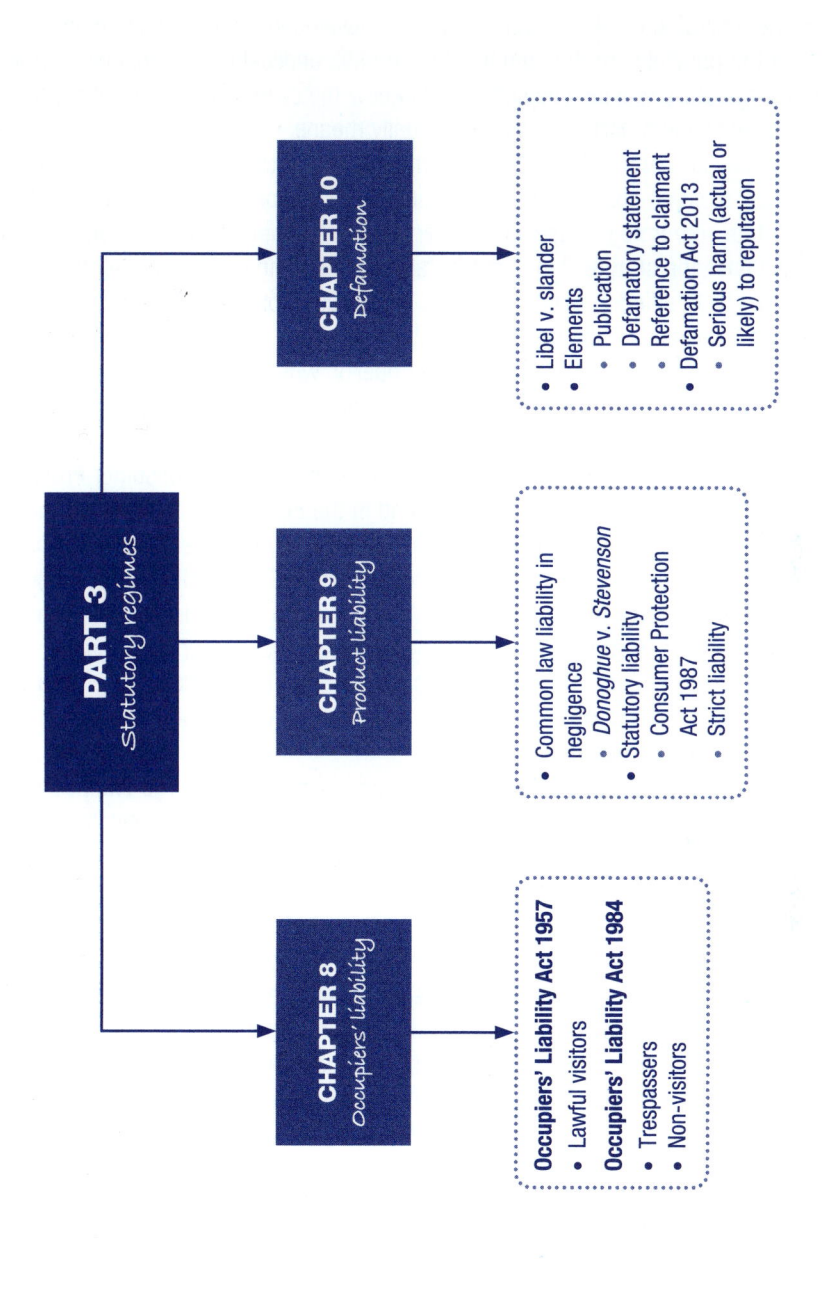

CHAPTER 8
Occupiers' liability

- **Occupiers' Liability Act 1957**
  - Lawful visitors
- **Occupiers' Liability Act 1984**
  - Trespassers
  - Non-visitors

CHAPTER 9
Product liability

- Common law liability in negligence
- *Donoghue v. Stevenson*
- Statutory liability
- Consumer Protection Act 1987
- Strict liability

CHAPTER 10
Defamation

- Libel v. slander
- Elements
- Publication
- Defamatory statement
- Reference to claimant
- Defamation Act 2013
- Serious harm (actual or likely) to reputation

PART 3 INTRODUCTION

In the third part of this book we look at torts that have been legislated upon to a greater extent than some of the others. You will see that all of them developed out of the common law, and in many instances the principles of the common law are still applicable. So even where there is a highly developed statutory regime, you still need to know the cases, sometimes in order to make sense of what a section in a particular statute actually means.

Occupiers' liability and product liability sometimes, to a greater or lesser extent, overlap with negligence. In fact, in some instances a claim could (and if you are a prudent lawyer, *should*) be based on the statute and/or negligence, in the alternative. Why then, if the common law principles still apply, do we have the statutes? In some instances, the common law crystallised to such an extent that it could be codified in statute. In many instances, though, the legislature got involved for policy reasons. For example, the Occupiers' Liability Act 1984 was aimed to give some protection to trespassers injured whilst on somebody's property, where it would otherwise have been harsh to refuse them a remedy – for instance, child trespassers. We look at occupiers' liability to people injured whilst on their property in Chapter 8.

Product liability is another good example of a statutory regime. The Consumer Protection Act 1987 was the result of recognition both in the UK and in the EU that the fault requirement in the common law made it very difficult for deserving claimants to prove their cases against manufacturers of consumer products. For example, people born with birth defects because of their mothers having taken the drug Thalidomide in the 1970s found it almost impossible to prove their claims against the manufacturers of the drug – and yet there was general recognition that their injuries should be compensated. The result was legislation that made such manufacturers liable to consumers without them having to prove fault, i.e. intention or negligence. We call this *strict liability*. We examine product liability in Chapter 9.

More recently, Parliament decided to change the common law to a large extent by enacting the Defamation Act 2013. This was largely the result of pressure by free speech activists who pointed out that the UK defamation laws have a chilling (or stifling) effect on freedom of expression, as it is argued that rich and powerful claimants are favoured in defamation actions. We will look at the famous 'McLibel' case, where a few almost penniless protesters were sued by the giant corporation McDonalds over a span of years and in an action costing millions of pounds, and how this kind of litigation can serve as a means to silence protest or criticism. As the UK became known as the 'libel capital' of Europe, the legislature decided to act and in the new Defamation Act 2013, certain hurdles for prospective litigants will now attempt to redress the balance between freedom of speech and protection of reputation. At the time of writing this book, the 2013 Act is not yet fully in effect, so in Chapter 10 we will look at the common law as well as the statute.

CHAPTER 8
Occupiers' liability

BLUEPRINT
Occupiers' liability

KEY QUESTIONS

LEGISLATION
- Occupiers' Liability Act 1957, s. 2(1)
- Occupiers' Liability Act 1957, s. 2(4)(a)
- Occupiers' Liability Act 1984, s. 1(1)(a)

CONTEXT
- The common law has long accepted that the occupier of premises has a duty of care towards visitors. This area of law has now been largely codified by the Occupiers' Liability Acts 1957 and 1984.

CONCEPTS
- Occupier
- Common duty of care
- Lawful visitors
- 'Persons other than visitors'

- The Occupiers' Liability Act 1984 enables trespassers to sue for injury suffered whilst trespassing. Is the law too generous to trespassers?

- Can a person sue for personal injury and damage to property suffered due to the state of premises she visited?
- What may be claimed under the Occupiers' Liability Acts 1957 and 1984 respectively?
- What is meant by the 'occupier' of premises?

CASES

- *Wheat* v. *E Lacon & Co Ltd* [1966]
- *Lowery* v. *Walker* [1911]
- *Tomlinson* v. *Congleton Borough Council* [2003]

REFORM

- Liability towards trespassers cannot be excluded in the same way as it can be towards lawful visitors. Should this be addressed by the law?

SPECIAL CHARACTERISTICS

- Control test to determine occupier
- OLA 1957 applies to lawful visitors, defined in s. 1 and the common law
- ss. 1(1)(a) and (7) determine the scope of OLA 1984

CRITICAL ISSUES

Setting the scene

Occupiers of land (e.g. owners or tenants) have a duty to visitors to ensure that their land is not hazardous. Or, seen from the other side, visitors who are injured, or who in some cases suffer damage to their property while on somebody's land, may sue the occupier. They can only sue if the damage or injury is due to the state of the land or activities closely related to it. The common law used to govern this area of law, but from 1957 the Occupiers' Liability Act 1957 governed liability towards lawful visitors. The common law continued to govern liability towards others, such as trespassers, but this proved unsatisfactory and there followed a second statute, the Occupiers' Liability Act 1984, dealing with mainly trespassers. Some common law principles still apply, and many concepts from the common law were incorporated in the two Acts; for this reason we need to examine both the common law as well as the two important statutes.

INTRODUCTION

An occupier of premises may be liable in tort to a person who, whilst on the premises, suffered harm due to the premises being defective or dangerous. In limited circumstances, and only where there is some connection to the premises itself, liability could also flow from activities on the premises. Occupiers' liability is governed by two Acts: the Occupiers' Liability Act (1957) (OLA 1957), which concerns the duty of care owed to all lawful visitors; and the Occupiers' Liability Act (1984) (OLA 1984), which concerns the duty owed to people *other* than lawful visitors. Usually, for the purposes of OLA 1984, these others will be trespassers.

From this, we can see that three concepts are important and need further scrutiny: who is an '**occupier**'; what do we understand 'premises' to mean; and finally who would qualify as claimants? We look at these concepts below, but for now take note that liability under the two Acts depends on the *legal status of the claimant*. We need to ask in what capacity the claimant was on the premises. For example, was she there as a guest, as a trespasser, as a tenant or as a purchaser?

INTERSECTION

For the principles surrounding occupiers' liability to be applicable, it is not enough to show that the damage or injury occurred on premises occupied by someone – there has to be some connection to the state of the premises. For example, in *Revill* v. *Newbery* [1996] QB 567 an elderly man guarded his shed from the frequent attentions of vandals and thieves and accidentally shot a trespasser. The Court of Appeal held that the mere fact that the occupier of property caused injury to a person coming onto his land did not mean that occupiers' liability is relevant – the common law principles of negligence were applied. Other areas of tort may also be applicable, for example: trespass, statute law such as the Defective Premises Act 1972, and nuisance. Apart from tort, there could also, for example, potentially be contractual obligations, or equitable or proprietary rights, or criminal sanctions. Liability could be held by, for example, a vendor/lessor to a purchaser/tenant, in respect of defects which exist at the time of sale/lease; a builder to a purchaser/tenant; or by local authorities for design faults or negligent inspection, to purchasers or otherwise.

OCCUPIER

If it is established that the state of the premises contributed to or caused the injury or damage, the next question is who to sue? Both Acts make it clear that 'the occupier' will be liable, but who is an occupier? The statutes point us to the common law definition of an occupier.

CORNERSTONE

Occupier

The term 'occupier' is a bit deceptive, as under common law you do not need to physically occupy premises to count as 'an occupier', nor do you need to be the owner. The main question is whether you have sufficient control over the premises to control who can enter.

There may also be more than one occupier at the same time. This is illustrated well in the following case.

CORNERSTONE

Wheat v. *E Lacon & Co Ltd* [1966] AC 552

In this case, where a punter fell down unlit stairs in a pub, both the owners and the managers of a pub were held to be potentially liable as 'occupiers' because both controlled access to the premises.

The key issue is whether or not the person had control over the premises. Essentially, it boils down to how the courts interpret the facts of each case. For example, in *Bailey* v. *Armes* [1999] EGCS 21 a child fell from the roof of a supermarket which he accessed via a window of a flat above the supermarket. The Court of Appeal held that neither the supermarket nor the tenants of the flat had sufficient control over the roof area. They could therefore not be occupiers.

The occupier could also be an absentee and need not have taken actual or symbolic steps to take possession. In *Harris* v. *Birkenhead Corporation* [1976] 1 WLR 279 (CA) the council served a notice of compulsory purchase on the owner of a property. A child entered the derelict house before the council took physical possession, and was injured. The court held that the council was the occupier of the empty house as it was best placed to control who could go into the house.

Take note

The concept 'lawful interest in land' is important in nuisance where it is a requirement for a claimant in private nuisance. You can only claim in private nuisance if you can prove that you have a proprietary interest in the use and enjoyment of the affected land or premises affected. You therefore need to be the →

CHAPTER 8 Occupiers' liability

> owner or tenant of the affected fixed property; a lesser interest such as that of a lodger will not be enough to enable you to sue. We look at nuisance in Chapter 10.

An occupier may also include an independent contractor. In *AMF International Ltd* v. *Magnet Bowling* Ltd [1968] 1 WLR 1028 a contractor, as well as the owner, was held to be the occupier of the whole building although part of the building was separated by a screen beyond which the contractor went only to attend to heating and lighting.

These are all examples of who could potentially be seen as occupiers for purposes of occupiers' liability. We have already seen that an occupier does not need to be in actual physical occupation of the land. The occupier also does not need to have a proprietary or lawful interest in the land in order to be held liable. The main criterion is that of control.

Whether or not somebody is an 'occupier' (and therefore a potential defendant in terms of occupiers' liability) can be represented as follows:

Occupier flowchart

- No definition in statutes – look to common law
  - *Wheat* v. *E Lacon & Co Ltd*
    - Sufficient degree of control over premises
- What is **NOT** needed to be an occupier?
  - Estate in land
  - Physical possession
    - Don't confuse this with private nuisance
      - (See Chapter 10) **Nuisance** CLAIMANT needs to have lawful interest in land
      - **Occupiers' liability** Occupier is **DEFENDANT** and need **NOT** have lawful interest in land

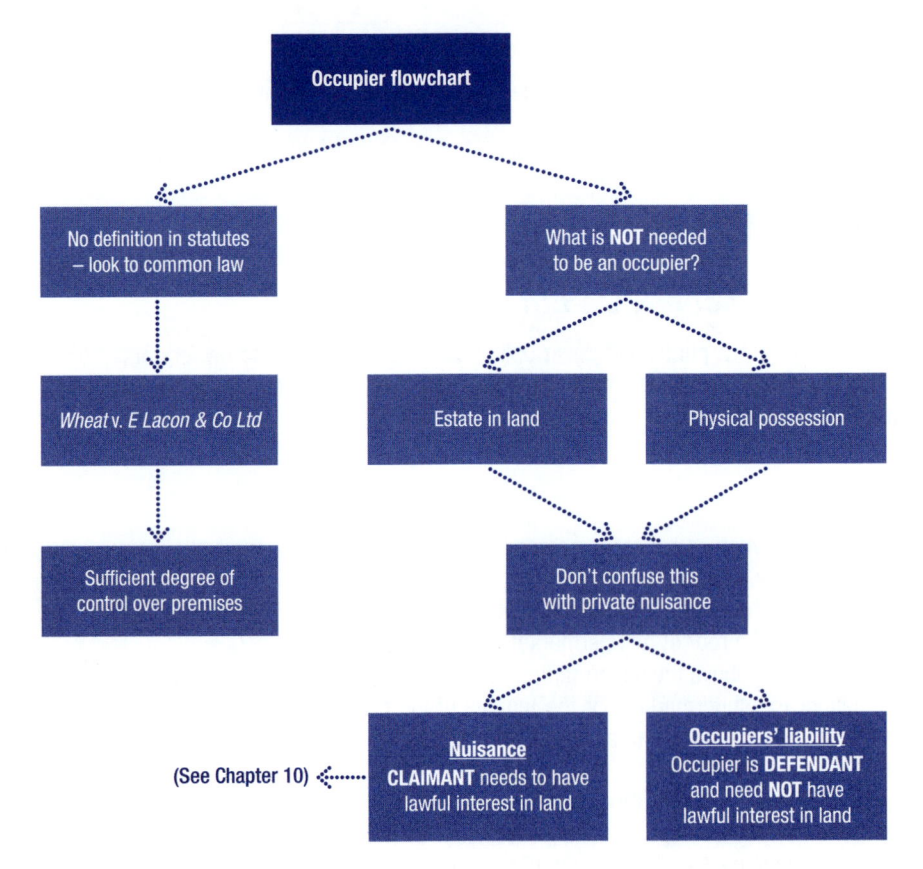

Figure 8.1 Occupier flowchart

OCCUPIERS' LIABILITY ACT 1957: OCCUPIERS' LIABILITY TO LAWFUL VISITORS

> **CONTEXT**
>
> Before 1957, the common law prescribed that you owed a duty to lawful visitors, but that duty varied according to whether the visitor entered by contract or as an invitee or licensee. Thus, varying levels of duty were owed to various kinds of visitors. The Occupiers' Liability Act 1957(OLA 1957) simplified matters by abolishing these 'occupancy duties' and replacing them with the single common duty of care, owed to a single category of visitor, the lawful visitor.

People other than lawful visitors are not protected by the 1957 Act. Most of them are now protected by the 1984 Act (see below).

CORNERSTONE

Common duty of care

Section 2(1) of the 1957 Act forms its core, and states that an occupier of premises owes a common duty of care to visitors.

Lawful visitors

Section 1 of the Act provides that the duty of care is owed to 'visitors' and specifically that a visitor for purposes of the Act is the same as a licensee or invitee under the common law. The terms 'invitee' (people invited to enter the premises) and 'licensees' (people who are merely permitted to be on the premises) are not important save that they help us to understand case law from before the Act. Added to people invited onto and permitted on premises, certain people are allowed onto premises 'as of right', such as policemen, postmen, meter-readers, etc. Further, section 1(4) states who is *not* a visitor, namely a person entering the premises 'in exercise of rights conferred by virtue of section 2(1) of the Countryside and Rights of Way Act 2000 or an access agreement or order under the National Parks and Access to the Countryside Act 1949' – in other words, people using rights of way. In the case of private rights of way, the 1984 Act applies, but for public rights of way, principles of the common law operate.

CORNERSTONE

Lawful visitors

It is important to determine whether the claimant is a lawful visitor or not, as the 1957 Act is only applicable to lawful visitors. If the claimant is not a lawful visitor, the 1984 Act may be applicable.

Express or implied permission

The 1957 Act will regard someone with implied permission to enter as a lawful visitor. The obvious problem is to determine whether a person indeed has such implied permission to enter. This will be determined on the facts of each case, and the burden of proof is on the person who claims implied permission. Let us consider a few examples.

CORNERSTONE

Lowery v. *Walker* [1911] AC 10

Trespassers frequently crossed the occupier's field and although he objected to this he did not take legal proceedings against them, as many of them were his customers. However, he then put a wild horse in the field without giving warning to the public, and the claimant was injured. The House of Lords held that the claimant had implied permission to be on the premises.

Thus implied permission would cover instances where people have not been invited to enter but their presence is not seen as objectionable to the occupier. However, it is necessary to show permission and not mere tolerance, as the following case illustrates.

In *Edwards* v. *Railway Executive* [1952] AC 737 boys habitually broke through a fence along a railway and played on the embankment. One boy was injured and sued the occupier railway. The railway denied giving an implied licence to trespassers, as it repaired the fence whenever it noticed damage to it. The House of Lords held that a licence may not be implied merely because the occupier knows of the entrant's presence or has failed to take every possible step to prevent his entry. According to Lord Goddard, repeated trespass of itself confers no licence:

> '. . . there must be evidence either of express permission or that the landowner has so conducted himself that he cannot be heard to say that he did not give it.'

Finally, a person may be a trespasser without knowing it. It is the mind (and actions or lack of action) of the occupier that are relevant, not the beliefs of the visitor. A visitor may also become a trespasser when she exceeds her invitation or strays into areas where she had not been invited because section 2(2) states that the common duty of care applies only to 'the purposes for which [the visitor] is invited or permitted by the occupier to be there'. This can relate to areas to which the visit is constrained, length of stay and also activities permitted while on the premises. Scrutton LJ famously said, in *The Calgarth* [1927] P 93:

> 'When you invite a person into your house to use the staircase, you do not invite him to slide down the bannisters.'

INTERSECTION

We already saw in *Wheat* v. *E Lacon & Co Ltd*, above, that there can be more than one occupier of premises, and we also know that an independent contractor can be regarded as an occupier together with the owners of the premises. *Ferguson* v. *Welsh* [1987] 1 WLR 1553 is significant as it illustrates how the 1957 Act is applied and how it intersects with other torts.

Let us look at the *Ferguson* case step by step. A local council contracted with S to demolish a building. S, contrary to the council's express prohibition, subcontracted the work to W, who in their turn employed the claimant. Due to unsafe practices, the building collapsed and severely injured the claimant. The House of Lords' decision is important in several ways.

First, it made clear that it is possible for a claimant to be a trespasser to one occupier, but a lawful visitor to another. In this case, the benefit of the doubt was given to the claimant, and he was regarded as a visitor for both the occupiers (the council and the contractor).

Secondly, having established that the claimant was a visitor under the Act, and that the defendants were to be regarded as occupiers, the next step was to determine whether the occupiers fell foul of the common duty of care (discussed below) prescribed by section 2(2) of the Act. The common duty of care entails that occupiers should try to keep visitors safe not only from dangers due to the state of the premises but also known dangers due to things done or omitted to be done on them. This would seem to make the occupiers liable, but the court went on to examine the special situation governing independent contractors contained in section 2(4) (discussed below).

In considering section 2(4)(b) the court held:

> 'It would be going a very long way to hold that an occupier of premises is liable to the employee of an independent contractor engaged to do work on the premises in respect of dangers arising not from the physical state of the premises but from an unsafe system of work adopted by the contractor.'

The court held that as long as the council had no reason to suspect that the independent contractor was not to be trusted, they could not be held liable.

The final significance of this case is that it illustrates how occupiers' liability intersects with another tort, employer's liability, in that the employer failed to provide a safe system of work and was held liable on that basis. We examine this tort in Chapter 12.

Premises

The term 'premises' within the Act includes land and buildings and section 1(3) includes 'any fixed or movable structure, including any vessel, vehicle or aircraft'. Examples of what were held by courts to be 'premises', include pylons, grandstands, lifts, tunnels and even a ladder.

It is very important to note that occupiers' liability arises from defective premises, or the state of the premises, and not from what is *done* on the premises. The following cases illustrate the difference.

CORNERSTONE

Tomlinson v. Congleton Borough Council [2003] 3 WLR 705

The claimant dived into the shallow end of a lake owned by the defendant council, struck his head and suffered a severe spinal injury. The council had put up warning signs prohibiting swimming and diving and was planning to destroy the beach on the shores of the lake as the warning signs were frequently ignored by members of the public. At first instance the council was held not liable, but on appeal the Court of Appeal decided that all three elements of section 1(3) were satisfied. The House of Lords, however, overruled that decision and held the defendants not liable, for several reasons including that the risk was not due to the state of the premises but rather due to the activity that the defendant himself chose to pursue. Importantly, the House addressed an interesting →

debate: how far should the law go in protecting people against themselves? The court stressed that paternalism should not be taken too far, and that individuals should take responsibility for their own actions. Lord Hoffmann's thoughts are noteworthy:

> 'I think that there is an important question of freedom at stake. It is unjust that the harmless recreation of responsible parents and children with buckets and spades on the beaches should be prohibited in order to comply with what is thought to be a legal duty to safeguard irresponsible visitors against dangers which are perfectly obvious. The fact that such people take no notice of warnings cannot create a duty to take other steps to protect them . . . A duty to protect against obvious risks or self-inflicted harm exists only in cases in which there is no genuine and informed choice, or in the case of employees, or some lack of capacity, such as the inability of children to recognise danger (*British Railways Board* v. *Herrington* [1972] AC 877) or the despair of prisoners which may lead them to inflict injury on themselves (*Reeves* v. *Commissioner of Police* [2000] 1 AC 360) . . . The Borough Leisure Officer said that he regretted the need to destroy the beaches but saw no alternative if the Council was not to be held liable for an accident to a swimmer. So this appeal gives your Lordships the opportunity to say clearly that local authorities and other occupiers of land are ordinarily under no duty to incur such social and financial costs to protect a minority (or even a majority) against obvious dangers.'

More recently in *Geary* v. *JD Wetherspoon plc* [2011] EWHC 1506 (QB) the claimant slid down a bannister in the defendant's pub, fell and broke her back. The court held that the defendant was not liable. The injury resulted from what the claimant had decided, voluntarily, to do whilst in the premises, and not from the state of the premises as such. Her voluntary assumption of the risk of injury was fatal to her claim.

The 'common duty of care'

Section 2(1) of the 1957 Act states:

> 'An occupier owes the same duty, the "common duty of care", to all his visitors . . .'

Section 2(2) goes on to define the common duty of care as:

> '. . . a duty to take such care as in all the circumstances of the case is reasonable to see that the visitor will be reasonably safe in using the premises for the purposes for which he is invited or permitted by the occupier to be there.'

INTERSECTION

You will remember from the discussion of the tort of negligence (Chapter 2) that the first step in a claim for negligence is to *establish* a duty of care on the defendant. In occupiers' liability this step, which can be very difficult to prove, is cut out, as the 'common duty of care' is assumed when all the other elements of the tort (such as injury due to the state of the premises, the claimant being a visitor and the defendant the occupier) are present. The intersection with negligence is important as many of the principles, such as causation, are the same.

It is a question of fact to determine in each case whether the common duty of care had been fulfilled. Revise the principles relating to breach of duty in negligence claims (Chapter 3) because they are similar. The standard of care is the same, namely that of the reasonable person. The word 'common' merely means that the Act does not make a distinction between *types* of visitors in the way the common law did (licensees, invitees, etc.). In brief, the common duty of care means that the occupier of premises has a duty to ensure that the premises are safe for visitors and, importantly, that they are safe for the purpose/s for which the visitors are present. The occupier must guard against foreseeable risks. When deciding on what is required in a specific case for the duty to be discharged by the occupier, the courts also take into account whether the claimant had knowledge of any danger or risk.

The Act gives some specific guidance on the standard of care in section 2(3) by providing that an occupier must be prepared for children to be less careful than adults; and that an occupier may expect that a person who enters her premises in the exercise of a calling, will appreciate and guard against any special risks ordinarily incidental to such calling.

> **Take note**
>
> While the principles of the duty of care are similar for negligence and occupiers' liability, the differences are significant. For the latter, the duty is assumed, as pointed out above, while for negligence it has to be proved. An occupier can exclude or limit her duty of care towards visitors (discussed below).

Children

According to section 2(3)(a) of the OLA 1957, 'an occupier must be prepared for children to be less careful than adults'. This means that the premises must be reasonably safe for a child of that age (the visitor). Therefore, we measure the standard of care owed to children subjectively (by looking at the relevant child and its age). In *Glasgow Corporation* v. *Taylor* [1922] 1 AC 44 a seven-year-old child ate poisonous berries in a public park from a shrub that was easily accessible to children. The court held that it was to be expected that a young child would be attracted by the brightly coloured berries, and that the occupier should have taken adequate measures to prevent access to them. In contrast, it was held in *Keown* v. *Coventry Healthcare NHS Trust* [2006] EWCA Civ 39 that there was no liability when an 11-year-old boy fell while climbing on a fire escape, as at that age the child knew the risk of what he was doing. We will revisit this case when we look at the OLA 1984, as the boy was a trespasser.

Glasgow Corporation v. *Taylor* also gave us the concept of 'allurement', which denotes something on a premises which is both 'fascinating and fatal' to the young, such as the poisonous berries in the park. Since the OLA 1984 (see below), the concept of allurement is used in order to assess whether or not the relevant duty of care has been adequately discharged.

What may be safe for an adult may be dangerous to a child. In *Moloney* v. *Lambeth London Borough Council* (1966) 64 LGR 440 a child fell into a gap in a stairwell that was too small for an adult. The court held the council liable.

The courts may take all relevant circumstances into account – such as an expectation that very young children will be under a reasonable degree of parental control. The court held an occupier not liable when a five-year-old child fell into a trench on its premises, as the parents should have supervised a child of that age properly (*Phipps* v. *Rochester Corporation* [1955] 1 QB 450).

Finally, liability only arises if the damage is foreseeable. In *Jolley* v. *London Borough of Sutton* [2000] 3 All ER 409 the defendant occupier failed to remove an abandoned boat, which formed an allurement to children as a place to play. A 14-year-old boy was injured when he and his friends jacked the boat up and it fell on him. The Court of Appeal held that although it was reasonably foreseeable that children would play on the boat and be injured, it was not foreseeable that they would prop up the boat and be injured by its falling off the prop. The House of Lords reversed this decision and held that it was sufficient that injury in general was foreseeable.

INTERSECTION

> The House of Lords in *Jolley* applied the foreseeability principles from the case of *The Wagon Mound*, which we discussed (in Chapter 4) when we looked at causation as an element for negligence.

To sum up: the level of care expected regarding children depends on the age and awareness of the child, as well as the nature of the risk itself.

Skilled visitors

Section 2(3)(b) determines that:

> '(a)n occupier may expect that a person, in the exercise of his calling, will appreciate and guard against any special risks ordinarily incidental to it, so far as the occupier leaves him free to do so.'

An occupier may thus expect that a skilled visitor, employed to undertake work on the premises, will take appropriate precautions against risks ordinarily associated with her work.

So, where occupiers had to be more vigilant where children visited the premises, the opposite is true for skilled visitors, where the assumption is that they know what they are doing.

For example, in *Roles* v. *Nathan* [1963] 1 WLR 1117 the court held an occupier not liable when chimney sweeps died from carbon monoxide inhalation, as it could be assumed that sweeps would know of this danger due to the nature of their work. Note that this only covers risks associated with the job the professional is engaged to do.

APPLICATION

> Consider the case of *Roles* v. *Nathan* again. The sweeps' injury was incidental to their work. If the injury had been caused by something unrelated to their work, such as for example, a faulty stairway giving way under them, the occupier could be held liable.

Also note that the mere fact that a claimant has a particular skill is not enough for the occupier to escape liability. Cases where firemen successfully sued for injuries sustained while fighting fires negligently started by occupiers illustrate this. In *Ogwo* v. *Taylor* [1988] AC 431 the court held that an out of control fire was inherently dangerous even to men with special skills, training and equipment.

Warning signs

An occupier can discharge her common duty of care by issuing a warning. However, there are requirements that have to be fulfilled.

CORNERSTONE

Occupiers' Liability Act 1957, section 2(4)(a)

The OLA, in section 2(4)(a), determines that:

'. . . where damage is caused to a visitor by a danger of which he had been warned by the occupier, the warning is not to be treated without more as absolving the occupier from liability, unless in all the circumstances it was enough to enable the visitor to be reasonably safe.'

Because the warning must be enough to enable the visitor to be reasonably safe, we must look at how adequate the warning is. It must state clearly the nature of the danger, and the visitor must have an option, for example alternative access that will be safe. If the visitor has no alternative but to use the premises, a warning will not be adequate. The warning must also be precise enough so that the visitor knows what risk she is facing. Some common sense factors are also taken into account: if the danger is obvious, for example slippery algae on a high wall, a warning may not be necessary; if the visitors are mostly young children, on the other hand, warning signs may be totally ineffective. In some cases of extreme danger, even a specific warning will not be enough; it must be accompanied by an appropriate barrier.

It is important to distinguish between a warning notice, which is subject to the criteria of 'adequacy' under section 2(4)(a) and an exclusion of liability notice. Exclusion clauses are contractual terms and therefore the Unfair Contract Terms Act 1977 applies to them. Section 2(1) of the OLA 1957 recognises that the occupier can exclude her duty of care towards visitors by means of such contractual exclusion, but note that, arguably, they cannot go below the minimum standard of care owed to trespassers by the OLA 1984. If this were not so, trespassers would be better protected than lawful visitors. Also note that of course, exclusion clauses will not be effective against children who cannot read, or against strangers who have not had the opportunity to read the exclusion clause, or against persons who enter the premises as of right. Liability for death or personal injury caused by negligence also cannot be excluded.

Independent contractors

In general, an occupier is not liable for the negligence of an independent contractor. However, there are three exceptions contained in section 2(4)(b). The occupier may be held liable for her independent contractor's harm to a visitor if she had not acted reasonably in entrusting the work to an independent contractor, or taken reasonable care to see that the contractor was competent, or (where feasible) that the work was properly done. It would be easy, for example, to check whether a simple task had been done, but the courts will not expect a layperson to check work of a highly technical nature. To illustrate, in *Haseldine* v. *Daw* [1941] 2 KB 343 an occupier was not held liable for damage caused by an independent contractor's faulty servicing of a lift, while in *Woodward* v. *Mayor of Hastings* [1954] KB 74 the occupier was held liable to an injured child who slipped on a step that was icy due to the cleaners' failure to clean up properly.

Remember that should it prove impossible to sue the occupier, there may still be the option to sue directly the contractor, either in a claim for negligence or if the contractor can be regarded as an occupier, under either of the Occupiers' Liability Acts.

Defences

Consent

According to section 2(5), the occupier has no liability to a visitor in respect of risks willingly accepted by the visitor. The general principles of consent, or *volenti non fit injuria*, apply. However, there are certain requirements. The visitor must have fully understood the risk. Not only must the visitor have known the risk, but also have accepted it and such knowledge must have been sufficient to make her safe. What is more, if the claimant had no choice but to enter the premises, she cannot be said to have accepted the risk and thus to have consented to it.

Contributory negligence

The court could hold that the claimant contributed to her own damage or injury and in such a case the award of damage will be reduced in proportion to the extent that she so contributed.

Exclusion

A properly worded, effective warning or exclusion notice could be a valid defence – see the discussion above under 'warnings'.

OCCUPIERS' LIABILITY ACT 1984: LIABILITY TO TRESPASSERS AND NON-VISITORS

> **CONTEXT**
>
> Traditionally, the common law tended to operate harshly against trespassers. The only duty an occupier owed to a trespasser was not intentionally or recklessly to injure her, and what is more, this was only accorded to trespassers known to be present. The problem with this was that not all trespass is morally reprehensible. For example, it often happened that children trespassed onto land, got injured and then had no remedy. This offended against justice, and the common law's response was to circumvent this by using legal fictions such as the concept of allurement, which we examined in the case of *Glasgow Corporation* v. *Taylor* above. Later, it was decided that occupiers owe at least a 'duty of common humanity' to trespassers (*British Railways Board* v. *Herrington* [1972] AC 877), but the situation remained unsatisfactory until 1984, when with the enactment of the Occupiers' Liability Act 1984, liability to trespassers was formally recognised.

Scope of the Act

The OLA 1984 extends the duty of care owed by an occupier to go beyond that of a duty to a lawful visitor – now the duty is also owed to 'persons other than visitors'.

CORNERSTONE

Claimants under the Occupiers' Liability Act 1984

In terms of section 1(1)(a) 'persons other than visitors' include trespassers, persons using a private right of way, persons entering the land under an access agreement or order under the National Parks and Access to the Countryside Act 1949. Section 1(7) explicitly excludes users of public rights of way from the protection afforded by the Act.

According to section 1(1), an occupier has a duty of care in respect of people other than visitors for 'injury on the premises by reason of any danger due to the state of the premises or the things done or omitted to be done to them'. From this it is clear that the OLA 1984 provides compensation for injuries only and not for damages to property.

When does the OLA 1984 apply?

An occupier will only owe a duty if:

- she is aware of the danger or has reasonable grounds to believe that it exists;
- she knows or has reasonable grounds to believe that the other is in the vicinity of the danger concerned or that she may come into the vicinity of the danger (in either case, whether the other has lawful authority for being in that vicinity or not); and
- the risk is one against which, in all the circumstances of the case, she may reasonably be expected to offer the other some protection.

The tests under the first two elements are subjective, but the test under the third is objective. Section 1(4) determines that 'the duty is to take such care as is reasonable in all the circumstances of the case to see that he does not suffer injury on the premises by reason of the danger concerned'. The standard of care is thus an objective standard based on negligence (the reasonable person, or in this instance, the reasonable occupier). It is a question of fact in each case, but the courts are likely to take into account:

- the nature of the premises;
- the degree of danger;
- the practicality of taking precautions; and
- the age of the trespasser.

In *Keown* v. *Coventry Healthcare NHS Trust* (discussed above) the court looked at the age of the child to determine whether he ought to have realised the risk of his behaviour, but they also made an important distinction between potential danger due to the state of the building and the dangerous use of premises that may be in good repair. You will remember that the defendant was held not liable. Contrast this to the decision in *Young* v. *Kent County Council* [2005] EWHC 1342 (QB), where a child of similar age fell through a skylight that was known to the defendant council to be in a flimsy state of repair. The council was held liable, although the damages award against it was reduced due to the child's contributory negligence.

Also remember that occupiers' liability arises out of the *state* of the premises, and *not* what the claimant chose to do whilst there. Revise the previous discussion of *Tomlinson* and *Wetherspoon*.

The courts must take all the circumstances at the time the injury occurred into account. Echoing the common sense approach taken in *Tomlinson*, the court decided in *Donoghue* v. *Folkestone Properties Ltd* [2003] EWCA Civ 231 that there was no liability towards a trespasser who sustained a diving injury while trespassing on a slipway in a harbour, at midnight, and in the middle of winter.

Furthermore, there is no liability if the occupier had no reason to suspect a trespasser to be present. In *Higgs* v. *WH Foster* [2004] EWCA Civ 843 an occupier owed no duty of care to a trespasser who had fallen into an uncovered inspection pit on his land since he did not know or have reasonable grounds for believing that a trespasser would enter his premises and come into the vicinity of the pit. There is also no liability if the occupier was unaware of the danger or had no reason to suspect the danger.

Exclusion of liability

Section 1(5) states that the duty of the occupier can be discharged by 'taking such steps as are reasonable in all the circumstances of the case to give warning of the danger concerned or to discourage persons from incurring the risk'. The principles relating to warning signs discussed under the 1957 Act are applicable. However, note that the reference to exclusion clauses made in the OLA 1957 is absent from the OLA 1984. The reason given for this is that the OLA 1984 creates a minimum standard of care and no occupier should be allowed to go below this.

> It is possible to use an exclusion clause to exclude liability to lawful visitors, but not towards trespassers. This means, logically, that trespassers are accorded greater protection by the law as liability to them cannot be excluded. Think about the reason given for this above. Do you think it is good enough? Does the law need to address this issue?

REFLECTION

Defences

The defence of *volenti* is possible if the trespasser is fully aware of and consents to the risk. The defence of contributory negligence has also been accepted in relation to the OLA 1984.

The following flowchart illustrates how to determine liability for occupiers under the two Acts and the common law.

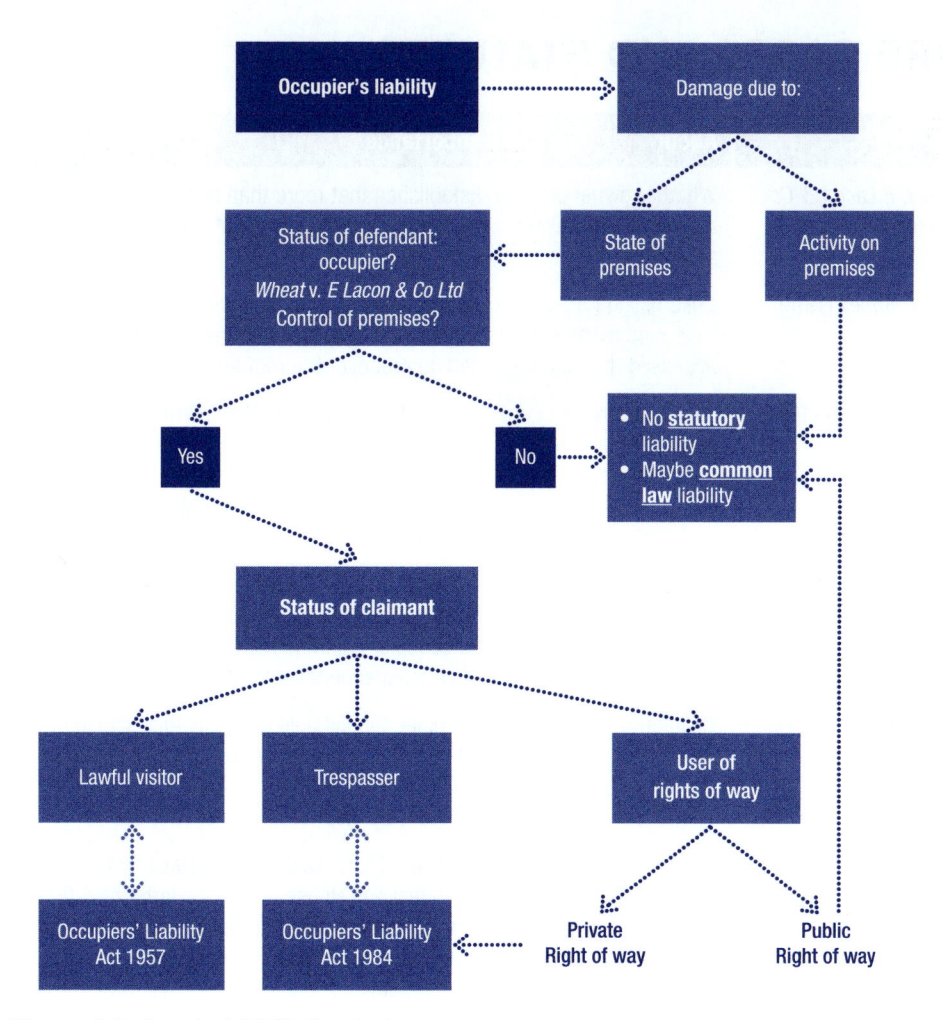

Figure 8.2 Occupiers' liability flowchart

KEY POINTS

- Under certain circumstances, occupiers of premises may be held liable to persons injured whilst on their premises.
- The Occupiers' Liability Act 1957 relates to lawful visitors and enables them to sue for both personal injury as well as damage to property.
- The Occupiers' Liability Act 1984 relates to visitors other than lawful visitors. In most instances, this means trespassers. Under this Act, personal injury only may be claimed.
- Occupiers' liability branched out of the general principles of negligence.
- An 'occupier' is the person who has control over the state of the premises and could be, for example, the landlord or the tenant, or both, of premises.
- Liability for defective premises can also arise under the Defective Premises Act 1972.

CORE CASES AND STATUTES

Case	About	Importance
Wheat v. *E Lacon & Co Ltd* [1966] AC 552	Whether owner or manager of pub were occupiers	Established that more than one person could be the occupier for purposes of occupiers' liability.
Bailey v. *Armes* [1999] EGCS 21	Child falling through roof of supermarket accessed through flat	Neither supermarket nor tenants of the flat held liable, court held that the key was whether they had control over the roof area.
Lowery v. *Walker* [1911] AC 10	Tolerated trespassers suddenly confronted with wild horse	House of Lords held implied permission covers instances where people had not been invited to enter but their presence were not seen as objectionable to the occupier. Mere tolerance not enough.
Ferguson v. *Welsh* [1987] 1 WLR 1553	Contractors subcontracted unlawfully, employee hurt	Claimant can be a trespasser to one occupier, but a lawful visitor to another. Discussed when an occupier could be held liable for the actions of an independent contractor.
Glasgow Corporation v. *Taylor* [1922] 1 AC 44	Child ate poisonous berries in public park	Occupier council held liable, as they should have taken proper care to prevent children eating the berries, higher standard of care owed to children. Concept of allurement set out.
Jolley v. *London Borough of Sutton* [2000] 3 All ER 409 (HL)	Abandoned boat fell on teenage boy playing under it	Concept of foreseeability discussed by Court of Appeal and House of Lords – latter held that foreseeability of injury in general is enough, do not need to prove foreseeability of the specific kind of injury.
Keown v. *Coventry Healthcare NHS Trust* [2006] EWCA Civ 39	11-year-old injured while playing on fire escape	Age of child taken into account – he was old enough to know the risk of what he was doing.
Tomlinson v. *Congleton Borough Council* [2003] 3 WLR 705	Despite warning signs, claimant dived into lake and injured his spine	House of Lords held council not liable as risk was not due to state of premises but due to (prohibited) activity claimant himself chose to do. Important decision in the debate about the so called 'compensation culture'.

Statute	About	Importance
Occupiers' Liability Act 1957	Occupiers' liability to lawful visitors	Gives a remedy against an occupier of premises for personal injury or damage to property due to the state of the premises visited.
Occupiers' Liability Act 1984	Occupiers' liability to people other than visitors	Gives a remedy against an occupier of premises for personal injury only sustained by mostly trespassers to the premises.

FURTHER READING

Bundock, M. and Farrelly, M. (2001) Dangerous premises and liability to trespassers. *NLJ* **151, p. 309**
This article discusses an Appeal Court judgment relating to an occupier's duty of care towards trespassers and the causation requirement under the 1984 Act.

Jaffey, A.J.E. (1985) *Volenti non fit injuria.* **CLJ 44, p. 87**
You need to understand when and how liability for injury or damage can be excluded for occupiers of premises. This article examines some of the problems that are encountered with exclusion of liability and specifically the concept of consent in occupiers' liability.

Jones, M. (1984) The Occupiers' Liability Act 1984. *MLR* **47, p. 713**
This article discusses the 1984 Act in context and will give you a solid understanding of the duties of care owed by occupiers to trespassers.

Murphy, J. (1997) Public rights of way and private law wrongs. *Conv* **p. 362**
The author gives a good explanation of the reasons why both the Occupiers' Liability Acts were promulgated, examines how far they replace or supplement the common law, and importantly, explains the problem encountered with public rights of way.

CHAPTER 9
Product liability

BLUEPRINT
Product liability

KEY QUESTIONS

LEGISLATION
- Consumer Protection Act 1987
- Council Directive 85/374/EEC on liability for defective products

CONTEXT
- On policy grounds, due to the difficulties presented by the fault requirement under negligence, legislation was enacted creating a strict liability tort for product liability.

CONCEPTS
- Manufacturer
- Ultimate consumer
- Intermediate inspection
- Producer

- Why should defective products give rise to strict liability?

- Who can be held liable in negligence for damage by defective products to consumers?
- How does liability for defective products differ under the common law on the one hand and statute on the other hand?

CASES

- *Donoghue v. Stevenson* [1932]
- *O'Byrne v. Aventis Pasteur SA* [2010]
- *Pollard v. Tesco Stores* [2006]
- *A v. National Blood Authority* [2001]
- *Abouzaid v. Mothercare* [2000]

REFORM

- Meaning of 'producer' in terms of the EC Directive was unclear and had to be referred to the ECJ by the House of Lords for clarification in *O'Byrne*.

SPECIAL CHARACTERISTICS

- Liability for damage due to defective product can arise either:
  - Under common law – negligence principles (i.e. fault-based liability)
  - Under statute – strict liability

CRITICAL ISSUES

Setting the scene

Arguably the most famous case in the common law, *Donoghue* v. *Stevenson* is commonly regarded as the case that firmly established negligence as the most important tort of our time. In this case, the claimant's friend gave her a bottle of ginger beer, from which she drank before discovering a half decomposed snail emerging from the opaque bottle. The claimant could not claim in contract, as she did not buy the drink for herself (in contract law terms she was not party to the contract, and the rule of privity states that only parties to a contract may sue upon the contract). Did that mean that she had no claim at all?

Well, the court thought that she ought to have one, and Lord Atkin formulated the famous 'neighbour principle', which kicked off the long modern development of the tort of negligence. This well-known passage is referred to as the 'wide *ratio*' of *Donoghue* – wide, because it deals with *all* potential instances of when a duty of care could be owed by one person to another.

But the court also focused its attention on the narrow issue before it, namely the manufacturer of the bottle of ginger beer, and the potential liability towards the ultimate consumer. The 'narrow *ratio*' in *Donoghue*, dealing with the duties of manufacturers towards consumers, clarified the common law position regarding product liability. Since then the law in this area developed apace, and was eventually codified in statute. Defective products nowadays can therefore give rise to liability both from statutory provisions and from the common law of contract and tort.

LIABILITY IN CONTRACT AND CONSUMER LAW

This area of law lends itself to large overlap with, especially, the law of contract and consumer law.

INTERSECTION

> Consumers were first protected by the Sale of Goods Act 1893. Now protection is found in the Sale of Goods Act 1979, as amended by the Sale and Supply of Goods Act 1994. In terms of this Act, the seller is strictly liable to the buyer under certain circumstances. If successful under this Act, the buyer can reclaim the purchase price and also claim further damage. This is one example of consumer protection under contract law.

Other legislation such as, amongst others, the Unfair Contract Terms Act 1977 and the Unfair Terms in Consumer Contract Regulations 1999, provides further protection to consumers. However, there is one fundamental proviso to most of this protection: only a party to the contract can generally sue for breach of that contract. So the person receiving a defective product as a gift, for example, cannot claim under the Sale of Goods Act 1979. This is because of the doctrine of privity of contract. This doctrine also means that only the person (or company) that actually sold the product can be sued. The Contracts (Rights of Third Parties) Act 1999 goes some way to alleviate this problem as it does provide that a third party can have rights under the contract, under certain conditions. Once again, though, this is very limited and is not likely to be applicable in many cases.

So, whilst a detailed discussion of contract and consumer law lies beyond the scope of this book, hopefully it is clear from this limited mention that the consumer is not fully protected by them – the law of tort still plays an important role.

Consumer protection in tort can arise under either the common law and/or the Consumer Protection Act 1987.

COMMON LAW LIABILITY IN NEGLIGENCE

So what can a person who is injured by a defective product and who is not the buyer of that product do? She might be able to sue for negligence.

CORNERSTONE

Donoghue v. Stevenson [1932] AC 562

Donoghue v. *Stevenson* established not only the neighbour test but also the principle that a manufacturer owes a duty of care to the consumer. As Lord Atkin stated (the 'narrow ratio'):

'. . . a manufacturer of products, which he sells in such a form as to show that he intends them to reach the ultimate consumer in the form in which they left him with no reasonable possibility of intermediate examination, and with the knowledge that the absence of reasonable care in the preparation or putting up of the products will result in an injury to the consumer's life or property, owes a duty to the consumer to take that reasonable care.'

From this we can tease out some key terms to consider. What is meant by a **manufacturer**, for example? Also, what is meant by 'ultimate consumer', 'with no possibility of intermediate examination' and, last but not least, a 'product'? The courts have grappled with these, so let's look at what has been said about them.

Manufacturer

Remember that *Donoghue* was actually concerned with the question whether a manufacturer was under a legal duty to the ultimate consumer who had suffered damage as a result of a defective product. Subsequently, the principle in *Donoghue* has been extended in the case law to include not only manufacturers in the strict sense of the word, but also a variety of other occupations. The key is whether the party created the danger in the product which was then put into circulation. So, for example, in *Haseldine* v. *Daw* [1941] 2 KB 343 the court said that the repairers of a lift could be held liable.

INTERSECTION

> We looked at *Haseldine* v. *Daw* when we discussed occupiers' liability (in Chapter 8). You will remember that the question was whether the occupier of the premises would be held liable for the defective lift. Several torts, as well as several key concepts in tort, had to be considered: occupiers' liability, product liability, vicarious liability, etc. As you read more tort cases, you will note that this is something that often happens. It also often happens that from one set of facts, two (or more) causes of action may arise. For example, it is entirely possible to plead both product liability as well as in the alternative, negligence. We return to this strategy towards the end of this chapter.

From case law on this issue we see that the courts therefore interpreted 'manufacturer' widely.

CORNERSTONE

'Manufacturer'

The fact that the courts interpreted the term 'manufacturer' widely means that it now includes but is not limited to such disparate categories as fitters, erectors, water suppliers, second-hand dealers, assemblers, retailers and wholesalers.

Ultimate consumer

Donoghue protects the 'ultimate consumer' by stating that she is owed a duty of care by the manufacturer of the product that caused the injury. So who do we include under 'ultimate consumer'? Once again, the courts interpret this term widely. Anyone injured or suffering loss caused by a defective product can bring an action for negligence: the buyer; those who have received the product as a gift; those using a product belonging to someone else; or someone injured by a product while not actually using it themselves. Here are two examples from case law where there was held to be liability: in *Stennett* v. *Hancock* [1939] 2 All ER 578, a bystander was hit by a lorry wheel flying off a passing lorry; and in *Brown* v. *Cotterill* (1934) 51 TLR 21 a tombstone fell on a child who was lawfully in a graveyard.

CORNERSTONE

'Ultimate consumer'

In this area of law (the liability in negligence of manufacturers to consumers) the term 'consumer' includes almost anyone that the defendant could foresee may be affected by the defective product.

Product

What is a product? Yet again, this term is interpreted widely. We already saw in *Haseldine* v. *Daw* (above) that it includes lifts. Another example is clothing. In *Grant* v. *Australian Knitting Mills* [1936]

AC 85 the court held liable the manufacturers of dermatitis-causing underpants. A 'product' can therefore be seen as any kind of manufactured article which can cause injury or damage. It includes such diverse articles as gas, food and drink, hair-dye and towing-hitches.

Intermediate examination: causation

The final phrase from the narrow rule in *Donoghue* that we need to examine has to do with causation. What does 'with no reasonable possibility of intermediate examination' mean?

CORNERSTONE

'Intermediate inspection'

In practice, the term 'intermediate inspection' entails that if an intermediary is reasonably expected to examine the product, and if such inspection would or should have revealed the defect, but failed to do so, the chain of causation may have been broken.

In such an instance the chain of events linking the manufacturer with the ultimate consumer is broken by somebody else (let's call her 'X') because X did not properly inspect the product. In such an instance it could be X who would be held liable, not the manufacturer.

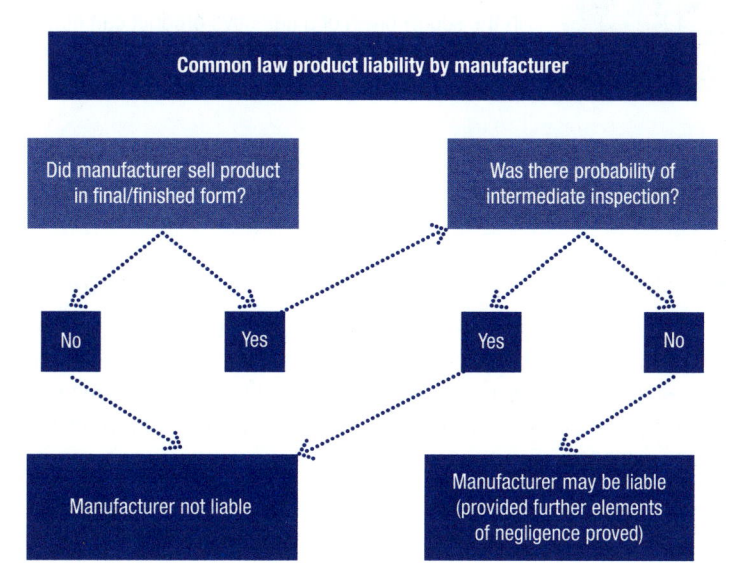

Figure 9.1 Intermediate inspection

Since *Donoghue* the term has been refined to mean reasonable *probability* rather than a reasonable *possibility* of intermediate examination. If there is any probability of intermediate examination and a possibility that some intervening event has caused the product to be faulty, it will be difficult for the defendant to show that the damage was caused by the *manufacturer's* negligence. This is even more so if there is a clear warning by the manufacturer that the product should be inspected. In *Kubach* v. *Hollands* [1937] 3 All ER 907 a schoolgirl was injured when the chemicals she used at school in an experiment caused an explosion. It turned out that the retailer who supplied the chemicals to the school had not tested the product as per the manufacturer's instructions. The court held that the retailer could be held liable but not the manufacturer.

Take note

Intermediate examination is only relevant if it would be reasonable to expect somebody (such as the retailer, or the consumer, or anybody else) actually to inspect the product. If a product is supposed to go onto the market 'as is', it would not be reasonable to expect an examination. Let's contrast the two cases we have looked at to illustrate the point: In *Grant v. Australian Knitting Mills* nobody would expect anyone to test or inspect underpants when they've been put on the market. In contrast, it was reasonable to expect the retailer in *Kubach v. Hollands* to inspect the chemicals before selling it on to the public.

Exclusion of liability

Kubach also brings us to the final issue to examine before leaving the common law and looking at the statutory regime. In that case the manufacturer, by requiring the product to be tested before use, effectively excluded its own liability. Similarly, for example, the defendant's liability may be excluded where the claimant has full appreciation of the danger or has misused the product.

Common law product liability as a form of negligence

What we have seen from the above is that almost anyone involved in the supply chain of a defective product can potentially be sued by a claimant who has suffered damage due to such defective product.

CORNERSTONE

Product liability – common law negligence principles

What you need to be clear about is that this (common law product liability under negligence) is not a tort in its own right, it forms part of negligence. That means that all the rules around negligence apply here as well. (Revise the elements we discussed in Chapters 2–4.) You will remember that the claimant has to prove that she was owed a duty of care, breach of that duty of care, causation, foreseeability and damages.

All of these elements also need to be proved in a common law product liability claim, with one important exception: it is already established law that a 'manufacturer' (in its wide sense as discussed above) owes a duty of care to the ultimate consumer. So one potential step is cut out for the claimant (of course, there are now so many established instances of recognised duties of care that it is not much of an advantage).

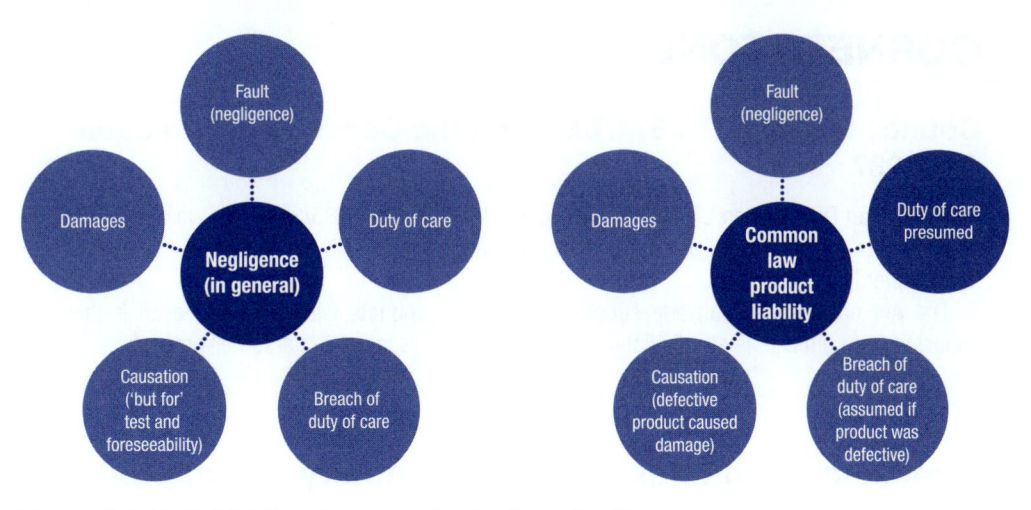

Figure 9.2 Product liability under common law is a form of negligence

Look at Figure 9.2. Note that 'fault' in the form of negligence needs to be proved for negligence, and thus also for product liability under common law. The need to prove fault, as well as the further task of proving breach of duty of care, is fairly difficult for claimants. The converse of this is that a person will not be liable if she has taken all reasonable steps to avoid injuring someone else and it is therefore relatively easy for manufacturers to exclude their potential liability. Given the unequal footing that manufacturers, on the one hand, and consumers on the other usually find themselves in, the need eventually arose to legislate in this area.

STATUTORY LIABILITY – THE CONSUMER PROTECTION ACT 1987

In many cases the fault requirement in negligence proved to be an insurmountable obstacle to claimants in product liability cases under the common law.

> There were several instances where society's sense of justice demanded that people should have a remedy, despite their inability to prove fault. For example, during the 1960s a number of babies, whose mothers had taken the drug Thalidomide during pregnancy, were born with birth defects. It proved to be virtually impossible to hold the manufacturers liable.
>
> This, together with other concerns prompted the EU to take action to protect consumers injured by defective products and to make it easier for them to claim compensation. The idea was to introduce strict liability for defective products. The EU and in turn the UK Parliament therefore enacted legislation to try and aid consumers.

CORNERSTONE

Council Directive 85/374/EEC and the Consumer Protection Act 1987

The European Directive on Liability for Defective Products 1985 (85/374/EEC) was passed which in turn led to the enactment of the Consumer Protection Act 1987. (We'll refer to it as 'the Act' in this chapter.)

The Act provides that anyone supplying defective products within the EU, even if they are imported from outside, is strictly liable if the defect causes injury to person or property.

Common law (fault-based) versus statutory (strict) product liability

The Act does not preclude any other liability arising in contract or tort generally. It does not replace the common law, but complements it. It tries to assist the consumer-claimant by doing away with the fault requirement. Generally it would therefore be easier to proceed with a claim in terms of the Act because you do not need to prove negligence or intention (the fault requirement under common law) – it imposes strict liability by creating a statutory tort.

The difference between the common law and the statutory tort can be represented like this:

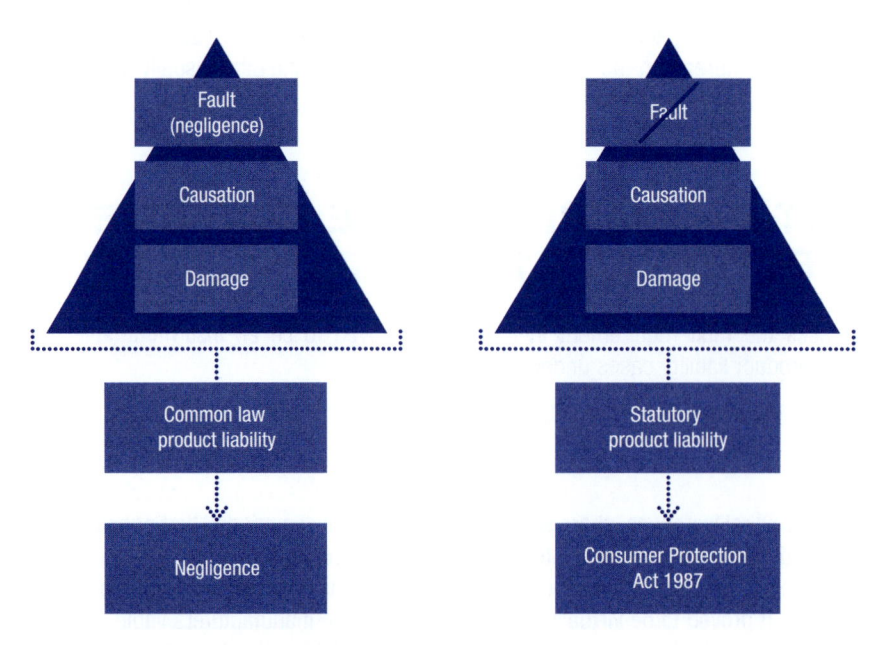

Figure 9.3 Common law v. statutory product liability

Let's look at the elements you need to prove to succeed with the statutory tort in more detail.

Who can sue?

Section 2(1) of the Act states that that there will be liability 'where any damage is caused wholly or partly by a defect in a product'. Thus anyone who suffers personal injury or damage caused by a defective product can sue.

Potential defendants

Section 2(2) lists the potentially liable people: producers, the 'own-brander' and the importer of goods originating from outside the EU.

Producers

The producer of a product is usually its manufacturer, but could also include people who manufacture parts that are in turn used by other manufacturers to produce something else.

If the finished product is defective, who will be held liable?

> **Take note**
> Remember that apart from fault, the claimant still has to establish, for the statutory tort: that it is the defendant that is to be held liable (i.e. she has to identify the correct defendant); that there is a defect in the product; that she suffered damage; and that the defect caused the damage.

APPLICATION

X provides microchips to Y, who in turn uses the microchips in its production of smart phones. Later the smart phones tend to explode. It turns out that the microchips were defective. Who will be held liable? In terms of the Act both the manufacturers are liable.

What about suppliers of goods? Do they count as 'producers'? The Act says that suppliers can be held liable *only if* the producer (or importer or own-brander) cannot be identified. The Act further requires that, if the consumer herself cannot identify the manufacturer, she has to first provide the supplier the opportunity to try and identify the manufacturer. Only if the manufacturer really cannot be identified, can the supplier be held liable. Think of this as going back along the chain of causation.

CORNERSTONE

O'Byrne v. Aventis Pasteur SA [2010] 4 All ER

Both the House of Lords and eventually the European Court of Justice had to grapple with the meaning of 'producer'. In *O'Byrne* v. *Aventis Pasteur SA* the claimant suffered brain damage after being administered a vaccine supplied by a wholly owned subsidiary of the defendant. The claimant therefore sued the subsidiary, but it was raised as a defence that the proper defendant should have been the parent company, who manufactured the vaccine. The claimant therefore wanted to substitute as defendant the parent company, but by that time his claim was time barred.

The matter went all the way up to the House of Lords (on various grounds) who, because of the fact that the relevant EC directive had to be interpreted, referred it to the European Court of Justice (ECJ) for clarification.

→

176 CHAPTER 9 Product liability

> The ECJ (at Paras. 54–58 and 64) held that where the person injured by an allegedly defective product was not reasonably able to identify the producer of the product, the supplier was under a duty promptly, and on its own initiative, to inform the injured person of the identity of the producer or of its own supplier. If it failed to do so, it could be treated as a 'producer' (and sued). The court also held that it was not enough for the supplier to merely inform the injured party that it was not the producer of the product – it had a positive duty to reveal the identity of the producer.

Own-branders
Supermarkets often use this kind of branding: somebody else produces the product but the supermarket sells it as their 'own brand'. In such an instance the supermarket itself can be sued in liability, the claimant does not need to try and find out who really manufactured the product.

Importers
Finally, anyone who has imported the product into the EU from another country may be held liable for the product.

Damage
What damage can you claim for? Section 5(1) provides that damage includes death or personal injury or any loss of or damage to property. However, sections 5(3) and (4) give restrictions to the liability for damage to property. There is no liability for loss or damage to the product *itself* or to any product of which the defective product forms part, and the Act does not cover damage to commercial interests. As far as property damage is concerned, the damage must be valued above £275.

APPLICATION
Let's say that Ben is given, and Hassan and Grace buy, the defective smart phones in our previous example. Ben's phone explodes in his hands and he suffers injuries to his hands and eyes. Hassan places his phone on his desk where it explodes, damaging the desk and Hassan's computer to such an extent that they have to be thrown away. Grace leaves her phone on the lawn at university whilst she plays an impromptu game of football with her friends. The phone explodes, but luckily nobody is injured and nothing damaged. Who can claim in terms of the Act? And what can they claim?

Ben can claim for his personal injuries.

Hassan can claim for the damage to his desk and computer.

Grace will not be able to claim in terms of the Act. The reason for this is because the Act does not provide a claim for damages to the product itself. (Grace may be able to claim in contract, maybe in terms of the Sale of Goods Act. She may also be able to claim in terms of the common law, maybe in terms of negligence if she can prove fault on the part of the manufacturer.)

Product
The Act is fairly specific about what is included and what is not included as a 'product'. See the following table.

Included in the Act	Not included in the Act
'Goods' (s. 1(2) including s. 45(1)): • substances • growing crops • things comprised in land by virtue of being attached to it • any ship, aircraft or vehicle	A building supplied by way of a creation or disposal of an interest in land (s. 46(4))
Electricity (s. 1(2))	Nuclear power (s. 6(8))
A product which is comprised in another product, whether by virtue of being a component part or raw material or otherwise (s. 1(2))	
Human blood and organs (*A* v. *National Blood Authority* [2001] 3 All ER 289)	

Defective

At this stage it is worth thinking about what the Act tries to protect, namely consumer safety. Section 3 deals with the meaning of 'defect' and states that a product is defective 'if the *safety* of the product is not such as persons generally are entitled to expect' (emphasis added). The Act thus only covers defects that make the product dangerous and not those that merely make the product perform less well or become less valuable. Put another way, 'defect' relates to the safety, not the quality, of the product.

Safety is considered in the context of risks of damage to property, and risks of death or personal injury. To decide whether a product is defective, section 3 directs the courts to take account of all the circumstances including the manner in and purposes for which the product was marketed, its get-up, any instructions or warnings accompanying it, what may reasonably be expected to be done with the product, and also the time when the product was supplied by the producer.

What this boils down to is that the court has to look at how safe the product was (taking into account the nature of the product and its intended use, amongst others). The reference to the time when the product was supplied means that the courts also have to take into account that times change, and that what is deemed unsafe today (with modern, up-to-date knowledge), may have been deemed safe a few years ago, judged against the knowledge of the time. (This relates to the 'state of the art' defence we examine later on.) Let's look at a few cases for examples of defective products.

In *Richardson* v. *LRC Products* [2000] Lloyd's Rep Med 280 the claimant had an unwanted pregnancy after her husband's condom split, and she sued the condom manufacturers. The court applied section 3 of the Act (examining the meaning of 'defect') and held that it was not possible to pinpoint why the condom had split, and that scientific research at that time merely showed that condoms did burst on occasion for no readily discernible reason. So the claimant had not proved that the condom was defective for purposes of the Act – it could have been damaged while it was stored at the claimant's house.

The following case illustrates how the courts deal with section 3 of the Act, and further illustrates how, on the same set of facts, a negligence claim may also be pursued. Further, in terms of section 2(5) of the act more than one defendant may be sued, and liability is joint and several. In this case we have three defendants.

CORNERSTONE

Pollard v. Tesco Stores [2006] EWCA Civ 393

In this case we deal with an own brander. A one-year-old child, C, got hold of a bottle containing washing powder, managed to open it and ingested some of the powder, which made him seriously ill. A claim on his behalf was instituted against both the own brander and the manufacturer in terms of the Act. It was alleged that the 'child-proof' bottle top had turned out not to be child-proof and was therefore defective for purposes of the Act.

The defendants then joined C's mother as a third defendant in the claim, by stating that she must have left the top off the bottle, or not fastened it properly, and furthermore that the bottle should not have been left where C could reach it. This, they alleged, must have been the real reason little C got to ingest the powder. So now there was, in addition to the tortious claim *in terms of the Act* against the 'producers', also a claim in *negligence* against C's mother.

The bottle top was tested and found to be not up to the British Standard, but also not as easy to open as an ordinary bottle top. In the court of first instance, the judge found in favour of C as to the claim against the producers, and held his mother, on the facts, to be not liable in negligence. The first and second defendants (i.e. the own brander and the manufacturer) appealed against this.

In the Court of Appeal Laws LJ gave the unanimous judgment. He stated that the case turned on whether there was a breach of the 1987 Act which was *causative* of C's injuries, and quoted the critical provision namely section 3(1): 'There is a defect in a product for the purposes of this Part if the safety of the product is not such as persons generally are entitled to expect . . .' He then asked what was meant by the phrase 'such as persons generally are entitled to expect' – did it mean that they were entitled to expect, in this instance, that the child-proof cap was up to British Certificate standards? The court was of the opinion that they were not – what they were entitled to expect was what they could be expected to understand, and that did not encompass the technical details of industry standards. So what persons could expect in the instant case was that the cap should be more difficult to open than an ordinary screw-top – which it was.

On that basis the claim in terms of the Act against the own brander and the manufacturer failed.

What about the claim against C's mother? The court held that, on the facts, although there were some doubts about the evidence given about where the bottle was left, etc., it could not be proved that the mother *caused* C's injuries. Therefore, the claim in negligence also failed.

No exclusion of liability

Note that liability, if the product is found to be defective, cannot be excluded under the Unfair Contract Terms Act 1977 by virtue of section 7 of the Consumer Protection Act. Producers who have business liability cannot exclude liability for death or personal injury caused by their negligence. However, note that sometimes a notice may prevent liability arising because it gives sufficient warning of the risk inherent to the product. For example: 'The contents of this bottle are poisonous. Do not drink them.' Make sure you understand that there is a difference here: if the product itself is dangerous, notice of its danger is sufficient, but if the danger arises because the product is *defective*, liability cannot be excluded.

Remember, finally, that liability is to a 'consumer' (i.e. anyone who suffers damage as a result of the defect(s) in question; the claimant need not be a 'user' of the product in question).

Causation

Just as in negligence, the claimant has the burden to prove causation, and the usual 'but for' test is used. More precisely, the claimant has to show that the producer put the product into circulation, that the product itself was defective in terms of the Act, and finally that the claimant suffered damage because of the defectiveness of the product.

DEFENCES UNDER THE CONSUMER PROTECTION ACT 1987

Section 4 of the Act lists the defences that can be raised. Let's first look at it in table format.

Section 4(1), subsection	Defence
(a) Legal requirements	It is a defence to show that you had complied with legal requirements. For example, if the manufacturer in *Pollard* could show that the bottle top was up to British Standard, it would have been a defence.
(b) Not supplied	It is a defence to prove that you had not 'supplied' the product – this relates to stolen or counterfeit goods.
(c) Not supplied in course of business	For example, if you supply products as a charity (e.g. you bake cakes and give them to a church which sells them at a fund-raising fete).
(d) Not defective at time of supply	If the defect arises after the date of supply, the manufacturer will not be liable. It is up to the manufacturer to prove the product was not defective at the time of supply.
(e) State of the art	Here the defendant proves that at the time of the supply, the state of scientific or technological knowledge was such that the defect could not have been known or foreseen. This takes into account that what is known today may not be the same as what is discovered tomorrow, and you are only judged against what is known at the time you supply the goods. See the discussion of *A* v. *National Blood Authority* [2001] EWHC 446 (QB) and *Abouzaid* v. *Mothercare (UK) Ltd* [2000] EWCA Civ 348 below.
(f) Component not defective	Here we deal with manufactured products comprising several components. If it can be shown that the defect is wholly attributable to the design of the finished product, the manufacturer of a component will not be liable.

CORNERSTONE

A v. *National Blood Authority* [2001] EWHC 446 (QB)

The claimants were infected with Hepatitis C because the blood transfusion service had taken blood from infected donors. The blood transfusion service argued that it was not liable: although there was a known risk of infection, there was also not any screening test available, due to the extent of scientific knowledge at the time the transfusions had taken place. They therefore argued that the risk was unavoidable.

On this point, the court took into account that the Act imposed *strict* liability. For this reason, the question of avoidability of the harm, the impracticability of taking precautionary measures and the benefit of the product to society as a whole, were not factors which the court was required to consider when determining liability under the Act.

Remember how the court in *Pollard* v. *Tesco* said that, in terms of the Act (s. 3) the question is not what the industry, or technical, standard is, but what the consumer could expect regarding the safety of the product? In a similar vein the court here held that the question is not what the medical profession understood about the risks inherent in the blood. Rather, the only relevant consideration for the court was what the public knowledge of the risks consisted of. In the instant case, while the risks had been appreciated by the medical profession, they had not been made known to, or accepted by, the wider public. Put another way, the Blood Authority had known about the risk but nevertheless continued to supply it to the public, who had an expectation that the blood would be safe. As such the Blood Authority could not evade responsibility.

In short, the defendants tried to rely on, but failed with, the state of the art defence.

In the following case the court again reiterated that liability hinged upon the expectations of the public at large about safety.

CORNERSTONE

Abouzaid v. *Mothercare (UK) Ltd* [2000] EWCA Civ 348

The claimant was injured when he tried to fasten his brother's pushchair. The defendant pointed out that this was the first time that such an accident had been reported about the product. It therefore argued that, as it had not been reported before, the state of technical knowledge at the time did not allow it to take steps to prevent the accident.

The court held that 'technical knowledge' for the purposes of the statute did not include previous accident reports. Mothercare was held liable. Also note that once again the court emphasised that we look not at what the *defendant* had known about the safety of the product, but that the test is what the public at large expected as to safety.

In addition to these defences, contributory negligence may also be raised. Also remember that, as in negligence, there is a prescription period. Action must be taken within three years from the date of the damage or from the date on which it could reasonably have been discovered. In the case of latent damage, there is a long stop of ten years after the product was put into circulation.

KEY POINTS

- 'Product liability' refers to the liability of manufacturers for products causing harm to consumers.
- Liability for defective products at common law developed from the narrow ratio of *Donoghue* v. *Stevenson* and therefore forms a category of negligence.
- Under the common law, a manufacturer of finished product put into circulation without the possibility of intermediate examination, owes a duty of care to consumers to ensure that the product will not cause foreseeable injury to the consumer's life or property.
- The fault requirement under the common law on product liability proved to be controversial, resulting in the European Union (EC Directive 85/372/EEC) and thereupon the Consumer Protection Act 1987 ushering in strict liability for defective products.
- In terms of the Consumer Protection Act 1987 fault does not need to be proved but the claimant still needs to correctly identify the defendant and prove that the product caused her damage.

CORE CASES AND STATUTES

Case	About	Importance
Donoghue v. *Stevenson* [1932] AC 562	Liability of manufacturer to ultimate consumer	A manufacturer owes a duty of care to the ultimate consumer if: the product was sold in the condition and form in which it was intended to reach the consumer; there was no reasonable possibility of intermediate inspection; and the manufacturer knew that the absence of reasonable care in the preparation of the product will result in damage or injury to the consumer.
Haseldine v. *Daw* [1941] 1 WLR 1375	Liability of repairer to person injured due to defective lift	Illustrates that 'manufacturer' is widely interpreted by the courts, including amongst others, 'repairers'.

Case	About	Importance
O'Byrne v. Aventis Pasteur SA [2010] 1 WLR 1375	Claimant was injured due to a defective vaccine. He sued the subsidiary, who raised the defence that the parent company should have been sued.	Where the person injured by an allegedly defective product was not reasonably able to identify the producer of the product, the supplier was under a duty promptly, and on its own initiative, to inform the injured person of the identity of the producer or of its own supplier. If it failed to do so it could be treated as a 'producer' (and sued).
Abouzaid v. Mothercare [2000] EWCA Civ 348	Claimant injured by pushchair snapping. Such defect had not been reported before, so the defendant argued that the state of technical knowledge at the time did not allow it to take steps to prevent the accident.	The court held that 'technical knowledge' for the purposes of the statute did not include previous accident reports. Defendant held liable.
Pollard v. Tesco Stores [2006] EWCA Civ 393	Toddler opened 'child-proof' top of bottle and was injured; case examined whether the top was 'defective' in the meaning of s. 3(1) of the Consumer Protection Act 1987.	Court held that '. . . what the public in general are entitled to expect' in section 3(1) meant that they would expect the bottle top to be more difficult to undo than an ordinary screw top, not that it would have been up to British Standard. In other words, the test is general, not specialist.

Statute	About	Importance
Consumer Protection Act 1987, s. 3	Meaning of 'defective product'	Interpreted in cases such as *Pollard v. Tesco Stores* and *A v. National Blood Authority* to mean what the public in general would expect about the safety of the product (not what a specialist would take it to be).
Consumer Protection Act 1987, s. 4	Defences	Includes defences such as the 'state of the art' defence which was examined in cases such as *Abouzaid v. Mothercare* and *A v. National Blood Authority*.

FURTHER READING

Gilliker, P. (2003) Strict liability for defective goods: the ongoing debate. *Business Law Review* 87
This article will deepen your understanding of how far the law implements the strict liability regime for consumers under the Consumer Protection Act 1987.

Fairgrieve, D. and Howells, G. (2007) Rethinking product liability: a missing element in the European Commission's Third Review of the Product Liability Directive. *Modern Law Review* 70, p. 962
European Union law have been instrumental in the development of English law in this regard. Reading articles such as these will keep you abreast of developments that influence UK legislation and court decisions.

Hodges, C. (2001) *A* v. *National Blood Authority. LQR* **117, p. 405**
One of the areas where the Act has had an impact is in liability for medical products. This article discusses the ground-breaking case of *A* v. *National Blood Authority*, which in its turn discussed issues central to the Act, such as strict liability. Reading this article together with the case will deepen your insight into both the case itself as well as the way in which one has to read a case in order to extract the most salient points.

Horsey, K. and Rackley, E. (2011) *Tort Law.* **Oxford: Oxford University Press**
Chapter 13 in this text provides a thorough and critical discussion of both the common law and statutory regime governing product liability.

CHAPTER 10
Defamation

BLUEPRINT
Defamation

KEY QUESTIONS

LEGISLATION
- Defamation Act 2013
- Defamation Act 1996

CONTEXT
- The ancient tort of defamation is adapting to the changed landscape focusing on human rights such as privacy protection and freedom of expression.

CONCEPTS
- Libel
- Slander
- Presumption of harm

- Several areas of concern about defamation were not addressed or were only partially addressed by the recent attempt at reformation in the Defamation Act 2013.

- What interest does defamation protect?
- What are the defences against a claim in defamation?

CASES
- *Cassidy* v. *Daily Mirror Newspaper* [1929]
- *Jameel* v. *Dow Jones & Co Inc* [2005]
- *Reynolds* v. *Times Newspapers Ltd* [1999]

REFORM
- Defamation Act 2013.
- The Act is still to come fully into operation and needs to be fleshed out by regulations and judicial interpretation.

SPECIAL CHARACTERISTICS
- Defamation protects one's reputation
- Libel is in permanent form and actionable *per se*
- Slander is in transitory form and mostly only actionable if special damage is proven

CRITICAL ISSUES

Setting the scene

If asked to give a snappy definition of defamation, one could say it means 'untrue and unjustified public disparaging of another'. The tort of defamation is in many ways very unlike any of the other torts. Most torts are there to protect your person or your property, and if they protect your person that usually means your right to safety or bodily integrity. Defamation, however, protects your *reputation*. Take note right at the start that it protects reputation and not privacy! This ties in with the strongest defence to an allegation of defamation, namely that what is being said is the truth: if so, there is no defamation. There is also no defamation if there is no publication. This means that a statement made between only the claimant and the defendant, with nobody else there to overhear it, cannot be defamation, regardless of how much it impugns the claimant. The reason for this is that reputation consists of what others think about you. So, if I make a statement about you causing others to think less of you, that would be defamation – provided that I have no defence such as that I was telling the truth.

There are various other ways in which defamation differs from most other torts. For example, there are many defamation-specific defences which play a very important role in defamation actions.

For many years commentators and free speech activists (such as for example scientists who were prevented from publishing critiques of certain practices by the threat of libel actions) severely criticised the common law tort as it stood on the tort of defamation. For this reason (which we will examine below) Parliament enacted the Defamation Act 2013.

INTRODUCTION

In many ways, the tort of defamation differs substantially from other torts. It has also recently been subjected to severe criticism, to such an extent that Parliament had to act by reforming the law through enactment of the Defamation Act 2013 (in this chapter, 'the Act'). At the time of writing this book, most of the provisions in the Act are not yet in force, and regulations intended to clarify and flesh out certain provisions have not yet been published. What we will do, therefore, is to look not only at the Act and how it changes the common law (or not!), but also why it was deemed necessary in the first place for Parliament to transform the law of defamation.

CORNERSTONE

Definition of defamation

Based on Lord Atkin's test for the word 'defamatory' in *Sim* v. *Stretch* [1936] 2 All ER 1237, defamation can be defined as '. . . the publication of a statement which reflects on a person's reputation and tends to lower him in the estimation of right-thinking members of society generally or tends to make them shun or avoid him'. (W.V.H. Rogers (2010) *Winfield and Jolowicz on Tort* 18th edn, London: Sweet & Maxwell, Para. 12.3.)

We can add to this definition the requirement that the statement should be untrue. Put another way, defamation is the publication of a false statement that injures the reputation of the person to whom it refers.

CORNERSTONE

Protection of reputation

Take note that defamation protects a person's *reputation* (and not privacy).

Students often make the mistake of confusing privacy protection with defamation. Be aware from the start that defamation does *not* protect privacy. In fact, English common law does not recognise a general right to privacy, nor is there a specific tort of invasion of privacy: *Wainwright* v. *Home Office* [2003] 4 All ER 969. Instead, breach of privacy is protected, but only to a limited extent, by the tort of 'breach of confidence'. This tort protects against the disclosure of confidential information (and is therefore to some extent equivalent to privacy protection). A few examples where celebrities succeeded in using breach of confidence to sue after their privacy had been invaded include Catherine Zeta Jones in *Douglas, Zeta Jones and Northern and Shell plc* v. *Hello! Ltd (No 1)* [2001] QB 967) and Naomi Campbell in *Campbell* v. *Mirror Group Newspapers plc* [2004] 2 AC 457. Remember that this is a tort in its own right and that the main difference is that it protects confidentiality, whereas defamation protects reputation.

Freedom of expression and defamation

Article 10 of the European Convention on Human Rights contains the right to freedom of expression. This Article is now incorporated through the Human Rights Act 1998, section 12. Freedom of expression includes the right to criticise, to debate, and to air opinions which may not be to everyone's liking.

On the other hand, defamation protects a person's right to her reputation. It is not surprising that these competing protected interests, for example reputation/privacy and freedom of speech often conflict. One of the main areas of concern leading to the reform of defamation law through the 2013 Act was that these competing interests were not fairly balanced, and that freedom of expression was being stifled.

LIBEL AND SLANDER

There are two types of defamation – **libel** and **slander**. They differ in form and effect.

CORNERSTONE

Libel v. slander

Libel and slander differ in *form* and *effect*. Libel consists of a statement in permanent form whereas slander is in transitory form. As to effect, the tort of libel is actionable *per se*, meaning that the claimant does not have to prove damages (unless it is a business). In contrast, slander is not actionable *per se* and special damages must be proved.

Form of defamation

There are various ways in which a statement could be captured in permanent form, for the purpose of defamation. The most common example is when something is written, but libel could also consist of a statement captured in another way, such as a broadcast, a picture, a statue, a recording, etc. Slander, in contrast, occurs when the statement is in a transitory or non-permanent form: for example, it could consist of spoken words or a gesture. Nowadays, when there always seems to be somebody around, ready to record anything with a mobile phone, slander is becoming much rarer.

Effect of defamatory statement

Libel is actionable *per se*, but slander is not. What this means is that for slander, the claimant will have to prove that she suffered some kind of *monetary loss because of* her damaged reputation. There are two exceptions to this (there used to be four, but section 14 of the 2013 Act abolishes two): slander is actionable *per se* if the allegation made was that the claimant had committed a serious crime, or if the allegation was that the claimant is incompetent, unfit or dishonest in her business, profession or trade. For these two instances, and for libel, all the claimant has to prove therefore is that there was a defamatory statement impugning her reputation. But does she also have to prove that her reputation *was in fact damaged*? The 2013 Act provides clarity.

Actual or likely serious harm to reputation

> Section 1 of the Defamation Act 2013 states that a statement is not defamatory unless it causes (or is likely to cause) serious harm to the reputation of the claimant.

CONTEXT

So the claimant will have to prove that the statement did or could indeed damage her reputation. This would automatically exclude a person who has already built up a bad reputation! However, the question as to what constitutes serious harm is left open and will be open to interpretation.

Corporate claimants

The 2013 Act adds another exception to the general rule that libel is actionable *per se*. Section 1(2) states that in the case of 'bodies that trade for profit,' serious harm to its reputation is not 'serious harm' unless it has caused or is likely to cause the body serious financial loss. This in effect means that libel is *not* actionable *per se* for businesses. Still, the business does not need to prove *actual* harm – it can also convince the court that there is *likely* to be harm to its reputation.

One of the main criticisms against the UK's libel laws is that it accords legal persons the same status as human beings, i.e. corporations are regarded as persons whose reputations may be defended in courts of law. Another hallmark of defamation is that legal aid is not available to either parties. Therefore, if a powerful corporation sues an ordinary person, the playing field is very unequal. A prime example is the lengthy and expensive court battle waged by a big corporation with teams of lawyers, against two indigent individuals dependent on the goodwill of *pro bono* lawyers in *McDonalds Corp.* v. *Steel* [1995] 3 All ER 615. McDonalds sued two environmental campaigners for allegedly defamatory statements about the company. The 'McLibel' case is famous for being the longest civil action in English history, and for the large amount of damages (£60,000) awarded to McDonalds. It was rumoured that McDonalds' legal costs ran into the millions of pounds. The case eventually ended up at the European Court of Human Rights in Strasbourg (*Steel and Morris* v. *UK* [2005] 18 BHRC 545), where it was held that the UK's laws on defamation not only infringed the defendants' rights to freedom of expression but also, by denying them legal aid, their right to a fair trial.

> **REFLECTION**
>
> Do you think that the requirement of corporations having to prove financial loss before being able to sue in section 1 of the Defamation Act 2013 addresses the inequality between 'ordinary' people and corporate claimants in defamation, as illustrated in the McLibel litigation?

ELEMENTS OF DEFAMATION

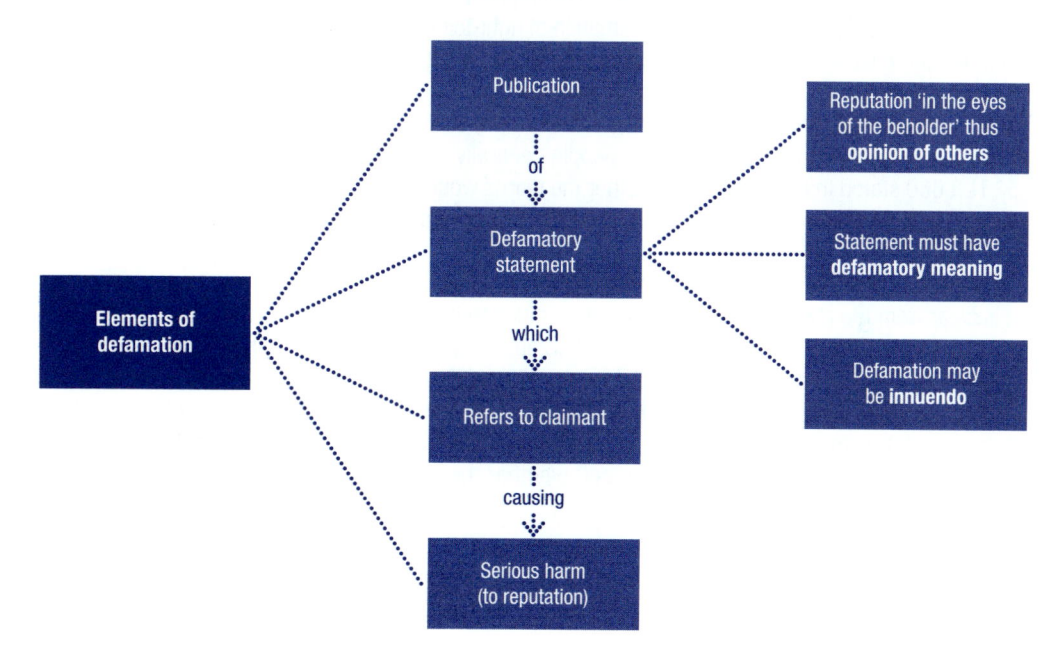

Figure 10.1 Elements of defamation

For a successful action in defamation, the claimant has to prove the publication of a defamatory statement referring to the claimant and which (in terms of the new Act) caused (or is likely to cause) serious harm to the reputation of the claimant. Let's look at these individual elements.

Publication

To establish publication for defamation, you need only one person (apart from the person allegedly defamed) to have heard or seen the statement – do not confuse the term 'publication' with the generally accepted meaning of transmission to many people! (There is one exception to the 'at least one other person' rule, and that is that the 'other person' cannot be the claimant's spouse.)

A statement made solely to the claimant, without anybody else hearing it, can therefore not be defamatory, regardless of how insulting it is. This is because defamation is concerned with protecting an individual's reputation, not her feelings – and a reputation consists of what other people think of a person.

INTERSECTION

See the discussion of the 'single publication rule' below under the discussion of who may be sued in defamation.

Defamatory statement

To decide whether or not a statement is 'defamatory' we need to reconsider what we understand the concept of 'defamatory' to be. Let's revisit the definition of defamation above, namely a statement that '. . . tends to lower [the claimant] in the estimation of right-thinking members of society generally or tends to make them shun or avoid him'. It also helps to look at some other ideas about what constitutes a defamatory statement: the Faulks Committee (Report of the Committee on Defamation CMND 5909, 1975, at Para. 65) regards a statement as defamatory if it: '. . . would be likely to affect a person adversely in the estimation of reasonable people generally.' Finally, Lord Atkin in *Sim* v. *Stretch* [1936] 52 TLR 669 stated that the test was whether the words would tend to lower the plaintiff in the estimation of right-thinking members of society generally. Let's unpack these concepts a bit more.

Reputation reflects opinion of others

It is clear from the above that reputation is very much to be found in the eyes of the beholder. It does not depend on what the individual thinks of herself, but what society, or 'right thinking members of society', or 'reasonable people generally' think of the claimant. This could be a very difficult test to apply, especially in a very diverse and multicultural society. Certain statements may be considered defamatory in some cultures and not in others, or at certain periods of history and not at others. Consider the following case and ask yourself whether the same set of facts could lead to a claim in defamation today:

CORNERSTONE

Cassidy v. *Daily Mirror Newspaper* [1929] 2 KB 331 (CA)

An article implied that the claimant was living with a man without being married to him. 'Living in sin' at that time was socially unacceptable and a statement to that effect about an unmarried woman was very damaging to her reputation.

Defamatory meaning

Some words are in and of themselves clearly defamatory: think of words such as 'liar', 'murderer', 'criminal', 'adulterer', etc. Other words are more ambiguous and one then has to look at the context in which they were uttered. The meaning of some words also change over time. 'Gay', for example, used to mean carefree and jolly, but nowadays most people understand it to refer to a homosexual person. It is up to the claimant to convince the court of the meaning of the words she alleges to be defamatory. We call relying on an additional meaning to words 'setting up a false innuendo'. Contrast this to words or phrases that make up a 'true' innuendo, below.

('True') innuendo

It may happen that words are totally innocent in *all* of their alternative meanings, but are nevertheless defamatory because of the context in which they are uttered, or because of extrinsic facts known to the recipient.

APPLICATION

> Imagine that Jenny tells Ahmed that she saw Fay kissing and cuddling X. This may look like a perfectly innocent statement, but if X happens to be an under-age pupil in Fay's class, things might look different! If the claimant is relying on such an additional meaning to be given to the words, we say that she is setting up a true innuendo.

To repeat the difference between true and false innuendo: in a 'false' innuendo, anybody who happens to know the alternative meanings of the words complained of may deduce the defamatory meaning. In a 'true' innuendo, only 'insiders' will be able to figure out that the statement is disparaging. In the example above, if Ahmed did not know Fay, he would not be able to grasp that there was any implication of impropriety. In both instances of innuendo, the claimant will have to inform (and convince) the court of the alternative meaning or the alternative interpretation of the statement.

Reference to claimant

If the claimant cannot be identified from the statement, there is no defamation. This does not mean that the claimant has to be specifically named, however. Just as the statement may be defamatory by innuendo (above), the claimant may be identified by implication. The test is whether the hypothetical reasonable reader/viewer, with knowledge of any special circumstances would believe that the claimant is being referred to.

Sometimes it would be easy to deduce that somebody is being referred to, even if that person is not identified in the statement. At other times it will be up to the claimant to convince the court that she is the person being referred to. In *Morgan* v. *Odhams Press* [1971] 1 WLR 1239 it was alleged in an article that a (named) girl had been abducted, but nobody else was named in the article. At the time the girl was staying with the claimant. The House of Lords held that, in such circumstances, if the words themselves did not identify the claimant, extrinsic evidence could be brought to show that the claimant was identified by implication. In this instance, the claimant had called witnesses who testified that after reading the article, they had thought the article referred to the claimant.

What if a class of people is referred to in the statement? If you were a member of that class, would you be able to sue in defamation? The courts' somewhat vague answer to this is, only if the claimant is identifiable personally, or if the group is so small and narrowly defined that each member of it could be identified personally. So how small does a group need to be for its members to be able to sue? In *Knupffer* v. *London Express* [1944] AC 116 an article was published which called the movement which the claimant belonged to 'fascist' (something clearly defamatory in the context of the Second World War era). At the time there were only 24 members of the movement in the UK. The House of Lords added that in a small, identifiable group, the aggrieved statement will need to be interpreted as referring to *each* of the members before an individual member can sue. The House held:

> '. . . it is an essential element of the cause of action for defamation that the words complained of should be published "of the plaintiff".'

Where he is not named, the test of this is whether the words would reasonably lead people acquainted with him to the conclusion that he was the person referred to. The question whether they did so in fact does not arise if they cannot in law be regarded as capable of referring to him. If a defamatory statement made of a class or group can reasonably be understood to refer to every member of it, each one has a cause of action.

In this instance, it was held that the words referred to a class (the movement was some 2,000 members strong internationally) and that the claimant was not individually identifiable.

Serious harm to reputation

We have seen that defamation is actionable *per se*, which means that the claimant does not have to prove actual *damage*. It used to be enough merely to show that there was a defamatory statement – the law then presumed harm to the claimant's reputation.

CORNERSTONE

Presumption of harm

Harm to reputation in itself is seen as defensible. There is a presumption that if it is proved that a statement is defamatory, the claimant's reputation is automatically harmed.

'Harm' here could mean anything from completely destroying somebody's reputation to only tarnishing it a little bit – so there are degrees of harm. Harm to your reputation does not necessarily mean damage in the sense of loss of income or personal injury, of course – but loss of income could, in turn, indicate that there was damage to reputation, especially if your income is related to your good reputation.

In recent years, and in some measure as a result of the realisation of having to balance protection of individuals' reputations with human rights such as the right to freedom of expression, the presumption of harm to reputation (following a defamatory statement) has been challenged. The Court of Appeal tested the presumption against the right to freedom of speech in the following case.

CORNERSTONE

Jameel v. *Dow Jones & Co Inc* [2005] 2 WLR 1614 (CA)

The claimant, a Saudi national, issued defamation proceedings in England against the publisher of the *Wall Street Journal* based on an article it posted on its website in the USA, which was available to subscribers in England. The claimant alleged that the article and its hyperlinks identified him as a funder of Al Qaeda. The defendant pointed out to the court that very few (as few as five) people in England had accessed the article, and that the claimant had therefore in fact suffered no or minimal damage to his reputation. This brought them to the issue of presumption of harm. The defendant argued that this presumption of harm was in conflict with Article 10 of the Human Rights Convention (the right to freedom of speech), as scheduled to the Human Rights Act 1998.

The Court of Appeal held that the presumption of harm in the law of tort relating to defamation was an *irrebuttable* presumption. This means it is a presumption that cannot be challenged and disproved – if a defamatory statement is proved, the automatic presumption is that the relevant reputation was harmed. However, the court then held that in cases where *actual* damage to the claimant's reputation was minimal, the claim could be struck out as an abuse of process (which means that the court regards it as a frivolous claim that should not have been pursued).

The courts, although stopping short of removing the presumption of harm, therefore now require as a minimum threshold for defamation actions that the claimant must have, in fact, suffered harm to her reputation. This 'seriousness' requirement further serves to prevent frivolous claims from clogging up the courts.

These developments are reflected in the first section of the 2013 Act, which seemingly does away with the presumption of harm. Section 1(1) states:

> 'A statement is not defamatory unless its publication has caused or is likely to cause serious harm to the reputation of the claimant.'

Remember that 'harm' in this sense does not necessarily mean *monetary* loss. This is, however, exactly what it does mean if the claimant is a corporation: section 1(2) goes on to say:

> '. . . harm to the reputation of a body that trades for profit is not "serious harm" unless it has caused or is likely to cause serious financial loss.'

> Re-read the discussion of the McLibel case above. Do you think that if section 1 of the 2013 Act had been in operation at the time, the matter would have followed the same trajectory as it did?

REFLECTION

WHO CAN CLAIM?

Any individual referred to in the statement may sue, so there can be situations where there is more than one claimant. From our discussion so far you will have noted that it is not only human beings but also legal persons such as corporations that have legal standing to sue. The idea is that, if it is

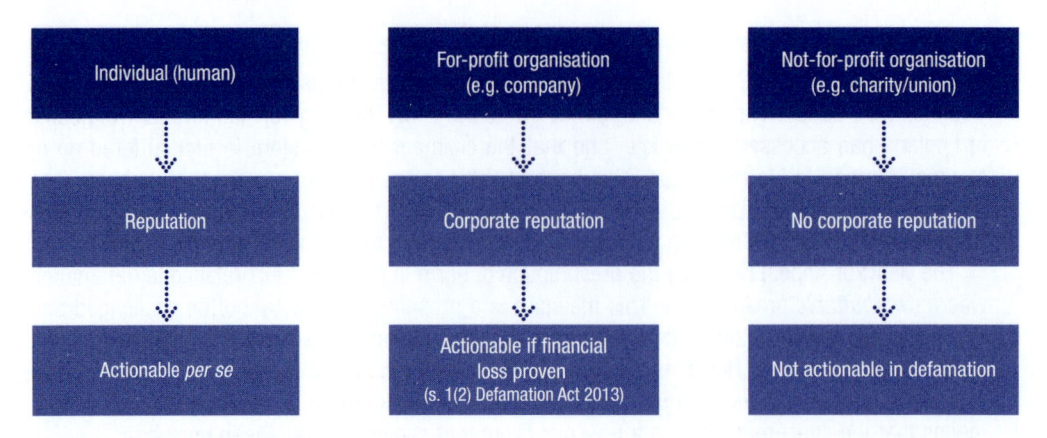

Figure 10.2 Defamation: who can claim?

Individual (human)	For-profit organisation (e.g. company)	Not-for-profit organisation (e.g. charity/union)
↓	↓	↓
Reputation	Corporate reputation	No corporate reputation
↓	↓	↓
Actionable *per se*	Actionable if financial loss proven (s. 1(2) Defamation Act 2013)	Not actionable in defamation

possible for you to have a reputation, it is possible to sue in defamation. For businesses, their reputation largely consists of goodwill, and 'brand protection' is taken very seriously: think back to our earlier discussion of the McLibel case (*McDonalds Corp.* v. *Steel*). Now think about the requirement in section 1(2) of the 2013 Act, which requires that a 'body that trades for profit' cannot sue unless it can show that the defamation caused it serious harm consisting of *serious financial loss*. What about not-for-profit organisations? Trade unions do not have a corporate reputation and cannot sue in defamation.

For policy reasons, political parties cannot sue and neither can local authorities. It is thought that it would be against the public interest in free debate to allow democratically elected bodies to sue for libel. This is not as far-reaching as it may seem, however, because although a political party may not sue, nothing prevents an individual member of such a party to sue (provided she can prove that the defamatory statement referred to her and not just to the party as a group – revise the discussion of group defamation above).

WHO MAY BE SUED?

The net of defamation is very wide, and there may be several possible defendants and several possible actions. The originator of the statement is liable for her own intended or negligent publication. What if other people then repeat the defamatory statement?

Repeat publication: multiple *v.* single publication rule

The common law position used to be that each publication of defamatory material gave rise to a separate cause of action – the so-called 'multiple publication rule'. Each repetition was therefore seen as a fresh defamation and actionable in its own right. That also meant that the limitation period (which is only a year in defamation actions, and therefore very important) was calculated from various times depending on when the original and the repetitions occurred. Therefore, given various repetitions, an originally prescribed defamation action may revive as a new prescription period started afresh after each repetition. There were common law defences to this, but they were not satisfactory. Section 8 of the 2013 Act now changes the law to reflect the 'single publication rule'. The prescription period for defamation actions will in future be calculated from the date of publication of the *original* defamatory statement. Subsequent repetitions falling outside of the prescription period will not be defamatory provided that they are not 'materially different' from the manner of the first publication.

> **REFLECTION**
>
> Libel law critics have long campaigned against the multiple publication rule and agitated for it to be replaced by the single publication rule. The 2013 Act contains this rule, but with the proviso that repetitions that are 'materially different' will be excluded and therefore actionable. In the government's Explanatory Notes to the Defamation Bill, it was stated that the term 'materially different' relates not only to the content of the statement but also the manner of publication. For example, if the original statement was obscure, perhaps in a small local paper, and the subsequent repetition was in a prominent national newspaper, that would be regarded as 'materially different' even if the statement was repeated verbatim. The repetition would then be actionable in its own right.
> Do you think that this waters down the 'single publication rule'?

What about the internet?

In *Bunt* v. *Tilley* [2006] 3 All ER 336 the claimant alleged that internet service providers (ISPs) should be liable for defamatory statements published on their websites. The defendant ISP successfully argued that the claims against them should be struck out because they were not, at common law, the publishers. ISPs are regarded as mere conduit intermediaries who carry particular internet communications from one computer to another. The law regards ISPs in the same way as postal services – like a postman, they facilitate communication by delivering statements, but they do not create the statement and almost never know what the content is of what they are delivering.

WHAT MAKES/MADE DEFAMATION SPECIAL?

Before moving on to the defences to defamation, it is important to look at some of the reasons why defamation is different from most of the other torts.

Short prescription period

In terms of section 4A of the Limitation Act 1980, claims must be brought within 12 months, after which they would prescribe. This is much shorter than most claims in tort, but was countered by the multiple publication rule. The new single publication rule in section 8 of the 2013 Act (see above) replaces this, but remember that any further publication that is 'materially different' from the original counts as a new publication.

Expensive to sue and defend

Suing and being sued in defamation is in general very expensive. In addition, there is no legal aid for defamation (subject to one exception, which we look at below). Although legal aid in general is being

CHAPTER 10 Defamation

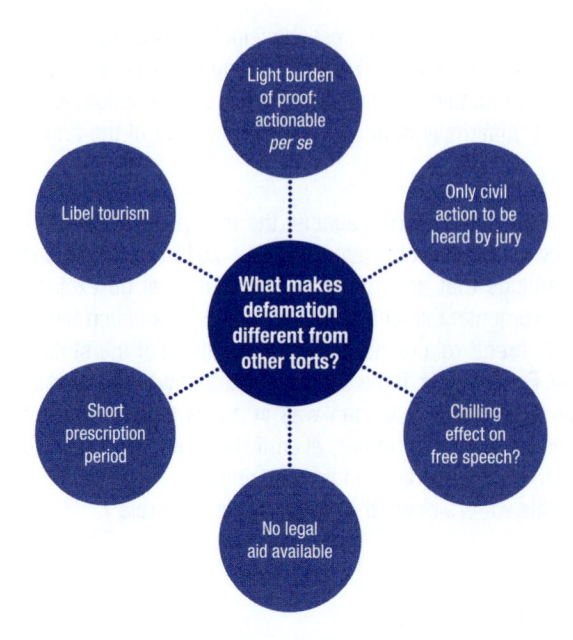

Figure 10.3 What makes defamation different from other torts?

- Light burden of proof: actionable *per se*
- Only civil action to be heard by jury
- Chilling effect on free speech?
- No legal aid available
- Short prescription period
- Libel tourism

What makes defamation different from other torts?

cut, and this has an impact on society, campaigners have pointed out that the fact that there is no legal aid for defamation actions impacts disproportionately on ordinary or poorer people. First, it is expensive to go to court and, in the absence of a tribunal or other alternative dispute resolution forum for defamation, court remains the only option for such a claim. Conditional fee arrangements only address this partially, with the result that it seems that only the rich and powerful have unfettered access to legal protection of their reputations.

Secondly, it is also expensive to *defend* a claim of defamation. Free speech advocates (including academics, journalists, NGOs and consumer groups) point out that, in many instances, the mere threat of a libel action is enough to silence criticism.

> **REFLECTION**
>
> It is argued that the costs involved in defending a defamation claim have a 'chilling effect' on free speech, which in turn has dire consequences for scientific or academic discourse, consumer awareness, legitimate criticism, etc. Put another way, people are silenced because they are scared of having to defend themselves without adequate funds.

You will remember that the defendants in the McLibel case took the matter to the European Court of Human Rights (*Steel and Morris* v. *UK* [2005] 18 BHRC 545), where it was held that the fact that they had received no legal aid when they were defending themselves in the UK courts was an infringement of their right to a fair trial. As a consequence of this decision by the Strasbourg court, legal aid is now available to the defendant in a libel action, but only if the action was brought by a multinational corporation.

Trial by jury

There was historically a right to jury trial in the High Court for defamation actions. This makes it the only civil action in English law potentially heard by a jury. There was a definite tendency for juries to award disproportionately high damages. To name but one example: in *John* v. *Mirror Group Newspapers* [1996] 2 All ER 35 the jury awarded Elton John a total of £350,000 in damages. The Court of Appeal later reduced this to £75,000 and directed that, in future, judges should give clear guidance to juries on damages.

Libel reform activists argued that these high awards, coupled with the extra layer of complexity added by jury trials, further tended to have a chilling effect on free speech. The European Court of Human Rights seemed to agree: in *Tolstoy Miloslavsky* v. *United Kingdom* [1996] EMLR 152 it held that an award of £1.5 million made by a jury against the defendant was an infringement of Article 10 of the European Convention on Human Rights.

Parliament took note of these concerns and section 11 of the 2013 Act now directs that defamation trials are to be conducted without a jury unless the court orders otherwise. In addition, even if there is a trial by jury, the maximum award is now set at £200,000.

Chilling effect on free speech?

The cases on defamation represent a constant conflict between a defendant's demands for free speech and a claimant's interests in her reputation. The potential chilling effect on free speech of current defamation laws is one of the main reasons for the enactment of the Defamation Act 2013, which attempts to redress the balance. Keep in mind that the courts are required to give effect to Article 10 of the European Convention on Human Rights as enacted in the Human Rights Act 1998.

Libel tourism

The government's Explanatory Notes to the Defamation Bill accepted that concern about libel tourism was valid. Libel tourism means that cases with only a tenuous link to England and Wales are instituted here because the jurisdiction is seen as very favourable to defamation claimants. The fact that libel claims are actionable *per se* made this jurisdiction particularly attractive. Let's look at two examples.

> In *Bin Mahfouz* v. *Ehrenfeld* [2005] EWHC 1156 (QB) a wealthy Arab businessman sued an American academic, Dr Rachel Ehrenfeld, in London for defamatory statements about him in her book entitled *Funding Evil*. Only 23 copies of her book had been sold in the UK, and it was pointed out that the claimant chose England rather than the USA to sue, because the latter's constitutional protection of freedom of speech effectively cancelled his suit's prospect of success. When he won his case in England, the USA reacted by passing the Securing the Protection of our Enduring and Established Constitutional Heritage (SPEECH) Act 2010. This Act makes foreign libel judgments unenforceable in US courts, unless those judgments are compliant with the US constitutional protection of freedom of speech.
>
> The fact that a traditional ally such as the United States deemed it necessary to protect its citizens' right to freedom of speech against English laws by enacting legislation to that effect was seen as hugely embarrassing: the House of Commons Culture Select Committee Report on Press Standards, Privacy and Libel 2010 termed it a 'national humiliation'.

The same factors (mainly the low threshold set by defamation actions being actionable *per se*) also made suing (or silencing critics by threatening to sue) in London attractive to multinational corporations with only the most tenuous link to the UK. For example, in *Jameel* v. *Wall Street Journal Europe SPRL (No. 3)* [2006] UKHL 44, the House of Lords held that a company which had a trading reputation in England and Wales was entitled to pursue a remedy in a defamation action *without being required to allege or prove that the publication complained of had caused it actual damage*. The Law Lords pointed out that this just meant that companies are being treated in the same way as individuals, i.e. that there was no need to prove harm in cases of defamation.

Section 9

Criticism of libel tourism led to the inclusion of section 9 of the 2013 Act, which states that if the defendant is *not* domiciled in the UK or EU, the court would not normally be able to adjudicate a defamation action, unless (in subsection (2)):

'. . . the court is satisfied that, of all the places in which the statement complained of had been published, England and Wales is clearly the most appropriate place in which to bring an action in respect of the statement.'

This section is not yet in force.

Burden of proof

It is an ancient principle of the law of England and Wales that 'he who avers has to prove', meaning that the burden of proof should, in all but exceptional circumstances, be on the claimant. In defamation, this burden is lightened by the fact that what the claimant has to prove is relatively easy: she merely has to provide proof of a defamatory statement. Because of the *presumption of harm*, from that point onward the burden shifts to the defendant to prove that she has a valid defence using one of several defences that are particular to defamation. The presumption of harm is of course (as we saw above) abolished in section 1 of the 2013 Act, which requires proof of serious harm to reputation: however, this is not yet in force. Even when the presumption is abolished, the defendant will still carry a significant burden in defending herself, as defamation remains actionable *per se*.

This quasi-reverse burden of proof is the reason why the defences are so important in defamation law. This is also reflected in the 2013 Act, whose bulk deals with defences to defamation actions. As they are important, we will look at the defences in some detail. The table below summarises the main areas changed by the new Act.

Pre-2013 defamation law	Defamation Act 2013
Presumption of harm (if defamatory statement proved)	Requirement of serious harm to reputation (s. 1)
Libel actionable *per se*, also for corporations	For-profit organisations to prove (actual or likely) serious financial loss (s. 1)
Multiple publication rule	Single publication rule (with exceptions) (s. 8)
Allegedly promotes 'libel tourism'	Restricts actions against defendants not domiciled in the UK (s. 9)
Right to trial by jury	Trial to be without jury unless court orders otherwise (s. 11)

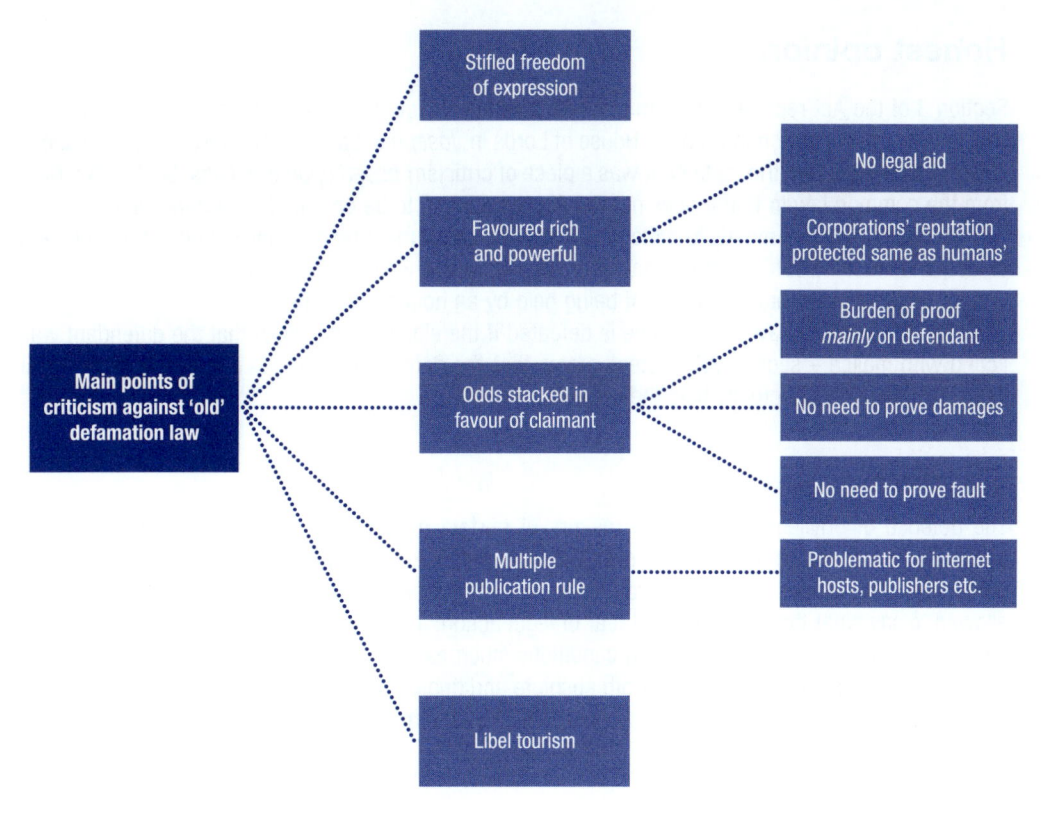

Figure 10.4 Criticism of 'old' defamation law

DEFENCES

The Defamation Act 2013 retains and expands most of the common law defences to defamation. The importance of these defences is reflected in the fact that they make up the bulk of the 2013 Act. At time of writing, none of the defences set out in the Act is in force yet. We will therefore refer to a defence by its new name in terms of the Act, and point out what its common law predecessor was called, and how they differ.

In addition to the defences, the Act sets a hurdle to claimants in section 1 by requiring proof of (actual or likely) damage to reputation, and in section 1(2) by requiring corporations suing in libel to prove (actual or likely) financial loss.

Truth

The common law name for this defence is 'justification', and its successor remains the most powerful and complete defence against a claim in defamation. Section 2 of the Act provides that it is a defence for the defendant to show that the imputation conveyed by the statement complained of is *substantially true*. This means that, as long as the substance of the statement is true, the defence will not fail if some part of the statement is untrue. If the imputation consists of two or more statements, of which some are true and some untrue, the Act directs the court in section 2(3) to allow the defence if the untrue imputations do not seriously harm the claimant's reputation.

Honest opinion

Section 3 of the Act replaces the common law defence of 'fair comment' (or 'honest comment' as it was known since a direction from the House of Lords in *Joseph* v. *Spiller* [2010] UKSC 53). In essence it allows a defence that the statement was a piece of criticism *based upon true facts*. Section 3 differs from the common law in that it does not require the opinion to be on a matter of public interest.

This defence relates mostly to editorial comments, etc. It must be an opinion, and not a statement of fact, and must indicate, in either general or specific terms, what the basis for the opinion is. Further, it must be an opinion that is capable of being held by an honest person.

Under the common law this defence is defeated if the claimant can show that the defendant was acting with malice – section 3(5) instead states that the defence is defeated if it can be shown that the defendant did not actually hold the opinion.

Privilege

The defence of privilege protects the makers of certain defamatory statements because the law considers that, in the circumstances covered by this defence, free expression is more important than protection of reputation. In other words, there are occasions where it is important that people are allowed to say what they think without fear of legal action. In some instances the protection is absolute, and in others qualified by certain conditions (such as that the maker of the statement should actually hold the opinion she utters). Both absolute and qualified privilege were mostly codified in the Defamation Act 1996, which is still in operation. The Defamation Act 2013 *extends* the protection given by the 1996 Act in section 7.

Absolute privilege

The law gives some statements absolute privilege, which means that it is impossible to sue the person who makes that statement – the statement cannot be used in a court of law. The most important instance of absolute privilege relates to statements made in Parliament or in any parliamentary report.

> Article 9 of the Bill of Rights 1688 declares:
>
> 'That the Freedome of Speech and Debates or Proceedings in Parlyament ought not to be impeached or questioned in any Court or Place out of Parlyament.'

CONTEXT

Other examples of absolute privileged statements include those made in the course of proceedings before any court or tribunal (s. 7 extends the protection to courts in most countries), fair and accurate media reports of such public judicial proceedings and any statement made by one spouse to another.

Qualified privilege

This is a more limited form of privilege but it has the same effect as absolute privilege: it means that the statement cannot be used in a court of law.

At common law, the traditional statement of when qualified privilege will apply comes from Lord Atkinson in *Adam* v. *Ward* [1917] AC 309:

> 'A privileged occasion is . . . an occasion where the person who makes the communication has an interest or a duty, legal, social or moral, to make it to the person to whom it is made, and the person to whom it is so made has a corresponding interest or duty to receive it. This reciprocity is essential.'

A good example of qualified privilege would be when an employment reference is given. However, keep in mind that qualified privilege is subject to one important restriction: it does not cover statements made with malice or with a bad motive, or if the person making it did not honestly believe it was true, or both.

CORNERSTONE

Defamation Acts 1996 and 2013

Section 6 of the 2013 Act expressly provides privilege to statements published in peer reviewed scientific or academic journals.

Section 15 of the Defamation Act 1996 (now extended by s. 7 of the 2013 Act) provides that certain types of statements are subject to qualified privilege. These include fair and accurate reports of 'proceedings in public', which include, amongst others, proceedings of legislatures, courts, public inquiries, international organisations or conferences, publicly listed companies etc.

An important caveat to section 15 is that the matter reported must be of public interest – which brings us to the next defence.

Publication on matter of public interest

A specialised 'responsible journalism' defence developed, under the common law, out of qualified privilege into a defence in its own right. This defence is commonly known as the 'Reynolds defence'. Let's look at the case from which it arose.

CORNERSTONE

Reynolds v. *Times Newspapers Ltd* [1999] 4 All ER 609 (HL)

This case concerned a defamation claim by a politician against a newspaper. The question was raised whether there should be a generic category for media reports covering political information and debate. The House of Lords emphasised the importance of freedom of expression and acknowledged the importance of the role played by the media to inform the public at large of political matters so they could make informed choices about, for example, whom to vote for. But they also pointed out that it was in the public interest for individuals such as politicians to be able to defend their reputation against false allegations, so that voters could make informed choices. →

> The Law Lords developed a new form of the qualified privilege defence for responsible journalism which seeks to protect information published fairly and responsibly in the public interest.
> The Lords listed ten factors which should be taken into account when deciding whether the defence would succeed:
>
> 1. the seriousness of the allegation;
> 2. the nature of the information and whether it is of public concern;
> 3. the source of the information;
> 4. the steps taken to verify the information;
> 5. the status of the information;
> 6. the urgency of the matter;
> 7. whether the claimant was asked to comment on the story;
> 8. whether the article contained at least the gist of the claimant's side of the story;
> 9. the tone of the article;
> 10. the circumstances of the publication including the timing.
>
> The Law Lords also stressed that the list is not exhaustive and that other factors might be taken into account.

Section 4 of the 2013 Act is clearly based on, but *abolishes*, the Reynolds defence. This section (which is not in operation at the time of writing) simply states that it is a defence to show that the statement was on a matter of public interest and that the defendant reasonably believed that publishing the statement was in the public interest. Further, subsection (2) simply states that when a court has to decide whether the statement was in the public interest, it '... must have regard to all the circumstances of the case'. It remains to be seen how the courts will interpret this section when it comes into operation – most probably they will continue to use the factors listed in *Reynolds*.

Author, editor or publisher (s. 10) and operators of websites (s. 5)

This used to be known in the common law as 'innocent publication' and aims to protect those who do not have any editorial control over the material they handle. The defence extends to those who provide access to information on the internet where the information is provided by a person over whom the service provider has no control.

Section 5 of the Defamation Act 2013 now deals with actions that are brought in defamation against operators of websites in respect of a statement posted on the website. In such an instance the operator can raise as a defence that it was not the operator who posted the statement. If the real author cannot be identified (and therefore sued) by the claimant, however, the claimant will be entitled to complain to the operator and if the operator does not respond to the complaint, it may be sued in defamation. The law around internet defamation is complex and evolving and this is reflected in the fact that detailed regulations are to be drafted fleshing out section 5, which is itself not in force yet (like most of the 2013 Act). Section 10 deals with more 'traditional' publishers but provide basically the same as it relates to defendants who do not exercise editorial control.

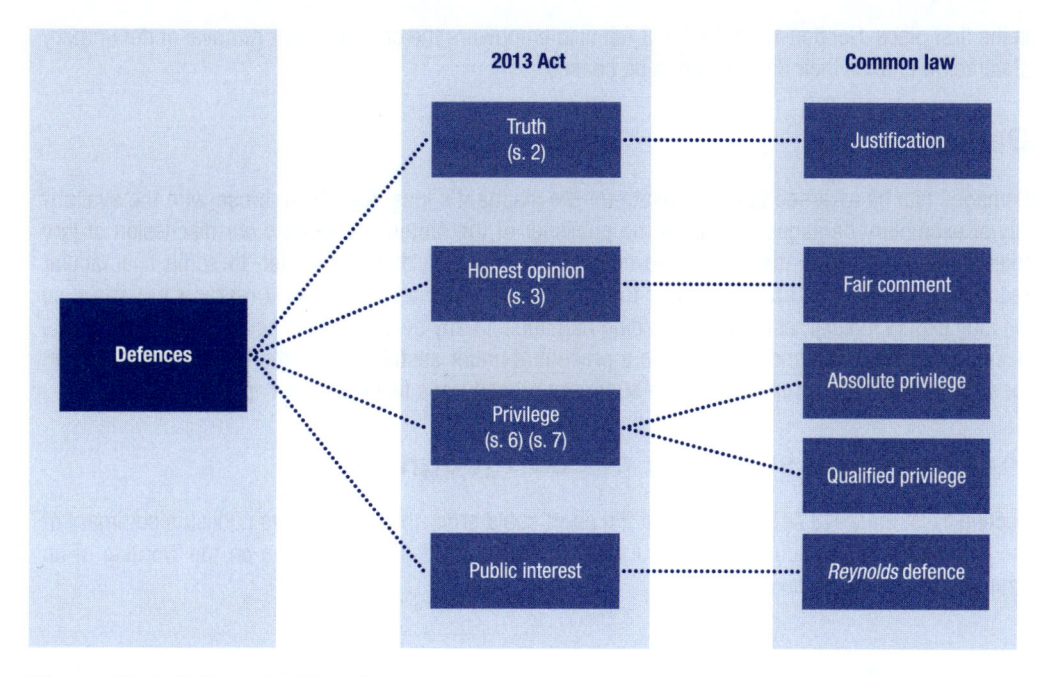

Figure 10.5 Defences to defamation

Offer of amends

This is not strictly a defence, but it can have a similar effect. It is contained in section 2 of the Defamation Act 1996 and is a procedure whereby a person who has published an allegedly defamatory statement can make an offer of amends in the form of a correction, an apology and, where appropriate, a payment of damages. As such the offer of amends procedure provides a means of settling cases promptly where the defendant accepts that she is wrong and also provides a way for claimants to get an apology and compensation at an early stage, so avoiding the costs of a trial. Acceptance of the offer of amends means that the action for defamation against that particular publication ends. If the claimant does not accept the offer, it can then be pleaded as a defence later on. The court may decide that the claimant had been unreasonable in declining to accept the offer. An offer of amends can also be used in mitigation of damages, whether or not it has been relied on as a defence.

REMEDIES

The main remedies for defamation are injunctions and damages.

Injunctions

Injunctions can be used either to stop a continuing defamation (such as for example a defamatory statement which appears on a website), or to prevent a defamatory statement from being published in the first place. Section 13 of the 2013 Act also empowers the court to order removal of defamatory statements and for their distribution to be ceased.

Damages

Damages can be awarded to compensate for the claimant's loss. A problem arose with the availability of exemplary damages, to punish the publisher of the statement. Review our discussion of jury trials, where it was pointed out that excessive damage awards by juries led to some spectacular reductions by higher courts. Remember though that the 2013 Act in section 11 restricts jury trials, so we may expect judicial restraint in awarding damages. In any event, there is now a ceiling on general damages of £200,000 and there is also a procedure under section 8(3) of the Defamation Act 1996 for summary disposal of claims – if the summary procedure is followed, the cap is at £10,000.

Publication of summary of court judgment

Section 12 of the 2013 Act provides that the court could order the defendant to publish a summary of the judgment. This of course is a useful tool where the parties cannot agree on the wording of an appropriate apology to be published.

KEY POINTS

- Defamation protects an individual's reputation and is the defamatory publication of an untrue statement which lowers the claimant in the eyes of society.
- The law of defamation has recently been the subject of major reform, resulting in the enactment of the Defamation Act 2013.
- There are two kinds of defamation: libel and slander, of which the former is more important.
- Libel is defamation in permanent form, whereas slander consists of a transitory statement.
- Libel is actionable *per se* but section 1 of the 2013 Act now requires that the claimant at least proves that her reputation was seriously harmed before being allowed to sue.
- For slander and for-profit bodies, there is a requirement of special damages to be proved.
- The defences to defamation are very important and have been extended and potentially strengthened by the 2013 Act.
- The main defence against defamation is that the statement is the truth. This is an absolute defence.
- Certain statements are privileged, such as statements made in Parliament or in a court of law, and cannot be used in defamation proceedings.
- Other defences include publication in the public interest, publication of honest opinions based on facts, and publication in peer-reviewed academic and scientific journals.
- The main remedies in defamation include injunctions, damages and the publication of an apology.

CORE CASES AND STATUTES

Case	About	Importance
Cassidy v. *Daily Mirror Newspaper* [1929] 2 KB 331 (CA)	Innuendo	Illustrates that the requirement of the claimant being identified/identifiable from the defamatory statement, could be satisfied by proving innuendo.
Jameel v. *Dow Jones & Co Inc* [2005] 2 WLR 1614 (CA)	Defamation cases actionable *per se*; presumption of harm	The court held that the presumption of harm was an irrebuttable component of defamation law. Nevertheless the court has the discretion to strike out claims where little or no actual harm could be proved.
Reynolds v. *Times Newspapers Ltd* [1999] 4 All ER 609 (HL)	Responsible journalism defence	Sets out guidelines for and establishes the responsible journalism defence, which developed out of the common law defence of qualified privilege.

Statute	About	Importance
Defamation Act 2013, s. 1	Requirement of harm	Abolishes common law presumption of harm and requires claimant to prove serious harm to reputation. In case of for-profit organisations, this requires proof of serious financial harm.
Defamation Act 2013, s. 2	Defence of truth	Abolishes common law defence of justification but retains its essence, i.e. truth as absolute defence.
Defamation Act 2013, s. 3	Honest opinion	Replaces common law defence of fair comment.
Defamation Act 2013, s. 4	Publication on matter of public interest	Replaces Reynolds defence and is aimed at journalism.
Defamation Act 2013, s. 8	Single publication rule	Replaces the multiple publication rule with a conditional single publication rule.
Defamation Act 2013, s. 9	Action against person not domiciled in UK	Aims to prevent libel tourism.

Statute	About	Importance
Defamation Act 2013, s. 11	Trial to be without jury	Makes the default position a trial without a jury, except where the court orders otherwise.
Defamation Act 1996, s. 14	Absolute privilege	Sets out instances of absolute privilege, such as court proceedings.
Defamation Act 1996, s. 15	Qualified privilege	Sets out instances of qualified privilege.

FURTHER READING

Defamation Act 2013, annotated
As this is such a new statute, with several sections still to come into operation, and which is yet to be extensively tested in the courts and commented upon in the academic literature, it is best to look at the Act itself as well as the explanatory notes accompanying it. The explanatory notes are particularly useful as they explain the law as it was, why it was deemed necessary to change the law, what the concerns were, and how the Act attempts to address these concerns.

www.libelreform.org
This website contains material documenting the problems created under the old regime dealing with defamation, mostly in layman's terms, but also addressing problems with the law. Reading the reports and case studies contained here will give you an insight into the most pressing reasons for the recent change in the law on defamation.

***Jameel* v. *Dow Jones & Co Inc* [2005] 2 WLR 1614**
The decision of the Court of Appeal in this case sets out the legal position relating to jurisdiction. This is important to understand so as to grasp the criticism that current English defamation law makes England a prime destination for libel tourism/forum shopping. It is also important to read the case to understand how it changed the 'presumption of damage' rule.

Handman, L. Reid, E. and Balin, R. (2009) Libel tourism and the Duke's manservant – an American perspective. *EHRLR* **3, pp. 303–31**
This article discusses the concept of 'libel tourism' and how it boils down to international forum shopping for allegedly libellous statements. Reading it and understanding the impact of libel tourism, including the US response to the potential threat to free speech posed by English libel judgments, will help you understand some of the main reasons for the enactment of the Defamation Act 2013. The authors also examine the significance of the multiple publication rule.

PART 4
Miscellaneous torts

PART 4
Miscellaneous torts

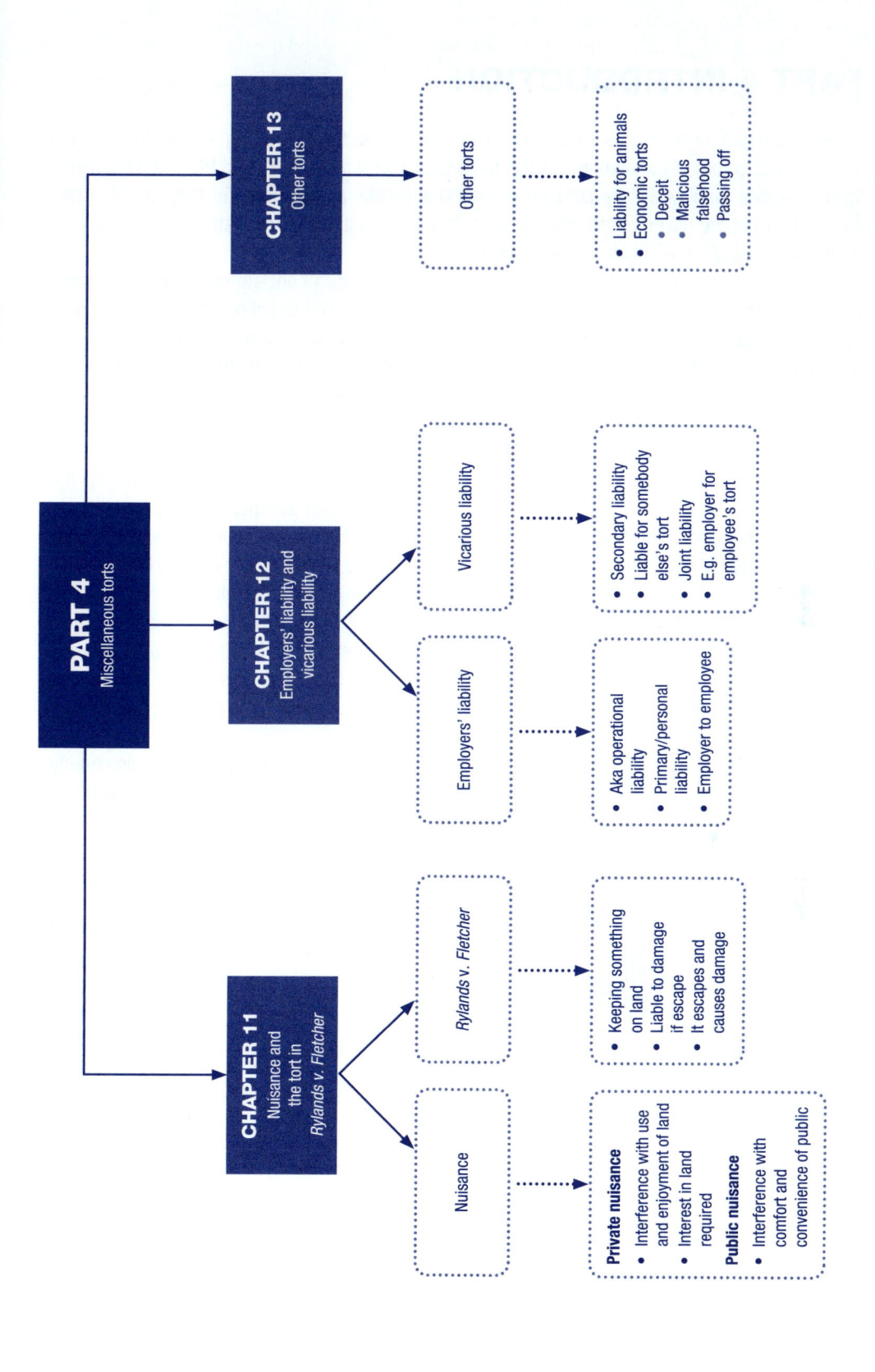

CHAPTER 11
Nuisance and the tort in *Rylands v. Fletcher*

Nuisance

Private nuisance
- Interference with use and enjoyment of land
- Interest in land required

Public nuisance
- Interference with comfort and convenience of public

Rylands v. Fletcher
- Keeping something on land
- Liable to damage if escape
- It escapes and causes damage

CHAPTER 12
Employers' liability and vicarious liability

Employers' liability
- Aka operational liability
- Primary/personal liability
- Employer to employee

Vicarious liability
- Secondary liability
- Liable for somebody else's tort
- Joint liability
- E.g. employer for employee's tort

CHAPTER 13
Other torts

Other torts
- Liability for animals
- Economic torts
  - Deceit
  - Malicious falsehood
  - Passing off

PART 4 INTRODUCTION

In the final part of this book you are introduced to the tort of nuisance, the tort dealing with escapes commonly known as the tort in *Rylands* v. *Fletcher* (1868) LRJ HL 330, employers' liability to their employees, the concept of vicarious liability and some other torts that are discussed less but are nevertheless important as they crop up at court. The latter include the torts of deceit, passing off, and liability for animals.

In Chapter 11 we look at the tort of nuisance, which in turn consists of private and public nuisance. The two torts differ fundamentally, although both relate to actions about behaviour or occurrences that constitute a nuisance. The main difference is that private nuisance is there only for people who are disturbed in their *property rights*, i.e. owners or tenants of property. An example is where I cannot use my garden because my neighbour is constantly burning rubbish in his back yard and the smell and smoke is unbearable. For public nuisance, however, the claimant does not need to be the owner or tenant of property. An example would be where somebody obstructs a road so that the road users cannot park or drive on the road. Finally, we look at the tort of *Rylands* v. *Fletcher*. In this tort, we deal with something that escapes from a person's land and causes damage when it escapes. For example, if you store large amounts of water on your property and the tank bursts and floods your neighbour's house, this would be a tort in *Rylands*.

In Chapter 12 we look at employers' liability *towards* their employees, which is a form of primary or personal liability, and contrast it to an employer's liability for actions by their employees, which is a good example of vicarious liability. Vicarious liability in turn is a form of secondary liability. It is important always to keep in mind that there could be vicarious liability – if there is any kind of relationship where the tortfeasor was under the authority of somebody else, such as an employer, or a parent, or a principal in an agency situation.

Finally, in Chapter 13 we look at some other torts, such as liability for animals. We also briefly look at the so-called 'economic' torts. For example, if you intentionally tell lies about somebody with the aim of hurting them financially, this could be malicious falsehood; or if you market a product very like a leading brand, with a similar-sounding name, this could be 'passing off'. We look at how they relate to other torts and at the gaps in the law that they fill.

CHAPTER 11

Nuisance and the tort in Rylands v. Fletcher

BLUEPRINT

Nuisance and the tort in Rylands v. Fletcher

KEY QUESTIONS

LEGISLATION
- Civil Aviation Act 1982, s. 77

CONTEXT
- Private nuisance is a tort against land, whereas public nuisance is concerned with the interests of classes of people.

CONCEPTS
- Private nuisance
- Public nuisance
- The tort in *Rylands* v. *Fletcher*

- Nuisance and the tort in *Rylands* v. *Fletcher* mainly aim to balance the conflicting rights or interests of various users of land.

- What interests are protected by the three different types of nuisance respectively?
- Why did the courts deem it necessary to create the tort in *Rylands* v. *Fletcher*?

CASES

- *Hunter* v. *Canary Wharf Ltd* [1997]
- *Sedleigh Denfield* v. *O'Callaghan* [1940]
- *Halsey* v. *Esso Petroleum* [1961]
- *Attorney-General* v. *PYA Quarries* [1957]
- *Rylands* v. *Fletcher* [1868]

REFORM

- Courts have to grapple with whether the tort of private nuisance should be extended to give a right to claim to persons other than those with lawful interest in land – whether the protection accorded by the Human Rights Act (Right to respect of family and home life) is adequate.

SPECIAL CHARACTERISTICS

- Standing in private nuisance limited to claimants with legal interest in the affected land
- Public nuisance is a tort against the comfort and convenience of a class of people
- Tort in *Rylands* v. *Fletcher* applies where something that was brought onto land and is likely to do damage if it escapes, does in fact so escape

CRITICAL ISSUES

Setting the scene

Trouble with the neighbours . . . At some stage, many of us will experience such annoyance. For the most part, many of these everyday annoyances remain just that: annoyances, part of the give and take of living in proximity to other people. In few instances, however, matters get out of hand and people have to turn to the law to redress the balance. One of the legal methods to address this type of problem is a civil or criminal action based on the tort of nuisance.

From the outset you must note a few things about the tort of nuisance. The first is the distinction between private and public nuisance. These are really two very distinct torts, with separate requirements. Typically, for 'neighbour disputes', private nuisance is the appropriate remedy, as it is aimed at protecting your proprietary rights in land. On the other hand, public nuisance is mainly a crime from which a tortious action may follow, and is aimed at the protection of wider interests than private nuisance

However, there was also a gap in the law where interests were not protected by either public or private nuisance, or indeed negligence. To fill this gap, the courts created a new tort in the case of *Rylands* v. *Fletcher*.

INTRODUCTION

There are several forms of the tort of nuisance:

1. *Statutory nuisance* refers to nuisances created as such, and dealt with in, Acts of Parliament.
2. *Public nuisance* is a crime, but from which an individual in limited circumstances may also claim in tort. The most common example is obstructing the highway.
3. *Private nuisance* is a tort only, and covers indirect interference with land. Examples include making such noise that a neighbour cannot sit out in her garden, or emitting noxious fumes, or bad smells, such as from a pig farm. Since it is purely a tort and not a crime as well, we will discuss private nuisance in the most detail.

STATUTORY NUISANCE

A statutory nuisance is created by an Act of Parliament. With certain exceptions, individuals cannot sue in respect of statutory nuisance. Instead the relevant statute usually creates or nominates a statutory or other body and then tasks it with enforcement of the statutory standards. Therefore, if you are affected by, say, sewage leaking onto your property, you should complain to the relevant body dealing with such an occurrence. For example, in *Marcic* v. *Thames Water Utilities Ltd* [2003] UKHL 66 the claimant, Mr Marcic, owned a house that was regularly flooded by effluent from a sewerage system operated by the defendant water company. He claimed damages against the company in nuisance, amongst others. One of the main reasons the claimant failed was because there was a statutory regime covering the facts, and he should have claimed under that scheme.

PRIVATE NUISANCE

Definition

We can use Lord Atkin's definition in *Sedleigh Denfield* v. *O'Callaghan* [1940] AC 880 at 896:

'. . . nuisance is . . . defined as a wrongful interference with another's enjoyment of his land or premises by the use of land or premises either occupied or in some cases owned by oneself.'

It is very important to note that the main aim for private nuisance is to protect the claimant's *interest in land* (and not, for example, her comfort) – the tort is linked to the land and is indeed a tort committed *against* land. That explains why the right to sue is limited to certain classes of people.

Claimant

Who can sue in private nuisance?

CORNERSTONE

Standing of claimant

Only a claimant who has an interest in land or who has exclusive possession of the land can sue for private nuisance. Lawyers refer to the legally recognised right to sue as 'standing' (or also, still, as '*locus standi*'). In private nuisance actions, only a person with a legal interest in the affected land has standing.

For example, the wife and children of a homeowner may have lived with him in the house for decades and feel a deep connection to the property but, nevertheless, for a nuisance action, the law will only recognise the husband's interest in land as lawful owner. In *Malone* v. *Laskey* [1907] 2 KB 141, it was held that the wife of the tenant could not claim in nuisance as she had no legal interest in the property. In the years following this decision, the rule was repeatedly criticised in the courts and, finally, in *Khorasandjian* v. *Bush* [1993] 3 WLR 476, the Court of Appeal had to decide whether the daughter of a house-owner could claim in nuisance. (We also look at this case in Chapter 7, which deals with trespass to the person.) In brief, the daughter of the house owner was subjected to harassing phone calls. The court had to decide whether the actions complained of could amount to trespass to the person or nuisance. In Chapter 7 we see what happened to the trespass issue and how this case contributed to the eventual enactment of the Protection from Harassment Act 1997. As to nuisance, the court held that deliberate harassment may constitute an actionable nuisance and furthermore, that the daughter did indeed have standing to sue. Dillon LJ put it like this (at 734):

'To my mind, it is ridiculous if in this present age the law is that the making of deliberately harassing and pestering telephone calls to a person is only actionable in the civil courts if the recipient of the calls happens to have the freehold or a leasehold proprietary interest in the premises in which he or she has received the calls.'

However, this decision was decisively overruled by the House of Lords in the following leading case.

CORNERSTONE

Hunter v. Canary Wharf Ltd [1997] 2 All ER 426

The plaintiffs occupied dwellings in the London Docklands area, and complained of interference with their TV reception because of the construction of a Canary Wharf skyscraper, as well as deposits of dust on their properties caused by the construction of a link road. The court had to decide whether there was an action in nuisance and/or negligence. The judge of first instance ruled, amongst others, that interference with television reception was capable of constituting an actionable private nuisance but that to claim in private nuisance it was necessary to have a right to exclusive possession of the property. The House of Lords disagreed on the first point, but agreed with the judge on the second.

Therefore, the rule is still that only a claimant who has an interest in land can claim.

This does leave people who do not have exclusive possession – for example a lodger – without a remedy, unless the Protection from Harassment Act 1997 is applicable.

> Article 8 ECHR guarantees a right to respect for private and family life, home and correspondence. Human rights, of course, have as their focus the relevant human affected. As such, Article 8 does not make a distinction between people with and people without interests in land, as it is the person and not the person's land which is the focus. So, where the subject matter is unacceptable behaviour or emanations interfering with home life, the courts conduct a factual enquiry as to links with the home, rather than an enquiry as to legal or proprietary interests.

REFLECTION

For instance, the court in *McKenna* v. *British Aluminium* [2002] Env LR 30 as well as the Court of Appeal in *Dobson* v. *Thames Water Utilities Ltd* [2009] EWCA Civ 28 recognised that claimants (e.g. children) without proprietary interests living on the land affected by private nuisance may be able to claim for damage or injury suffered on their own account, based on the Human Rights Act 1998.

Finally, what do we include under 'land'? It is obvious that property such as farmland, houses, flats, etc. would be included. The courts have also shown willingness to extend the concept further to encompass less obvious property rights: in *Crown River Cruises Ltd* v. *Kimbolton Fireworks Ltd* [1999] 2 Lloyd's Rep 533 the court examined the definition of land and held that an interest in a permanently moored barge, occupied under a mooring licence, could sustain an action.

Defendant

The person to sue would usually be the one who caused the nuisance. Unlike for claimants, it seems that the defendant does not have to possess a legal interest in the land – usually, the defendant would be the occupier of the land from which the nuisance emanates.

Must the defendant have an interest in the land?

In *Hussain* v. *Lancaster City Council* [2000] QB1 the claimant was subjected to racial harassment from tenants on a council estate. When he sued the council as landlord of the tenants, the Court of Appeal held that, in a claim for nuisance, the person to be sued was the occupier of the property from which the nuisance emanated. In this case, the claimants were harassed whilst in their shop, so they satisfied the requirement of the claimant having an interest in land. The court pointed out that the acts complained of unquestionably interfered persistently and intolerably with the claimant's enjoyment of his land, but they did not involve the *tenants'* use of the *tenants'* land (the harassers were on the public highway outside the claimant's shop). The court therefore clearly requires that, for private nuisance, the nuisance needs to emanate from the defendant's land to the claimant's land. When the court refers to 'occupier', does that then imply that the defendant also must have a legal interest in the land?

Contrast this to the decision in *Lippiatt* v. *South Gloucestershire CC* [2000] QB 51, where the claimant complained of acts of nuisance committed on neighbouring land by travellers occupying the defendant's land. The Court of Appeal distinguished this case on the facts from *Hussain*. The principle, as stated by Lord Goff in *Hunter* v. *Canary Wharf Ltd* [1997] AC 655, with whom Lord Lloyd of Berwick agreed (at 700), is that as a general rule some form of 'emanation' from the defendant's land is required. On analysis, what 'emanated' in the *Lippiatt* was the travellers themselves.

The facts in *Hussain* were held to be materially different because the disturbance was a public nuisance for which the individual perpetrators could be held liable, and they were identified as individuals who lived in council property, but their conduct was not in any sense linked to, nor did it emanate from, the homes where they lived. In *Lippiatt* the travellers were allowed to congregate on the council's land and they used it as a base for the unlawful activities of which the plaintiffs, as neighbours, complained.

Vicarious liability

The occupier of the premises from which nuisance emanates will generally be liable for that nuisance. The normal rules of vicarious liability apply, so that means that an occupier may also be held liable if the nuisance is created by, for example, her employee. (We examine vicarious liability in detail in Chapter 12.)

It is uncontroversial that one could be held vicariously liable for the actions of certain people, such as employees. The main reason for this is because there is an assumed element of control. But what if the nuisance results from actions by people not under your control or supervision, or events out of your control such as an act of nature? In this instance the courts will ask whether the occupier knew of the state of affairs and whether she should or could have done something about it. Let's look at some examples.

CORNERSTONE

Sedleigh Denfield v. *O'Callaghan* [1940] AC 880

In *Sedleigh Denfield* v. *O'Callaghan* (from which we took our definition of private nuisance at the start of this chapter), a ditch on the defendant's land was converted, without his permission or knowledge, into a culvert. The ditch where it ran into the culvert became blocked and caused flooding on the claimant's property. When sued in nuisance, the defendant raised as a defence that →

the construction of the culvert was a trespass but the House of Lords found the defendant liable in nuisance. As the pipe had been laid almost three years prior to the flood, and the defendant's workers cleared out the ditch leading into the pipe at times, the court found that the defendant must have had knowledge of the existence of the pipe on his land. The court held that an occupier of land is liable for the *continuance* of a nuisance created by others, for example by trespassers. That is, if the occupier became aware of the nuisance and let it continue.

Take note

If you have studied negligence in detail you will be familiar with the fact that the 'reasonableness' requirement in negligence is objective. In contrast, the standard of reasonableness in nuisance is subjective: we look at the knowledge and ability of the relevant occupier. Did she know about the nuisance? Is it physically and financially possible for her to abate the nuisance?

The same reasoning – awareness of the nuisance and nevertheless continuing it – applies to acts of nature. For example, in *Goldman* v. *Hargrave* [1967] 1 AC 645 the defendant was aware of a fire on his property but did not take sufficient steps to prevent it spreading; whilst in *Leakey* v. *The National Trust* [1980] QB 485 debris from the defendants' land fell on that of the claimant. In both instances the defendants were found to have committed nuisance, even though the nuisance consisted of natural states. The law expects the defendant to take reasonable care to either stop or abate the nuisance.

The duty to abate the nuisance is also limited by foreseeability. For example, in *Holbeck Hall Hotel Ltd* v. *Scarborough Borough Council* [2000] 2 All ER 705, despite minor landslips, it was held that the defendants could not have foreseen (and could therefore not be held liable in nuisance for) a major landslide from their property which damaged the claimant's hotel.

Landlords

What about landlords? Can they be held liable for nuisances created by their tenants? To answer this question, you need first to keep in mind the rule that, in general, people are held liable for their own actions. If a tenant caused a nuisance, in principle it would be the tenant who is held liable. That is, as soon as the tenant takes occupation or control of the land from which the nuisance emanates, the landlord will cease to be held liable.

REFLECTION

Revise the courts' reasoning in the cases of *Hussain* and *Lippiatt*, discussed earlier. Why were the landlords in the latter case held liable in nuisance, and those in the former not? Do you agree with the court's reasoning in *Lippiatt* that the travellers themselves constituted the nuisance emanating from the defendants' land?

A landlord can be held liable in nuisance if the very purpose for which she grants a lease constitutes a nuisance. For example, in *Tetley and others* v. *Chitty and others* [1986] 1 All ER 663 the court held that, by allowing the tenants to operate a go-cart club on its land, the landlord had consented to the nuisance.

Elements to prove

To determine what you need to prove to succeed in an action, let's revise the definition of private nuisance: wrongful interference with another's use and enjoyment of his land or premises. Usually 'interference with enjoyment of land' is taken as meaning some form of damage. (Therefore, this is not a tort that is actionable *per se*.) Secondly, 'wrongful' interference is taken as meaning unreasonable and substantial interference. Take note that the action itself does not need to be unlawful – something lawful may be a nuisance if it is done unreasonably. Finally, it is important also to note that the interference has to be *indirect*.

Interference with use and enjoyment of land

The interest protected by the tort of private nuisance is the 'use and enjoyment of land'. What precisely does this mean? It is fairly obvious that this would include physical damage to property, but what about damage that falls short of this – such as, for example, being unable to sleep in your house's front bedroom due to noise, or being unable to sit out in your garden due to noxious smells? Further, what about personal injury? The answer to these questions is logical when you keep in mind that this tort is aimed at protecting an *interest in land* and is not aimed at protecting individuals as individuals. For this reason, you cannot claim personal injury under private nuisance. Loss of amenity in the property and physical damage to the property can be claimed. Where the claimant suffers loss of amenity, she does not sue for any personal injury sustained but rather for the inability to use her property to its fullest.

INTERSECTION

> Because nuisance is a tort concerned with *land*, it should come as no surprise that it overlaps with land law to a large extent. For example, you will note that many cases dealing with nuisance are adjudicated in the tribunal called the Lands Chamber, which deals mostly with land law cases.

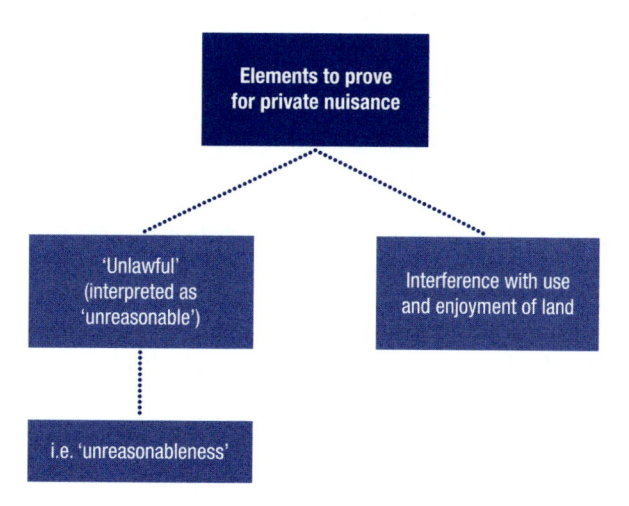

Figure 11.1 Elements to prove for private nuisance

The recoverable damage may therefore be either loss of amenity in the claimant's use of the premises, or physical damage to the property as in *St Helen's Smelting Co* v. *Tipping* (1865) 11 HLC 642, where the claimant's crops and trees were damaged by the acid rain from the defendant's smelting works. It is important to distinguish between the two, as *locality* is important for the former, but disregarded if there is physical damage present. We return to this below when we look at the reasonableness test to determine whether the interference was unjustified.

CORNERSTONE

Halsey v. *Esso Petroleum* [1961] 2 WLR 683

Halsey v. *Esso Petroleum* is a useful case to read because from its facts we find an example of both types of damage in private nuisance. (Its facts also contain an example of public nuisance and the tort of *Rylands* v. *Fletcher*.)

The claimant was the owner and occupier of a house in a residential area bordering a strip of light industrial land. The defendants ran a depot located on that strip of land, opposite the claimant's house. The depot emitted a foul smell as well as noxious acid smuts, which damaged the plaintiff's washing hung out to dry, and also damaged the paintwork of his car standing in the street outside his house. In addition to this, the depot ran through the night and tankers entered its premises opposite the claimant's house. The noise was sometimes so great that the claimant's windows and doors vibrated, and he could not sleep.

The court held that that the defendants were liable in private nuisance for damage done to the plaintiff's washing (physical damage). The defendants were also held liable for the noise at night, which the court held to be an interference with the enjoyment by the claimant of his house.

Obviously, it is easier to prove physical damage than loss of amenity! Further, loss of amenity entails something substantial. The closer it gets to actually diminishing the value of the land, the more likely it is that it will be actionable in private nuisance. On the other hand, if the court finds the loss of amenity to be closer in nature to recreational use, the less likely it is to be actionable. A house in which one cannot sleep through the night clearly entails a loss of amenity (as in *Halsey* v. *Esso Petroleum* above). What about loss of television reception? The older cases regarded this as not actionable. In *Bridlington Relay Ltd.* v. *Yorkshire Electricity Board* [1965] Ch 436, for example, Buckley J held that electrical interference with television signals did not constitute a legal nuisance, because it was interference with a purely recreational facility, as opposed to interference with the health or physical comfort or well-being of the claimants. Newer cases seem to differ from this.

In *Hunter* v. *Canary Wharf Ltd* (above) it was also held that interference with television reception, due to the construction of a tall tower, was not actionable in either public or private nuisance. However, in contrast to *Bridlington Relay Ltd*, the reason was not because of the *nature of the amenity* (of television reception), but because the construction of a skyscraper in and of itself is not a nuisance that *emanates* from the defendant's land. The House of Lords seemed to accept that loss of television reception *could* be an actionable loss of amenity in property. In *Hunter*, the House likened the loss of television reception to the loss of a view due to another building being constructed by a neighbour: while the loss of view is a pity for the person losing it, it is not a nuisance. So, make sure you understand that the reason why the House of Lords denied loss of television reception to be actionable is different from the reasoning in the earlier cases, namely that it was a mere recreational facility.

Unreasonableness

Once the claimant has proven interference in the sense discussed above, she needs further to prove that the interference was *unreasonable*.

> Make sure that you do not assume that the concept of unreasonableness in nuisance means the same as in negligence! In negligence, we ask whether the *defendant's conduct* was unreasonable. In nuisance, on the other hand, we look at the interference that the claimant suffers and asks whether the *interference itself* is unreasonable, and whether it is reasonable to expect the defendant to do something about it.

What this boils down to in most instances is a balancing exercise where the interests of two neighbours in using and enjoying their land as they please come into conflict. Lord Wright put it like this in *Sedleigh-Denfield* v. *O'Callaghan* [1940] AC 880:

> 'A balance has to be maintained between the right of the occupier to do what he likes with his own and the right of his neighbour not to be interfered with . . . A useful test is what is reasonable according to the ordinary usages of mankind living in society.'

What exactly is meant by 'reasonable' very much depends on the facts of each individual case, but the courts do take certain factors into account in assessing the reasonableness of the action complained of. These factors include locality of the claimant, time at which the aggrieving action occurs, duration of the alleged nuisance, the danger it poses, and the nature and purpose of the action. The courts also examine whether the claimant is particularly sensitive to the alleged nuisance. Let's consider these factors in more detail.

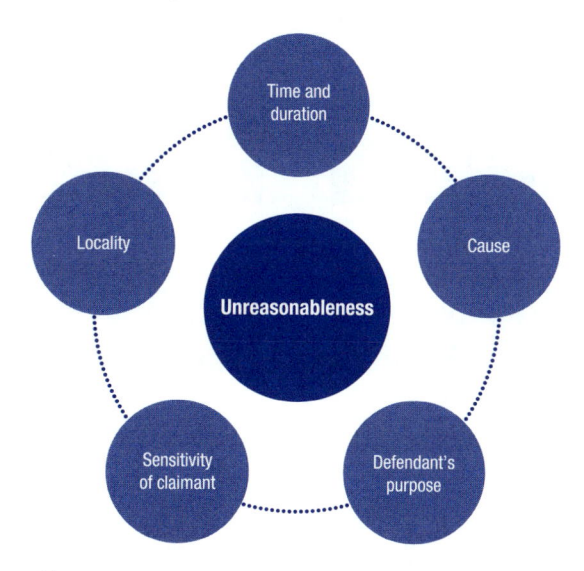

Figure 11.2 Unreasonableness

> **Take note**
>
> If the alleged nuisance caused physical damage, locality is not a consideration. However, as we saw earlier, one can also claim for loss of enjoyment or loss of amenity in land. In this instance, the locality is crucial. This was decided in *St Helen's Smelting Co v. Tipping* and confirmed in later cases such as *Halsey v. Esso Petroleum* (both discussed above).

Locality

It could be crucial to ascertain the *nature of the area* in which the alleged nuisance takes place because, in the famous words of Thesiger LJ in *Sturges* v. *Bridgman* (1879) 11 Ch D 852, 'what would be a nuisance in Belgrave Square would not necessarily be so in Bermondsey'.

What are the implications of this? If you happen to live in an industrial area, or on a busy high street, it would be less likely that you would succeed in claiming for loss of sleep or noise, for instance. But even if you lived in an industrial area, you would be able to claim in nuisance if your property suffered *physical* damage.

What if you live in a residential area, but planning permission is granted for a business which then proceeds to create a nuisance? We look at this issue again when we look at possible defences, but suffice it to say here that planning permission in itself is not a defence. However, if the nature of the locality changes because of such planning permission, the claimant may stand less of a chance in an action for nuisance.

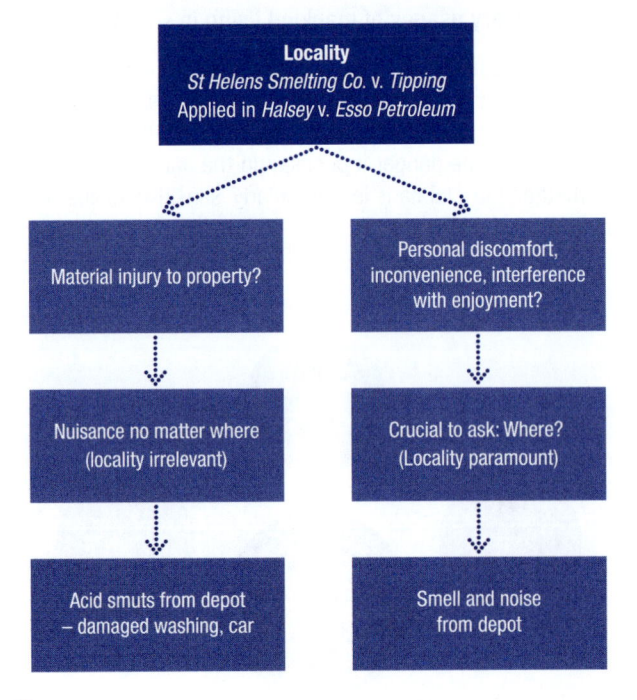

Figure 11.3 Locality

Time and duration

Another important question is when, and for how long, the alleged nuisance takes place. We expect certain events to take place during the day, when most people are awake, but when they take place at night, disturbing people's sleep, it may constitute a nuisance. Furthermore, even a low-level activity which would usually be merely annoying, may become a nuisance when it is repeated for long periods of time. *Halsey* v. *Esso Petroleum* pointed out that the filling of oil tankers at 10 am was reasonable, but it was a nuisance to do so at 10 pm.

How long does something have to continue in order to become a nuisance? Usually a continuous state of affairs is needed for nuisance. Can a single isolated escape of something that affects the claimant's property be a nuisance? It could be a tort under *Rylands* v. *Fletcher*, which we discuss below, or it could of course be actionable in negligence. But can it be nuisance? It is unlikely, under normal circumstances. For example, the isolated escape of a cricket ball out of the grounds was held not to be a nuisance in *Bolton* v. *Stone* [1951] 1 All ER 1078. However, if the isolated escape is connected to a state of affairs on the defendant's land, it may be a nuisance. For example, in *Spicer* v. *Smee* [1946] 1 All ER 489 faulty wiring in the defendant's property caused a fire which destroyed a neighbour's bungalow. The court held that the state of the electric wiring in the defendant's bungalow constituted a nuisance on her property for which she was liable.

Clearly, the longer something continues the more likely it is that it will be unreasonable and a nuisance, but even temporary measures can be nuisances. For example, in *Barr* v. *Biffa Waste Services Ltd* [2012] EWCA Civ 312 the Court of Appeal found in favour of residents affected by smells from a waste site, even after the situation improved. The residents had suffered from bad smells during the years that the waste site operators had dumped the waste close by, and during that period this constituted a nuisance. Another example can be found in *Andreae* v. *Selfridge & Co Ltd* [1938] Ch 1, where temporary noise arising from building activities which caused loss of sleep was held to be a nuisance.

INTERSECTION

Here we see that the court looks at the duration and time of the aggrieving occurrence to decide whether it is a nuisance in the first place. If so, the court returns to this issue again at the end, i.e. when the claimant has been successful. Then the temporary or occasional nature of the activity may affect the remedy that is available to the claimant. If it is clear that the nuisance will come to an end at some stage, or has already come to an end, it is more likely that damages will be granted in lieu of an injunction. This is only logical – why would the court grant an order for something to stop if it was going to stop (soon) in any case? It is also fair – people who have suffered nuisance should be entitled to compensation.

Take note, however, that the courts have on several occasions reiterated that damages in lieu of an injunction should be used only by exception – otherwise it may lead to the temptation for people to commit nuisances in the belief that they could then simply 'pay off' the victims. The first remedy for nuisance should always be an injunction – see below.

Cause of and control over the nuisance

The court will examine what caused the nuisance. Was it something the defendant did? Or was it something caused by nature? If the latter, the court will look at how much control the defendant had over the occurrence, whether it was practicable to control the event, etc., because a natural occurrence is more likely to be a reasonable state of affairs and so not a nuisance. For example, in *Goldman* v. *Hargrave* [1967] 1 AC 645 the defendant was held liable when he did not fully extinguish a fire on his property which then spread to his neighbour's land. The court reasoned that he had a duty to act in respect of hazards on his land and his failure to do so adequately was unreasonable.

Defendant's purpose

The basic principle in tort law is that malice is irrelevant. For example, it was held in *Bradford Corporation* v. *Pickles* [1895] AC 587 that malice did not make an otherwise lawful action unlawful. There are certain exceptions, however. One of them is found in private nuisance, and the other in defamation (which we examine in Chapter 11). Here, if the defendant acts out of spite or with hostile intentions, her actions may be seen as *unreasonable*, which is of course precisely the necessary element of private nuisance we are looking at now. The following two cases illustrate how something which is usually lawful, or even reasonable, may become unreasonable and therefore actionable because of malicious intent.

In *Christie* v. *Davey* [1893] 1 Ch 316 the defendant tried to disrupt music lessons conducted by his neighbour by making noises in his own home, such as banging on pots. This was held to be nuisance. In *Hollywood Silver Fox Farm* v. *Emmett* [1936] 2 KB 468 the defendant regularly fired his shotgun on his farm. This is not something unusual for a farmer to do, but the defendant fired the shots at times calculated to prevent his neighbour's foxes to mate, so depriving him of his fox fur business. The court pointed out that deliberate action and malicious intention made an interference *prima facie* unreasonable.

Sensitivity

From the above we see that the court examines the occurrence and the defendant's actions to determine whether they are reasonable. In addition, the court will also look at whether the *claimant's* reaction to the event was reasonable. Put another way, this is a kind of 'reasonable claimant' test: would any other reasonable person also have experienced the event as a nuisance? Or is there some characteristic of this particular claimant that makes her unduly sensitive (in which case the claim will not stand)? For example, in *Robinson* v. *Kilvert* (1889) 41 Ch D 88 the claimant and defendant both ran businesses in the same building. The claimant's trade involved heat sensitive paper, which was damaged by the activities of the defendant's trade. The court held that in this case there was a particular sensitivity and therefore the claim could not succeed.

PUBLIC NUISANCE

Take care to understand that public and private nuisance may be present in the same set of circumstances. Revise *Halsey* v. *Esso Petroleum* to see how this may happen. In our discussion of public nuisance, you must therefore remember that most of the principles (such as reasonableness) that are relevant to private nuisance also apply to public nuisance. Instead of repeating these, we will therefore focus on the *differences*, so that you are able to distinguish public from private nuisance. The first and most significant difference is that whereas private nuisance is a tort that infringes an interest in land, public nuisance infringes upon the comfort and convenience of a class of people. Secondly, whereas private nuisance protects an interest in land, this is not the case in public nuisance, which protects classes of people. Thirdly, and tying in with the group nature of public nuisance, this is always also a crime. The civil claim aspect of public nuisance builds on the group injury as a starting point – to claim as an individual in public nuisance, you first have to prove that you belong to the group affected, but that you as an individual suffered additional injury or damages *over and above* those suffered by the group.

Definition

The classic definition of public nuisance comes from the following case.

CORNERSTONE

Attorney-General v. PYA Quarries [1957] 2 QB 169

In this case a quarry caused dust, noise, vibrations, and flying rocks and stones. This disturbed the local community. In finding for the claimants, Romer J defined a public nuisance as: 'any nuisance which materially affects the reasonable comfort and convenience of life of a class of Her Majesty's subjects.'

Elements

Public nuisance is a crime and could lead to prosecution and criminal sanctions. It could also be a tort. How then does it work in practice? First, it is necessary that a group of people needs to be affected. Such a group will be represented by the Attorney General, who will sue the offender on their behalf in what is called a *relator action* (as in the *PYA Quarries* case above). It is also possible for local authorities to apply on behalf of the local community (Local Government Act 1972, s. 222).

Then, if a member of that group can prove that she suffered *special damage*, i.e. that she suffered more than the others (either in physical damage or injury, or in terms of inconvenience), she will be able to sue in her own name in tort.

Therefore, we can say that the two essential elements of the tort of public nuisance are, first, that a class of people is affected, and secondly that the claimant member of that class suffered special damages. Apart from that, she will also have to prove, just as in private nuisance, that the action complained of was unreasonable.

Claimant is member of an affected group of people

For public nuisance (unlike in private nuisance), the claimant does not need a legal interest in land in order to be able to sue (nor is it necessary that the defendant be a neighbour). The claimant does need to prove, however, that she is a member of the group of people affected by the alleged nuisance.

The courts interpret the notion of a group very widely for this purpose: the group could, for example, be a local community, spectators at a sporting event, users of the highway such as drivers or pedestrians, etc. The key is that the group should be an identifiable group and not an indiscriminate number of people. This was illustrated very well in the following case.

In *R* v. *Rimmington* [2005] UKHL 63, the defendant sent more than 500 separate letters and packages containing racially offensive material to several different people. At first instance, on a charge of public nuisance, he was found guilty (remember public nuisance is a crime). The House of Lords, however, overturned the decision, mainly because the group to which the defendant sent the material was an indiscriminate collection of people and not an identifiable group. The House pointed out that what we had here was individual acts causing injury to several different people rather than to the community as a whole or a significant section of it. As such it lacked an essential ingredient of the offence of causing a public nuisance: it did not cause *common injury* to a *section of the public*.

(If this offends your sense of justice, read Baroness Hale of Richmond's *dicta* from paragraph 58 in the judgment, in which she points out that the kind of 'poison pen' communications such as we saw in this case, are covered by the statutory offence contained in the Malicious Communications Act 1985.)

How many people need to be affected before an action can be brought? This is to be determined on a case-by-case basis – there is no minimum, objective threshold. The nuisance must be shown to injure a representative cross-section of the class.

Special damage

An individual suing in public nuisance must prove that she suffered damage which is 'particular, direct and substantial' beyond that suffered by others affected. What is meant by this? *Benjamin* v. *Storr* (1874) LR 9 CP 400 illustrates how a claimant in public nuisance needs to prove damages over and above those suffered by the group affected. The claimant kept a coffee house in Covent Garden. The defendants constantly loaded and unloaded goods into and from (given the year 1874) horse-drawn vans, which blocked out light, obstructed access to the claimant's shop and caused a stench (horses of course not being toilet-trained!) The court agreed that this affected the claimant's business (as being a member of a group of inhabitants and business owners of Covent Garden) disproportionately and he won his case.

The damage could be damage to property, as in *Halsey* above, where the claimant's car parked on the public highway was damaged by smuts from the factory and the claimant therefore suffered more damage than other road users. Unlike in private nuisance, in public nuisance one can also claim for personal injury. Why? The Court of Appeal gave an answer in the following case.

> In *Corby Group Litigation Claimants* v. *Corby BC* [2008] EWCA Civ 463 the claimants had all been born with upper limb deformities. Their mothers all lived close to land under the control of the local authority, who in turn allowed the relevant land to be developed as contaminated land. The claimants contended that exposure to this contaminated land during their mothers' pregnancies had caused their deformities. The question before the Court of Appeal was whether they could claim for their personal injuries under public nuisance.
>
> It was argued by the defence that because personal injury is not recoverable in private nuisance, it should also not be recoverable in public nuisance. It was also argued that personal injury should be confined to claims in negligence.
>
> The court held that the essence of the right that was protected by the tort of public nuisance was the right not to be adversely affected by an unlawful act or omission whose effect was to endanger the life and health of the public. The reference to life and health necessarily implies that personal injury is recoverable – and this is also what the established law says about public nuisance. The court did say that it is possible for the law to develop in such a manner that personal injury should be confined to negligence claims, but if that is the case it should be clearly stated either by Parliament or by the House of Lords (now of course the Supreme Court). Do you think it advisable? Note that a claimant who sues in public nuisance for personal injury must in any case show that the defendant's conduct was negligent. Would it therefore make any difference to the claimant whether she should base her claim on public nuisance or negligence?

You can also recover (consequential) economic loss in public nuisance: in *Tate and Lyle Industries* v. *Greater London Council* [1983] 2 AC 509 the defendant's constructing of terminals for the Woolwich Ferry silted up the claimant's jetty, and they had to spend money on dredging. The House of Lords held that there was an interference with the public's right of navigation of the Thames constituting a public nuisance, and that the claimant could recover their expenditure.

DEFENCES TO NUISANCE

Apart from prescription, which is not available as a defence to public nuisance, the availability and operation of defences are the same for both types of nuisance. There are three defences that are particular to nuisance, but before we get to that it is important to note that there are also some 'false' defences; i.e. people tend to think that they constitute proper defences whereas in reality they do not. Take note of them in Figure 11.4, and keep them in mind as we look at the relevant cases because more than one defence, as well as some non-defences, come up in their findings.

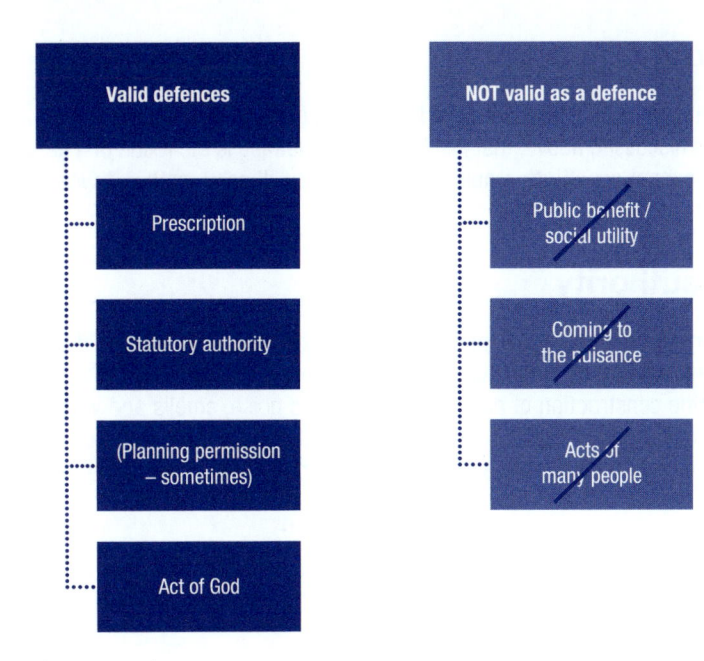

Valid defences
- Prescription
- Statutory authority
- (Planning permission – sometimes)
- Act of God

NOT valid as a defence
- Public benefit / social utility
- Coming to the nuisance
- Acts of many people

Figure 11.4 Defences to nuisance

Prescription

Prescription means that a claim runs out of time. Put another way, if your claim has prescribed, it means that you have run out of the time in which the law allows you to institute your claim. This concept is also referred to as the statute of limitations, or time-barring. The prescription period for private nuisance is 20 years, during which time the action complained of *must have constituted a nuisance*.

APPLICATION

To understand prescription in private nuisance, imagine the following scenario: Jane suffered an accident in childhood which left her without hearing. In 1985 she moved into a house next to Dave, who plays drums in a rock band. Dave suffers from insomnia and likes to practise his drumming when he cannot sleep, from approximately midnight to 5 am. In 2006, due to an advance in science, Jane underwent an operation and her hearing was restored. She then became aware of, and complained about, Dave's nocturnal drumming. Has her claim in nuisance prescribed?

> According to case law such as *Sturges* v. *Bridgman* (1879) 11 ChD 852, the answer is no. In *Sturges*, a doctor lived without complaint next door to a neighbour with a noisy business for several years, but when he built a consulting room on his property, the noise became a problem. The court held that his claim had not prescribed: we calculate the prescription period not from the date the action started, but from the date on which it *started to be a nuisance*. For Jane, that date was in 2006 – not 1985.

Act of God

True natural disasters, out of the control of human beings, would of course not be actionable. Take note, however, as discussed above, that just because something is the result of a natural state, it does not mean that it cannot constitute a nuisance. The court will ask whether it was practicable and to be expected of the defendant to do something about the state of affairs.

Statutory authority

It is a good defence to a claim in nuisance if you can show that what you are doing is authorised by statute, or is the inevitable consequence of such statutory authority. In *Allen* v. *Gulf Oil Refining Ltd* [1981] AC 1001 the construction of an oil refinery caused noise, smells and vibration, for which the claimants sued in nuisance. The House of Lords upheld the defence of statutory authority, as the defendants had been given statutory authority to build and operate the refinery.

CORNERSTONE

Civil Aviation Act 1982

Section 77 of this Act provides a good example of how statutory authority works as a defence. Section 77(1) states that there should be regulations about noise made by aircraft at aerodromes, and section 77(2) states that as long as these regulations are adhered to, there will be no possibility of a claim in nuisance.

The Court of Appeal recently reflected on the interplay between statutory and common law principles affecting the tort of nuisance in *Barr* v. *Biffa Waste Services Ltd* [2012] EWCA Civ 312. The claimants lived in a housing estate close to a quarry which was being used as a landfill site. In terms of a permit granted under a relevant environmental statute, the defendants then started to dump a different kind of waste in the site, with the result that the smell became such that the residents of the housing estate sued them in nuisance.

One of the issues before the court was whether the permit that was granted was enough to constitute the defence of statutory authority and, if not, whether the permit changed the nature of the neighbourhood in a way that changed it to a neighbourhood where smells from a waste dump could not be considered a nuisance. (We look at planning permission as a defence directly below.)

The Court of Appeal confirmed that statutory authority confers a defence, but also found that the mere fact that there is a statute (dealing with the activity) does not automatically negate common law rights in nuisance. In other words, one has to study the statute and then compare what is being done against the statutory regime to find out whether the statute actually does permit the activity.

LJ Carnwath put it like this (at 48):

'... Short of express or implied statutory authority to commit a nuisance ... there is no basis, in principle or authority, for using such a statutory scheme to cut down private law rights ...'

As to whether the permit changed the neighbourhood to a kind in which smells could not reasonably be regarded as a nuisance, he continued:

'... the 2003 permit was not "strategic" in nature, nor did it change the essential "character" of the neighbourhood, which had long included tipping. The only change was the introduction of a more offensive form of waste, producing a new type of smell emission.'

The defence of statutory authority therefore failed in *Barr*.

This decision clearly sends out the message that the common law will not be ousted easily by a statutory regime – the common law prevails unless it is very clear in the relevant statute that a nuisance is permitted.

Planning permission – sometimes!

Planning permission in and of itself does *not* constitute a valid defence to a claim in nuisance. It is only if the planning permission has the result that the neighbourhood changes in character, that it *may* be relevant to a defence. That is, if the neighbourhood changes into the kind of neighbourhood where the action for which planning permission was granted would not constitute a nuisance, then only would the fact that planning permission was given be relevant in raising a defence to a claim in nuisance.

> **REFLECTION**
>
> The defendants in *Lawrence* v. *Fen Tigers Ltd* [2012] EWCA Civ 26 (which is also known as *Lawrence* v. *Coventry (t/a RDC Promotions)*) operated a motorsport track on their property and at some stage obtained planning permission to run a motocross track on its agricultural land. The claimants subsequently bought residential property nearby and instituted a claim in nuisance due mainly to noise. The Court of Appeal rejected the claim. It emphasised that although a planning authority could not by the grant of planning permission authorise the commission of a nuisance, the permission, coupled with the activities it permitted, could have the effect of changing the character of a locality. In such an instance, the question whether particular activities in that locality constituted a nuisance then has to be decided against the background of its changed character.
>
> The court also pointed out that the motorsport activities in the area had been going on for 13 years before the claimants started complaining.
>
> At the time of writing, this case was pending an appeal to the Supreme Court. Do you agree with the Court of Appeal's reasoning? Or do you think that this is an example of 'coming to the nuisance' (discussed below) and should have been decided otherwise?

So, planning permission could be given that would, for example, have the effect of changing a residential area into an industrial area. In a subsequent nuisance suit, the court could then take into account that planning permission was given – but it will still be only one of several possible factors that the court will consider.

Not defences to nuisance

Do not mistake the following for defences to nuisance.

First, there is what is known as '*coming to the nuisance*'. The defendant cannot argue (as a defence) that the claimant was aware of the nuisance when they moved into the area. The defendant can, however, raise it as a factor that the court should take into consideration when deciding upon either the reasonableness of the action or the claimant's response, or when deciding upon a suitable remedy.

Secondly, you cannot raise a defence that your *action is of public benefit* or has some social utility. In other words, it is not a defence to say that the greater good of the public should outweigh the specific rights of the individual claimant. An extreme example is the case of *Bellew* v. *Cement Co* [1948] Ir R 61, where Ireland's (then) only cement factory was closed down because it constituted a nuisance. Again, note that although social utility is not a *defence*, it might be taken into account in deciding upon the remedy. For example, in *Miller* v. *Jackson* [1977] QB 966 cricket balls often landed in the claimant's garden from the defendant cricket club's grounds. The court held that this did indeed constitute a nuisance, but decided not to grant an injunction on the grounds of the club's social utility to the public.

Finally, it is no defence that there were *many people causing the nuisance*, and the defendant just happened to be one of them. As long as the defendant knowingly participated in the collective nuisance, she can be held liable.

REMEDIES FOR NUISANCE

Injunction

It should come as no surprise that the primary remedy in nuisance is the injunction: most people when faced with a nuisance want nothing more than for it to just *stop* – stop the smell from waste being dumped nearby, stop the noise from oil tankers thundering past in the small hours of the night, etc. The aim is to prevent the nuisance from continuing or recurring.

> **Take note**
> Remember that equitable remedies (such as injunctions) are at the discretion of the court. This means that the court can decide not to grant the remedy, even if the claimant is successful. Common law remedies (such as damages), on the other hand, are not discretionary, and have to be awarded if proven.

An injunction could, instead of prohibiting the activity altogether, also limit it. This is a concession to the notion of balancing the interests of the parties concerned. For example, noise may be permitted, but only during certain hours. In *Watson and Others* v. *Croft Promo-Sport Ltd* [2009] 3 All ER 249 the defendant was ordered to limit its use of a motorsport circuit to 40 days a year.

Does this mean that courts can and often do award damages in lieu of an injunction? The courts have grappled with this in several cases and have come to the conclusion that even though an injunction is discretionary, it still remains the primary remedy for nuisance – even where the claimant is more than willing to receive damages instead of an injunction. The policy reason for this is because it would be wrong to allow people to 'purchase' (by paying damages) the right to commit a nuisance.

Nevertheless, in some instances an injunction would not be a proper or even possible remedy. In such an instance damages may be awarded.

Damages

In private nuisance, damages are limited to physical damage to the land, or loss of value of the land. Because, as we know, the tort is a tort against *land*, you cannot claim for personal injury. As we have seen in our discussion of public nuisance, in that instance personal injury can be claimed also.

Abatement

This means that the claimant stops the nuisance herself, and thus it amounts to self-help. Because this may complicate matters – for example in doing so the claimant may expose herself to a charge of trespass – it is usually only advisable in emergencies or when permission is given.

THE TORT IN *RYLANDS* v. *FLETCHER*

The tort in *Rylands* v. *Fletcher*, as it is generally known, fills a gap in the law protecting landowners or occupiers of land.

> **Take note**
> Before we move on to the tort in *Rylands* v. *Fletcher*, take a moment to contrast nuisance with negligence. In negligence, we focus on the defendant's conduct: Did she have a duty of care? Did she breach that duty by falling under the required standard? Did her action cause harm? In contrast, nuisance focuses on the interests that are invaded. You might say that the two torts approach a set of facts from two different angles. This is a good habit to cultivate: when faced with a set of facts, approach it from different angles as you need to ensure that you cover all possibilities.

> **CONTEXT**
> Think about the following: landowners and occupiers of land are protected by a number of torts – trespass, negligence and nuisance. But each of these torts, as you know, has requirements (or elements) that limit their operation to only certain instances: trespass to land requires a direct and intentional interference; negligence requires negligence or carelessness as to risk; nuisance generally requires the occurrence to continue over a period of time. The gap (or lacuna) left would be instances where damage was caused by a single occurrence of something that was unintentional and non-negligent.

More specifically, as far as occupiers are concerned, the torts of negligence, nuisance and trespass do not cover instances where their land is damaged by a non-negligent and isolated escape from their neighbour's land.

Let's look at the case from which we got this tort.

CORNERSTONE

Rylands v. *Fletcher* (1868) LR 3 HL 330

In *Rylands* v. *Fletcher* water from a reservoir escaped from the defendant's land and flooded the neighbouring claimant's colliery. It was accepted that the defendant had not been negligent. Nevertheless the House of Lords found the defendant liable. The definition of this cause of action can be found in the judgment of Mr Justice Blackburn, modified by Lord Cairns in the House of Lords: →

234 CHAPTER 11 Nuisance and the tort in *Rylands v. Fletcher*

> 'A person who for his own purpose brings onto his land and collects and keeps there anything likely to do mischief if it escapes, must keep it in at his peril, and if he does not do so, is . . . answerable for all the damage which is the natural consequence of its escape. The use of the land must amount to a non-natural use.'

Gap left by negligence, nuisance and trespass filled by tort in *Rylands* v. *Fletcher*

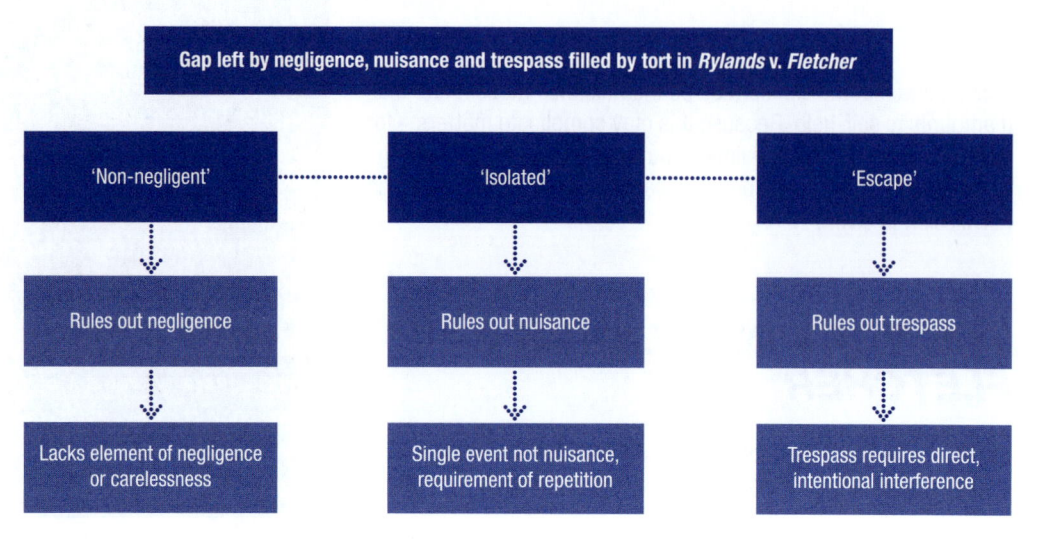

'Non-negligent'	'Isolated'	'Escape'
Rules out negligence	Rules out nuisance	Rules out trespass
Lacks element of negligence or carelessness	Single event not nuisance, requirement of repetition	Trespass requires direct, intentional interference

Figure 11.5 The gap filled by the tort in *Rylands* v. *Fletcher*

Take note

Do not get confused here. Something which is in itself not dangerous, such as water, could become dangerous under certain circumstances. In other words, something which is 'natural' could still escape or cause an escape that is dangerous. So do not equate 'naturally there' with 'natural'. What is meant by 'naturally there' is that the thing is present on the property as a result of natural phenomena. For ➔

Elements of *Rylands* v. *Fletcher*

From the definition above we can tease out four elements to the tort of *Rylands* v. *Fletcher*, that is, four things that have to be proven to succeed in a claim:

1. bringing onto land and keeping there;
2. something likely to do mischief when it escapes;
3. the thing must escape; and
4. non-natural use of the land.

Bringing onto land and keeping there

In *Rylands* the thing brought onto and kept on the land was water. Note the requirement that the thing must be 'brought onto' the land. This means that anything which is naturally there, cannot give rise to an action in *Rylands*. Note that it *could* give rise to an action based on, for instance, negligence or nuisance: revise the decisions in *Goldman* v. *Hargrave* and *Leakey* v. *National Trust* discussed under private nuisance above.

Something likely to do mischief when it escapes

The thing need not be dangerous in itself, but it must be likely to cause damage should an escape happen. What is dangerous is decided in each particular case on the facts. If you think about it, almost anything, however innocuous, may be dangerous under the right circumstances. A tree in itself is not dangerous – but if it blows over onto a neighbour's house it could well be. Similarly, water is not dangerous in itself, but collect together a whole reservoir full and then let it loose and it could kill. This means we have to look not only at the thing itself, but also at how much of it there is, how it is stored, etc.

> example, water could be on a property because of rainfall, or a spring. In such an instance there would be no liability (under Rylands!) if the water escaped – there would only be liability under Rylands if the water was brought onto and kept on the land by humans.

It follows that there is a requirement of foreseeability. In *Transco plc* v. *Stockport Metropolitan Borough Council* [2003] UKHL 61 the defendants were in charge of providing a water supply to a block of flats by means of a connecting pipe from the water main. This burst and extensive damage followed. The court held that, though water supplied by means of pipes was capable of causing damage in the event of an escape, it did not amount to the creation of a special hazard constituting an extraordinary use of land for the purposes of *Ryland*. On the topic of foreseeability, Lord Bingham remarked:

> 'I do not think the mischief or danger test should be at all easily satisfied. It must be shown that the defendant has done something which he recognised, or judged by the standards appropriate at the relevant place and time, he ought reasonably to have recognised, as giving rise to an exceptionally high risk of danger or mischief if there should be an escape, however unlikely an escape may have been thought to be.'

The thing must escape

The claimant will have to prove that an actual escape took place.

Must it be the thing *itself* that escapes? What if the 'dangerous' thing itself does not escape, but causes something else to escape? Older cases include this scenario as falling under *Rylands*. For example, in *Miles* v. *Forest Rock Granite Co (Leicestershire) Ltd* (1918) 34 TLR 500 (CA) the defendant was held liable under *Rylands* when explosives kept on his land (obviously a dangerous thing) exploded and caused rocks to escape.

However, the Court of Appeal recently held in *Stannard (t/a Wyvern Tyres)* v. *Gore* [2012] EWCA Civ 1248, when a fire broke out amongst tyres kept on the defendant's property and spread to the claimant's, that the escape had to be of the thing itself. Because the tyres had not escaped, it was held, *Rylands* did not apply.

Commentators see this as proof of the diminishing importance of the tort of *Rylands* v. *Fletcher*.

Also, note that 'escape' means going from one property to another. If the occurrence is confined to one property we cannot speak of an escape and a claim will not lie in *Rylands*: in *Read* v. *J Lyons & Co Ltd* [1947] AC 156 the claimant, a weapons inspector, was injured in the course of her duties when a shell exploded while she was inspecting it at the defendants' munitions factory. The defendants were not liable under *Rylands*, since there had been no escape of any dangerous thing from their premises.

Non-natural use

Natural use has essentially been interpreted as 'ordinary use'. But what is meant by 'non-natural use'? Lord Moulton in *Rickards* v. *Lothian* [1913] AC 280:

'It is not every use to which land is put . . . It must be some special use bringing with it increased danger to others and must not merely be the ordinary use of the land or such a use as is proper for the general benefit of the community.'

If we look at the comments from the House of Lords in cases such as *Cambridge Water* v. *Eastern Counties Leather plc* [1994] 2 WLR 53 and *Transco plc* v. *Stockport Metropolitan Borough Council* [2003] UKHL 61, we see that foreseeability of damage is a prerequisite of liability under *Rylands*. So, the requirements of non-natural use and dangerousness can be seen as interlinked. There has to be an exceptionally high risk of danger and the activity must be unusual or special for the possibility of liability to arise. In the case of *Cambridge Water*, the defendant polluted groundwater, but at the time it was not foreseeable when the then applicable environmental laws were considered. Because of the foreseeability requirement, there was no liability in *Rylands*.

Claimant and defendant

Rylands v. *Fletcher* has its roots in – and is still seen as a kind of sub-species of – nuisance. Therefore, as in *Hunter* v. *Canary Wharf Ltd* [1997] 2 All ER 426, it is likely that a person can only claim if she has a proprietary interest in the land. As for the defendant, an owner or occupier of land, including whoever stores or collects the dangerous substance in question, can be sued. Note that the claimant and defendant do not have to be neighbours.

Defences to *Rylands*

The following defences are available against a claim in *Rylands* and operate in the same manner as for other torts: statutory authority; consent; act of God; act of a stranger; and contributory negligence.

Remedies for a claim based on *Rylands* v. *Fletcher*

The main remedy in a claim based on *Rylands* is an injunction, but note that under exceptional circumstances damages may be awarded in lieu of injunction. The same policy issues as in nuisance are at play. Abatement is a form of self-help where the claimant intervenes. Again, this works the same way as in nuisance and except if it is an emergency, the claimant should give notice if entry is necessary to avoid liability for trespass to land. Finally, damages may be recovered for damage to property or for consequential economic loss, but personal injury is not recoverable.

KEY POINTS

- The tort of nuisance takes three forms: private nuisance, public nuisance and statutory nuisance.
- Private nuisance aims at protecting an interest in land; it therefore protects *land* rather than individuals. For this reason the tort of private nuisance overlaps with land law to a large extent, and you will note that many cases involving private nuisance are heard in the land tribunal. For the same reason personal injury is not recoverable in private nuisance.
- Public nuisance is a crime out of which a claim in tort may arise. The aim is to protect the affected group of people by removing or abating the nuisance. An *individual* member of such group can further claim for damages provided she can prove that she suffered damages over and above those

of the relevant group. Because of its nature, this tort overlaps with criminal law. Unlike private nuisance, personal injury is recoverable.
- Statutory nuisance refers to nuisances created as such, and dealt with in, Acts of Parliament.
- The tort in *Rylands* v. *Fletcher* protects against indirectly caused harm due to a non-negligent and isolated escape from a neighbour's land.

CORE CASES AND STATUTES

Case	About	Importance
Marcic v. *Thames Water Utilities Ltd* [2003] UKHL 66	Claim in nuisance	Where a statutory regime covers a nuisance situation, the claim has to be instituted in terms of the statute.
Hunter v. *Canary Wharf Ltd* [1997] 2 All ER 426	*Locus standi* in private nuisance	One has to have a legal right in the affected land in order to be able to sue in private nuisance.
Sedleigh Denfield v. *O'Callaghan* [1940] AC 880	Private nuisance	Even if you did not create a nuisance, you could be held liable for its continuance.
Attorney-General v. *PYA Quarries* [1957] 2 QB 169	Public nuisance	Defined public nuisance as any nuisance which materially affects the reasonable comfort and convenience of life of a class of Her Majesty's subjects.
Rylands v. *Fletcher* (1868) LR 3 HL 330	Escape from land causing damage	Filled a lacuna left by nuisance, negligence and trespass for providing liability for damage caused by non-negligent escape of something that was brought onto a neighbour's land likely to cause damage if it so escaped.

Statute	About	Importance
Civil Aviation Act 1982, s. 77	Defence of statutory authority	Section 77 illustrates how statutory authority works as a defence against a claim in nuisance. Section 77(1) states that there should be regulations about noise made by aircraft at aerodromes, and s. 77(2) states that as long as these regulations are adhered to, there will be no possibility of a claim in nuisance.

FURTHER READING

Barr and others v. Biffa Waste Services Ltd [2012] EWCA Civ 312
Again, this case provides a good general discussion of nuisance, but it is particularly worth reading for the way it clarifies what happens when there is a nuisance, but also a statutory regime covering the matter. Does the statute supplant the age-old common law principles in nuisance? Or are the common law rules inalienable? The court explains that unless there were express or implied statutory authority to commit a nuisance, such a statutory scheme would not cut down private law rights.

Gearty, C. (1989) The place of private nuisance in a modern law of torts. CLJ, p. 215
This article examines the relationship between the torts of private nuisance and other torts such as negligence. It is important that you understand the differences and similarities between these torts, and reading this article will aid your grasp of the subtle interplay between them.

Halsey v. Esso Petroleum Co. Ltd [1961] 1 WLR 683
This case provides a good discussion of all the torts discussed in this chapter: private nuisance, public nuisance and also the tort in *Rylands* v. *Fletcher*. The facts and findings illustrate how one set of related actions can give rise to liability in both public and private nuisance. You need to know how to distinguish between public and private nuisance, and reading this case will make the distinction clearer.

Hunter v. Canary Wharf Ltd [1997] 2 All ER 426
You will benefit from the House of Lords' discussion of the rules relating to both public and private nuisance in this case in general. More specifically, note the explanation for the court's confirmation that only those with a proprietary interest in land could claim in private nuisance – the remarks by Lord Goff from 687–95 in particular will help you understand the reasoning behind this.

Lee, M. and Waite, A.J. (2003) What is private nuisance? LQR, p. 298
This article provides an in depth discussion of the theory of private nuisance.

Murphy, J. (2004) The Merits of Rylands v. Fletcher. OJLS 24, p. 643
Every so often there are statements that the tort in *Rylands* v. *Fletcher* serves no further purpose and should be subsumed into, for example, negligence. This article argues otherwise, and in so doing will aid your understanding of this often overlooked tort.

Spencer, J.R. (1989) Public nuisance – a critical examination. CLJ, p. 55
It is important that you understand the differences between private and public nuisance. This article will aid your understanding.

CHAPTER 12

Employers' (operational) liability and vicarious liability

BLUEPRINT

Employer's operational liability and vicarious liability

KEY QUESTIONS

CONTEXT

- Employers have a particular duty of care towards their employees because of the frequency and added risk inherent in many workplaces.
- Vicarious liability as a concept recognises that in some instances justice or policy demands that somebody other than the tortfeasor be held liable for the latter's actions.

LEGISLATION

- Law Reform (Personal Injuries) Act 1948
- Employers' Liability (Defective Equipment) Act 1969, s. 1

CONCEPTS

- Personal (primary) liability
- Vicarious (secondary) liability
- Employers' liability/operational liability
- Breach of statutory duty

- If the common law still requires fault to be proven if a claimant sues her employer for injury at work, why do many statutes impose strict liability?
- The general rule is that you are held liable only for your own actions. Why does the law make an exception to this rule in employer/employee relationships?

CRITICAL ISSUES

- What are the responsibilities that employers have towards their employees?
- Can these responsibilities be delegated?
- Are employers held liable for torts committed by their employees?
- What are the requirements for employers to be held vicariously liable for torts committed by their employees?

CASES

- Wilsons & Clyde Coal Co v. English [1938]
- Ready-Mixed Concrete (South East) Ltd v. Minister of Pensions and National Insurance [1965]
- Lister v. Hesley Hall Ltd [2002]

SPECIAL CHARACTERISTICS

- Employers may be personally liable to employees under operational liability
- Employers may be vicariously liable to third parties for torts committed by employees
- Employers will only be vicariously liable if:
  1. an employee
  2. committed a tort
  3. within the course and scope of employment

REFORM

- Much of the employee-favourable legislation originates from EU law – if the UK leaves the EU, will this protection continue?
- Will popular disaffection with the perceived 'overkill' of health and safety regulations impact on employee protection?

Setting the scene

As a rule, you are only held liable for torts that you yourself commit. This is called personal liability. We also refer to this as primary liability. Sometimes, however, you can be held liable for a tort committed by someone else. In that case we refer to it as **vicarious liability**. We also refer to this as secondary liability. Vicarious liability arises often in circumstances where one person is in a position of authority or responsibility over another. For example, a parent can be held liable for the actions of a child, or a prison officer can be held liable for a tort committed by a prisoner under her supervision. Similarly, it often happens that an employer can be held liable for a tort committed by her employee.

If there is vicarious (secondary) liability, there is always *also* personal (primary) liability. This means that the claimant can sue two persons – the person who committed the tort (who is primarily or personally liable) as well as the person who can be held vicariously liable.

Vicarious liability often arises in the workplace, where the employer is responsible *for* actions committed by an employee *to* a third party. Here the employer is vicariously liable to the third party. However, in the workplace, the law also recognises that the employer is responsible *to* an employee. In this instance the employer is personally (or primarily) liable to the employee. This responsibility arose from and is recognised in the common law, but is also now extensively regulated in statute law.

DISTINCTION BETWEEN PERSONAL (PRIMARY) AND VICARIOUS (SECONDARY) LIABILITY

We are going to look at these two concepts from the perspective of the workplace, i.e. where employers and employees are involved, because this is a scenario which readily lends itself to both concepts and is therefore useful as an illustrative tool. Remember, though, that there are many other contexts in which there could be either personal and/or vicarious liability – it is not confined to the employer–employee situation! For example, a parent could be vicariously liable for her child's actions, a company can be held liable for the actions of its director, a principal for its agent, etc.

CORNERSTONE

Personal (primary) liability v. vicarious (secondary) liability

The general rule is that an individual is held liable for her own actions. This is called personal (or primary) liability. There are two parties involved: the 'victim' (claimant) and the tortfeasor (defendant).

Under exceptional circumstances somebody else can be held liable for a tort committed by an individual. There are three parties involved: the 'victim' (claimant), the tortfeasor and the person responsible for the tortfeasor. In this instance, both the tortfeasor and the person responsible for her may be defendants, either jointly or severally. The reason is that even though the claimant may hold the third party liable for the tortfeasor's actions, in most instances the law still recognises that the tortfeasor is personally liable. We call this vicarious (or secondary) liability.

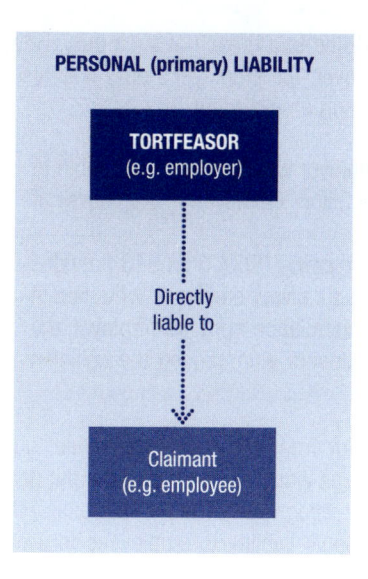

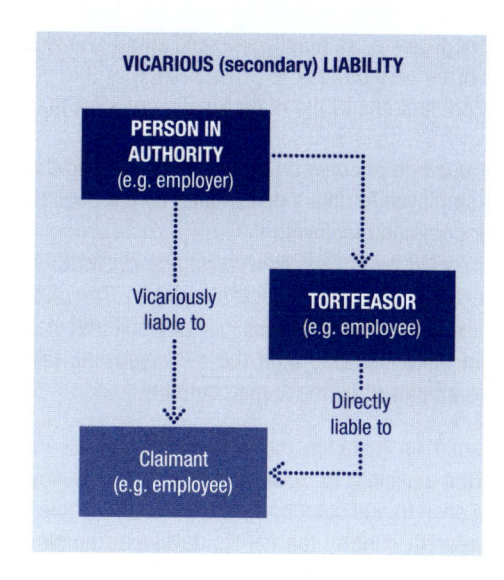

Figure 12.1 Personal (primary) liability v. vicarious (secondary) liability

Note that:

- If A commits a tort, she is *personally* liable.
- If A employs B to commit a tort, or authorises B to commit a tort, A is *personally* liable.
- If A employs B and B commits a tort in the course of her employment, A can be *vicariously* liable, whilst B could also be held personally liable.

The distinction between personal and vicarious liability can be visually represented as shown in Figure 12.1.

When you are sure that you grasp the difference between personal and vicarious liability, let's enter the workplace and look at how this translates to real life. We start with personal liability, and use the employer as an example. An employer's personal liability to an employee is also called **operational liability**.

EMPLOYER'S LIABILITY/ PRINCIPLES OF OPERATIONAL LIABILITY

Employer's liability relates to the employer's personal liability for the management of the organisation including the safety of the employees.

Origins of employers' liability

People often joke about 'Health and Safety', but not so long ago things were very different. In the nineteenth century an employer did owe a duty of care at common law to his employees and, just

> **Take note**
> It is a good idea always mentally to add the word 'personal' to the term 'employers' liability' in order not to get confused with 'employers' vicarious liability'. Or keep the two concepts separate by calling one 'organisational liability' and the other 'vicarious liability'.

like in negligence, an employee could sue if she was injured due to a breach of such duty. However, it was often very difficult to prove breach of this duty. Moreover, the employer's duty was also very restricted, and one of the main restrictions was that of common employment.

> **CONTEXT**
>
> The *doctrine of common employment* entailed that an employer would not be held liable to her employee for injury occasioned by the negligence of a fellow-employee in the course of their common employment.
>
> Hutchinson v. *York, Newcastle and Berwick Railway Company* (1850) 5 Ex 343 provides an example of how the doctrine worked. The claimant was a railway employee who died in a railway collision. When his wife and children claimed compensation from his employer, the claim failed because both the deceased and the engine drivers who caused the collision were employed by the same company.

In such an instance the employee could of course claim from the fellow employee, but this was often a useless exercise as the claimant's fellow employees would not be well off and it does not make sense to sue somebody who will not be able to pay. In recognition of the unfairness of this, in the twentieth century the courts developed employers' personal liability to employees to avoid the doctrine of common employment. In 1938 the House of Lords in *Wilsons and Clyde Coal Company* v. *English* [1938] AC 57 held that an employer had a personal duty to take reasonable care for the safety of his employees. More importantly, the court held that this duty was non-delegable: this meant that when that duty was relied upon the defence of common employment could not arise.

The doctrine of common employment was finally abolished by the Law Reform (Personal Injuries) Act 1948. In fact, development of workplace liability in the courts was at the same time mirrored by the enactment of several pieces of legislation also dealing with safety in the workplace. Today this is an area that is highly regulated by legislation, and we will therefore need to look at breach of statutory duty too. However, let's first examine the common law.

Non-delegable duty

The employer's duty is personal and non-delegable, in that if it is not performed, it is no defence for the employer to show that she delegated its performance to another person. It does not matter whether the duty was delegated to an employee or another person; the employer remains liable for non-performance of the duty.

CORNERSTONE

Wilsons and Clyde Coal Co v. *English* [1938] AC 57

The defendants, who owned a coalmine, attempted to delegate their responsibilities and liability under various industrial safety laws in operation at the time to their manager by contractually making him entirely responsible for safety in the mine. When a miner was injured, the owners tried to avoid liability on this basis, i.e. by using the doctrine of common employment.

The House of Lords held the owners liable on the basis that their personal liability could not be delegated to a third party. Lord Wright spelled it out:

> '. . . a failure to perform such a duty is the employer's personal negligence . . . whether he performs or can perform it himself, or whether he does not perform it or cannot perform it save by servants or agents . . .'

Elements

In *Wilsons & Clyde Coal Co* v. *English* the court held that the employer had a duty to provide four components:

1. competent staff as colleagues;
2. adequate plant and equipment;
3. a proper system of work and effective supervision; and
4. a safe place of work.

Competent staff as work colleagues

This includes the selection of competent employees and giving those employees proper instructions and supervision.

> **APPLICATION**
>
> Imagine that Firm A employs B to operate a crane which she is not properly qualified or trained to do. B then proceeds to crash the crane, injuring C, a fellow employee. In this scenario, C would have three options:
>
> 1. she could sue B as B is personally liable to her;
> 2. she could sue her employer A under employers' liability (as A had breached the duty to provide competent staff); or
> 3. she could sue A as being vicariously liable for B's actions (see our discussion of vicarious liability below).

Adequate plant and equipment

The duty to provide necessary equipment includes a duty to inspect, maintain and safeguard such plant and equipment. Section 1(1) of the Employers' Liability (Defective Equipment) Act 1969 enables an employee to sue her employer if injured by equipment that is defective as a result of the manufacturer's negligence. Equipment is defined by this Act as including any plant and machinery, vehicle, aircraft and clothing.

From the decision by the House of Lords in *Knowles* v. *Liverpool CC* [1993] 1 WLR 1428 we can see that the courts interpret 'equipment' widely. The claimant was injured by a defective flagstone. The court held the employer liable under the Employers' Liability (Defective Equipment) Act 1969, applying the provision that an employer could be held liable for a defect not of its own making. The court also held a flagstone to be 'equipment' for the provisions of the Act.

See also the Provision and Use of Work Equipment Regulations 1998, which impose strict criminal and civil liability and requires employers, in addition to other protective measures, to train employees in the safe use of equipment.

A proper system of work and effective supervision

This is an area of the law that is particularly open to interpretation.

In *Speed* v. *Thomas Swift & Co Ltd* [1943] KB 557 (applying the decision in *Wilsons and Clyde Coal*) a dockworker was injured whilst loading a ship. In deciding in favour of the claimant, Lord Green described 'system' as including:

'. . . the physical lay-out of the job, the setting of the stage, so to speak, the sequence in which the work is to be carried out, the provision in proper cases of warnings and notices, and the issue of special instructions.'

A safe system of work can mean different things and depends on the context of the particular trade. Trade practices, i.e. the general practice of a particular trade, will be relevant, but not conclusive in deciding whether or not the duty has been breached.

As to effective supervision, this includes a duty to give proper safety instructions. In *General Cleaning Contractors* v. *Christmas* [1953] AC 180 it was held that where a practice of ignoring an obvious danger has grown up it is not reasonable to expect an individual employee to take the initiative in devising and using precautions; the employer should put the matter right. The occupiers of premises engaged window-cleaning contractors to clean their windows. One of the cleaners supported himself in an unsafe manner and fell. The court held the employers liable as they had not ensured that the system of work adopted was as reasonably safe as it could be made and for failing to take reasonable steps to see that their instructions were carried out.

A safe place of work

Be careful to distinguish this requirement from safe equipment (perhaps found inside or on the premises of work) and a safe way of doing work (safe system and supervision). In *Latimer* v. *AEC Ltd* [1953] AC 643, after its premises were flooded, the defendant employer put down sawdust but this did not cover the whole floor and the claimant slipped and fell. The court held that the employer had taken reasonable steps to guard against the risk and was therefore not liable.

We therefore have to consider the workplace itself, the premises on which the work is done. This relates to the building itself, etc. but could also include what is done on the premises. A workplace can also be unsafe if the operations regularly carried out in it made it so. In *Baker* v. *Quantum Clothing Group* [2011] UKSC 17 the Supreme Court held that, in the defendants' knitting factory, noise generated by the knitting machines was a permanent feature of the operations intrinsic to the workplace. (We return to this case when we look at 'fault' below.)

All four duties overlap and a claim against an employer will often contain elements of more than one duty.

Fault

The common law duty of care of an employer for the safety of her employee is not a strict liability; fault has to be proved and even foreseeable damage sometimes does not give rise to liability when an employer has done all that is reasonably required in the circumstances, such as we saw in *Latimer* v. *AEC* above.

In *Baker* v. *Quantum Clothing Group* [2011] UKSC 17 factory workers' hearing was damaged due to noise in their workplace (knitting factories) and they sued for damages under the common law or the Factories Act 1961. The Supreme Court held that the question of whether a place is safe is objective, but the onus remains on the employee to show that the workplace is unsafe. To show that, one has to look at the knowledge and standards *of the time*, because, as the court pointed out, there is no such thing as an unchanging concept of safety.

In this instance, the claimants worked at a large and a smaller company. During the 1970s and 1980s, a 1972 industry code was followed by the employers, indicating the acceptable level of noise. During the mid to late 1980s, however, there were consultations about the level of noise, culminating in a 1986 Industry Directive, and finally the Noise at Work Regulations 1989, which set a higher standard, and based upon this the employers had to give their employees ear protection as the noise levels in their factories exceeded the Regulations' standards. The Regulations came into effect in

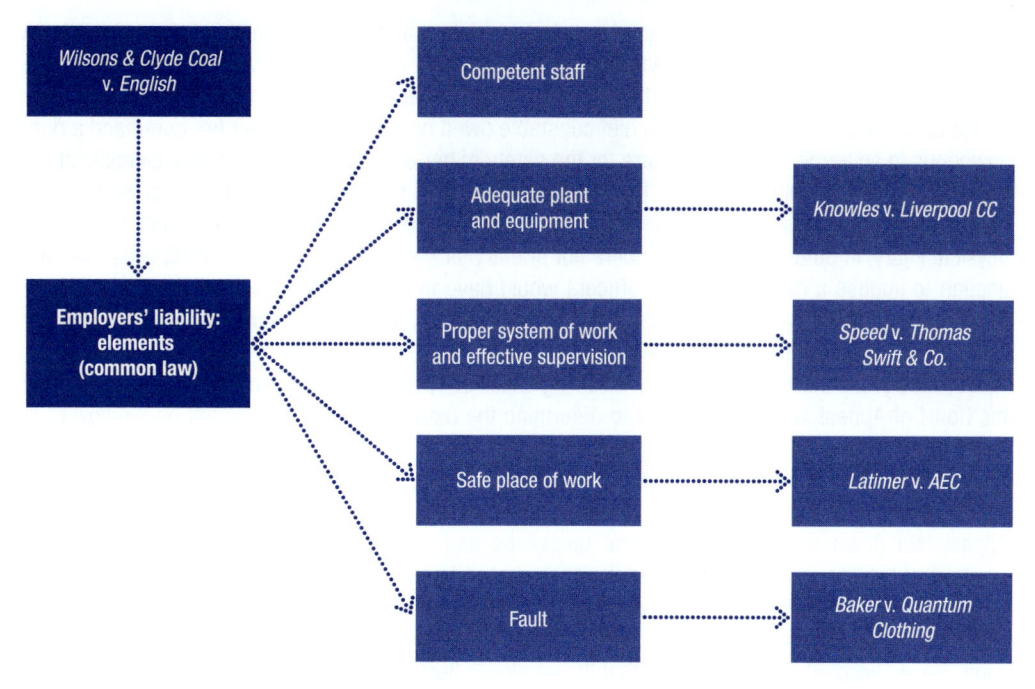

Figure 12.2 Elements of employers' liability

1990. The question before the courts was whether the employers could be held liable for injury sustained *before* the 1989 Regulations came into effect in 1990.

The Supreme Court ruled that the employers could only be held liable from the date that they should have been aware that it was no longer enough to comply with the 1972 industry code, i.e. when the terms of the 1986 Directive became generally known. In the case of the smaller company, this meant when the Regulations came into effect, so they were not liable. However, the court held that the larger company was in a position to know about this change earlier, so they were held liable for the portion of time that they had known of the change but not provided the required protection.

Psychiatric injury

Most of the cases turn on issues of physical danger, but in *Walker* v. *Northumberland County Council* [1995] 1 All ER 737 an area social services officer successfully claimed damages for psychiatric injury caused by the stress of his workload.

INTERSECTION

In our discussion of the tort of negligence we examined the decision in *Alcock* v. *Chief Constable of South Yorkshire Police* [1991] 4 All ER 907 and you will remember that the court decided that, for claims in psychiatric injury, if you are a primary victim you can claim psychiatric injury in the same way as physical injury, but if you are a secondary victim (i.e. if you are not in danger of physical injury) you have to satisfy certain criteria, such as a close tie of love and affection with the primary victim, etc. The same principles apply for psychiatric injury in the workplace.

The following case is a good example of the principles relating to psychiatric injury at work. In *White* v. *Chief Constable of South Yorkshire* [1999] 1 All ER 1 police officers who assisted during the Hillsborough football disaster claimed for psychiatric injury because of what they had witnessed. The House of Lords acknowledged that a chief constable owed police officers under her command a duty analogous to an employer's duty to care for the safety of her employees and to take reasonable steps to protect them from physical harm. However, the court held that such a duty did not extend to protecting them from psychiatric injury when there was no breach of the duty to protect them from physical injury. In other words, if they were not primary victims, the employment relationship was not enough to impose a duty. The police officers would have to satisfy the *Alcock* criteria and because they could not, their claim failed. Note that, had they been in physical danger (and therefore primary victims) their claim would have succeeded.

Because of the increase in litigation involving cases of stress at work since the decision in *Walker*, the Court of Appeal set out guidelines to determine the nature of the duty imposed on employers in cases of excessive stress in the workplace.

Hatton v. *Sutherland* [2002] 2 All ER 1 involved four conjoined appeals by employers against judgments holding them liable for psychiatric injury as the result of stress at work. The Court of Appeal laid down a number of general guidelines and stressed that the ordinary principles of employers' liability applied. The main criterion is that of foreseeability. The court ruled that there are no intrinsically stressful occupations and that unless an employer knows of some particular problem or vulnerability it is usually entitled to assume that an employee can withstand the normal pressures of a job. Taking account of any concerns that the employee herself has raised, foreseeability of the injury depends on what the employer knows (or reasonably ought to know) about the individual employee. In cases where an employee is known to be vulnerable, she will not be at fault for failing to inform the employer.

Once the risk of harm from stresses in the workplace is foreseeable, the question then arises as to what it is reasonable to expect the employer to do. According to Hale LJ, the employer's duty is then to:

'. . . take reasonable care. What is reasonable depends . . . upon the foreseeability of harm, the magnitude of the risk of that harm occurring, the gravity of the harm which may take place, the cost and practicability of preventing it, and the justifications for running the risk .'

One of the unsuccessful claimants in *Hatton* appealed against the Court of Appeal decision and his appeal was allowed (mostly on the facts) by the House of Lords in *Barber* v. *Somerset* [2004] UKHL 13. Their Lordships agreed with LJ Hale's ruling but noted that '. . . in every case it is necessary to consider what the employer not only could but should have done'. In assessing this, the court held that the size and scope of the employer's operation will be relevant, as will its resources, whether it was in the public or private sector, and the other demands placed upon it. Among those other demands are the interests of other employees in the workplace.

Statutory protection: breach of statutory duty

You will remember that the development of employers' duty towards employees in the common law was mirrored by legislative recognition. Today, employers also have extensive statutory duties, for example under the Health and Safety at Work etc. Act 1974. The duties above might also overlap with these statutory duties. Remember that under the common law, the claimant still has to prove *fault* on the part of the defendant employer. Some (but not all!) statutes provide for strict liability, however, which makes proving a claim much easier for the claimant.

CORNERSTONE

Breach of statutory duty

Because there are so many pieces of legislation dealing with employers' liability, we need to briefly look at the tort referred to as 'breach of statutory duty' in order to understand how liability works in those instances. This tort deals with civil liability arising from a breach of a duty imposed by statute.

In many statutes duties are imposed on, for example, public bodies, individuals, companies, etc. The question is what happens when such duties are not performed or are not performed properly. Be careful to note that the mere fact that a statute imposes a duty does not automatically confer a corresponding right to sue if such duty was not performed. You need to look at the relevant statute itself to determine whether such a right exists.

Statutes fall into three broad types:

1. Those that clearly state that failure to perform a specified duty will confer the right to sue (such as the Race Relations Act 1976). Added to that are statutes that clearly concern civil liability, more often than not because they served to codify the common law where civil liability was already established. The two Occupiers' Liability Acts (see Chapter 8) are good examples, and so are several statutes dealing with employers' liability.
2. Statutes that clearly state that failure to perform a specified duty will *not* confer a right to sue (e.g. Safety of Sports Grounds Act 1975).
3. Statutes silent on the issue.

Statutes falling in the first two categories are unproblematic, but where a statute is silent on whether breach of a duty is actionable, it is up to the courts to decide. The House of Lords confirmed in *X* v. *Bedfordshire County Council* [1995] 2 AC 633 that breach of a duty laid down in statute does not give those affected a right to sue, unless the statute makes it clear that *Parliament intended to create such a right*. The court held that to decide whether it is possible to claim based on breach of statutory duty, several factors need to be assessed such as the words of the relevant statute and whether they confer an action for damages; who was intended to benefit by the statute; whether there was a duty of care owed to them; whether any other remedies are available; the degree of detail with which the duty is set out; background to the legislation; type of harm involved, etc. What it boils down to, therefore, is that the courts will have to use the rules of statutory interpretation to decide upon the intention.

Recently, the Enterprise and Regulatory Reform Act 2013 in section 69 enacts that there will be no civil right of action for breach of a duty imposed by certain health and safety legislation (such as the Health and Safety at Work, etc. Act), other than where such a right is specifically provided for. This section only came into effect in April 2013 but, given its content, will probably have a significant impact on what is written and decided about breach of statutory duty.

A full discussion of this tort (breach of statutory duty) falls outside the scope of this book, but be aware of the fact that breach of statutory duty is seen as a type of tort in its own right, and has been the subject of much judicial consideration.

Let's get back to employers' duties. Assume that the relevant statute allows a civil claim (either expressly or interpreted as conferring same). The claimant will have to prove that: the defendant owed her a statutory duty; that there was breach of this duty; and that: this caused her to suffer the *type of damages covered by* the relevant statute.

INTERSECTION

> Duty, breach of duty, causation, damage: these concepts should sound familiar to you, as they are some of the essential elements of the tort of negligence. The main difference lies in the type of damage recoverable: in employers' liability if your claim is based upon a statute you have to check to see whether your damage is of the type covered by the statute. Another difference is that many statutes dealing with employers' liability impose strict liability (whereas in negligence of course you have to prove fault).

In *John Summers and Sons Ltd* v. *Frost* [1955] AC 740 the claimant was employed as a machine operator. Statutory regulations applying to the industry stated that all machines must be fitted with a guard. The guard on the claimant's machine was removed for cleaning and inadvertently not replaced before the machine was used. The claimant put his hand into the machine and lost a finger. The relevant statutory duty was contained in section 14(1) of the Factories Act 1937, which provided that every dangerous part of machinery should be securely fenced. This was enough for the court to prove that there was breach of duty by the defendant, and they were held strictly liable – the claimant did not have to prove fault (e.g. carelessness) on the part of the employer.

Remedies and defences

Given the fact that this is related to negligence, it should come as no surprise that the main remedy is an award of damages, and that the main defences are consent and contributory negligence. Of course this is subject to the provisions of individual applicable statutes.

Turning from common law and statutory regulation of an employer's duty towards her employees, we next look at vicarious liability.

VICARIOUS LIABILITY

Vicarious liability, as we saw at the beginning of this chapter, arises where under certain circumstances, and contrary to the general rule of personal/primary liability, one person can be held liable for a tort committed by another. This usually happens where one person is in a position of control or authority over another, but also in agency situations. An example of the former is where prison authorities are held liable for torts committed by prisoners under their control (review the facts of *Home Office* v. *Dorset Yacht Club* [1970] AC 1004 discussed in Chapter 2) and an example of the latter is where a partnership is held liable for actions of a partner.

The most common relationship that could give rise to vicarious liability is the employer/employee relationship. This scenario, which we'll look at in the remainder of this chapter, entails that the employer is held liable for the tort committed by her employee (the tortfeasor) in the course of her employment, against a third party (whether a fellow employee or not). The employer will be held liable even though she had not expressly instructed the employee to do the wrongful act. In this situation the third party can sue the employer and/or the employee (i.e. liability is joint).

Vicarious liability is strict

True vicarious liability is strict liability. In other words, the defendant is liable even though she herself has done nothing wrong personally. The proviso is that the tortfeasor for whom the defendant is responsible, must have committed a tort. Put another way: D will not be liable to C unless E has committed a tort (against C). The actual tort is perhaps not a tort of strict liability (e.g. negligence) but if E has committed it, D will be strictly liable.

Vicarious liability is a form of joint liability. For example if an employee, in the course of her employment, negligently injures somebody, that person may elect to sue either the employer or the employee or even make them joint defendants. The fact that the employer can be made liable does not exonerate the employee. If the claimant has joined both employer and employee as joint defendants the court may divide liability for damages between them according to their respective blameworthiness.

INTERSECTION

> Revise the concept of apportionment of damages, which we encountered in Part 1 under negligence and more specifically under contributory negligence.

In many cases it could happen that in circumstances where the employer is vicariously liable for a tort committed by an employee, that the employer might also have a personal duty to the claimant. It could be that both the employer and employee may have committed torts. For example, if A is an NHS Trust it can be personally liable for any negligent medical malpractice by medical professionals working for it (since the NHS Trust holds itself out as having a personal responsibility towards patients). At the same time the medical professionals themselves may be personally liable and a patient could make the NHS Trust vicariously liable.

Thus, in *Cassidy* v. *Ministry of Health* [1951] 1 All ER 574, Lord Denning took the view that it did not really matter whether the hospital staff were employees or not. The hospital was under a primary duty to treat patients correctly and so would have been liable for failing to do so in any event.

EMPLOYERS' VICARIOUS LIABILITY: ELEMENTS

There are three elements required to make an employer liable for a tort committed by an employee:

1. the employee must have committed a tort;
2. the employee must be an *employee* and not, for example, an independent contractor; and
3. the employee must have committed the tort within the course and scope of employment.

Tort committed

Remember that an important requirement for vicarious liability is that a tort should actually have been committed. There can be no vicarious (secondary) liability if there is no direct (primary) liability. It is not surprising that the tort that most commonly gives rise to vicarious liability is negligence –

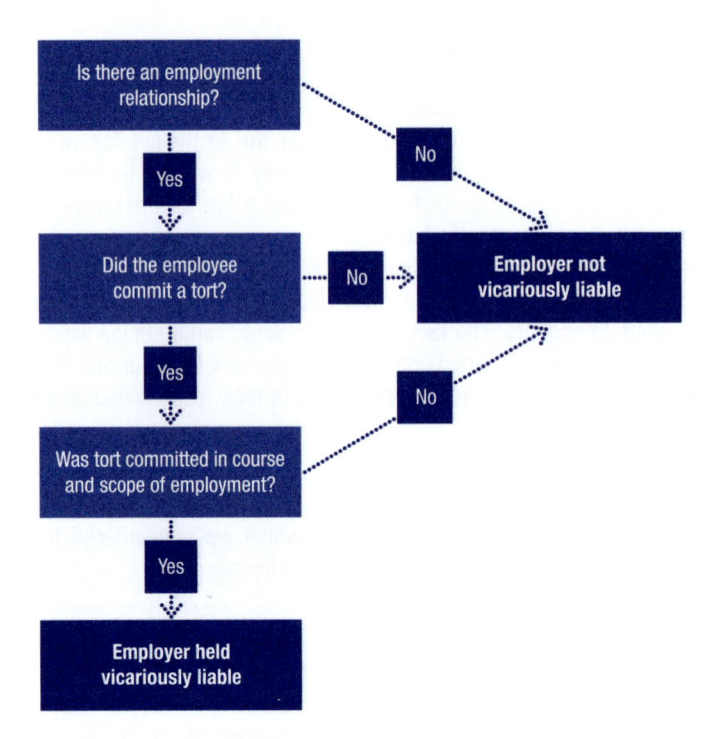

Figure 12.3 Elements of employers' vicarious liability

negligence is after all the most commonly encountered modern tort. But it could be any of the others too – trespass, defamation, etc.

You will see from the case law that we will be looking at later that it can happen that an employer is held liable for an employee's tort even if the employee disregarded instructions, or even if the employee did what she was expressly told *not* to. Therefore, it is entirely possible to impose vicarious liability on 'innocent' employers. The same goes in the case where a statutory duty was placed on the employ*ee* (and she breached it) – the 'innocent' employer can be held liable.

In *Majrowski* v. *Guy's and St Thomas's NHS Trust* [2006] UKHL 34 the claimant, Mr Majrowski worked for Guy's and St Thomas's NHS Trust and claimed that his manager harassed him. The NHS Trust investigated the matter and found that harassment did indeed take place. The claimant subsequently sued the employer NHS Trust in terms of section 3 of the Protection from Harassment Act 1997. Although this Act clearly placed a personal duty on individuals to refrain from harassment, it was held both in the Court of Appeal and in the House of Lords that nevertheless the employer could be vicariously liable for the breach by an employee in the course of employment of a statutory duty imposed solely on the employee.

Tort committed by an employee

It is imperative that there should be an *employment* relationship because employers are not held liable for torts committed by their independent contractors. It is therefore critical that you are able to identify whether you are dealing with an employee or not. As you will note from the case law, this is easier said than done, because it is not always possible to determine whether a person is an employee – there is no precise legal definition of an employee. Instead the courts have devised certain tests to try and determine employment status.

Control test

This is the oldest test that was used and asked whether the employer controlled the actual performance of the work done by the employee. The employer had to control what was done as well as *how* it was done. If the employee herself had the freedom to decide how to do the job, there was not sufficient control and she would be regarded as an independent contractor.

You can imagine that this test does not work well for high level or very skilled employees, but nevertheless it is still used to some extent today. For example in *Hawley* v. *Luminar Leisure Ltd* [2006] EWCA Civ 18 a nightclub was held vicariously liable for the act (an assault) of a doorman supplied to it under an agreement for the provision of security services, because the club had control not only over what the doorman did but also over how he had to do it.

Organisation or integration test

An alternative to the control test was developed, namely the organisation or integration test. It took into account the extent to which persons were integrated into the business in assessing whether or not they were employees. To do this the court looks at whether the person was working in terms of a *contract of service* (employee) or a *contract for services* (independent contractor). Lord Denning in *Stevenson Jordan & Harrison* v. *Macdonald & Evans* [1952] 1 TLR 101 put it thus:

> 'It is often easy to recognise a contract of service when you see it, but difficult to say where the difference lies. A ship's master, a chauffeur, and a reporter on the staff of a newspaper are all employed under a contract of service; but a ship's pilot, a taxi-man, and a newspaper contributor are employed under a contract for services. One feature which seems to run through the instances is that, under a contract of service, a man is employed as part of the business, and his work is done as an integral part of the business; whereas, under a contract for services, his work, although done for the business, is not integrated into it but is only accessory to it.'

Like the control test, this test was also limited as there were no clear criteria for identifying integration – the intuitive 'one knows it when one sees it' approach above is not foolproof. The courts today take a pragmatic approach in the following test.

Economic reality test

The economic reality (or multiple factor) test takes into account all the key relevant factors, including control and integration. This is also referred to as the 'pragmatic test', and is the test we use today to determine whether a worker is an employee or not.

CORNERSTONE

Ready-Mixed Concrete (South East) Ltd v. *Minister of Pensions and National Insurance* [1965] 2 QB 497

In this case it fell to the court to decide whether, for the purposes of National Insurance payments, truck drivers were employees of the defendant or not. The claimants had to buy and maintain the trucks themselves and had flexible working hours, but the trucks carried the logo of the defendant. McKenna J formulated the following test:

→

> 'A contract of service [i.e. employment] exists [when] three conditions are fulfilled:
>
> 1. The servant agrees that, in consideration of a wage or other remuneration, he will provide his own work and skill in the performance of some service for his master [employer];
> 2. He agrees, expressly or impliedly, that in the performance of that service he will be subject to the other's control in a sufficient degree to make that other master;
> 3. The other provisions of the contract are consistent with its being a contract of service.'

Conditions 1 and 2 in *Ready-Mixed Concrete* are in effect re-statements of tests formulated in earlier case law: there must be an employment contract in terms of which power to exercise control over the worker is given to her employer. If these two conditions are met, then there is a *presumption* that the contract is a contract of employment. This presumption may be rebutted if there are other factors that are inconsistent with the contract being a contract of employment. The third requirement is an extremely open provision, and means that courts can take various points into consideration, such as:

- *Level of independence and working hours*: independent contractors are usually more independent in how and when they do their job than employees.
- *National Insurance and tax*: independent contractors usually pay this for themselves, while deductions are usually made at source for employees.
- *Payment method*: employees usually get a regular (weekly or monthly etc.) salary while independent contractors usually get a lump sum for services rendered.
- *Equipment*: employees usually use equipment provided by their employers, whilst independent contractors usually own their own equipment.

Subsequent cases have identified other factors to take into account, such as the intention of the parties, the question of who takes the financial risk (i.e. is the worker running her own business) and whether there is any obligation for the employer regularly to provide, and the worker to undertake, work (e.g. an 'events' barman was not an employee).

As you can see, there is no scientific formula to determine whether somebody is an employee or not. All you can do is to attempt to convince the court using the factors listed above.

Take note

When an employer lends (or hires) an employee, who is regarded as the employer if the issue of vicarious liability arises? The answer is that it is a question of fact and which one is to be held responsible will have to be decided on the evidence.

Irregular situations

For example, in *Hawley* v. *Luminar Leisure Ltd* (above) it was held on the facts that the 'borrowing' employer was liable. In *Thompson* v. *T Lohan (Plant Hire) Ltd* [1987] 1 WLR 649 Company A hired an excavator and driver from Company B. The contract between them said that such drivers 'shall for all purposes in connection with their employment in the working of the plant be regarded as the servants or agents of the hirer . . . who alone shall be responsible for all claims arising in connection with the operation of the plant' by the drivers. The driver concerned was killed at work, and his widow successfully sued Company A (i.e. the 'borrowing' company identified as responsible by the indemnity in the contract).

The court rejected Company A's contention that such indemnity would be contrary to the Unfair Contract Terms Act 1977.

Take note that it could also happen that, on the facts, *both* employers should be held liable, if both were entitled to exercise control.

Can an employer 'contract out' of liability?

As noted earlier, it is important to distinguish clearly between vicarious and personal liability. The former arises only if the tortfeasor is an employee of the defendant. The latter relates to the employer's responsibility for the management of its organisation. So an employer could be liable if it had selected what was obviously an incompetent firm to do maintenance works and took no steps to ensure the work was carried out properly. Thus, in *Cassidy* v. *Ministry of Health* (above) Lord Denning took the view that it did not really matter whether hospital staff were employees or not. The hospital was under a personal duty to treat patients correctly and so would have been liable for failing to do so in any event.

It follows from the reasoning in *Cassidy* that the courts are prepared as a matter of social policy, to impose a kind of non-delegable duty on an employer (whether a natural person or organisation) who undertakes responsibility for the provision of a service for the benefit of another despite the existence of any independent contract. Thus it owes a primary duty not only to exercise care personally, but also to ensure that the person who actually carries out that service performs it carefully.

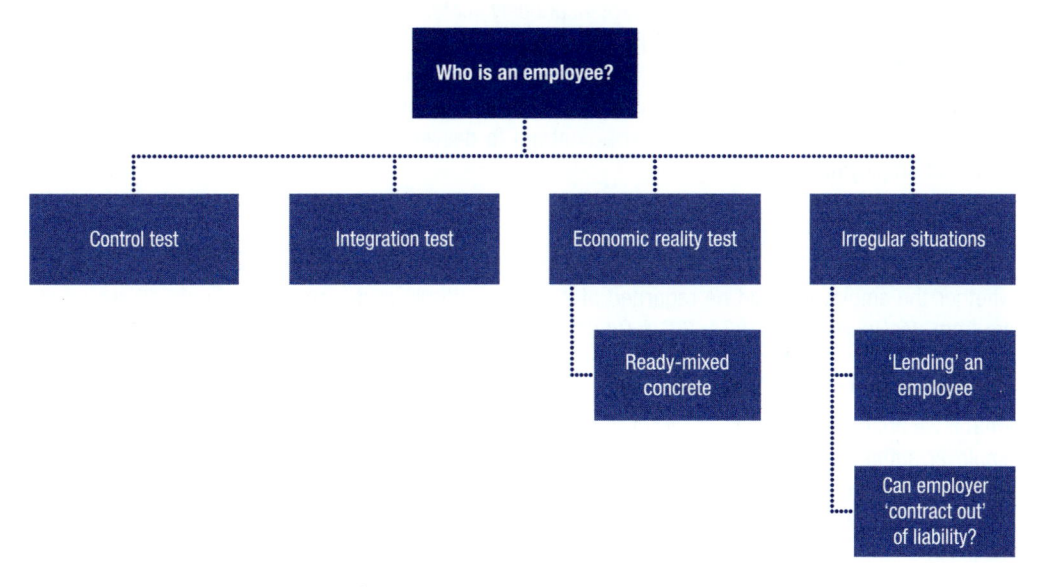

Figure 12.4 Who is an employee?

Some support for this principle is implicit in the decision of *Lister* v. *Hesley Hall Ltd* [2002] 1 AC 215 (see below).

Tort committed by an employee within the course and scope of employment

Finally, the claimant has to prove that the employee committed the tort whilst acting *in the course and scope of her employment.*

The Salmond test

The traditional starting point has been the 'Salmond test':

> Sir John Salmond, *Torts* (1st edn, 1907), at p. 83, devised the following test to determine whether a tort was committed within the course and scope of employment:
>
> 'It is deemed to be so done if it is either (a) a wrongful act authorised by the master, or (b) a wrongful and unauthorised *mode* of doing some act authorised by the master.'

The first leg is uncontroversial. The second leg is a bit trickier, so let's look at some cases. Negligent conduct cases concerned with actions contrary to instructions, or negligently performed duties, shed some light: in *Rose* v. *Plenty* [1976] 1 WLR 141 a milkman, contrary to instructions not to, engaged a young boy to help him in his milk-round. When the boy got injured, the question was whether the milkman's employer could be held liable. The Court of Appeal said yes: the milkman had been acting in pursuance of his employer's business and had not engaged the claimant for his own purposes; accordingly the employers were vicariously liable. In *Century Insurance* v. *Northern Ireland Regional Transport Board* [1942] AC 509 the driver of a petrol lorry lit a cigarette and negligently threw away a lighted match whilst delivering petrol, causing an explosion and fire. Viscount Simon LC held that even though the act of smoking was not part of the performance of the job, it was an incidental activity whilst serving his master under a contract to deliver petrol and therefore it was within the course of employment.

Unauthorised actions

What happens if the employee, during working hours, does something unauthorised? The test is whether the employee could be regarded of acting in a 'frolic of the employee's own' (these words are from *Joel* v. *Morrison* (1834) 6 C & P 501) – if so, the employer will not be held liable.

Unlawful or criminal acts

What if we are dealing with an unlawful or criminal act? Look at the Salmond test again. Clearly if the employer authorised the criminal act, it would be held liable with the employee. But if there was no authority, and the employee committed a crime during working hours, could the employer be held vicariously liable? The following is the leading case on this, and provides a useful test for determining the issue.

CORNERSTONE

Lister v. *Hesley Hall Ltd* [2002] 1 AC 215

The warden of a boarding school for children with problems systematically abused the claimants, who were children in the boarding school. The question before the court was whether the employers could be held vicariously liable for this. The claimants averred that the school had actual or constructive knowledge of the abuse and failed to prevent it. The problem lay in the fact that what the warden had done could not be described as an unauthorised method of doing some act authorised by the employers (Salmond's second leg). It was the opposite of what he was employed to do.

Nevertheless, the school were held vicariously liable. The House of Lords held that the appropriate test was whether there was a sufficient connection between the employment and the torts carried out by the employee: was the employee's tort so closely connected to his employment that it would be fair and just to hold the employer vicariously liable? Here the torts were carried out on the school's premises and at times when the employee should have been caring for the claimants. The court accepted that there was an inherent risk of abuse that the employer should have guarded against so that vicarious liability was appropriate in the circumstances.

In effect, what the House of Lords did here was to rephrase the 'course of employment' test in terms of 'close connection'.

The 'close connection' test has also been applied in vicarious liability decisions outside of the clear-cut employer/employee situation. For example, in a series of cases dealing with a very topical issue, sexual abuse by clergy, the close connection test indicated liability. In *E* v. *English Province of Our Lady of Charity and another* [2013] 2 WLR 958 the Court of Appeal held that the relationship between a parish priest and his bishop was similar enough to that of an employer and her employee for the 'close connection' test to also apply in the former. In this case, the priest had sexually abused the claimant. Because the court held that the church stood in a relationship to the priest that is similar to an employment situation, the church was held vicariously liable for the priest's actions – in deciding this the court applied the 'close connection' test.

The Supreme Court confirmed this in *Various Claimants* v. *Institute of the Brothers of the Christian Schools* [2012] 3 WLR 1319, where the defendant Institute was held vicariously liable for sexual abuse at residential schools carried out by lay brothers of the Catholic Church who taught at the schools. The court confirmed that vicarious liability involved a two-stage test. First, we have to examine the relationship between the defendant and the tortfeasor to see whether it is one that can give rise to vicarious liability, such as an employer-employee relationship. Here, the court held that the lay brothers' relationship to the Catholic Church and the Institute was close enough to that of an employer and an employee to satisfy this requirement. Second, we must ascertain whether there was a 'close connection' between the acts done by the tortfeasor, and her relationship with the defendant, to establish liability. The court decided that both were satisfied and the Institute was held vicariously liable.

Finally, we have already seen above, under the personal liability of employers, that an employer could be held liable for an employee's breach of statutory duty imposed on the employee personally – *Majrowski* v. *Guy's and St Thomas NHS Trust*.

So what you need to take away from this discussion is the three elements for the vicarious liability of an employer: the employee must have committed a tort; within the course and scope of her employment (or after *Lister*, closely connected to her employment); and the tortfeasor must have been an *employee*. And, finally, remember that these same principles apply for vicarious liability in situations that are *akin* to an employer–employee relationship (such as a priest in the Catholic Church).

KEY POINTS

- The general principle in civil liability is that you are responsible only for your own actions. The exception is vicarious liability, where under certain circumstances, you could be held liable for a tort committed by another. This often happens in employer–employee relationships.
- Employers are placed under a direct duty of care for the safety of their employees, both in terms of the common law and statute. This duty is non-delegable.
- Employers may also be held vicariously liable for torts committed by their employees during the course and scope of, or closely connected to, their employment.

CORE CASES AND STATUTES

Case	About	Importance
Wilsons & Clyde Coal Co. v. *English* [1938] AC 57	Doctrine of common employment	Court departed from the doctrine of common employment and held that an employer has a non-delegable duty towards her employees.
Latimer v. *AEC Ltd* [1953] AC 643	Safe place of work	Court will consider what employer did to make the workplace safe – if she had done all that could reasonably be expected, no liability.
Baker v. *Quantum Clothing Group* [2011] UKSC 17	Fault requirement	Onus remains on claimant to prove that workplace was unsafe.
Hatton v. *Sutherland* [2002] 2 All ER 1	Psychiatric injury at work	Employer only to be held liable if such injury was reasonably foreseeable and the employee did not take reasonable steps to address the issue.
John Summers and Sons Ltd v. *Frost* [1955] AC 740	Strict liability in terms of statute	Interpreted regulations about safe equipment – if employee proved equipment faulty, do not have to prove fault on part of employer.
Majrowski v. *Guy's and St Thomas's NHS Trust* [2006] UKHL 34	Vicarious liability is strict liability	If employee committed tort and requirements for vicarious liability fulfilled, employer held liable even if employer is 'innocent'.
Ready-Mixed Concrete (South East) Ltd v. *Minister of Pensions and National Insurance* [1965] 2 QB 497	Integration test	Test of whether person is an employee is pragmatic and we look at how far the person is integrated into the business of the employer.

Case	About	Importance
Lister v. Hesley Hall Ltd [2002] 1 AC 215	Close connection test	Revised the Salmond test to reflect that an employer can be held liable even for illegal, unauthorised acts of an employee, as long as the acts were closely connected to such employment.

Statute	About	Importance
Law Reform (Personal Injuries) Act 1948	Injuries at work	Abolished doctrine of common employment.
Employers' Liability (Defective Equipment) Act 1969, s. 1	Employer's liability for defective equipment	Employer to be held liable for defective equipment even if defect result of third party, e.g. manufacturer.

FURTHER READING

Barrett, B. (2006) Vicarious liability for harassment by an employee. *ILJ* **35(4), p. 431**
This is a case comment on the House of Lords' decision in *Majrowski* v. *Guy's and St Thomas's NHS Trust* [2006] UKHL 34, and explains in clear terms how employers are held vicariously liable for both common law and statutory torts committed by an employee.

Brodie, D. (2007) Enterprise liability: Justifying vicarious liability. *OJLS* **27(3), p. 493**
This article examines Canadian influence on the issue of vicarious liability in the UK courts. As it looks at the theoretical justifications for holding employers liable for torts committed by employees, it will help you understand this area of the law in more depth.

Mullany, N.J. (2002) Containing claims for workplace mental illness. *LQR* **118, p. 373**
This article examines the impact of the Court of Appeal decision in *Sutherland* v. *Hatton*, which narrows the limits for damages awards for stress-induced psychiatric illness caused by employment. Reading this discussion will help you understand not only the case but also general principles relating to employers' liability towards their employees.

Pawlowska, C. (2012) Vicarious liability is now more about value judgment than law. *SJ* **156(11), pp. 12–13**
In this easy-to-read article in the *Solicitors' Journal*, the author examines cases after the decision in *Lister* v. *Hesley Hall*, where the test of 'close connection' was established for vicarious liability for an employee's action. It is important for you to understand when an employer will be held liable for an employee's action, and also to decide whether you agree that this potential liability is being expanded, as the author argues.

Weddall v. Barchester Healthcare Ltd [2012] EWCA Civ 25
It is useful to read the judgment in this conjoined appeal because in the one appeal, the court held that the employee was acting in a 'frolic of his own' while in the other it was held that the employee was acting in the course and scope of his employment. Reading the Court of Appeal's reasoning will help you understand and contrast the difference.

CHAPTER 13
Other torts

BLUEPRINT
Other torts

KEY QUESTIONS

LEGISLATION
- Animals Act 1971, s. 6(2)
- Animals Act 1971, s. 2(2)
- Animals Act 1971, s. 5

CONTEXT
- There are various torts that are discussed less in textbooks, mainly because they come before the courts less.
- Many torts are also contained in statutes, necessitating knowledge of how the tort 'breach of statutory duty' works.

CONCEPTS
- Dangerous animals
- Deceit
- Malicious falsehood
- Passing off

- Should liability for damage or injury caused by animals always be strict?
- Is the distinction between dangerous and non-dangerous animals in the Animals Act 1971 logical when it only includes as non-dangerous animals domesticated in the British Isles?

- In which ways can the owner or person in control of an animal be held liable for damage or injury caused by the animal?
- What are the elements necessary to prove the tort of deceit?
- How does malicious falsehood differ from libel or slander?
- What do you need to prove in a claim based on 'passing off'?

CASES

- *Draper v. Hodder* [1972]
- *Turnbull v. Warrener* [2012]
- *Derry v. Peek* [1889]
- *Erven Warnink BV v. J Townend & Sons (Hull) Ltd* [1979]

REFORM

- Section 2(2) of the Animals Act 1971 has been criticised as being so vague that it is difficult to interpret. Legislative clarity on this point is desirable.

SPECIAL CHARACTERISTICS

- Animals could be 'dangerous' in terms of the Animals Act either because of their species or characteristics
- Deceit is a tort of fraud
- Malicious falsehood requires intent
- Passing off commonly refers to brand imitation

CRITICAL ISSUES

Setting the scene

When confronted with the word 'tort', many non-lawyers often frown in puzzlement. But if one then mentions examples such as 'negligence', 'personal injury', 'defamation', 'assault' or 'trespass', for example, most people would have a fair idea of what you are talking about, and the mystery vanishes.

Yet there are many more recognised categories in which civil liability may arise. There are various ways in which people could be held accountable for damage caused by animals in their control. Sometimes this would fall under negligence, but in other instances there could be a statute that applies to the situation. You need to know this because sometimes the statute could, for example, provide for strict liability, which gives a claimant an advantage as she does not have to prove fault (which is a major hurdle to be cleared in negligence claims).

In fact, it is important to remember the tort of breach of statutory duty (which we examined in Chapter 12), as it often goes hand in hand with employers' liability.

Other less discussed torts include the so-called 'economic torts', which come before our courts quite frequently. These include the tort of **deceit** (which boils down to fraud), **malicious falsehood** (which is a close cousin of defamation), **passing off** (which is a kind of commercial copycat) and interference with trade.

LIABILITY FOR ANIMALS

A person could be held liable for damage caused by animals under the common law and also under statute. Usually the person held accountable would be the owner, or the person under whose control the animal was when it caused the damage.

Liability at common law

The owner or controller of an animal may be held liable under negligence, nuisance or trespass. Let's look at an example of each to see how it works.

Negligence

The owner or handler, or person in control of an animal at the time of the relevant incident, could be held liable in negligence.

CORNERSTONE

Draper v. Hodder [1972] 2 QB 556

A child had been savaged by a pack of Jack Russells which lived next door. The owner was held liable in negligence. Think of this decision in terms of the elements of negligence: the owner, an experienced dog breeder owning a pack of dogs, had a duty of care towards people with whom his dogs might come into contact. When his Jack Russells, as a pack, rushed next door and attacked the claimant, the owner had breached his duty of care by falling under the standard of care that was to be expected of a breeder who should have known that Jack Russells, as a breed,

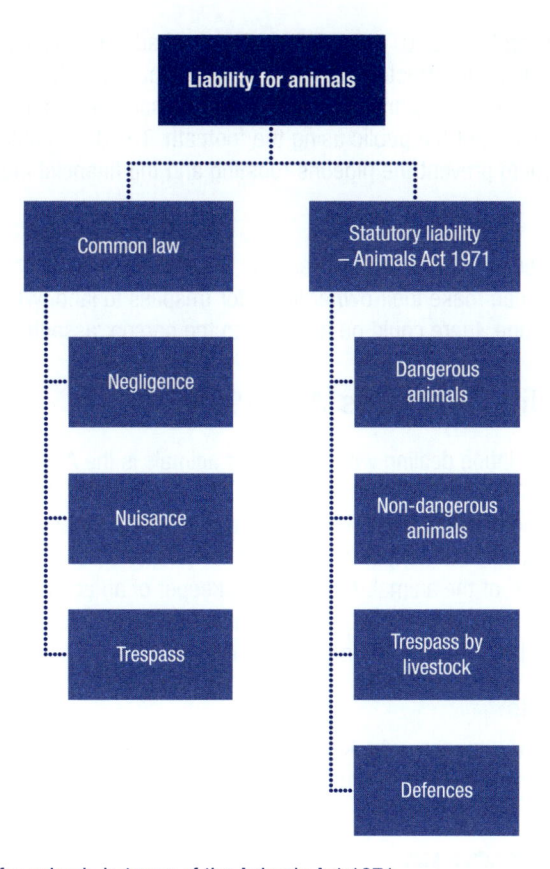

Figure 13.1 Liability for animals in terms of the Animals Act 1971

> and specifically when they are not alone but in a pack, have a tendency to attack moving persons or objects. This is exacerbated by the fact that he also knew that his dogs had a habit of running next door, so he should have fenced them in. As to causation: it was clear that there was factual causation; the dogs did cause the injuries, and as to legal causation; it was reasonably foreseeable that someone might be injured by the pack of dogs.

As we can see from this example, it is not at all far-fetched for a person to be held liable in negligence because of something her animals did. The problem in claims like this almost always lie with the fault requirement, namely the breach of duty of care. If the defendant can show that she did everything reasonably possible to prevent the harm, she may not be held liable.

Nuisance

Animals can give rise to a claim in nuisance because of noise, smell and general disruption.

In *Leeman* v. *Montague* [1936] 2 All ER 1677 the defendant was held liable in private nuisance for noise made by cockerels in the early hours of the morning. An example of public nuisance is found in

Wandsworth LBC v. *Railtrack plc* [2001] 1 WLR 368. Pigeons had been roosting under the defendant's bridge and their droppings had affected pedestrians using the footpath below. The court held the defendants liable: the pigeon fouling amounted to a public nuisance as it substantially interfered with the comfort and convenience of the public using the footpath. The defendants' liability lay in the fact that they had the control to prevent the pigeons roosting and the financial means to do so.

Trespass

Animals could be the cause of an action in trespass to land, trespass to the person or trespass to goods. Straying animals can make their owner liable for trespass to land. Where an animal is used to threaten or attack someone, there could be trespass to the person: assault or battery.

Statutory liability: Animals Act 1971

The primary piece of legislation dealing with liability for animals is the Animals Act 1971, but you also need to be aware of the Dangerous Dogs Act 1991. The Animals Act 1971 distinguishes between dangerous and non-dangerous animals. For dangerous animals, there is strict liability. For non-dangerous animals, the court has to look into the matter further before liability is imposed. Liability is imposed on the 'keeper' of the animal. A person is a keeper of an animal if she owns the animal or has it in her possession. If the person who has the animal in her possession is a child or minor, then the head of such child's household is taken to be the keeper.

Dangerous animals

The basic principle is that a person, who keeps a dangerous animal, as defined by section 6(2), has strict liability for any damage this animal may cause.

CORNERSTONE

Dangerous animals: Animals Act 1971, section 6(2)

'A dangerous species is a species—

(a) which is not commonly domesticated in the British Islands; and

(b) whose fully grown animals normally have such characteristics that they are likely, unless restrained, to cause severe damage or that any damage they may cause is likely to be severe.'

The question whether an animal is of a dangerous species is a question of law, not a question of fact. So here the court looks at the species itself and not at the individual animal. First the court asks itself whether the animal is normally domesticated in the British Isles. Dogs, cats, rabbits, horses, sheep, cattle, etc. are all domesticated and therefore do not fall under this section. Animals such as camels are not. If it is not a (British) domesticated animal, the court then goes over to the second subsection and asks whether an adult of that species is likely to cause severe damage. To look at two extreme examples: a tiger is likely to do such damage, whereas a non-native type of, say, parrot, would be unlikely to do so. Thus the tiger would be classed as dangerous but the parrot would not. This does not mean that if an animal is not classed as dangerous there can be no liability – it simply means that if the animal is of a non-dangerous species, the court will have to look at the characteristics of the individual animal itself, to determine whether that specific animal was dangerous at the time of the relevant incident (see the discussion of 'non-dangerous animals' below).

Strict liability, of course, means that the claimant does not need to prove fault on the part of the defendant, and also that the court does not concern itself with examining the individual animal's character. If the animal is of a species regarded as 'dangerous', and it causes damage or injury, its keeper will be held liable regardless of whether the animal happened to normally be a particularly docile or inoffensive animal.

Non-dangerous animals

A person who keeps a domesticated animal which is usually regarded as harmless, will only be liable if the animal has given cause to fear that it has unusual characteristics which make it potentially dangerous. Here the court *does* concern itself with looking at the individual animal and what was known about that animal.

CORNERSTONE

Liability for damage done by animals not of a dangerous species: Animals Act 1971, section 2(2)

Section 2(2) deals with liability for animals that do not belong to a dangerous species. In such instances, it will have to be proved that the animal itself was dangerous. The section reads as follows:

'Where damage is caused by an animal which does not belong to a dangerous species, a keeper of the animal is liable for the damage, except as otherwise provided by this Act, if—

(a) the damage is of a kind which the animal, unless restrained, was likely to cause or which, if caused by the animal, was likely to be severe; and

(b) the likelihood of the damage or of its being severe was due to characteristics of the animal which are not normally found in animals of the same species or are not normally so found except at particular times or in particular circumstances; and

(c) those characteristics were known to that keeper or were at any time known to a person who at that time had charge of the animal as that keeper's servant or, where that keeper is the head of a household, were known to another keeper of the animal who is a member of that household and under the age of sixteen.'

All three conditions must be fulfilled. If all three conditions are fulfilled, the keeper is held *strictly* liable. If not, the keeper could still be held liable, but the claimant will have to prove fault.

Section 2(2) has caused the courts some difficulty in interpretation, and you will note that the courts are not very impressed with the way in which section 2(2) is drafted. Let's look at a few examples.

In *Welsh* v. *Stokes* [2007] EWCA Civ 796 the claimant, a trainee groom at the defendants' stables, was injured when a horse she was riding unexpectedly reared, threw her, and subsequently fell on her. The question before the court was whether the horse could be regarded as 'dangerous' in terms of section 2(2) of the Animals Act 1971. This was an important question because if the answer to that question was 'yes', the defendants were to be held strictly liable – if 'no', the claimant would have to prove fault on the part of the defendants, and in this case it looked at least possible that the defendants were not negligent in letting the claimant ride the horse, as that particular horse was known to be a docile and obedient horse – under normal circumstances. So, was the horse dangerous under section 2(2)?

The decision turned on the interpretation of section 2(2)(b) – whether the likelihood of the damage or of its being severe was due to characteristics of the animal which are not normally found in animals of the same species or are not normally so found except at particular times or in particular circumstances, and section 2(2)(c) – whether this was known to the defendant.

The defendant argued that in interpreting section 2(2)(b) the court had to confine itself to examining the *particular individual animal* (who did not normally rear up), but the court disagreed, holding that it could also refer to behaviour normal in the species. In this instance, it was normal for horses (as a species) to rear up from time to time.

Therefore, in this case the horse was held to be 'dangerous' for the purposes of section 2(2) because it did something which its species normally do under certain circumstances – and the defendants were held strictly liable.

Does the decision in this case 'feel' a bit unfair to you? Remember that the defendants had only allowed the claimant to ride the horse because they had known the horse to be particularly well tempered, so it was unlikely that anyone could have foreseen the unfortunate incident. If liability had not been strict, it is arguable that they would not have been held liable.

Dissatisfaction with section 2(2) was explicitly expressed in the next case we look at, also concerning a horse-riding accident.

CORNERSTONE

Turnbull v. *Warrener* [2012] EWCA Civ 412

In this case both claimant and defendant were experienced horse-riders. The claimant was injured when the horse did not respond as expected. The court again had to look at the interpretation of section 2(2) and found that the defendant was strictly liable, following the same reasoning as in *Welsh* v. *Stokes*.

The court commented that, at the time of its judgment, the way in which section 2(2) was drafted had attracted 40 years of judicial and academic criticism, and that it was 'grotesque' because it made owners of non-dangerous animals strictly liable for damage done by the animal where the prescribed conditions under section 2(2) were all satisfied.

The defendant, however, did manage to escape liability as she was able to raise a valid defence in terms of the Act (see below).

Remember that section 2 relates to dangerous animals – either because they are of a dangerous species (s. 2(1)) or because they 'turned dangerous' under certain circumstances (s. 2(2)). If an animal is considered dangerous for the purposes of section 2, then there is strict liability. If the animal is considered *not* to have been dangerous, the keeper could still be held liable but then not strictly – fault will need to be proved.

Liability for animals

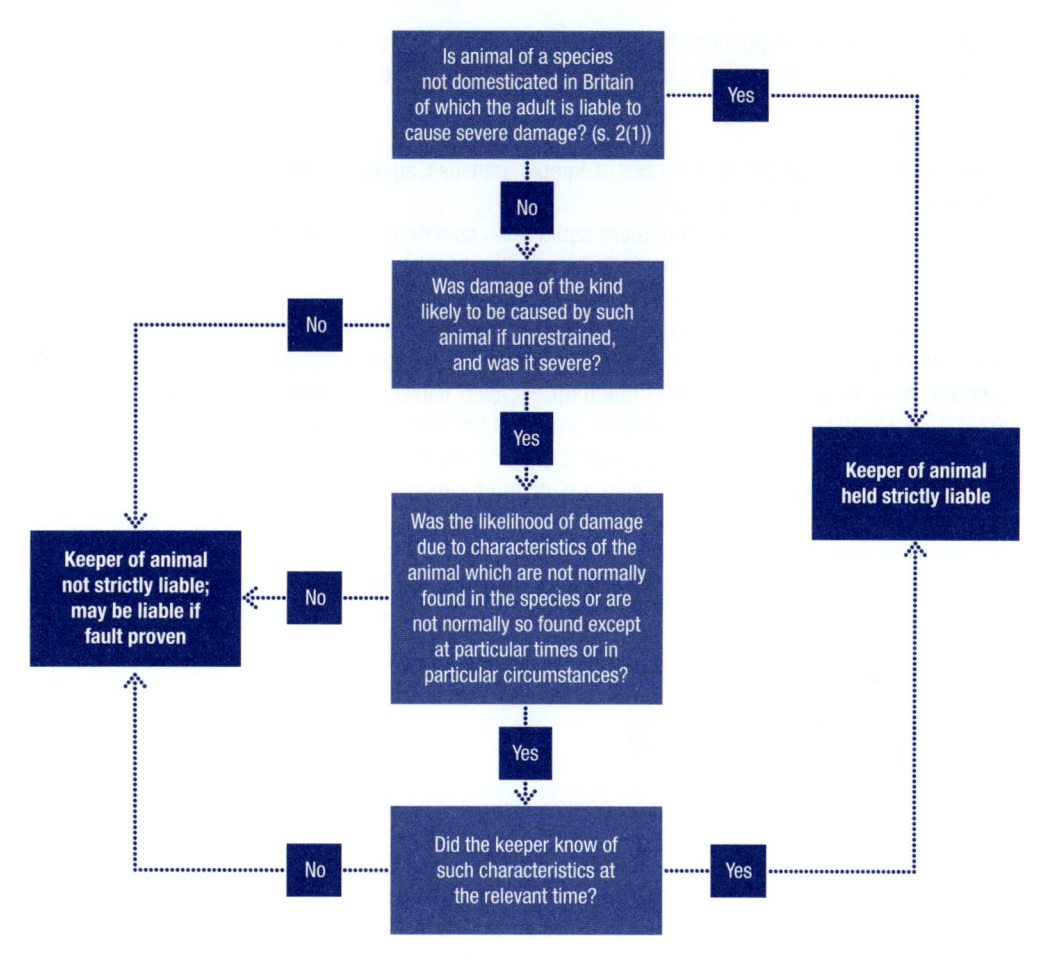

Figure 13.2 Liability for animals

Trespass by livestock

The Animals Act 1971 also covers liability for livestock damaging someone's land or property onto which the animals have strayed (s. 4).

> **CONTEXT**
> 'Livestock' is defined in the Animals Act 1971 as including cattle, horses, asses, mules, hinnies, sheep, pigs, goats and poultry, deer not in the wild state and also captive pheasants, partridges and grouse.

The owner of the land is entitled to retain the livestock until the damage had been paid.
Section 8 imposes a general duty to prevent livestock from straying onto the highway, with some areas excepted. The keeper of a dog that causes damage to livestock is liable for that damage under

section 3, while section 9 provides that a person who kills or injures a dog in these circumstances is not liable for that damage provided certain conditions are satisfied.

Defences

The Act sets out a number of defences a keeper can use against claims for damage caused by dangerous or non-dangerous animals:

Section 5(1) provides that the defendant could raise as a defence that the claimant was herself at fault. However, the claimant would have to be wholly at fault, which would be a difficult burden to prove.

Section 5(2) concerns voluntary assumption of risk by the defendant. For example, the experienced horsewoman who was injured in the case we looked at above (*Turnbull* v. *Warrener*) was held to have accepted the risk, and therefore the defendant escaped liability. Similarly in *Cummings* v. *Granger* [1977] 1 All ER 104 a woman who entered premises knowing them to be patrolled by a guard dog and who subsequently was attacked by that dog, was held to have voluntarily accepted the risk.

Section 5(3) deals with trespassers who are injured by animals on the premises they are trespassing on, *provided* that the trespasser is injured by an animal which is not being kept for the purpose of protection of persons or property, or, if it is kept for the purpose of protection, where it was not unreasonable to do so. Note that the Guard Dogs Act 1975 now imposes stringent conditions for the use of guard dogs.

ECONOMIC TORTS

These torts relate to interference with a person's economic interests or livelihood.

Deceit

This tort is closely related to fraud.

CORNERSTONE

Deceit

The tort of deceit is committed when the defendant makes a false statement to the claimant, knowing it to be false, or reckless as to its truth, with the intention that the claimant acts on it, the claimant does act and suffers damage as a result.

If you have studied negligence already, this will sound familiar to you. We have looked at a type of negligence (in Chapter 2) called negligent misrepresentation, and specifically at the case of *Hedley Byrne & Co* v. *Heller & Partners* [1964] AC 465, and we saw that in such an instance the claimant can sue for pure economic loss (something that is not ordinarily claimable in tort). So how does negligent misrepresentation differ from deceit? In *Hedley Byrne*, it is pointed out to us (at 502) that in an action founded on deceit, actual dishonesty, involving intention, must be proved. In negligent misrepresentation we have something less than intention, namely negligence.

```
                    ┌─────────────────────┐
                    │ Elements of deceit  │
                    └─────────────────────┘
        ┌──────────────┬──────────────┬──────────────┐
┌───────────────┐ ┌──────────────────┐ ┌───────────────────┐ ┌──────────────┐
│False statement│ │Recklessly/        │ │Intention that     │ │Damage caused │
│ to claimant   │ │intentionally false│ │claimant relies on │ │              │
│               │ │                   │ │statement          │ │              │
└───────────────┘ └──────────────────┘ └───────────────────┘ └──────────────┘
```

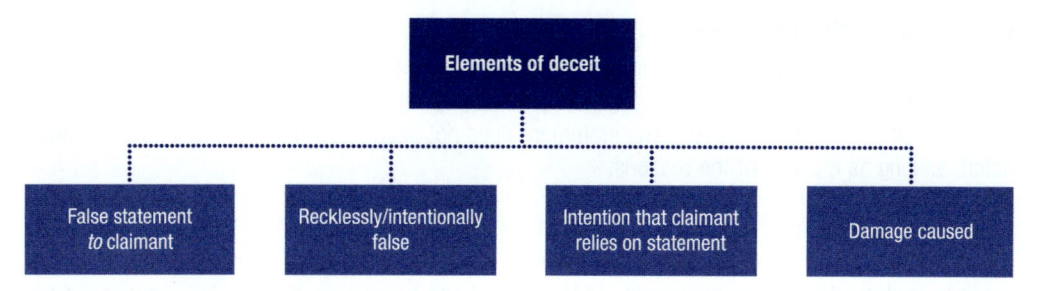

Figure 13.3 Elements of deceit

The significance of the tort of deceit is that a successful claimant is able to recover not just for financial loss but also for physical loss or injury. Let's look at the elements of this tort in more detail.

False statement to claimant

First, the claimant has to prove that the defendant had made a false statement to her, or to a class of people which included her. This element also implies that it needs to be a positive statement, not an omission, although omissions could be actionable in instances where there was a duty of disclosure.

Intention or recklessness

This element could mean two things. The defendant will clearly be liable if she intentionally made a false statement. However, what happens if the false statement was not made intentionally? In *Ludsin Overseas Ltd* v. *Eco3 Capital Ltd* [2013] EWCA Civ 413 the defendants raised as a defence that there was no intention to deceive on their part. The Court of Appeal dismissed this, holding that 'intention to deceive' was not a separate element of the tort, but merely another way of describing the mental element of the tort which consists of the following two parts: (1) the defendant knew the representation was false or was reckless as to its truth; (2) the defendant intended that the claimant should act in reliance on it. In finding thus, the court was applying the decision in the following well-known case.

To be reckless as to the truth therefore means to be indifferent whether the statement is true or not.

CORNERSTONE

Derry v. *Peek* (1889) 14 App Cas 337

In this case it was held that deceit would arise where a false representation was made, either knowingly, without belief in its truth, or recklessly or carelessly as to whether it was true or false. The defendants raised money for a venture to run trams by publishing a prospectus, on the strength of which people subscribed to their company. The prospectus stated that they had the authority to run steam trams – in fact, the defendants still had to obtain such authority. They believed that they would have obtained such authority but in the event it was turned down. The claimant, who had invested based on the information contained in the prospectus, sued, and the court held in his favour. The statement in the prospectus had been made recklessly as to its truth.

Reliance on the statement

The third requirement for deceit is that the defendant must intend that the claimant will rely for her conduct on the false statement. The claimant must then show that she did in fact act on the statement and suffered detriment as a result. The statement does not need to be the only reason the claimant acted, as long as it is one of the reasons.

Damage

Deceit is not actionable *per se*. Therefore, the claimant must prove that she suffered damage as a result of having relied on the statement. All losses that can be seen as a direct consequence of the deceit can be recovered, including economic loss, personal injury, property damage or distress and inconvenience. The following recent case illustrates the potentially wide net for damages in deceit.

In *Parabola Investments Ltd* v. *Browallia Cal Ltd* [2010] EWCA Civ 486 the defendant stockbroker defrauded its client, the claimant. The defendant falsely represented to the claimant that its trading was profitable when it was not and lied about how much money was in the claimant's account. The period of trading until the truth was discovered was just over seven months. In that time, the defendant had lost a large chunk of the claimant's money, and it was uncontroversial that this could be recovered. However, the claimant also claimed to have suffered considerably greater loss than would be satisfied by an award of interest, first, from its lost opportunity to have traded with the fund as it would otherwise have done during the seven month period, and secondly from its lost opportunities for trading during the period from the termination of its relationship with the defendant, until the trial. The Court of Appeal held that the claimant was entitled to recover lost profits for both stages.

Malicious falsehood

This is sometimes referred to as injurious falsehood, and is closely related to defamation. In fact, you will often see allegations of malicious falsehood jointly alleged in defamation actions. Just as with defamation, it covers loss of reputation through false statements. So how does it differ from defamation? Let's first look at a definition for malicious falsehood as this may give us an idea.

CORNERSTONE

Malicious falsehood

Cooke (2013: 524) defines malicious falsehood as: '. . . false statements made to third parties about the claimant with the intention that loss will be caused to the claimant'.

Here we already have one significant difference from defamation, namely that it is not actionable *per se*. In fact, the interest protected under malicious falsehood is not so much the reputation of the claimant, but her financial or economic interests.

The elements that need to be proved are, first, a false statement of fact; secondly, that there was intention to harm the claimant (i.e. malice); and thirdly, this caused the claimant to suffer damage.

False statement about claimant

Just as in defamation, it is a requirement that the statement that is made about the claimant should be false. Truth, in other words, would likewise be a defence. The false statement could relate to almost anything, provided of course that it ended up harming the claimant's economic interests. For example, in *De Beers Abrasive Products Ltd* v. *International General Electric Co of New York* [1975] 1 WLR 972 an advertisement disparaged a competitor's product, and was held to constitute a malicious falsehood.

```
                    ┌─────────────────────┐
                    │ Elements of malicious│
                    │     falsehood       │
                    └──────────┬──────────┘
         ┌────────────┬────────┴────────┬────────────┐
┌────────────────┐ ┌──────────┐ ┌──────────────┐ ┌──────────────┐
│False statement │ │Publication│ │Intention to harm│ │Damage caused│
│about claimant  │ │          │ │  claimant     │ │              │
└────────────────┘ └──────────┘ └──────────────┘ └──────────────┘
```

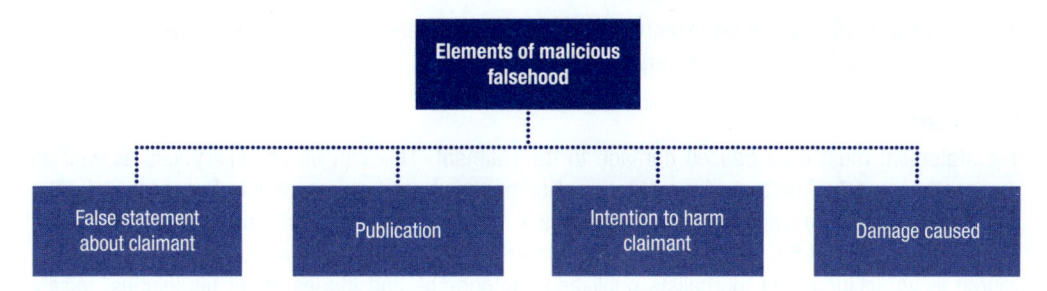

Figure 13.4 Elements of malicious falsehood

One important difference from defamation is that in defamation, the court is concerned with finding one or a main meaning of the statement complained of. This could be a straightforward meaning, but could also be a message conveyed by innuendo, in which case the search for the 'true' meaning of the statement could be quite a task! This rule is called the 'single meaning rule'. In malicious falsehood, this rule does not apply, which means that the court can look at all the alternative meanings of the statement. The implications of this difference are illustrated in the following case.

In *Cruddas* v. *Calvert* [2013] EWCA Civ 748 the claimant, a Tory politician, sued the defendant newspaper in libel and malicious falsehood because of an article they had published in terms of which it was alleged that the claimant had 'corruptly' in exchange for cash donations to the Conservative Party, offered for sale the opportunity to influence governmental policy and gain unfair advantage through secret meetings with ministers. At issue was the meaning of the phrase containing the word 'corruptly'. If it was taken to mean 'criminally corrupt', or that a crime had been committed, the defendants would have no defence against a claim in defamation, but if it was taken as meaning corruption short of criminal corruption, they would be able to rely on the defence of justification (truth).

The Court of Appeal pointed out, for the purposes of the defamation claim, that it was imperative to ascertain *one* meaning of the statement, as that was the sole meaning upon which the question of defamation turned. In this instance, the court held that the words complained of did not infer criminal corruption but something less.

However, turning to malicious falsehood, the court pointed out that all alternative meanings of the statement had to be considered. In this instance, the possibility that the statement could be understood by many people as referring to a crime, had to be considered by the court (together with other interpretations).

(The Court of Appeal did not itself decide upon the meaning/s for the purposes of malicious falsehood, but referred the matter back for trial on that issue, where it was decided that there *was* malicious falsehood.)

Publication

Just as in defamation, the statement had to be publicised, which simply means that the statement had to be witnessed by at least one other person (apart from the claimant and defendant). Bear in mind that proving a possible false statement is not the end, the claimant still then has to prove the other elements, namely that the statement was calculated to cause harm, and that she suffered damages as a result.

Intention to harm claimant

This means that the statement must have been calculated to cause damage to the claimant. Of course this further means that the damage was foreseeable. Usually this also means that there must have been the element of malice, which the claimant will have to prove – not always an easy task! Malice does not necessarily involve dishonesty on the part of the defendant, but it does involve the absence of just cause or belief in the statement

Damage

The statement must have caused damage to the claimant. This can be pecuniary loss as well as damage to property. The test of remoteness of damage is based on reasonable foreseeability. Take note that damage here could also include the loss of a chance. This is illustrated in the case of *Kaye* v. *Robertson* [1991] FSR 62, which involved the famous television actor Gordon Kaye. He was seriously injured in an accident and journalists published photographs and stories about his injuries, falsely stating that the story was produced with the actor's permission. An action for malicious falsehood succeeded, the loss being that it prevented the claimant from marketing the story himself and receiving payment for it.

INTERSECTION

In Chapter 10, where we looked at defamation, it was pointed out that the English law does not recognise a tort for invasion of privacy, the reasoning being that there are other torts which protect privacy via different routes. One such tort was 'breach of confidence'. Another is malicious falsehood, as illustrated in the case of *Kaye*.

Finally, let's briefly recap the differences between defamation and malicious falsehood.

Defamation	Malicious falsehood
Actionable *per se*	Damage needs to be proved
Protects reputation	Protects economic interests
Single meaning rule	Multiple meaning rule

Passing off

At the risk of over-simplifying things a bit, this tort could be thought of as the 'copy-cat' tort. The defendant commits the tort by passing her goods off as those of the claimant and thus profiting from the claimant's goodwill or commercial reputation.

CORNERSTONE

Passing off

The tort of passing off is similar to deceit and malicious falsehood because like those torts, it protects the claimant's financial interest in her property. The fact that the law recognises economic interests in brand name and goodwill is evidenced in the fact that, for example, one cannot market sparkling wine as 'champagne' if it was not actually produced in the French region of the same name – to name but one example. Usually allegations of passing off would involve not identical but similar names given to competitor products.

So what do you need to prove to succeed with a claim in passing off?

CORNERSTONE

Erven Warnink BV v. J Townend & Sons (Hull) Ltd [1979] AC 731

The House of Lords had to decide whether a drink marketed as 'Old English Advocaat' was passing off as there was a well-known Dutch product called 'Advocaat'. The House produced the following five elements that need to be present to establish the tort of passing off:

1. A basic misrepresentation;
2. made by a trader in the course of pursuing her trade;
3. directed towards prospective customers or ultimate consumers;
4. calculated to cause, or foreseeably capable of causing damage to the business or goodwill of another trader; and
5. which caused actual damage to the business or goodwill of the claimant or would probably do so. Therefore, the claimant does not need to show actual damage, it is sufficient that damage is the probable result of the passing off.

The House of Lords held that these requirements had been met and therefore granted the claimants an injunction against the defendants.

Let's look at a couple of further examples.

In *Reckitt & Colman Products* v. *Borden Inc* [1990] 1 All ER 873 the claimants were producers of lemon juice which they had marketed for more than 30 years in a yellow plastic container shaped like a lemon and which the public very clearly identified with their product. When the defendants also sold lemon juice in similar containers, the House of Lords held that this was passing off. The claimants were entitled to protect the very distinctive and original packaging of the product as well as the product itself. The court felt that it was clear that the public would be induced into believing that the lemon juice was produced by the same manufacturer and that the claimant's trade and goodwill was therefore threatened by the imitation.

Another example of passing of was found in *Woolley* v. *Ultimate Products Ltd* [2012] EWCA Civ 1038. The defendant sold watches bearing the name 'Henleys', whereas the claimant sold clothes and watches, amongst others under the name 'Henley'. The Court of Appeal carefully considered the various elements and came to the conclusion that there was a misrepresentation satisfying the criteria for passing off.

Remember that the damage that the claimant has to prove could include possible future loss of earnings.

KEY POINTS

- If an animal under your control causes damage or injury to someone you may be held liable under common law or statute.
- Common law liability for damage caused by animals can be found under negligence, nuisance, and trespass.
- The main piece of legislation dealing with liability for animals is the Animals Act 1971. This Act makes you strictly liable for damage caused by an animal regarded to be of a dangerous species, or by a domesticated animal that became dangerous due to circumstances.
- The defences to liability under the Animals Act 1971 include fault on the part of the defendant, and acceptance of the risk.
- Economic torts differ from torts that they closely resemble in the interest that they protect. Malicious falsehood, for example, differs from its close cousin defamation in that the former protects economic/financial interests whereas the latter protects reputation.
- The main economic torts include malicious falsehood, deceit and passing off.
- Deceit protects claimants who have suffered loss due to fraudulent misrepresentations.
- Passing off protects brand names and goodwill.

CORE CASES AND STATUTES

Case	About	Importance
Draper v. *Hodder* [1972] 2 QB 556	Liability for animals in negligence	Shows how the elements of negligence (duty of care, breach, causation) are applied to cases involving damage caused by animals.
Welsh v. *Stokes* [2007] EWCA Civ 796	Animals Act 1971, s. 2(2) – dangerous animals	Illustrates that an animal not of a dangerous breed can be considered dangerous under certain circumstances, leading to strict liability under the Animals Act 1971.
Turnbull v. *Warrener* [2012] EWCA Civ 412	Animals Act, s. 5 – defences	This case sets out the defences that may be raised under the Animals Act 1971.
Cruddas v. *Calvert* [2013] EWCA Civ 748	Malicious falsehood	Illustrates difference in operation between defamation and malicious falsehood.
Erven Warnink BV v. *J Townend & Sons (Hull) Ltd* [1979] AC 731	Passing off	House of Lords set out the elements to be proved for a claim in 'passing off'.

Statute	About	Importance
Animals Act 1971, s. 2	Dangerous animals	Keepers are held strictly liable for dangerous animals. This section sets out that certain animals are always seen as 'dangerous' whereas others are considered to be so under certain circumstances.
Animals Act 1971, s. 5	Defences to liability in terms of the Act	Sets out the defences to a claim for liability in terms of the Act, including the defence of voluntary acceptance of the risk.

FURTHER READING

Amirthalingam, A. (2003) Animal liability – equine, canine and asinine. *LQR* **119, p. 565**
This article offers a good explanation of not only the law relating to liability for animals, but also the problems encountered in interpreting the Animals Act 1971. You need to be able to show where the difficulty lies and this article is helpful in explaining this issue.

Cooke, J. (2013) *Law of Tort***. Harlow: Pearson, pp. 463, 498 and 523–5**
Students often confuse the tort of defamation with that of malicious falsehood. Professor Cooke clearly and concisely explains what malicious falsehood means, as well as the subtle yet fundamental differences between this tort and defamation. It is important for you to know the differences because a claim may succeed on the basis of one tort whilst failing on the other – as a lawyer it is your duty to cover all your client's bases by stating *all* of his/her claims in the alternative.

Deakin, S. and Randall, J. (2009) Rethinking the economic torts. *MLR* **72(4), p. 519**
This article discusses the conceptual basis for the economic torts in the light of their function namely to regulate fair competition. It will help you understand the reason why these torts exist.

Paterson, S., Fitzherbert, A. and Corrie, J. (2009) Deceit: welcome developments for victims of fraud? *Bus LR* **30(10), p. 212**
This article explains the ingredients for a successful claim under the tort of deceit.

***Woolley* v. *Ultimate Products Ltd* [2012] EWCA Civ 1038**
In this case, dealing with the tort of passing off, the Court of Appeal deals with the various elements that have to be proved very clearly, and also indicates the weight accorded to each in weighing up the evidence. Reading this case will cement your understanding of 'passing off'.

Glossary

actionable *per se* A claim which is actionable without proof of damage.

assault Tort consisting of the threat of immediate harm to the claimant.

battery Tort consisting of unlawful touching or touching with hostile intent.

burden of proof This indicates who has the burden or duty to prove something in court.

causation The element needed in most torts showing that the action forming the tort caused the damage sued for.

civil liability Liability that one person has towards another arising from an obligation incurred either in contract, for example, or because a tort has been committed.

contributory negligence A partial defence to torts such as negligence, meaning that the claimant's damages recovered will be reduced in proportion to her own contribution to her damage or injury.

deceit This tort is committed when the defendant makes a false statement to the claimant, knowing it to be false, or reckless as to its truth, with the intention that the claimant acts on it, the claimant does act and suffers damage as a result.

defamation Publication of a false statement about another identifying that person and injuring his/her reputation. See also 'libel' and 'slander'.

employer's liability Also known as 'operational liability'; this refers to an employer's liability for the management of the organisation including the safety of the employees.

ex turpi causa (non oritur actio) The defence of illegality. Loosely translated as meaning 'from a bad cause, no action can arise'.

false imprisonment Tort consisting of fully restricting a person's ability to move from a place.

fault A requirement for many torts, consisting of either intention or negligence.

harassment A course of conduct causing distress or alarm, in terms of the Protection from Harassment Act 1997.

injunction A court order to prevent something from happening, or if it is happening already, to stop it from recurring or continuing.

joint and several liability Where there are several defendants, the claimant could choose to hold one or more of them liable for the full amount, and these defendants will then have to try and recover the other defendants' proportional shares of the damage amongst themselves. This is favourable to the claimant as she could choose to sue, for example, only one (of several) defendants and recover her whole amount of damages from such defendant. See also proportional liability.

kettling Police practice in the UK of confining protesters to a cordoned-off area and preventing them from leaving.

libel A form of defamation captured in permanent format and actionable *per se*.

malicious falsehood This tort is committed by making a false statement to third parties about the claimant with the intention of causing loss to the claimant.

manufacturer Possible defendant in a product liability action in terms of the common law, and includes but is not limited to such disparate categories as fitters, erectors, water suppliers, second-hand dealers, assemblers, retailers and wholesalers. In terms of the Consumer Protection Act 1987 the term is accorded its more common meaning but liability is extended to producers, importers and retailers in case the manufacturer cannot be identified.

negligence This could be an element of fault but it also refers to the tort of negligence.

nervous shock Archaic term for 'psychiatric injury' below.

novus actus interveniens A Latin phrase that means 'a new act intervenes' in the chain of causation, breaking it. If this happens, the new intervening act would be the cause of the damage, not the original act.

nuisance This tort has two forms: private nuisance which is the indirect, unlawful interference with the use and enjoyment of property, and public nuisance which relates indirect unlawful interference with the comfort and convenience of the public.

occupier The person in control of premises for the purposes of the Occupiers' Liability Acts 1957 and 1984.

operational liability See 'employer's liability'.

passing off This tort is committed by passing goods off as those of the claimant and thus profiting from the claimant's goodwill or commercial reputation.

prescription Time-barring of claims – if you run out of time to institute your claim, it has 'prescribed'.

prima facie Literally translated: 'On the face of it' meaning that the facts are so obvious that they speak for themselves, and therefore need not be proved.

proportional liability In this instance, in the case of several defendants, each defendant will only be held liable for its own proportion of the damage, according to the portion of the damage it caused.

psychiatric injury Kind of injury which can be claimed for in damages consisting of a medically recognised condition (such as post-traumatic stress disorder), but subject to stringent conditions

'pure' economic loss Also referred to as 'expectation loss' – economic loss suffered that is not the direct result of physical damage or injury

ratio decidendi Reasons for the decision in a court judgment.

res ipsa loquitur Latin term meaning 'the facts speak for themselves' – facts that are seen as so obvious that they do not need proof in court.

slander A form of defamation in transitory format.

standard of proof This indicates to what extent proof is needed in court. For crimes, the standard is 'beyond reasonable doubt' (i.e. almost 100 per cent), whereas for civil matters the standard is 'on a balance of probabilities' (i.e. just more than 50 per cent).

strict liability Liability is strict if it is established without having to prove the element of fault (intention or negligence).

tortfeasor The person who commits a tort.

trespass Direct, intentional and unlawful interference with land, goods or person of another. Trespass to the person includes assault, battery and false imprisonment.

vicarious liability This is where one person can be held liable for a tort committed by another. This usually happens where one person is in a position of control or authority over another, but also in agency situations.

volenti non fit injuria The defence of consent. Loosely translated as meaning 'there can be no injury to one who consents'.

Index

act of God 230
act or omission 11–12
aims and objectives of tort law 17
animals 264–70
    Animals Act 1971 266–70
        dangerous animals 266–7
        defences 270
        non-dangerous animals 267–9
    common law liability 264–6
    dangerous 266–7
    negligence 264–5
    non-dangerous 267–9
    nuisance 265–6
    statutory liability 266–70
    trespass 266
    trespass by livestock 269–70
apportionment of blame 21
arrest
    false imprisonment, and 134
assault 124–6
    consent 128–9
    contributory negligence 132
    defences 128–33
    fear of immediate harm 125–6
    informed consent 129
    lawful authority 130
    limitation 131–3
    necessity 130
    parental authority 130
    self-defence 130
    words 124–5

background reading xxxv
battery 126–8
    consent 128–9
    contributory negligence 132
    defences 128–33
    direct and intentional application of force 126
    examples 126
    hostile intent 127
    informed consent 129
    lawful authority 130
    limitation 131–3
    medical cases 127–8
    necessity 130
    nonconsensual consent 126–7
    parental authority 130
    self-defence 130

boundaries of tort law 20
breach of duty 60–4; *see also* negligence
breach of statutory duty
    employers' liability, and 248–50

Caparo Industries plc v. *Dickman* 33–4
case law xxxiii–xxiv
causation 12, 65–82; *see also* negligence
    Consumer Protection Act 1987 179
    contributory negligence *see* contributory negligence
children
    occupiers' liability 155–6
civil liability 9
consent
    occupiers' liability 158
    trespass to land 113
    trespass to the person, and 128–9
Consumer Protection Act 1987 173–80
    causation 179
    damage 176
    defective, meaning 177–8
    defences 179–80
    importers 176
    no exclusion of liability 178–9
    own-branders 176
    potential defendants 175
    producers 175
    product 176
    risks, knowledge of 180
    suppliers 175
    who can sue 175
contract law 19
contributory negligence 22, 92–7
    apportionment of damages 96
    causation 94–5
    fault 93
    forseeability, and 95
    occupiers' liability 158
    partial defence, as 93, 96–7
    standard of care 94
        exceptional instances 94
        objective 94
    trespass to the person 132
conversion 115–16
    defences 116
    remedies 116
coursework xxxvi
criminal law 18

Index

damage 13
deceit 270–2
  damage 272
  false statement to claimant 271
  intention or recklessness 271
  reliance on statement 272
defamation 142, 185–208
  absolute privilege 202
  actual or likely serious harm to reputation 190
  author, editor or publisher 204
  burden of proof 200
  chilling effect on free speech 199
  corporate claimants 190–1
  costs 197–8
  criticism of old law 201
  damages 206
  defamatory meaning 193
  defamatory statement 192
  defences 201–5
  definition 188
  distinguishing characteristics 197–201
  effect of statement 190
  elements 191
  expensive to sue and defend 197–8
  form 190
  freedom of expression, and 189
  harm 194–5
  honest opinion 202
  injunctions 205–6
  innocent publication 204–5
  innuendo 193
  internet 197
  libel tourism 199–200
  multiple v. single publication rule 196–7
  offer of amends 205
  presumption of harm 194–5
  privilege 202
  protection of reputation 189
  publication 192
  publication of summary of court judgment 206
  publication on matter of public interest 203–4
  qualified privilege 202–3
  reference to claimant 193–4
  remedies 205–6
  repeat publication 196–17
  reputation reflects opinion of others 192
  section 9 of 2013 Act 200
  serious harm to reputation 194
  short prescription period 197
  trial by jury 199
  truth 201
  websites, operation of 204
  who can claim 195–6
  who may be sued 196–7
Defamation Act 2013 xxxiv

Donoghue v. *Stevenson* 28–30
drunk drivers' passengers
  volenti non fit injuria 91
duty of care 31–5
  Anns test 32–3
  development 32
  flowchart 34
  neighbour principle 32
  statutes 32
  three-stage *Caparo* test 33

economic loss 44–5
  not generally recoverable 44–5
    exceptions 45
economic torts 270–5
ejectment 115
employees
  volenti non fit injuria 89–90
employers' liability 212, 243–50
  adequate plant and equipment 245
  breach of statutory duty 248–50
  common employment, doctrine of 244
  competent staff as work colleagues 245
  defences 250
  effective supervision 245–6
  elements 245–7
  fault 246–7
  non-delegable duty 244
  origins 243–4
  proper system of work 245–6
  psychiatric injury 247–8
  remedies 250
  safe place of work 246
  statutory protection 248–50
  stress at work 247–8
essay questions xxxviii
European Convention of Human Rights
  Article 6 38
ex turpi causa non oritur see illegality
exams, preparation for xxxix–xl

false imprisonment 133–5
  actionable per se 134
  arrest 134
  defences 134–5
  lawful authority 134
  necessity 135
  strict liability 134
  total restraint 133–4
fault 13–14
foreseeability 78–80
  thin skull rule 79–80
  Wagon Mound (No. 1) 78–9

harassment 137
  Protection from Harassment Act 1997 137

Hillsborough litigation xxxiii–xxxiv
human rights 19–20, 38–9

illegality 97
   policy-based defence, as 97
injunctions
   defamation, and 205–6
   nuisance, and 232
   trespass to land 114
injurious falsehood *see* malicious falsehood
insurance 21
intention 14
interests protected by tort law 17
internet
   defamation 197
IPAC technique xxxviii

joint and several tortfeasors 22
journal rankings xxxi

law of torts 21
legal journal articles xxx–xxxii
   abbreviations xxxii
legally recognised liability 16–17
libel 189; *see also* defamation
limitation of actions 21
livestock
   trespass by 269–70
local authorities
   negligence, liability in 37

malice 14–15
malicious falsehood 272–4
   damage 274
   false statement about claimant 272–3
   intention to harm claimant 273–4
   publication 273

necessity
   false imprisonment 135
   trespass to land 113–14
   trespass to the person 130
negligence 4, 14
   animals, and 264–5
   breach of duty 50–64; *see also* breach of duty
      Civil Evidence Act 1968 60–1
      main legal points 62
   causation 65–82
      Bolitho case 77–8
      'but for' test 69
      chain 78
      factual 68, 69–77
      law 69
      legal 68, 77–9

      loss of chance 74
      materially contributed to damage 70
      materially increased risk of damage 70
      more than two or three possible causes 71
      multiple consecutive causes 71
      novus actus interveniens 75; *see also novus actus interveniens*
      omissions 74
   Compensation Act 2006, section 1 59–60
   consent 86
   contributory negligence 86
   defences 83–99
   Donoghue v. *Stevenson* 28–30
   duty of care 25–48
      elements xxxvii–xxix, 30–1
      focus on xxviii
      foreseeability 78–80
      illegality 86
      importance of 28
      local authority 37
      meaning 28
   mesothelioma cases 74
      Compensation Act 2006, s. 3 73
      Fairchild case 72–3
      joint and several versus proportional liability 72
   multiple causes of damage 70–1
   omissions 40–1
      assumption of responsibility 40–1
      creation of or failure to remove dangers or source of danger 41
      relationship of control between defendant and third party 41
   policy, role of 35–40
   public authorities, liability of 35–7
   public servants 38–40
   reasonable person test 52–3, 60
   remoteness of damage 69
   res ipsa loquitur 61
   standard of care 52–60
      Bolam test 54–5
      children 56
      common practice 58
      cost and practicability of precautions 57–8
      extent of possible harm 57
      likelihood of harm 56–7
      reasonable foreseeability 58
      skilled or professional defendants 53–4
      social value of activity 59–60
      sporting events 58–9
      state of the art defence 56
novus actus interveniens 75
   contributory negligence, and 76

intervening act of claimant 76
intervening act of nature 77
intervening act of third party 77
nuisance 212, 213–38
  abatement 233
  action of public benefit 232
  animals, and 265–6
  coming to 232
  damages 233
  defences 229–32
    act of God 230
    Civil Aviation Act 1982 230–1
    planning permission 231
    prescription 229–30
    statutory authority 230
  forms 216
  injunction 232
  private 217–26; *see also* private nuisance
  public 226–9; *see also* public nuisance
  remedies 232–3
  statutory 216

occupiers' liability 142, 145–63
  Act of 1984 158–60
    application 159–60
    exclusion of liability 160
    scope 158–9
  children 155–6
  common duty of care 151, 154
  consent 158
  contributory negligence 158
  defences 158, 160
  express or implied permission 152–3
  flowchart 161
  independent contractors 157–8
  lawful visitor 151
  non-visitors 158–60
  occupier 149–50
    control 149
    flowchart 150
    independent contractor 150
  premises 153–4
  skilled visitors 156
  state of premises 148
  statutes 146
  trespassers 158–60
  warning signs 156–7

passing off 274–5
planning permission
  nuisance, and 231
police
  liability in negligence 38–40

prescription 229–30
primary liability
  secondary liability, and 242–3
private nuisance 217–26
  cause 225
  claimant 217–18
  control over 225
  defendant 218–21
  defendant's purpose 226
  definition 217
  elements to prove 221–6
  interest in land, and 217–18
  interference with use and enjoyment of land 221–2
  landlords 220–1
  locality 224
  loss of amenity 222
  sensitivity 226
  time and duration 224–5
  unreasonableness 223–6
  vicarious liability 219–20
problem-type questions xxxvii
product liability xxxv, 142, 165–83
  common law v. statutory 174
  consumer law 168–9
  Consumer Protection Act 1987 173–80; *see also* Consumer Protection Act 1987
  contract law 168–9
  legislation 168–9
  negligence 169–73
    common law liability 172–3
    exclusion of liability 172
    intermediate inspection 171–2
    manufacturer 169–70
    product 170–1
    ultimate consumer 170
psychiatric injury 42–4
  employers' liability, and 247–8
  liability of 35–7
public nuisance 226–9
  claimant member of affected group of people 227–8
  definition 226
  elements 227–9
  special damage 228

reasonable person test 52–3, 60
remoteness of damage 77–8
  direct consequence 78
res ipsa loquitur 61
rescuers
  volenti non fit injuria 90
Rylands v. *Fletcher* 212, 233–7
  bringing onto land and keeping there 234

Rylands v. *Fletcher* (*continued*)
   claimant 236
   defences 236
   defendant 236
   elements 234–6
   non-natural use 235–6
   remedies 236
   something likely to do mischief when it escapes 235
   thing must escape 235

secondary liability
   primary liability, and 242–3
self-defence 130
slander 189; *see also* defamation
sport
   volenti non fit injuria 90–1
statutes xxxiv–xxxv
statutory regimes 142–208
strict liability 15–16
   vicarious liability, and 251

thin skull rule 79–80
tort
   basic elements 10–17
   importance of law xxvi
   justice, and xxii
   keeping up to date xxxiii–xxxv
   law in action xxix–xxx
   learning elements of xxviii
   meaning xxii, 8
   nominate xxvii, xxviii, 9
   reading about xxx
   reasons for studying xxxvi
   torts, and xxvi–xxvii
trespass 100–41
   animals, and 266
   common elements 102
   forms 106
   intention 106
   livestock, by 269–70
   meaning 106–8
   voluntary action 107
trespass to goods 115–16
   defences 116
   remedies 116
trespass to land 107
   ab initio 110–11
   abuse of right of entry 109
   consent 113
   damages 114
   defences 113–14
   distress damage feasant 114

ejectment 115
exceeding extent to which permission granted 110
forms 108–11
injunctions 114
lawful authority 113
necessity 113–14
physical entry 109
placing or projecting objects onto land 110, 111
possession of land 112
re-entry 114–15
remaining on land after permission revoked 110
remedies 114–15
self-help 114–15
squatters 112
title of claimant 112
trespass to land and goods 103
   actionable *per se* 108
trespass to the person 119–40
   actionable *per se* 122
   indirect harm *see Wilkinson* v. *Downton*
   intention 122–3, 124

vicarious liability 212, 242–3, 250–3
   employers' 251–7
      close connection test 257
      contracting out 255
      control test 235
      course and scope of employment 255–7
      criminal acts 256–7
      economic reality test 253–4
      irregular situations 254–5
      organisation or integration test 253
      Salmond test 256
      tort committed 251–2
      tort committed by employee 252–4
      unauthorised actions 256
      unlawful acts 256–7
   primary liability, and 242–3
   private nuisance 219–20
   strict 251
volenti non fit injuria 87–92
   complete and partial defences 87
   employees 89–90
   drunk drivers' passengers 91
   knowledge of risk 88–9
   rescuers 90
   sport 90–1
   statutory restrictions 92
   voluntary acceptance of risk 89

websites xxxvi
Wilkinson v. *Downton* 135–7, 138